A DICTIONARY
OF
ECCLESIASTICAL
TERMS

A DICTIONARY

OF

Ecclesiastical Terms

BEING

A HISTORY AND EXPLANATION

OF

Certain Terms used in Architecture, Ecclesiology
Liturgiology, Music, Ritual, Cathedral
Constitution, etc.

BY

JOHN S. BUMPUS

Hon. Librarian of S. Michael's College, Tenbury

LONDON
T. WERNER LAURIE

REPUBLISHED BY GALE RESEARCH COMPANY, BOOK TOWER, DETROIT, 1969

First published 1910

Library of Congress Catalog Card Number 68-30653

A DICTIONARY OF
ECCLESIASTICAL TERMS

Ablution. WASHING or purification, either of the hands or the sacred vessels. The word is generally used to signify the rinsing of the chalice after the Holy Communion with wine and water, which are reverently drunk by the celebrant (*cf.* 6th Rubric after Communion Service). In some churches it is customary to sing a short and appropriate sentence of Scripture, with the 117th Psalm— an antiphon, in fact—during the Ablutions. Such sentences have been set to music by various composers, notably Dr W. H. Monk, who, in 1869, wrote four, appropriate to various seasons, for the use of the Church of St Matthias, Stoke Newington, where, from 1852 to 1889, he was organist and director of the choir. They are unpublished. At St Paul's,·since 1892, the 150th Psalm has been sung in this place to an ancient chant, arranged by Sir George Martin, organist of the Cathedral. From Easter Day to Trinity Sunday, both inclusive, " Alleluia " is added, forming a very effective termination to the Communion Service at St Paul's, once described by Gounod as the finest thing of its kind on this side the Alps.

A Cappella or Alla Cappella. (1) The Italian term for the Church style; vocal music unaccompanied. (2) Church music in duple time, innumerable examples of which may be found among the masses, motetts, and anthems of the earlier English, Flemish, Italian and Spanish Schools of vocal composition. Our own countryman, Dr Nares (1715–1783), marks his excellent anthem, " Call to remembrance," *Alla Cappella*. The foreign *alla cappella* style, with English adaptations, has been much in vogue of late years in some of our principal choirs, such as those of St Paul's and Westminster Abbey. There can be no objection to this, so long as it is not overdone, and so long as the sterling and genuine cathedral music of the last three centuries is not excluded.

I

A DICTIONARY OF

Acolyte.
Gr. Ἀκόλουθος,
an attendant,
or minister ;
Old Eng.
collet.

The server at a low celebration, but the term is applied (in contradistinction to the singers) to all those who act as assistant ministers in the sanctuary and carry the cross, incense, tapers, etc., in processions. The server is generally a boy, the Church having from the earliest times consecrated *all ages* to the service of the sanctuary. Children were thus admitted to minister before the Lord, as was the child Samuel (1 Samuel i. 11). Fourteen was the usual age for admission. It is usual to admit boys into a choir with a form of prayer and blessing ; and to choose from among their number the steadiest and most devoutly disposed to act as servers and acolytes. " The Guild of Servants of the Sanctuary" is one of recent formation. In France, boys, without surplice or cassock, frequently serve as acolytes.

**Accentus
Ecclesiasticus.**

In plain-song, the inflections or intonations of the voice on reaching a comma, semicolon, or other stop. According to its position in the sentence, accent was said to be *immutabilis, medius, gravis, acutus, moderatus, interrogativus*, and *finalis*. Consult Rev. Thos. Helmore's " Primer of Plain-song " (Novello).

Agnus Dei.

An anthem sung by the choir during the Communion of the priest, and a prayer to Our Lord now present on the altar, " the Lamb as it had been slain." The choir sing thrice : " O Lamb of God, that takest away the sins of the world," adding twice : " Have mercy upon us," and the third time : " Grant us thy peace." Both the *Benedictus qui venit* before Consecration, and the *Agnus Dei*, after, were retained in Edward VI.'s First Prayer-Book, 1549 ; and so were among the things afterwards abandoned rather by the " curiosity of the minister and mistakers. than of any other worthy cause." The *Agnus Dei* is now permitted by the Lincoln Judgment, 1890, but it had long before been sung in many churches. It is now customary at Exeter, Manchester, Worcester, and some other cathedrals. The earliest arrangement to English words is in Merbecke's " Boke of Common Praier Noted " (1550). Of this book there are modern editions by Dyce, Rimbault, and others, and there is a beautiful reprint in facsimile by Pickering (1844). In the Roman rite the *Agnus Dei* is the last movement in a musical mass, and, as a rule, elaborately treated.

Aire.

A linen napkin, embroidered with coloured silks, to cover the chalice, used in Bishop Andrewes' Chapel and in Canterbury Cathedral, before the Rebellion. See the account of Bishop Andrewes' Chapel in " Hierugia Anglicana " (1848), p. 8.

ECCLESIASTICAL TERMS

Alb, or Albe. A linen vestment, much longer than the surplice, with tight sleeves like those of the cassock, and confined at the waist by a girdle or sash. It is employed in solemn celebrations of the Holy Eucharist; also by the " ministers "— *i.e.* the acolytes and thurifer—at solemn Matins and Evensong. They are engaged in assisting the priest at the offering of the Sacrifice; hence they wear the alb, which is the sacrificial vestment. The 58th Canon prescribes a surplice with sleeves to be worn at the Holy Communion, as well as at other services; and in the Rubric after the Communion in Edward VI.'s First Prayer-Book, regulating the Wednesday and Friday services, the priest is to wear a plain alb or surplice. This, however, does not imply that the surplice and alb were the same, the former being a modification of the latter. The intention of the canon evidently was to supersede all other vestments by the surplice, which has become the usual robe for the clergy in the English Church. Albs were of two kinds. Those wholly white and unadorned were called *purae simplices* (except it might be a border of gold lace). These, according to Honorius of Autun, were proper to the inferior clergy, doorkeepers, readers, exorcists, acolytes, and to boys in choir, but sometimes to priests on ferials. De Moleon ("Voyages Liturgiques," 62, 140, 150, 276) states, that the boys in choir, and the taper-bearers at Rouen, as late as 1756 put on their albs in their functions over their cottæ or surplices. The other kinds of albs, but always nearly of the same shape, were those which were ornamented, *paratae, frisiatae, fimbriatae,* which were for the bishop, priest, deacon and subdeacon. These rich decorations were not adopted till a later period. The first ornaments used were circular plaques, or fringes, or borders of gold, *Albae bullatae frisiatae.* These golden ornaments seem to have been gradually superseded by patches of various colours called apparels, which were accompanied by jewellery, embroidery, figures and inscriptions. The alb was originally, and still continues to be, white and of fine linen. Dr Simpson, in his charming book, " Old St Paul's and City Life " prints, at page 51, the pitiful remnant of the magnificent Treasury of 1552, " presented " to the Dean and Chapter at their request, being certain things of necessary use. The list contains " Thirty Albis, to make surplices for the Ministers and Choristers." J. D. Chambers describes the alb very fully in his beautiful work, " Divine Worship in the Church of England in the XIII., XIV. and XIX. Centuries " (1877), and cites innumerable examples from the Inventories of Sarum, Exeter, St Paul's, Rochester, Peterborough, Ely, Durham, etc. He also figures an alb of *c.* 1380 from Dr Bock's " Liturgische Gewänder " (ii. 3) and that of St Thomas of Canterbury, preserved at the Cathedral of Sens, from the " Mobilier Français " of Viollet-le-Duc (iii. 21).

It occurs at the beginning and end of many of the Psalms, and was always sung by the Jews on solemn days of rejoicing. In evident imitation of the Jewish custom, the Church

Alleluia. has, from very early times, at least during the season
Latin for of Easter, preceded the daily Psalms with " Alleluia "
" Hallelujah " or " Praise ye the Lord." It should be omitted during
(Hebrew)— the seventy days before Easter, beginning with
" Praise ye Septuagesima Sunday, and at other penitential times
the Lord," or and seasons. In the First Prayer-Book of Edward VI.
" Praise to " Alleluia " was sung after " Praise ye the Lord," from
the Lord." Easter to Trinity Sunday. The response, " The Lord's
Name be praised," was added at the last review (1662).

It had been inserted in the Scottish Liturgy in Charles I.'s time. Consult Jebb, " Choral Responses," etc. (1847–1857).

An officer in monasteries who had charge of the Almonry, a room where the alms were distributed, generally near the church, or a part of it. At St Paul's Cathedral, the almoner

Almoner. had the distribution of the alms, and it was his duty
Lat. *Eleemo-* to bury paupers dying in the precincts. Until 1872 he
synarius. educated from eight to twelve boys in music and
literature for the service of the choir. Since then the Almonry School has been entirely remodelled, and the number of boys increased to forty. For many years the office was practically that of Choirmaster or Master of the Boys, and was usually held by one of the vicars choral, but occasionally by a minor canon. The present headmaster of the Choristers' School represents the statutory *Magister Scholae Cantus* and the *Magister Scholae Grammaticae* in one. Consult Walcott's "Cathedralia" (1865) ; J. S. Bumpus' " Organists and Composers of St Paul's Cathedral" (1891), " The Choristers' School of St Paul's Cathedral" (1904), and " History of English Cathedral Music " (1908) ; Miss Hackett's " Brief Account of Cathedral Schools " (1827–1873) ; " Correspondence and Evidences respecting the Ancient Collegiate School attached to St Paul's Cathedral" (1832), and " Registrum Eleemosynariæ D. Pauli Londinensis " (1827) ; J. H. Lupton's " Life of Dean Colet " (1887).

The Lord High Almoner is a prelate who has the disposing of the King's Alms, and of other sums accruing to the Crown. It is still the custom on Maundy Thursday for the Lord High Almoner to distribute royal gifts of money and clothing to certain poor. This formerly took place at the Royal Chapel at Whitehall, but of late years (since the disuse of that building as a place of worship) this interesting and impressive ceremony has been transferred to Westminster Abbey. During the service several anthems are sung by the united choirs of the Chapel Royal and Westminster.

The choir tippet, formerly worn by all members of cathedral churches, of materials varying with the ecclesiastical rank of the wearer. G. J. French, in an interesting and curiously illustrated essay on "The Tippets of the Canons Ecclesiastical" (1850), observes that the hood part of the almuce was in the course of time disused, and a square cap substituted, the remaining parts giving way to the modern cape, worn in foreign churches, and perhaps the scarf now worn by bishops and dignitaries in our Church. The almuce, or "aumusse," is now an ornament of fur or other materials, carried over the arm by the canons of many French and other Continental cathedrals. The twelve minor canons of St Paul's wore almuces of calabrian fur, of a dark brown colour. On Whitsunday, 1549, on which feast the Book of Common Prayer was for the first time used, " the cannons and petie [minor] canons in Paules left of their grey and calabre amises and the cannons wore hoodes on their surpleses after the degrees of the Universities and the petie cannons tipittes like other priestes " (Wriothesley's Diary, ii. 144). Again : " 1559, Saturday, the 12 of August [ten months after the accession of Elizabeth], the aulter in Paules with the roode and Mary and John in the rood loft were taken down and the prebendaires and pettie canons commanded to leave of the grey amises of furre and to use onelye a surplesse in the service tyme by the commandement of Dr Grindall, bishop of London elect, and Dr May the new deane of Paules and others of the commissioners " (Wriothesley, ii. 146). The new rood was set up in Queen Mary's time, and was the object of a profane jest related by Foxe (Actes, iii. 114). The Rev. Percy Dearmer (" Parson's Handbook," 4th ed. p. 128) points out that the main difference between the almuce and the scarf is that the former is of fur ; originally it was made like a shawl, as shown in brasses at Hereford Cathedral, and worn scarf-wise ; later it was closed up or laced in front, and put on over the head, but it retained the scarf shape in the two pendants that hung down in front (see Plate IX. in the same book, showing a canon in choir habit). Some think that the black scarf lined or edged with fur, and shown in sixteenth-century portraits—e.g. those of Warham and Cranmer, as engraved by Lodge and others—represents a further development of the almuce, but this has been disputed.

Almuce.

5

A DICTIONARY OF

Mr Dearmer further observes that the grey almuce (of grey squirrel lined with miniver) was the highest mark of dignity ; it was worn by canons in the fourteenth, fifteenth and sixteenth centuries, as well as by bishops of Elizabeth's reign ; minor canons used black almuces, generally of calaber and lined with miniver (as those of St Paul's). At Sarum the vicars were restricted to the use of black cloth almuces lined with lambskin or goatskin ; the boys did not wear almuces. The same eminent ritualist is of opinion that it is certainly open to any bishop or cathedral chapter to invest themselves with grey almuces, and their chaplains with black ones ; and the practice, when it is adopted in the law-abiding days that are before us, will add much to the beauty and interest of our cathedral churches. Probably the form of almuce adopted will be that of a fur scarf, worn in cold weather, and carried, according to old custom, on the arm when the weather is hot. Consult further, Dr Wickham Legg, " The Black Scarf and Grey Almuce " (Transactions of the St Paul's Ecclesiological Society, iii.) ; also Fr. Robinson and Mr Cuthbert Atchley on the same subject (S. P. E. S. Trans. iv.).

The altar is surmounted by a cross to remind us of the death of Christ, which is especially shown forth in the Holy Eucharist. We **Altar Cross.** learn that when the Emperor Constantine and the Empress St Helena deposited the body of St Peter in the Basilica they placed over the shrine a cross of pure gold, weighing 150 lbs. (Parker, " Archæology of Rome," xi. p. 64) ; but we cannot be sure that this was in connection with the altar. Riddle (" Christian Antiquities," p. 706) states that crosses do not appear to have been set up in churches until about the middle of the fourth century. Haydn (" Dictionary of Dates," *s.v.*) says the cross was brought into use for devotional purposes in churches and chambers about the year 431. In fact, it would appear that, until about the tenth century, it was not customary to leave any ornament standing on the altar except during the time of Mass, but at that period a cross was usually kept there as a part of its ordinary furniture. In a MS. of the ninth century, upon the altar, covered with a white cloth, there are represented a chalice, wafer, and cross (Lacroix, " Military and Religious Life," p. 277). Dr Rock (" Church of our Fathers," i. p. 269) mentions that the cross always stood on the altar in the Anglo-Saxon period. Subsequently it at all times formed part of the *instrumenta* of the altar ; generally, though not invariably, flanked by candlesticks. In the Greek Church it always stands on the altar between two candlesticks. Gifts and bequests of crosses were very common, as *e.g.* the Duke of Bedford, Regent of France, bequeathed, in 1434, to the church in which he might be buried, "unam crucem argenteam deauratam, cum buretis, quas habuit de redemptione Johannis Alcurons" (Nichols, "Royal Wills," p. 272). At what time the figure was added to the cross, making it a crucifix, does not appear to be known with certainty. Haydn ("Dictionary of Dates," *s.v.*) says it was first used in the fourth century, and came into general use in the eighth century. The Sarum rite sometimes mentions the "cross" and at others the "crucifix." Thus : "After Evensong on the first Sunday in Lent all images, pictures, and *crosses* in the church are to be covered up with veils of white linen or silk. They remain covered till the first service of Easter Day exclusive, except that on Palm Sunday, from the commencement of the principal Mass till Evensong, crosses [and possibly other images and pictures] are exposed to view. One *crucifix* may be exposed on Good Friday till shortly before Evensong" ("Missale Sarum," p. 329, *Adoratio crucis in Parasceve*). Major Heales ("Adjuncts, Furniture, and Ornaments of the Altar," St Paul's Ecclesiological Society's Transactions, i. p. 161) says that "in the earlier representations of the crucifixion, Our Lord's Feet are invariably shown as affixed to the cross by separate nails, up to (roughly) the fourteenth century, and the change to the figure with one nail passing through both feet was not invariable for long afterwards. The single nail is clearly opposed to tradition ; and the removal of the hypopodion, and the substitution at the same time of one nail for two, was a change which has been attributed by some authorities to the Albigensian schismatics." Upon crosses of all kinds, and especially those for the altar, wealth of art and material was lavished in token of honour. Gold and silver-gilt were common up to the end of the twelfth century, and the whole was most usually covered with rich enamel ; afterwards chiefly metal gilt and enriched with gems. Lübke ("Eccles. Art in Germany") engraves a fine altar crucifix of the twelfth century in the Soltykoff Collection ; and another of about 1400, at the Katholischen Pfarrkirche, Dinslaken, is photogravured in Paul Clemen's "Die Kunstdenkmäler der Rheinprovinz" (1893), to mention two only out of the innumerable examples of such reproductions of *instrumenta ecclesiastica.* Heylyn ("History of the Reformation") tells us that the altar in the Chapel Royal of Queen Elizabeth was furnished with "rich plate, two fair gilt candlesticks with tapers in them, and a massy *crucifix* of silver in the midst thereof," and Strype ("Annals of the Reformation") says that "The Queen still to this year [1565] kept the *crucifix* in her chapel, as appears by a letter written to Secretary Cecil by a zealous gentleman, earnestly persuading him to use his interest with her Majesty to have it removed, as tending too much to idolatry." The altar in the chapel of Peterhouse, Cambridge, while Cosin was master of that college (1634–1644), had "a great crucifix, hanging over it." This was one of the articles exhibited against him by the Puritans. Again, Strype in his "Life of Archbishop Parker" (p. 310, fol. 1711) observes : (1570) "The *crucifix* which had been before removed out of the Queen's Chapel was now of late brought in again"; and in the Introduction to Heylyn's "Cyprianus Anglicus" (1668), we read that "a rich and massy crucifix was kept, for many years together, on the Table or Altar of the Chapel Royal in Whitehall, till it was broken to pieces by Pach, the Queen's fool (when no wise man could be got to do it), upon the secret instigation of Sir Francis Knollis." Charles I., "finding the *old crucifix* among the Regalia, caused it to be placed on the altar at his coronation, as in former times" (Heylyn "Cyprianus Anglicus," p. 144). At the Chapel Royal, Whitehall, "there was a fair crucifix in a piece of hangings hung up behind the Altar" ("Archbishop Laud's Answer, Troubles, etc.," p. 315). "At the Cathedral at Lichfield [1635], a very large crucifix, with a picture of Christ almost as big as a giant, was hanging over the high altar, with the pictures of men and women kneeling down before it and praying to it" ("Canterbury's Doom," p. 80). Amongst the contents of the treasury of St Paul's seized by the rapacious Edwardian Commissioners in 1553 were "a precious crosse of cristall set in silver and all gilte with many precious stones aboughte hym," etc. ; "a faire crosse with a crucifix and Marie and John, the bosse VI. square with ij anngelles upon the foote and iiij Evangelistes enamelled with iiij floure de luces in the iiij corners and a lambe on the backeside" ; "a great large crosse with the crucifix with Marie and John," etc., possibly that of the high altar ; "a crosse with the crucifix onlie with iiij ymages and iiij floure de luces adjoyning, silver and gilte" ; "a plaine crosse plated with silver and gilte with iiij redd stones in the iiij corners sett throughlie with perels and stones" ; and "ij cristal crosses with plates of silver at everie joynte, ordeinedd for processions." The same Cathedral possessed, in 1245, a large cross of wood ornamented with the not very usual subject of the resurrection of Adam. In an old legend Adam is said to have been buried in the precise spot on which the Cross was erected ; and the blood of the Crucified Redeemer falling upon Adam's tomb calls him back to life. In a fourteenth-century miniature figured by Mrs Jameson in her "History of Our Lord,"

Adam rises from his tomb at the foot of the Cross, and holds a chalice to catch the sacred Blood. It is related that the saintly Nicholas Ferrar had, in 1625, a crucifix on the altar in his church at Little Gidding.

The two lights which burn on the altar at the time of the Celebration signify that Christ is the true light of the world, and represent His two natures, the Human and the Divine, **Altar Lights.** both which He bears at the right hand of the Father in heaven. Other lights are lit round and about the altar in festal seasons as a sign of spiritual joy, as St Jerome testifies. The English (Sarum) Rule as to altar lights was as follows :—" I. At Celebrations of the Holy Eucharist. The number of lights on any given day should be the same whether the service be a High Mass, a Missa Cantata [Sung Mass] with incense, or a Missa Cantata without incense. (α) On Feasts, ranking as Principal or Greater Doubles, at the choral Celebrations *eight candles* lighted ' round about' the altar. (β) At all other choral Celebrations *four candles* lighted 'round about' the altar—' Alios duos (cereos) in gradu coram altari '—Registrum Osmundi, sect. v. (γ) At all Low Masses on any day in the year *two* lights and two only. II. At Mattins and Evensong. (α) On Feasts, ranking as Principal or Greater Doubles, at both first and second Evensong if choral, and at Mattins if choral, *eight candles* lighted ' round about' the altar. (β) On Lesser and Inferior Doubles, on Simples of the first class, on Advent Sunday, and on Palm Sunday at both first and second Evensong, on Wednesday in Holy Week at Evensong, on Maundy Thursday, and throughout Easter and Whitsun Weeks, whenever the service is choral, *four candles* ' round about' the altar. (γ) On every other occasion when Mattins and Evensong are said with or without music, *two candles* lighted ' on or about' the altar." The " Registrum Osmundi " directs only one candle to be lighted at Mattins on Ferias, but Mattins in our present Prayer-Book obviously represents Lauds rather than the ancient Mattins, which is a night office, and of a totally different structure. In 1547 King Edward VI.'s " Injunctions " ordered that, since images had been abused by pilgrimages, no lights should thenceforth be set before any image or picture," " but onely twoo lightes upon the high aulter, before the Sacrament, which for the signification that Christe is the very true lighte of the worlde, thei shall suffre to remain still." And so in Archbishop Cranmer's " Visitation Articles," he inquired whether they suffer any torches, candles, tapers, or other lights to be in the churches, but only two lights upon the high altar. The use of candles was restored during the Laudian revival (*temp.* Charles I.). Nicholas

Ferrar had them in his church at Little Gidding, and in Peter Smart's sermon at Durham, on 27th July 1628, Dr Cosin, one of the prebendaries, was charged, *inter alia*, with having tapers upon the altar. Cosin was compelled to explain that " in winter time upon the Communion Table were never set more than two fair candles, with a few small sizes near to them, which they put there of purpose that the people all about might have the better use of them for singing the Psalms and reading the Lessons out of the Bible, but 200 was a greater number than they used in all the church, either upon Candlemas night or any other" (" Works," lxxviii.). He did not, however, deny the article which charged him with allowing " the company of boys to come in with lighted torches in their hands at the choir door, bowing towards the altar at their first entrance, bowing thrice before they lighted their tapers, and withdraw, bowing so oft towards the altar, the organs all the time going." Old engravings of ceremonies in the choir of St Paul's early in the eighteenth century show two candles burning on the altar at services known to be held at noon, and they are so represented in the plate " Communion des Anglicans à Saint Paul," in Picart's " Cérémonies et Coutumes Religieuses de tous les Peuples du Monde " (7 vols., 1723–1737). Lord Mornington, of chant and glee fame, father of the Duke of Wellington, had candles upon the retable of the altar in his private chapel at Dangan Castle, Co. Meath ; and at Christ Church Cathedral, Dublin, the gradine of the altar formerly sustained massive silver-gilt candlesticks with wax candles in them, which were always lighted whenever the service was performed at dark. At Durham, at the beginning of the last century, the candles were regularly lighted on the altar on Sunday mornings, as if in anticipation of a Celebration. At St Paul's the candles have been lighted on the high altar for the Celebration on Sundays and Festivals for the past twenty years. On the Greater Festivals the two candles in the huge candelabra standing on the *gradus presbyterii* are also lighted, together with those on the altar, during the whole of Matins and Celebration. At the same cathedral it is the rule to have two lights on the altar at Evensong throughout the year. The number of candles adopted as the rule of the English Church appears to have been in this, as in so many other things, a re-enactment of the custom or practice of the very early Church ; and we find it still customary in the unchanging East. And the same use may be seen in North Italy, as at Venice and Lucca, for example, where the two altar candlesticks stand on a low step, while the four candles on the altar itself are not always lighted. In addition there is often a branch candlestick on a pivot at the outer end of a low wall running out at either end of the altar. In Spain, four candles are common; In France six candles may almost always be seen at Mass and Vespers. The most usual modern Roman practice is to have six large candles, but it may be doubted if this number were in any case introduced before the seventeenth century. Twelve may be found earlier. In a steel plate published in 1840, representing the interior of the choir of St George's Chapel, Windsor, during the ceremony of the Installation of the Knights of the Garter, six tall lighted candles are shown upon the altar. In referring to candlesticks, mention should not be omitted of " Judases." Candles being made of vast size and thickness, it became common to construct the lower part, standing upon the pricket of the candlestick, of wood painted to resemble wax, and possibly sometimes coated with it. Upon this the real candle was set. These false candles were called " Judases." St Margaret's, Westminster, furnishes an example : " 1524. Paid for twelve Judacis to stand with the tapers, ijs." (Nichols, " Illustrations," p. 9). We believe the name for these Judases is now " stocks." Lübke, a very eminent and careful authority, says that it can be proved that candles did not stand on altars before the twelfth century. He gives illustrations of Romanesque altar candlesticks (" Eccles. Art in Germ.," p. 175). Caumont (" Abécédaire," p. 290) gives the representation of an enamelled example dating in this (the twelfth) century. Walcott (" Sacred Archæology," s.v. " Altar ") says that before the thirteenth century no candles or crosses were permitted to be permanently set on altars, but that they were invariably brought in by two acolytes when Mass was to be said. We cannot, however, form an opinion whether Walcott's statement is trustworthy, owing to his system of omitting, for the sake of brevity, references to his authorities. There can be no doubt (as Bishop Cosin states in the second and third series of his " Notes on the Book of Common Prayer," originally edited by Bishop Nicholls, and cited by him in his Commentary on the same) that the two altar lights, and many other ornaments of the Church, disappeared in the latter part of the reign of King Edward VI., when private dwellings and dinner-tables were often seen fitted up with hangings, candlesticks and chalices taken from the churches ; but it is certain that many remained, and were in use in cathedrals and parish churches up to the time of Cromwell when, of course, they were destroyed. Fuller, in his " Church History," tells us that the Reformers " reduced candles, formerly six in number to two upon the high altar ; these being termed ' lights,' show they were not *lumina cæca*, but burning." Queen Elizabeth, and many of her bishops, used these lights during the whole of her reign, as is well known. Coxe, in his " Letters to the Queen," speaks of the "lights and cross remaining." In 1560, Sampson wrote to Peter Martyr, " the crucifix and candles are retained at Court." " These lights," says Bishop Cosin, "were, by virtue of the present rubric [*i.e.* in the Book of Common Prayer] afterwards continued in all the Queen's Chapels during her whole reign, and so they are in the King's [Charles II.] and in many cathedral churches, besides the chapels of divers noblemen, bishops and colleges, to this day." The Lord Treasurer Burleigh and Bishops Andrewes and Laud, as is well known, used them. They were used at a State christening in 1565 (Selden, *Collect.* ii. 691). In " Certain Demands," a Puritan book, printed *temp.* James I. (p. 29) : " We demand that copes, surplices, candles at noonday be taken away." That Cosin continued the practice of " Lights before the Sacrament " after the Restoration, is proved by a passage from Walter Brereton's Travels (Chetham Society), quoted by Mr Street in a lecture given at Durham (printed in *The Ecclesiologist*, October 1863). Brereton saw them so used. In 1643 the Cathedral of Peterborough had two pair of silver candlesticks in which tapers were burnt at the time of divine service (Gunton's *Hist. Peterb.*, 334). In 1736, in York Minster, were two silver candlesticks and two large tapers for the altar lit at the time of divine service (Drake's " Eboracum," 524). This list may conclude with an extract from the sermon of Dr Donne, the famous Dean of St Paul's, a man of unimpeachable Protestantism, whose biographer is Izaac Walton. In one of his celebrated sermons, dedicated to Charles I. and preached in St Paul's Cathedral, in defence of " Lights before the Sacrament " on Candlemas Day, after saying that " the Oblation of this Day's Purification is Light, so the day names it, Candlemas Day : so your custom celebrates it with many lights," he adds, " I would not be understood to condemn all use of candles by day in Divine Service, nor all churches that have or do use them, for so I might condemn the Primitive Church in her pure and innocent state. Lights were received into the Primitive Church to signify to the people that God, the Father of Lights, was otherwise present in that place than in any other ; and thus men came to offer Lights by way of sacrifice to God. We must not be hasty in condemning particular ceremonies, for, in so doing, we may condemn the Primitive Church that did use them to this day." The section " Lights " in J. D. Chambers' " Divine Worship in the Church of England in the XIII., XIV. and XIX.

ECCLESIASTICAL TERMS

Centuries" is well worth careful study, as showing the rules adopted as to lights at Salisbury, Lichfield, Wells, Aberdeen, etc. The ordinary rule, in the thirteenth century, in England, and indeed throughout the West, was to have two candlesticks of large size, with lighted candles. In the Inventory of St Paul's, 1295, were two candelabra of silver, given in 1195, with figures of animals, etc., weighing four pounds, and two others (1302) with gilt knobs resting on lions; and two other pairs of copper. As late as 1759, at the Cathedral of Rouen, there were no lights, either on the altar or its gradine, but the candelabra were held by four angels, standing on four columns of brass, immediately above the gradine (De Moleon, "Voyages Liturgiques," 126). Post-Restoration engravings in the Book of Common Prayer, and books of devotion, show that it was then customary to place the candles lighted upon the holy table. See a view of the east end of St Paul's Cathedral in " The Holidays of the Church of England throughout the Year," Keble, Fleet Street, 1719; and Dr Burnet's " Of the State of the Dead and of those that are to Rise, translated by Matthias Earbery, Presbyter of the Church of England," 1728, which contains a view of the altar in Magdalen College Chapel, Oxford. In this engraving, too, it should be noticed that the two books on the altar to be read from are placed facing east, and the drapery of the altar is so arranged as to preclude the possibility of kneeling at the altar facing north or facing south. In Wilkinson's " Londina Illustrata " (1819) is an engraving, after a drawing by Schnebbelie, which represents the interior of the Chapel Royal, St James's, looking east, or, to be strictly correct, north. Upon the altar are two massive candlesticks with lighted tapers in them. In the centre is the celebrated alms-dish, and on the wall beneath the window is emblazoned the Sacred Monogram, surrounded by a glory. St Paul's Cathedral had, before the wholesale plunder of the altar-plate in December 1810, a pair of silver-gilt candlesticks, three feet high, with these inscriptions : " In lumine Tuo videbimus lumen." " De tenebris vos vocavit in admirabile lumen Suum." " Sic luceat lux vestra coram hominibus," inscriptions certainly inconsistent with *lumina cæca*, and the various engravings which exist show them to have been lighted. St Paul's possessed two other candlesticks of the same materials, two feet three inches high. The present candlesticks on the high altar were the gift of the Hon. G. Cavendish Bentinck, Christmas 1874. An allusion to Candlemas Day recalls the fact that at Ripon, so late as 1790, on the Sunday before that festival (2nd February), "the Collegiate Church was one continued blaze

13

of light all the afternoon by an immense number of candles" (Walcott, "Traditions and Customs of Cathedrals," 199).

Alto-rellevo. Sculptures in which the figures considerably project.

Ambo.
From the Gr. ἀναβαίνειν, "to go up"; Fr. *ambon;* Ital. *ambone;* Ger. *lesepult.*

(1) A rostrum or kind of pulpit, usually of marble or some costly material, inlaid with mosaic patterns, connected with the choir and intended for the reading of the Epistle and Gospel. Examples: Pisa Cathedral; St Clemente, St Laurentius, and St Pancratius, Rome; Milan Cathedral (ancient); St Thomas, Upper Clapton, by W. Burges (modern). (2) The raised platform in Eastern churches on which the choir mount when they sing. The "Ambon," or pulpit, answers in its uses to the rood-loft of the Western Church: ὁ ἄμβων προ τῆς θύρας τοῦ βήματος ἵσταται, says Simeon of Thessalonica. That in the Church of the Holy Wisdom at Constantinople is described by Codinus as adorned with jewels and lights. For lights were fastened to crosses even as early as the time of St Chrysostom, if we may trust Nicephorus. To the ambo were two entrances, one east and the other west: for Codinus, speaking of the Emperor Constantine going up into it, says that he ascended, not on the side which fronted the Holy Doors, but on that which was opposite the Soleas or choir-steps. Symbolically, the ambo and its situation near the Holy Doors signified the stone that was rolled away from the Sepulchre: and the deacon mounted on the ambo, the angel seated on the throne. Ciampini ("Vetera Monumenta," 1647) figures (Pl. XII.) the Epistle and Gospel Ambons in St Clement's, Rome. The Epistle Ambon has, attached, the desk for the Lections at Matins, and the Gospel Ambon the great paschal candlestick.

Ambrosian Chant. The system of Church song introduced by St Ambrose, Bishop of Milan, in the fourth century. It formed the basis of the Gregorian system.

Ambrosian Hymn. The *Te Deum*, so called because its authorship is attributed by some to St Ambrose. See *sub voce* "Te Deum."

Ambrosian Te Deum. A musical setting of the *Te Deum* in plain-song. called after Bishop Ambrose. There are several versions, but that sung at the Church Pageant in June 1909 may be taken as the most authentic. Consult the "Service-Book for the Ninth Annual Festival of the London Gregorian Association at St Paul's," 19th May 1881; "The English Church Pageant Handbook" (1909). The *Te Deum* as noted

14

ECCLESIASTICAL TERMS

in Merbecke's book of 1550 is a form of the Ambrosian melody, and the *Te Deum* in Tallis' celebrated Service in the Dorian Mode is founded upon it.   See Boyce's " Cathedral Music," vol. i. (1760).

Amen.   This, in the phraseology of the Church, is denominated *orationis signaculum*, or *devotae conscionis responsio*, the token for prayer—the response of the worshippers.   It intimates that the prayer of the speaker is heard and approved by him who makes the response.   It is also used at the conclusion of a doxology.   To be perfectly correct, unless a hymn end with a doxology " Amen " should not be sung.   At the end of a prayer, as the Catechism teaches, it signifies " So be it."   After the repetition of the Creed it means " So it is."   Composers frequently append " Amen " to anthems where it can have no possible sense or significance.   Thus, Sir John Goss, Sir George Macfarren, and the Rev. W. H. Havergal in their settings of the antiphon, " O Saviour of the world."   This at once betrays liturgical ignorance.

Amice.   A piece of fine linen, oblong in shape, with an apparel or orphrey (*aurum Phrygiatum*—Phrygian gold-work [1]) sewn on its edges.   It was introduced in the eighth century as a covering for the neck—till then bare.   Derived from *amicere*, to bind.   It is worn by the celebrant at the Holy Eucharist, being put over the head, loosely tied, then slipped down on the shoulders beneath the alb.   It is supposed to represent the linen rag with which the Jews blindfolded our Saviour.   The corresponding garment in the Coptic Liturgy of St Basil is called 'Επωμὶs, and is reckoned by Gabriel, Patriarch of Alexandria, among the ecclesiastical vestments.   Other names are " superhumerale," " humerale," and " anabolagium."   Consult "Canonists on the Ecclesiastical Vestments," by Mackenzie E. C. Walcott, B.D., F.S.A., Precentor of Chichester (*The Ecclesiologist*, April, June, August, 1867).   See also *sub voce* " Bands."   Dr Bock (*Lit. Gewand.* ii. 17) and Viollet-le-Duc have exhausted the learning on the subject of this vestment. The former gives a plate (*lib.* ii.) representing the three modes in which it may be worn, and the latter (*Dict. Rais. du Mobil. Franc.*, iii. 17) figures the amice of St Thomas of Canterbury, preserved at Sens.   At Canterbury in 1295 there were in the sacristy sixty-four albs with their amices, plain without apparels (Dart, " Canterbury," Append.).   The amice of St Thomas was, however, adorned with gems.   So at St Paul's, 1295, there were many amices magnificently adorned—*e.g.* with nodules of gold and stars of silver, and letters

---

[1] Pliny, viii. 48.

inscribed round them : " An amice worked with red and blue silk, and with trees embroidered on it, etc., etc." At Sarum (A.D. 1222) were two amices adorned with gold and precious stones ; five embroidered amices, seven with gold, and four others of silk. At Exeter, Leofric gave white amices ; Brewere (Bishop, 1224) one " Indi coloris," sky-blue ; another of Archdeacon Pembroke (1263) was of white samite with angels and flowers in gold ; another of Bishop Berkeley, excellently adorned with large pearls, with others. J. D. Chambers (" Divine Worship," p. 35) mentions a German amice (fifteenth-century) with apparels of crimson and ornaments of silver four feet two inches by one foot eleven inches, as then (1876) in the South Kensington Museum. At the end of the sixteenth century we find the amice degenerated into the flowing neckcloth of the clergy, with the ends metamorphosed into large bands, which also have now vanished ; but there can be no reason why this ancient form of the clerical collar should not be revived.

The Angelical Salutation, or " Hail, Mary ! " A devotion recited three times a day in the Western Church, in honour of Our **Angelus.** Lord's Incarnation. The " Angelus bell " (which rings thrice at each of the three divisions of the form) is rung in some places at 6 A.M., at noon, and at 6 P.M. In others, as in Italy, the first and third Angelus take place respectively at sunrise and sunset. According to old English use the " Angelus " was said twice daily—viz. when the bell rang for Prime, and when the curfew bell rang at evening. The English form ran as follows : —(1) " The angel of the Lord brought the message to Mary, and she conceived of the Holy Ghost. Hail, Mary ! " (2) " Behold the handmaid of the Lord ; be it unto me according to Thy word. Hail, Mary ! " (3) " The Word was made Flesh, and dwelt among us. Hail, Mary ! " followed by the Collect for the Annunciation. In the Western Church the following is the form :—" Hail, Mary ! full of grace, the Lord is with thee : blessed art thou among women ; and blessed is the fruit of thy womb, Jesus." To this the reigning Pope added about the middle of the sixteenth century the clause, " Holy Mary, Mother of God, pray for us sinners now and at the hour of our death. Amen." In the Eastern Church the form is thus : " Hail, Virgin Mary ! Mother of God ! full of grace, the Lord is with thee : blessed art thou among women, and blessed is the fruit of thy womb which gave birth to the Saviour of our souls." The " Ave Maria " was not used before the Canonical Hours of Prayer (q.v.) until the sixteenth century, in the Latin Offices. It was then introduced by Cardinal Quignon into his " Reformed

ECCLESIASTICAL TERMS

Breviary" (1536). The words have been frequently used by composers of the Roman Church as a motett or anthem for festivals of the Blessed Virgin. The settings by Arcadelt and Palestrina (sixteenth century), Cherubini (early nineteenth century), and that by Mendelssohn (1832)—adapted to English words beginning "Saviour of sinners"—are celebrated. That by Cherubini is for a solo treble ; the others are for combinations of voices. There is a charming modern setting by Carl Oberthür, the harpist (d. 1895), adapted to English words beginning " Give ear, O Lord." Other hymns and antiphons to the Virgin are the *Alma Redemptoris, Alma Virgo, Ave Maris Stella, Ave Regina, O Sanctissima,* and *Regina cœli.* They have been set by numerous composers, ancient and modern. A very beautiful melody for the *Ave Maris Stella* is in use at the Cathedral of Beauvais.

Ante-Chapel. That portion of a college chapel westward of the screen upon which the organ is generally placed. Examples : Eton College ; All Souls', Magdalen, Merton, New, and Wadham Colleges, Oxford ; King's, Trinity, St John's, and Queens' Colleges, Cambridge. The usual form of an Oxford college chapel is a **T** ; that of the Cambridge ones an oblong. The word is often ignorantly spelt by newspaper reporters and guide-book manufacturers as " Anti-chapel." At Ely, from 1770 to 1847, there was an ante-choir of three bays immediately eastward of the octagon. At St Paul's, from 1697 to 1860, there was a short ante-choir which extended from the eastern piers of the dome to nearly the middle of the first bay of the choir. Then, in both cases, came the organ screen. At St Paul's, an iron grille, with gates, stood flush with the aforesaid dome piers, and there were also grilles, and gates opening into the aisles in the westernmost bay, partially occupied by the screen, on either side.

Antependium. See *sub voce* " Frontal."

Anthem. A composition for voices, with or without organ or other instrumental accompaniment, enjoined by the rubric of the English Church to be used at morning and evening service " in choirs and places where they sing." In our cathedral service the anthem holds an important place. A dissertation on this subject would be impossible here, and a history in all its fulness is yet unwritten. The word is derived from Ἀντίφωνον, originally a poem from some Psalm in which the choir responded to the priest (*ecloga ex Psalmo aliquo in Liturgiis Graecorum, qua sacerdoti chorus respondet*), from Ἀντίφωνος (*contra sonans, respondens,* from ἀντί, *contra,* opposite, and φωνή, *vox, sonus,* voice, sound).

17

A DICTIONARY OF

"Anthem" has been incorrectly derived from ἀντὶ and ὕμνος, a hymn, a thanksgiving offered to God for the blessings we enjoy (ὕμνος ἐστὶν ἡ ἐπὶ τοῖς ὑπάρχουσιν ἡμῖν ἀγαθοῖς ἀνατιθεμένη τῷ Θεῷ εὐφημία. Greg. Nys. in Ps. xi.). Dr Johnson wrongly said that the word should be spelled *anthym*. But a taste for music was one of the few characteristics of a noble mind which the great lexicographer possessed not. It is not necessary seriously to discuss other proposed derivations, such as ἀνάθεμα, in which the anthem is treated as an invocation ; or ἄνθημα, a flower, a word which seems to be found only in compounds. Since the ancient antiphons consisted of a short passage of Holy Writ set to music, it is not to be wondered at that the term *antiphon* was applied to signify any short passage of Scripture in general. Thus, it was used to designate the text of a sermon, as in the following passage from an old chronicler :—" He made unto them exhortacions or colacions, and took for his *anteleme* ' Haurietis aquas,' etc., ' Ye shall draw water out of the wells of salvation.' " In the account which Strype (" Annals of the Reformation ") gives of the solemn obsequies of Henry III. of France, memorialised in St Paul's Cathedral on the 8th and 9th of September 1559, we find : " The offering finished, the Sermon began, by the elect of Hereford [Bishop Scory] ; the elect of London, who should have preached, being sick ; his Anthem [*i.e.* his text] being *Veniet hora, et nunc est, quando mortui audient vocem Filii Dei*, etc. ' The hour shall come, and now is, when the dead shall hear the voice of God.' " Other instances of the kind might be adduced. In this sense it is that the short texts of Scripture, directed in our Prayer-Book to be sung instead of the *Venite* on Easter Day, are called " Anthems " ; the word anthems signifying texts, and not having reference to the way in which they should be sung or said. In the book of 1549, the sentence, " Remember not " in the Visitation of the Sick, the sentence, " O Saviour of the world," in the same office, and " Turn us, O Lord," in the Commination Service, are likewise called *anthems*. The term anthem in its modern and common sense signifies a composition for use in the Church, of a more or less varied and ornate character, and not a mere simple metrical tune. The anthem in our service corresponds to the motett in the Latin rite. The word " motett " is a diminutive from the Italian *moto*, signifying movement, and it is evident that the anthems of our earliest writers, such as Tye, Tallis, and Whyte, were suggested, as to form, by the motett of the Latin Church. Such compositions were abundant in the English Church before the Reformation. The place of the motett is at Mass (generally during

18

the offertory) and at Compline, the closing service of the day. The words of anthems are, in most cases, taken from Holy Writ, and are in prose. Sometimes they are derived from the collects, or other portions of the Book of Common Prayer, but most frequently of all from the Psalter. Occasionally portions of ancient liturgies, and metrical versions of the Psalms, are used. Sometimes they consist of various compositions in prose or verse, the works of private individuals ; and although it would seem preferable to derive them from the former four sources, yet we find the practice to have existed so constantly, ever since the Reformation, of using private compositions for the words of anthems, that it cannot be supposed unlawful. The well-known anthem, " Lord, for Thy tender mercies' sake," commonly ascribed to Farrant ; Tallis' " I call and cry " ; Gibbons' " See, see, the Word is Incarnate " ; and the numerous metrical anthems by various composers in Day's "Service-Book," (1565), and in Clifford's " Divine Services and Anthems " (1664), are proofs that no scruples existed on this point during the first century after the Reformation ; and every cathedral anthem-book contains instances enough to show that the licence to use uncanonical words has been freely acted upon, down to the present day. The music of anthems is, of course, of every possible variety. There are (1) the full anthem, intended to be sung by the whole choir in chorus, with perhaps some degree of antiphony between the *Decani* and *Cantoris* sides. Aldrich's " By the waters of Babylon," Batten's " Let my complaint," and " When the Lord turned again," Child's " O praise the Lord, laud ye," and Richardson's " O how amiable " —all full anthems—have the directions, " Decani," " Cantoris," and " Full," like Services for the Canticles ; (2) the verse anthem, which contains passages to be sung by two, three, or more select voices, with choruses interspersed, and (3) the solo anthem, in which the chorus is frequently a subordinate feature, though never omitted. Verse and solo anthems require the accompaniment of the organ. Full anthems, if constructed in the pure vocal style, are for the most part better without. Many of the movements from the oratorios, cantatas, etc., of Handel, Bach, Graun, Haydn. Beethoven, Mendelssohn, Spohr, Hiller, Gounod, Brahms, Sterndale Bennett, Julius Benedict, Macfarren, Sullivan, Stainer, and others, have now come to be recognised as integral parts of our anthem music, and adaptations have been made from the masses of Carissimi, Leo, Moreira, Pergolesi, Mozart, Hummel, and Novello, but with varying success. On the other hand, the adaptation to English words of the motetts of Anerio, Bach, Byrd, Deering, Eccard, Jacob

19

Händl, Orlando di Lasso, Lotti, Marenzio, Palestrina, Sweelinck, Tallis, Vittoria, and Samuel Wesley, is a healthy sign, and a practice now becoming very general. Leaving foreign compositions out of the question, we may say that the music of the English Church, as regards anthems, is a heritage of genius strictly national, and of unequalled excellence. Like that for the settings of the Canticles, technically termed "Services," and that for single and double chants to which the Psalms are sung, it has no duplicate in any Church in Christendom. The Prayer-Books of 1549 and 1552 contain no rubric directing the performance of the anthem, and Merbecke ("Book of Common Prayer Noted") is entirely silent on the subject. When the Liturgy was settled at the time of the Reformation, the usual place of the anthem seems to have been at the end of Matins and Evensong—that is, after the Third Collect, with which those offices then terminated. Strype ("Annals of the Reformation, "vol. i. c. 16) tells us that in 1560 he went to hear a sermon preached by Barlow before the Queen, and adds: "His sermon ended at five o'clock, and presently after her Chapel went to Evening song; the cross as before, standing on the altar, and two candlesticks, and two tapers burning in them, and service concluded, a good anthem was sung." The present rubric: "In Quires and Places where they sing, here followeth the Anthem," was not inserted until 1661, when the "State Prayers" were introduced. These last had, however, already appeared in Laud's Scottish Prayer-Book of 1637. The Rev. James Clifford's preface to his black-letter duodecimo, "The Divine Services and Anthems," published in 1664, informs us that four anthems were then sung at St Paul's on a Sunday: two at Matins and two at Evensong. They followed the Third Collect and the sermon at each service. It is impossible to say if this custom was kept up after the opening of the choir of the new Cathedral in 1697. At any rate, for the last century and a half, there has been only one regular anthem at St Paul's on Sundays—that at Evensong, though, since 1873, a short anthem, termed the Introit, has been sung between the Litany and the Communion Service. Formerly, the *Sanctus* was used in this place. There is no anthem at St Paul's on Litany mornings in the week— viz. Wednesday and Friday. Until 1869 the Sunday afternoon sermon was preached after the anthem, the service concluding with the "State Prayers." The omission of the anthem on Litany mornings at St Paul's is to be regretted. One of those short, solemn compositions in the short full style, and, in ferial seasons, of a penitential character, by our earlier writers, Tallis, Byrd, Farrant,

ECCLESIASTICAL TERMS

Batten, Rogers, or Aldrich, might occasionally be chosen, and thus form a fitting introduction to the deep supplication which follows. It should be observed that the anthem has, of late years, been restored in this place at Westminster Abbey, where irregularities of every kind formerly prevailed, but which the authorities of that church have, for some time past, done their best to ameliorate. At St Patrick's Cathedral, Dublin, four anthems of a high-class character are now sung every Sunday. Those in the morning precede the Communion Service and follow the Offertory ; and of the two in the evening service, the first is sung in its usual place after the Third Collect, the second after the sermon. Before 1900, the anthem in the morning service was sung after the Third Collect, but it was then ordered to be sung after the sermon, its former place being taken by a hymn. At the same time, the *Sanctus* which, until then, had ushered in the Communion Service, was replaced by a short anthem or introit. Jebb ("Choral Service of the Church," 1843) tells us that the place of the anthem had been frequently shifted at St Patrick's within his recollection. There was then only one anthem, at the one choral service on Sunday, that of Evensong. " At one time," he observes, " it was performed just before the [Apostolic] Benediction, and lastly after the sermon, where perhaps it still is." " The reason assigned for its postponement," he continues, " is the desire to prevent the congregation from leaving the church before the service is concluded. This reason is, in itself, altogether inadmissible ; besides, it would be quite within the power of the Chapter to obviate the careless behaviour, too visible in that Church, by stringent regulations, which indeed they have of late [1843] in part adopted." Thackeray mentions in his " Irish Sketch-Book," some three or four years later, that " the shameless English practice of the congregation retreating after the anthem, is prevented, at St Patrick's, by locking the gates, and having the music after the sermon." At Christ Church Cathedral, in the same city, the custom of having two anthems at Evensong obtained until comparatively recently, when a hymn was substituted for the shorter anthem after the Third Collect. In the middle of the last century the anthem was omitted altogether at York and some other cathedrals, on the Wednesdays and Fridays in Lent. At the cathedral of Oxford and at St George's Chapel, Windsor, a hymn is now sung in place of the anthem on Litany mornings, in defiance of all cathedral tradition and ritual propriety. At Westminster Abbey the anthem at Evensong on Sundays and Holy Days is sung at the conclusion of the sermon, which is preached after the Third Collect, the remaining prayers being said when the anthem is finished. This, apparently, has long been the custom at Westminster. Bishop Cleveland Coxe alludes to it in his book, " Impressions of England in 1851." See also *sub voce* " Full Anthem," " Solo Anthem," and " Verse Anthem."

Antiphon. In its earliest form this seems to have been a single verse out of any psalm, repeated after, or even before, the recitation of a Psalm or canticle, with a view of bringing into prominence, and fastening attention upon, some special idea connected with it, and giving the keynote, as it were, to the day's teaching. Afterwards, antiphons came to be selected, not exclusively from the particular Psalms to which they were affixed, but from appropriate passages of Scripture which might be similarly employed. The antiphon, " O Saviour of the world," in the Office of the Visitation of the Sick, is the only one left of the many antiphons with which our pre-Reformation service-books were studded. Consult " Parish Choir," vol. ii. p. 18 (1847) ; Rev. J. Baden Powell's " Choralia," p. 55. See also *sub voce* " Psalter."

Antiphonarium. Originally an anthem-book (see " Parish Choir," vol. i. p. 162), but, as time went on, it gradually collected other portions of the Divine Office, and contained not only antiphons, but also invitatories, responses, hymns, etc. Sometimes it was called Responsarium, or Responsoriale. Sometimes it contained only the antiphons which belonged to the Mass, but this was more generally called the *Gradual*. It was often very oddly spelt in English—*e.g. Antiphor, Antisyphonar.* In the accounts of St Margaret's, Westminster, for 1475, we find : " Item, for ye great bokes, called Antiphoners, £22."

Antiphonal Singing. The responsive or alternate singing of choirs, similar in some respects to the ἐπίρρημα and ἀντεπίρρημα of the old Tragedy. Although Christian authors give accounts of antiphonal singing as something new, there can be no doubt of its great antiquity. There are sufficient allusions to it in the Old Testament to show that it was well known to the Jews ; and the very structure of many of the Psalms implies its existence. In the cathedral worship of the Church Universal, the Psalms of the day are chanted throughout, and in order to preserve their responsive character, two full choirs (*Decani* and *Cantoris*) are stationed one on each side of the church. One of these having chanted one verse remains silent, while the opposite choir replies in the verse succeeding ; and at the end of each Psalm (and of each division of Psalm cxix.) the *Gloria Patri* is sung " Full " by the united choirs. The reading of the Psalms by parson and clerk in alternate verses, and the usage now prevalent in foreign churches subject to Rome, of chanting one verse by a single voice, or two voices, and the other by the full choir, is not ancient, and is admitted to be incorrect by some Continental ritualists themselves. So, too, in some of our own churches where Gregorian music prevails, an objectionable practice has crept in, of singing the verses of the Psalms by boys and men alternately, not even excepting the *Gloria Patri*. Such a method is quite destructive of the genuine effect of antiphonal chanting, which ought to be equally balanced on each side of the choir.

Apse. A semicircular or polygonal termination to, or projection from, a church, as at Canterbury, Lichfield, Norwich, Peterborough, St Paul's, Westminster. On the Continent the apse is almost universally the eastern termination. See also *sub voce* " Chevet."

Arcade. The technical term in architecture for a range of arches, supported on piers or columns, either open, or closed with masonry.

Architrave. The lowest division of the entablature (*q.v.*) in classical architecture, resting immediately on the abacus of the capital ; also the ornamental moulding running round the interior curve of an arch, and hence applied to the mouldings round the openings of doors, windows, etc.

Armariolum. A wardrobe in the treasury of cathedrals and monastic churches, for keeping the eucharistic and other vestments. Old St Paul's possessed such an armariolum, in which were twenty-four *perticae*, pegs, or rods, or frames, from which the copes, chasubles, frontals, etc., could be suspended, one *pertica* holding from three to six copes. There is an engraving of an Armariolum in Mueller's " Ornatus Ecclesiasticus," 1591.

Asperges, The. In the Church of Rome, immediately before the principal Mass on Sundays, a short service called the " Asperges " takes place. The celebrant, vested in a cope, enters the sanctuary with the deacon and sub-deacon, and a short procession is made, during which the holy water is sprinkled. While this ceremony is taking place the choir sing the antiphon, " Asperges me, Domine, hyssopo, et mundabor," etc. (" Thou shalt purge me with hyssop, and I shall be clean "), followed by the first verse of the 51st Psalm, " Miserere mei, Deus," etc. (" Have mercy upon me, O God "), and the *Gloria Patri*, after which the antiphon is repeated.

From Easter to Pentecost the antiphon is: "Vidi aquam egredientem, de templo a latere dextro, Alleluia," etc. ("I saw a stream of water flowing from the temple, out of the right side, Alleluia," etc.), followed by the first verse of Psalm cxviii. : "Confitemini Domino, quoniam bonus," etc. ("O give thanks unto the Lord, for He is gracious"), with *Gloria Patri*, and the antiphon repeated. This aspersion typifies the dew of God's blessing which is shed upon those who worship Him aright. The music to which these words are sung is generally plain-song, but there are settings in motett form by many of the distinguished composers for the Roman Church. There is an *Asperges* for four voices, attributed to Palestrina, printed in the 32nd volume of Breitkopf & Härtel's complete edition of his works, scored by Haberl, "*ex diversis Bibliothecis et Archivis*"; and a setting [1] by the Abbé Max Stadler (1748-1833), for four voices and organ, is somewhat celebrated. Other settings in the same form, interspersed with plain-song, by Vincent Novello and S. Webbe, will in found in the collection of "Motetts for the Offertory, etc.," published by the first-named while organist to the Chapel of the Portuguese Embassy, South Street, Grosvenor Square (1797-1822). In the Sarum rite the hallowing and sprinkling of the water took place immediately after the procession, and prior to the Office of Terce, by the priest, vested in alb, amice, and cope, and attended by deacon and sub-deacon duly vested (the former carrying the Book of the Holy Gospels), and by the thurifer and taper-bearers, and an acolyte bearing the processional cross, and two boys (one to hold the vessel of water, and the other the book). On Sundays that were Double Feasts the hallowing took place privately before some side altar, and the water was sprinkled after Sext, or the noonday office. Salt was cast into the water in the form of a cross, after having been, like the water, exorcised by the priest. The form for this blessing of the water will be found in "Notes on Ceremonial" (Pickering, 1882).

Aspergill, or Aspersol. The *sprinkle* or instrument (somewhat resembling a painter's brush) used in the Roman Church to sprinkle holy water at the "Asperges," before High Mass.

"Item; unum *Aspersol* cum hyssopo argenti"—Inventarium MS. Ecclesiæ Aniciencis, ann. 1444 (Ducange).
"There was also belonging to this service a portable vessel for the Holy-water, and an instrument attending it, called a *Sprinkle*. For we are told in Fox's Monuments, vol. iii. p. 262, that Dr Chadsey

---

[1] Of the *Vidi aquam*,

ECCLESIASTICAL TERMS

being to preach before Bishop Bonner in his chapel at Fulham, after putting the stole about his neck, carried the Holy-water *Sprinkle* to the Bishop, who blessed him and gave him Holy-water, and so he went to his sermon " (Delafield MS. in Bodleian Library, Oxford).

Aspersorium. The portable vessel to hold the holy water used at the "Asperges." In the Inventory of the Treasury of St Paul's, taken in 1552, we find : "One holye water stocke of sylver and parcell gylte viij. square ij. libardes (leopards') heddes at the socketts of the handle with a sprinkle allsoe of sylver and percell gylte, xlv. unc." This seems to have been the same vessel mentioned in an earlier inventory, 1402 : "A silver vase for holy water of Greek fabric," probably the gift of Bishop Richard de Belmeis I., 1127. The term " Aspersorium " is sometimes applied, though not quite correctly, to the "stoup," or fixed holy-water basin, to be found either in the porch or close to the entrance of a church. In the accounts of All Souls' College, Oxford, in 1485, there is a charge, " pro lapidibus ad *aspersorium* in introiter ecclesiæ," the remains of which may still be seen. The term also seems to have been sometimes applied to the " aspergill " or " sprinkle."

Athanasian Creed.
Lat.
Symbolum Athanasii.

Its liturgical title is *Quiqunque vult*, from the opening words, " Whosoever will be saved," etc. There is abundant and clear evidence that, at the commencement of the ninth century, the Athanasian Creed was not only extant in its entirety, as we now have it, but was used in the offices of the Church, and was commonly regarded as the genuine work of St Athanasius. Of the four MSS. at present extant, three are placed at the close of the ninth century, and of these three one is imperfect owing to mutilation. The fourth is the earliest-known MS. of the creed. It is deposited in the Ambrosian Library at Milan. Muratori, who was custodian of the library at the end of the seventeenth century, confidently assigned it to the close of the seventh century ; Montfaucon, the Benedictine, critic and antiquary (1655-1741), believed it to have been written in the eighth. No palæographical authority has ever placed it later than this. The Athanasian Creed has been used since the year 800 in the English Church, and probably some time before that date, for it is found in MS. psalters of the eighth century. In the Sarum Breviary it was appointed to be sung daily at Prime, after the Psalms and before the prayers. In the Roman Breviary it is ordered to be used on Sundays only. Cardinal Quignonez, in his Reformed Breviary of 1536, had appointed the Athanasian Creed on Sundays, and the Apostles' Creed on

week-days. In our first Prayer-Book of 1549 the Apostles' Creed was appointed to be said ordinarily at Matins, immediately after the *Benedictus*, and the Athanasian Creed in its stead upon the six festivals of Christmas, Epiphany, Easter, Ascension, Pentecost and Trinity.   In 1552 seven saints' days were added to these festivals, so that this creed should be used at intervals of about a month throughout the year.   The present English version is substantially the same as that given by Hilsey, Bishop of Rochester, in his Prymer of 1539.   In Bishop Cosin's "Durham Prayer-Book" there is a direction that it should be said "one verse by the priest, and another by the people ; or in colleges, and where there is a quire, by sides." Merbecke has set the Athanasian Creed very nobly to the 4th Tone, 1st Ending.   The chant usually sung, as given by Boyce, Bishop, Rimbault, Oliphant and others in their editions of Tallis' Service, has been incorrectly assigned to that composer, since it is not to be found in Barnard's collection of 1641, the earliest printed edition of the Service.   The tune called "Canterbury" in Edward Lowe's "Brief Directions" (1661) and in the "Review" of his "Brief Directions" (1664) will correspond with it, if the second counter-tenor be converted into the treble.   Lowe himself provides the 7th Tone, which, he tells us, was anciently used at Salisbury where he was a chorister before the Rebellion.   In this he is followed by Clifford ("Divine Services," etc., 1664) and Playford ("Introduction to Practical Music," 1672-1730).   Dean Aldrich in his Christ Church Oxford, MSS. also gives the 7th Tone, but with a different ending. The modern choral manuals—Mercer's "Church Psalter and Hymn-Book" (1854), Joule's "Directorium Chori Anglicanum" (1860), W. H. Monk's "Psalter and Canticles" (1878) and the "Cathedral Prayer-Book" (1891)—all provide the chant as given in Boyce's "Cathedral Music," the melody being assigned in some to the treble, in others to the tenor.   At Christ Church Cathedral, Dublin, an ornate double chant in the key of F by Sir John Stevenson (d. 1833) was formerly used.   This, with Stevenson's Preces and Responses, will be found in the "Short Service for Holy Days" (in C major), published in his score of 1825.   It was reprinted in "Chants, Ancient and Modern" (Dublin, 1883), and again (transposed to E) in a rearranged and greatly enlarged edition of the same book (1906). John Marsh, a once well-known amateur of Chichester (d. 1828), wrote a less florid double chant for this creed.   It appeared in his 'Twenty-four New Chants" (*c.* 1800) and again in the excellent collection edited by Alfred Bennett and William Marshall of Oxford (1829).   A writer in *The Parish Choir* (December 1849) quotes a curious chant for the Athanasian Creed which was at that time used at Lincoln. Notwithstanding all that has been written and spoken on the subject, the Church of England means to maintain *unmutilated*, the liturgical use of this creed. " The Catholic faith is this : that we worship "—not with intellectual assent alone, but with the movement of our entire being—" One God in Trinity and Trinity in Unity." It does not come within the scope of the present article to reply to the objections frequently alleged against the *Quiqunque vult*, especially the so-called damnatory clauses, upon dogmatic grounds. For a complete vindication of it from these objections the reader may be referred to a masterly paper by Professor Mozley, contained in his " Lectures and other Theological Papers " (Rivingtons, 1883), also to the fine sermon, " Trinity Sunday," by Canon Melvill, published in the second volume of sermons preached at St Paul's, etc., during the latter years of his life (Rivingtons, 1872). The date, authorship, original titles, reception and use, with full history of the Athanasian Creed, will be found in the able article by the Rev. G. D. W. Ommanney, Vicar of Draycot, and Prebendary of Wells, contributed to Hook's " Church Dictionary," 1896. The Athanasian Creed, when well chanted by the choir and accompanied on the organ with taste and skill, is a feature of our morning service on festivals. In the possession of the writer of this notice there is a chant for the Athanasian Creed, in quadruple form, by Gilbert Heathcote, Archdeacon of Winchester from 1819 to 1829. It is in vocal score, in the Archdeacon's autograph, and the MS. is thus subscribed : " This Chant for the Athanasian Creed is the old Chant of Tallis, as given by Boyce, with additional notes. The Creed is so written that four verses may be taken together without interrupting the connected sentences. The second and sixth divisions of the Chant are of short measure that they may be similar. The fourth and eighth divisions are long measure. G. Heathcote, Winton, May 1826." A chant, somewhat similar in construction, was written for this Creed by the late John Hopkins, organist of Rochester Cathedral from 1856 to 1900.

Aumbry, Almery, Aumery, or Ambry. A term defined by John Carter, the distinguished antiquary of the later eighteenth century, as " a niche or cupboard by the side of an Altar, to contain the utensils belonging thereunto." This would make it appear the same as the *locker*, a hollow space in the thickness of the wall, with a door to it. It is, however, evident from many passages in ancient writers, that a more extended signification must be given to the word aumbry, and that in the larger churches and cathedrals the almeries were very numerous, and placed in various parts of the church, and even in the cloisters. They were frequently of wood, and sometimes of considerable size, answering to what we should now call closets. The doors, and other parts that were seen, were usually richly carved and ornamented. Examples: Chapel of Chepstow Castle (stone), choir of Selby Abbey, Yorks, and St Peter's Church, Louvaine (wood). In some foreign churches the aumbry is too frequently made the receptacle for candle-ends and other refuse. Durham Cathedral contains a pair of interesting aumbries, immediately to the west of the quadruple sedilia, on the north and south sides of the sanctuary. Here, before the Dissolution of the Abbey various articles connected with the high altar and its services were deposited. The present doors, however, are modern. " In the north side of the quire there is an almerye near to the high altar, fastened in the wall, for to lay anything in pertaining to the high altar. Likewise there is another almerye in the south side of the quire nigh the high altar, enclosed in the wall, to set the chalices, the basins, and the cruets in, that they did minister withal at the high mass, with locks and keys for the said almeryes " (" Rites of Durham," p. 11). At the beautiful little Cathedral and Collegiate Church of the Holy Spirit, Isle of Cumbrae, built from the designs of W. Butterfield, 1849–1851, there is an aumbry in the north wall of the sanctuary, closed by a brass door, which is pierced with tracery work. At the Collegiate Church of St Michael, near Tenbury, there is one in the sacristy, with doors of oak.

A hymn whose text is found in Mone's *Lateinischer Hymnen des Mittelalters*, with the heading, " In elevatione Corporis Christi,"

Ave Verum Corpus Natum. and the statement that a Reichenau MS. of the fourteenth century says: " Pope Innocent composed the following salutation " and " this prayer has three years of indulgence granted by Pope Leo." In Horst's " Paradisus Animæ " (Cologne, 1644) it is printed as a private devotion at the Elevation of the Host in the Mass. It is anonymous. The most celebrated musical settings in motett form are those of Catalani and Josquin de Près (sixteenth and seventeenth centuries), Mozart (late eighteenth century), Cherubini (early nineteenth), Gounod (later nineteenth). Samuel Wesley contributed a fine setting for men's voices (A.T.T.B.) to Vincent Novello's " Motetts for the Offertory and Morning Service," book i. There are good modern settings by Sir Edward Elgar, F. A. W. Docker, W. S. Hoyte, B. Luard Selby, and the Rev. J. Baden Powell. Gounod wrote many settings, but the three finest are those known in this country beginning " Jesu, Word of God Incarnate," " Jesu, Blessed Word of God Incarnate," and " Word of God Incarnate," all published by Novello.   The translations of Mozart's and the other modern settings specified above are based on that of the first-named by Gounod. The ancient Gregorian melody used in the diocese of Paris will be found printed, with harmonies, in *The Sacristy*, February 1871.   It is arranged for tenor solo and chorus.   The translation begins : " Hail, True Body, born of Mary," and the whole is quite different from that to the other settings mentioned.   The *Ave Verum* is frequently sung as a motett in the comparatively modern Roman Office of Benediction.

Baldacchino. A canopy placed over an altar as an emblem of dignity and honour.   It usually rests on four pillars, but is occasionally bracketed out from the wall at the back, and three sides are frequently shut in by curtains.   At an early period it was by no means uncommon, and continued so in Italy until the fourteenth and perhaps the fifteenth century ; but in England, though examples up to the eleventh century may be found, it never seems to have been usual, and after that date, beyond perhaps isolated examples, they were no longer erected ; in fact, we have no term in the language conveying the meaning except the word *canopy*, which is of a general not specific nature, and not ordinarily used in ecclesiological language.   The word *baldacchino* is exclusively Italian, and its correlative was scarcely known here until the revival of ecclesiology led to the study and occasional introduction of foreign forms.   The Latin term *ciborium* (or canopy over the tabernacle) was occasionally applied to the structure when occurring in England, France and Germany.   Dr Rock (" Church of our Fathers," i. 199) gives an illustration of an example in use in the year A.D. 802, which had curtains hung from it, and says that on great festivals it was wreathed with garlands of evergreens and flowers.   Camille Enlart, in his " Manuel d'Archéologie Française " (1902), gives illustrations of the magnificent white marble and mosaic ciborium in the Church of St Maria in Cosmedin, Rome, the work of Diodato Cosimati (1296), and of the interesting fourteenth-century one at Marville (Meuse).   Other examples of the ciborium and baldacchino are those of St Peter's, St Paul Extra Muros, St Clement, and St John Lateran, Rome ; St Ambrogio, Milan ; the Cathedrals of Baretta and Viterbo ;   Parenzo, Istria ;   Valcabrere, Haute-Garonne ;   St Denis, Paris ;   the Cathedral of Ratisbon (Germany), and the Cathedrals of Sens, Nevers, Quimper, Moulins sur Allier, and Angers

(France). The introduction of the baldacchino into modern use was advocated very ably by Mr R. F. Pullan in his pamphlet, "The Altar, Baldacchino, and Reredos," and some thirty-five years ago there was a proposal to erect one in our Cathedral of St Paul, where, in a building of Italian type, it would not have been inappropriate. The altarpiece of carved oak in the Church of St Mary, Woolnoth, London, designed by Nicholas Hawksmoor in 1713, may well be described as a baldacchino. There are modern Renaissance examples in the Church of the Holy Redeemer, Clerkenwell, and in the new Cathedral at Westminster. That in the Church of St Barnabas, Oxford (1869), is Italian Romanesque in *motif*; while that in the cathedral at Peterborough is in the form of the mediæval ciborium.

An ornament in architecture resembling a ball placed in a circular flower, the three petals of which form a cup round it. It is **Ball-flower.** usually found inserted in a hollow moulding, and is generally characteristic of the Decorated style. Examples : Hereford Cathedral (where it is the prevailing ornament), Gloucester Cathedral (south aisle of nave), Grantham Church (west end), North Moreton Church, Berks (curious Early Decorated water-drain). It sometimes occurs, though rarely, in buildings of the thirteenth century, or Early English style, as in the west front of Salisbury Cathedral, where is it mixed with the tooth-ornament (*q.v.*)—an indication that the style is late.

Two oblong pieces of cambric or linen, four to nine inches long, and two or three wide, joined together and worn under the chin. **Bands.** They are said by some to be a relic of the amice ; but it is not an exclusively clerical vestment, being part of the full dress of the bar and of the universities, and of other bodies in which a more ancient habit is retained, as in some schools of old foundation, such as Christ's Hospital. Their use has been gradually discontinued by the clergy, but of late years they have been laudably revived by some. Cathedral choristers formerly wore them, and they still form part of the state dress of the Children of the Chapel Royal. Parish clerks frequently appeared in gown and bands. Bands were also worn by children attending parochial charity schools. Black bands, edged with white, form part of the dress of the French bishops and clergy. Dr Liddon, in his delightful little biography of Walter Kerr Hamilton, Bishop of Salisbury from 1856 to 1869, tells us that that saintly prelate would not allow his chaplains to follow the modern fashion of leaving off bands. "These things are all worth something," he said, "and it is very difficult, where it is not impossible, to restore any thing which has ever been given up."

ECCLESIASTICAL TERMS

Dr Liddon himself, for some time one of Bishop Hamilton's chaplains, invariably wore bands while Canon Residentiary of St Paul's (1870-1890).

Sometimes a separate building, sometimes the part of a church in which Holy Baptism was administered by immersion, of which **Baptistery.** a remarkable instance remains at Cranbrook, Kent, or merely the enclosure containing the font, as at Luton, Bedfordshire. At Canterbury, the font stood, until its removal to the nave a few years since, in a circular building, communicating with the north side of the church, called Bell Jesus. There is a good modern example at Escrick, Yorks, F. C. Penrose, architect, 1854 (see an excellent woodcut in *Illustrated London News* of that year). The font itself is by Tognoli, master of drawing to Canova. Others are at Christ Church Cathedral, Dublin (G. E. Street, architect, 1872-1878), and Truro Cathedral (J. L. Pearson, architect, 1887). Foreign examples : St John Lateran, Rome ; Cremona, Florence, Parma, Pisa, Pistoja, Ravenna, and Siena, at which last it is below the choir of the cathedral. In England, the baptistery was sometimes called the "Christening Pew." There was such a " Christening Pew " at the west end of Wren's fine church, St Andrew's, Holborn. It was destroyed by the mediævalist architect, S. S. Teulon, during his unfortunate " restoration " of the church in 1872. Teulon removed the font itself to an obscure south-eastern corner of the building, thus completely nullifying the beautiful symbolism of the entrance to the Spiritual Church by baptism. It has recently, however, been replaced in its proper position at the west end of the nave. At Trunch, Norfolk, a fine and interesting Decorated church, with considerable Perpendicular additions, and a noble hammer-beam nave roof with spandrels, there is an unusual arrangement of the font. It is placed within a remarkable baptistery or enclosure of carved wood, sufficiently spacious to accommodate several persons, the entire crocketed canopy resting on six slender pillars beyond it. The whole has been gilded and polychromatised, and is of Late Perpendicular date. At Terrington, St Clement's, another magnificent Perpendicular church in the same county, the cœval font has a very remarkable cover. The original tabernacle-work has been altered at some uncertain time. The interior is painted in a singular manner, *temp.* (it is supposed) Queen Anne. The lower part represents the Baptism of Our Lord. There are also two scenes from the Temptation. Above are the Four Evangelists with their symbols, and the mysterious inscription : " Voce Pater. Natus Corpore. Flamen ave. Mat. 3." The upper part

31

of the canopy has red and white roses. On the outside, groups of shafts, painted black, with gold streaking, support the rich tabernacle-work—painted black, white, and gold.

Barrel-vaulting or Waggon-headed Vaulting. A simple form of tunnel-like vaulting, deriving its name from its resemblance to half a barrel, or to the tilt often seen over large waggons. A good modern example may be seen in the chancel of St Matthias', Stoke Newington (W. Butterfield, architect, 1853), where the roof is vaulted in red and yellow brick, with stone ribs, the effect being excellent.

Basilica. **Fr.** *basilique;* **Ital. and Span.** *basilica.* The name applied by the Romans to their public halls, either of justice, of exchange, or other business. These were usually rectangular in plan with a division into aisles by rows of columns, that in the middle being the widest, with a semicircular apse at one end in which the tribunal was placed. Many of these buildings were afterwards converted into Christian churches ; and their ground plan was generally followed in all the early churches, which also long retained the name, and it is still applied to some of the churches in Rome by way of honorary distinction. Examples : St Maria Maggiore, St John Lateran, St Clemente, and St Paul Extra Muros, Rome ; St Apollinaris in Classe and St Apollinaris Nuova, Ravenna ; Torcello Cathedral (Italian) ; St Godehard and St Michael, Hildesheim, the Abbey Church, Quedlinburg (German) ; St Barnabas', Oxford—Sir A. Blomfield, architect (1869), St James', Leicester (modern English). Consult Beresford Hope, " The English Cathedral of the Nineteenth Century " (1861), pp. 133–157. De Vert (" Cérémonies," iii. 134) figures the interior of a basilica, with the positions of the bishop's throne, altar, baldacchino or ciborium, pulpitum, the two ambons or letterns, the paschal candlestick, the forms or rows of benches for the choir, and the places of the priests, deacons and subdeacons. J. D. Chambers reproduces this engraving as a woodcut in his " Divine Worship " (p. 3).

Bay. A principal compartment or division in the architectural arrangement of a building, marked either by the buttresses or pilasters on the walls, by the disposition of the main ribs of the vaulting of the interior, by the main arches and pillars, or by any other leading features that separate it into corresponding portions. The word is also sometimes used for the space between the mullions of a window, properly called a *light*. It is occasionally found corrupted into " Day."

32

ECCLESIASTICAL TERMS

Bedesmen. Almsmen in Cathedrals of the New, or Henry VIII.'s foundation, their number varying from six to twelve. They were usually in the patronage of the Crown (which appointed at Ely till 1670). They were to be poor, aged, or wounded soldiers, to attend daily service, to act as bellringers, sweep the church, to receive wages, and assist the vergers generally. Consult Precentor Mackenzie E. C. Walcott's " Cathedralia " (1865).

Bema. From the Greek βῆμα, the sanctuary, presbytery, or chancel of a church. In the Greek Church the primitive position of the bishop surrounded by his presbyters in the βῆμα or sanctuary is retained during the time of " Liturgy." The 56th Canon of Laodicea refers to this custom, when it orders that the priests shall not venture to sit down at the βῆμα before the entrance of the bishop. Simeon of Thessalonica explains the arrangement of the Saviour seated in the midst of His Apostles at the first celebration of the Holy Eucharist. This subject, often in mosaic or otherwise, decorates the apse : the great saints of the Eastern Church, as St Dionysius, St Basil, or St Chrysostom, are also here represented ; but deacons, when pictured, are only to be seen in the north and south apses. The north apse is appropriated to the προθέσις in the shape of a separate altar. A part of the Liturgy is here performed ; and the ceremony of the " Great Entrance," the offertory of the Elements, is one of considerable pomp. In the southern apse is the sacristy.

Bench-table. A low seat of stone on the inside of the walls of churches. It is also to be found sometimes in porches, cloisters, etc., and round pillars. Examples of the bench-table may be seen at Fotheringhay, Northants ; cloisters and entrance to chapter-house, Salisbury ; St Barnabas, Pimlico (1850) ; St Matthias', Stoke Newington (west end of nave), 1853.

Benedicite Omnia Opera. " The Song of the Three Children," a part of the Greek addition to the third chapter of Daniel. In this hymn of adoration, man undertakes, as Nature's priest and spokesman, to give utterance to the worship of silent service which the earth, through all its graduated activities, without speech or language, for ever fulfils. A paraphrastical exposition of the 148th Psalm, it was used as a hymn in the later Jewish Church, and was commonly sung in the Christian Church in the fourth century. In the old offices of the English Church, the Nocturns (*q.v.*) of Matins ended with the *Te Deum* and were immediately followed by Lauds (*q.v.*), beginning with the Psalms, among which *Benedicite* was sung. In 1549 it was ordered to be used in Lent instead of *Te Deum*.

A DICTIONARY OF

In 1552, when a Psalm was added to each canticle after the lessons of Matins and Evensong, the rubrics concerning *Te Deum* and *Benedicite* were altered, as it appears for uniformity, and these canticles were to be used at discretion, without being limited to particular seasons. *Benedicite* may be sung with great fitness on Septuagesima Sunday, when the First Lesson is the first chapter of Genesis, and on the twenty-first Sunday after Trinity, when the third chapter of Daniel is read. The following lines, given by C. A. Walker in his "Services of the Church, with Rubrical Directions according to the Use of the Illustrious Church of Sarum" (1868), will assist the memory as to the seasons in which *Te Deum* should be omitted and *Benedicite* sung :—

> Do not on Vigils through the year,
> Or in the Ember seasons,
> At Matins the *Te Deum* say,
> For penitential reasons.
>
> The same observe in Advent-tide,
> A feast-day notwithstanding :
> The rule to Septuagesima
> And Holy Lent extending.
>
> *One* Vigil and *one* Embertide
> Alone *Te Deum* graces ;
> Epiphany ; and Ember Week,
> With Whitsun-tide that paces.

Some liturgiologists are of opinion that there is no real authority for using *Benedicite* specially in penitential seasons, maintaining that the Roman and old English use was to make it a festal canticle : it was the canticle of Sunday Lauds, *Te Deum* belonging to Sunday Matins. In the Benedictine use it was the Sunday canticle. In the old use made by St Cæsarius of Arles, it was sung in Sunday Matins. In the old Spanish Church it was sung at Mass, according to the Council of Toledo in the seventh century. The five last verses are still part of the Roman Thanksgiving after Mass, as they were of that of Sarum. The version of *Benedicite* at present in use dates from the Prayer-Book of 1552. In the book of 1549, instead of "bless ye the Lord," we find "speak good of the Lord," and the burden, "praise Him and magnify Him for ever," ran "praise Him and set Him up for ever." Until almost our own day, *Benedicite* received but scant attention from composers, who wrote so copiously for other parts of the Church service. Indeed, during the Georgian period, the singing of it at all dropped out of use. The chant given to

34

ECCLESIASTICAL TERMS

Benedicite by Merbecke in his " Boke of Common Praier Noted " (1550) is essentially the same as that to which the hymn is set in the Sarum Breviary, but more simple. It is a slight modification of the irregular Gregorian Tone, known as the *Tonus Peregrinus.* Harmonies for this, by Chas. Child Spencer, will be found in the musical supplement to the eleventh number of *The Parish Choir* (December 1846), four different accompaniments being provided, in order to lessen the chance of weariness in singing the canticle to one chant. With the thirty-ninth number of the same useful periodical was printed a chant for *Benedicite* in the key of A minor. This is in triple time. It had previously appeared in the collection of chants compiled by Dr Beckwith, organist of Norwich Cathedral in 1808, and was there given anonymously. It is now generally acknowledged as the composition of Beckwith's master, Dr Philip Hayes. Sir Frederick Bridge has recently included this chant with others by James Turle and himself, in a setting of the *Benedicite.* No chant for this canticle is provided in the early post-Restoration choral manuals of Lowe, Clifford, or Playford, nor is it even mentioned. It may not be generally known that several settings of *Benedicite* arranged service-wise by eminent masters of the seventeenth century exist in MS. in our cathedral books. Instances occur in the services of Aldrich in E minor, Blow in E minor (omitted by Boyce in his printed copy of the service, 1778), Child in G (omitted by Goss and Turle in their edition of the service, 1845), Ferrabosco in B flat, Hawkins in A, Henry Loosemore in G, Purcell in B flat (printed by Boyce, 1778), and Tucker in F. The autograph score of Purcell's setting is in the Bodleian, Oxford. The existence of such settings is a proof that *Benedicite* was never intended to remain unsung from one year's end to another, as has been the custom within comparatively recent times. The canticle does not appear to have been much favoured by composers immediately succeeding the Reformation. There is, however, a setting service-wise in an organ-book belonging at one time to John Bishop, organist of Winchester Cathedral and College (1730), and now in the possession of the writer of this notice. To this setting (apparently for men's voices) the name of Farrant is appended. In the eighteenth century we meet with examples in the Services of Ralph Roseingrave and Richard Woodward, both organists of Christ Church Cathedral, Dublin—the former in 1727, the latter in 1765. Woodward's is given in the volume of " Cathedral Music," published by that composer in 1771. It is set chant-wise. Roseingrave's is more elaborate. John Marsh, the clever amateur of Chichester, provided a chant for *Benedicite* among his " Twenty-

A DICTIONARY OF

four New Chants," printed by Clementi, and dedicated to the Rev. Weldon Champneys, D.D., Sub-Dean and Succentor of St Paul's, Precentor of Westminster, etc. This book appeared about 1800. In a collection of " Cathedral Music," composed by Ralph Banks, organist of Rochester Cathedral, and published by Chappell shortly after his (Banks') death in 1841, appears a " Chant for the Benedicite, instead of the Te Deum, when the 1st Chap. of Genesis is the Lesson. From the Cath. Bristol. Harmonized by R. B." This is believed to be the composition of Richard Langdon, who was organist of Bristol from 1778 to 1781. All these chants are in triple measure. The first mid-nineteenth-century Services to contain *Benedicite* elaborately set were those of Hatton in E (1854) and Ouseley in C (1856). There are now, as we well know, innumerable arrangements. Many composers of simple settings in chant form have preferred to group their music into three divisions, into which the canticle seems to fall naturally. The first seventeen verses (verse 1 being introductory only) relate to the natural kingdom, in so far as it is, or in early days was thought to be, extra terrestrial ; the nine succeeding verses belonging to the terrestrial creation only. The remaining verses (27 to the end) refer to the spiritual kingdom—the Church. As an example, the change of construction at verses 18 and 27—" Benedicat," instead of " Benedicite "—first made in the setting by Stainer, Turle, and Irons, published by Novello in 1869, may seem to favour this suggestion, and in this arrangement an attempt was made to illustrate it musically by a change of chant at those verses. This has been since adopted by many other composers. Perhaps one of the most varied and attractive modern settings is that by the Rev. C. Hylton Stewart, sometime Precentor of Chester, who has divided his work into four sections, on the plan suggested by Bishop Westcott in his " Paragraph Psalter." In the admirable settings by W. T. Best, Sir George Martin, Mr Charles Macpherson, and Mr John E. West, we find the verses in groups of four, after the manner of a quadruple chant. Another setting, by Mr Myles B. Foster, equally admirable, is more varied. The words of *Benedicite*, being dactylic in rhythm, lend themselves more easily to triple time, and, as a rule, composers seem to have adopted this measure. In the settings of the hymn by certain of the composers of the later Stuart period, already mentioned, several verses are run into one another by the omission of the burden, " Praise Him, and magnify Him for ever." In Purcell's arrangement this is retained in 19, and in Tucker's in 16, verses out of the 32. In Aldrich's it appears only 12 times. Child, however, retains it in every verse. This treatment of the

36

words has been much censured ; but it was no innovation. On an examination of the Sarum and Roman office-books, it will be seen that the full refrain is only appointed to be sung in three verses (1, 18, 27), which open a fresh paragraph, and in the final verse. Perhaps, on the whole, the antiphonal character of *Benedicite*, and, indeed, its whole construction, makes it more suitable for a chant than for a " Service."

One of the canticles to be sung after the Second Lesson at Matins, taken from St Luke i. 68–79, being part of the song of Zacharias the

Benedictus. priest, concerning his son John the Baptist, who was to be the forerunner of Christ. It was exclusively appointed in 1549, the alternative of *Jubilate* being added in 1552, probably to avoid repetition. In churches where Matins are " solemnly sung " it is customary to use incense at *Benedictus*, as well as at *Magnificat* at Evensong. This is in honour of the Incarnation, which is specially celebrated in these, the " Evangelical " Canticles. Merbecke notes *Benedictus* (1) to Tone V., Ending I., (2) to Tone VIII., Ending I. In the Services of the composers who wrote for the English Church during the reign of Elizabeth the *Benedictus* is almost universally found—*e.g.* those of Causton, Farrant, Heath, Morley, Mundy, Parsley, Patrick, Strogers, and Tallis. Probably the oldest setting to English words is that of Barcroft, a MS. at Ely bearing date 1532, seventeen years before the appearance of the First Prayer-Book. In the reigns of James I. and Charles I. *Benedictus* continued to be set, as in the Services of Amner, Batten, Bevin, Byrd, Gibbons, Hilton, Parsons, Portman and Tomkins. During the later Stuart and the whole of the Georgian periods its inclusion among the canticles was almost dropped, but there are still some examples in the Services of Purcell, Blow, Aldrich, Nalson, Norris, Bishop, Roseingrave, Woodward, Philip Hayes, and Alcock. In the last century, the earliest composers to revive it were Dr Smith of Dublin, Sir George Elvey, Dr Edward Hodges, Professor T. A. Walmisley, Revs. T. H. Hawes, E. Fellowes, and G. M. Slatter, E. J. Hopkins, J. L. Hatton, and the Rev. Sir Frederick A. Gore Ouseley. Now, thanks to the influence of the Oxford Movement, it has entirely resumed its rightful place in the eyes of churchmen, and almost every modern composer includes *Benedictus* in his setting of the morning canticles. The compiler of a list of Cathedral Services, printed in *The Quarterly Musical Magazine and Review*, vol. vi. (1824), remarks in his preface, " The old masters frequently set the *Benedictus* (instead of the *Jubilate*) with the *Te Deum*, but the words are somewhat prosaic [!] and have rarely been adapted by the moderns." The author of these brilliant observations was probably R. M. Bacon, editor of the above-mentioned quarterly.

Bidding Prayer. Originally Bidding of Prayer. The custom of bidding prayers is very ancient, as may be seen in the Liturgy of St Chrysostom and others, where the " biddings " occur frequently, and are called Allocutiones, προσφωνήσεις. It was originally called " Bidding the bedes." The word " beads " or " bedes "—one of Saxon origin and signifying *prayers*—meant *desiring* the *prayers* of the congregation, and from the forms used at High Mass for this purpose, before the Reformation, is derived the " Bidding Prayer," prescribed by the English Canons of 1604. This formulary the Church directs to be used before all sermons, lectures, and homilies, because in it the preacher is directed to *bid* or exhort the people to pray for certain specified objects. Except in the universities, in the chapels of the Inns of Court, and in some cathedrals, the custom has now fallen into disuse. At St Paul's Cathedral, at the annual " Churching of the Judges " on the afternoon of the first Sunday after Trinity, the sermon is always prefaced by the " Bidding Prayer," which concludes with the Lord's Prayer. The form will be found in the Fifty-fifth Canon (1604). See also *sub voce* " Procession."

Bier. Saxon *baer*. A carriage on which the dead are carried to the grave. It is to be provided by the parish. A bier in the form of the ancient *herse* and of the shape approved by the Ecclesiological Society, as represented in the *Instrumenta Ecclesiastica* (1847–1850), has been for many years in use at the Church of St Matthias, Stoke Newington. Every church should be provided with this *instrumentum*, which may be carried or wheeled, thus obviating the horrible shouldering of the coffin in church by undertakers' men. Those approved by the Ecclesiological Society, and still made, have a properly shaped frame to carry the pall, which should, under no circumstances, be omitted.

Biretta. A square cap of black silk or other stuff, worn by persons in Holy Orders at processions, and other outdoor functions. The biretta is the non-episcopal form of the mitre, and both signify the helmet of salvation and the glory of the priesthood.

Bishop's Boy, or Bishop's Chorister. There is an ancient custom, peculiar to Salisbury Cathedral, of having one of the choristers especially appointed to attend on the bishop, and to precede him whenever he comes to the cathedral. The present bishop (Wordsworth) has drawn up a form of service which

he makes use of when he admits a chorister to be his
" Boy " or " Chorister." The bishop, before the altar, the
Custos Puerorum (Master of the Choristers' School), and all the boys
being present, the office begins with the Lesser Litany. This is
followed by the Lord's Prayer and Psalm lxxxiv. (*Quam dilecta*).
The bishop being seated in his chair, the *Custos* then presents the
boy to be admitted. Questions of examination are put by the
bishop, after which the chorister kneels down before the bishop, who
gives him a copy of the Book of Common Prayer, saying : " A. B.
admitto te in Puerum Episcopi, in Nomine Patris et Filii et Spiritus
Sancti. Amen." The bishop then gives him this blessing : " Deus
custodiat introitum tuum et exitum tuum, ex hoc nunc et usque in
sæculum : Deus aperiet labia tua verbo suo ad laudandum sanctum
nomen ejus : Deus sanctificet cor tuum omnes dies peregrinationis
tuæ terrestris, et perducat te in vitam æternam." A collect and
the blessing conclude the office, which will be found printed in full
in the " Register of Old Choristers of Salisbury Cathedral, 1810–
1897," compiled by E. E. Dorling, M.A., master of the Choristers'
School (1898). The oldest surviving " Bishop's Boy " is now Mr
C. G. Pittman, at present resident at Chichester, who went to Salisbury as chorister in 1843, and was " Bishop's Boy " from June 1848
to June 1850. At the enthronement of a bishop, the Bishop's
Boy (or Chorister), under a tree opposite the Choristers' School in
the Close, speaks a congratulatory address in Latin to the bishop,
and the prelate replies, also in Latin, beginning with " Boy of
eminent hope, and you white-robed scholars of our Church," and
concluding, before the Benediction, with " May God guard you in
school and in games, at table, and at your chambers." The traditional cambric frills worn by the Salisbury choristers cannot fail
to be noticed by the visitors to that cathedral. They are also
worn at York, Ripon and Southwark.

The minor festivals are so called because in all correctly printed
Black-letter Days. calendars their names are printed in black, while
those of the greater festivals are given in red letters.
Black-letter Days should be marked by change of
altar-frontal, vestments, etc.

A projecting mass of carving placed to conceal the intersection
of the ribs of a vault. Examples : nave, choir, and transepts,
Boss. Norwich Cathedral ; King's College Chapel, Cam-
bridge ; Oxford Cathedral (choir) ; Henry VII.'s
Chapel, Westminster ; Iffley Church, Oxon. Consult " The
Ancient Sculptures in the Roof of Norwich Cathedral," by

A DICTIONARY OF

E. M. Goulburn, Dean, and H. Symonds, Precentor, of Norwich (1876).

The discovery in 1680 of a monument in Salisbury Cathedral led to the knowledge of a singular, and as some think foolish and profane, custom, not only in this, but in other cathe-

Boy-Bishop drals and religious establishments, both in England (*Episcopus* and abroad. From the age of the monument (which *Puerorum*). lay long buried under the seats near the pulpit), the custom appears to have taken its rise, at least, as early as the beginning of the thirteenth century. It was certainly of subsequent date to the time of Osmund, otherwise some reference to it would have been found in his minute regulations for every part of divine service. On the Feast of St Nicholas (6th December), the day sacred to this patron of childhood, the choristers annually chose one of their number, who was called the Bishop of the Boys or Choristers. From his election till the night of Holy Innocents' Day he bore the name and state of a bishop, was pontifically habited, carried a pastoral staff, and wore a mitre. His fellow-choristers, likewise, vested in copes, assumed the style of canons. At St Paul's, " towards the end of vespers on St John Evangelist's Day, the boy-bishop and his clerks, arrayed in their copes and having burning tapers in their hands, and singing those words of the Apocalypse (ch. xiv.), *Centum quadraginta*, walked processionally from the choir to the Altar of the Blessed Trinity, which the boy-bishop incensed. Afterwards they all sang the anthem, and he recited the prayer commemorative of the Holy Innocents. Going back into the choir, these boys took possession of the upper canons' stalls, and those dignitaries themselves had to serve in the boys' places, and carry the candles, the thurible, the book, like acolytes, thurifers and lower clerks. Standing on high, wearing his mitre, and holding his pastoral staff in his left hand, the boy-bishop gave his benediction to all present : and, while making the sign of the cross over the kneeling crowd, he said :

> ' Crucis signo vos consigno ; vestra sit tuitio.
> Quos non emit et redemit suæ carnis pretio.'

The next day, the Feast of Holy Innocents, the boy-bishop preached a sermon. Two such sermons in English, delivered, the one at St Paul's, *temp*. Henry VII., and the other at Gloucester, *temp*. Mary, were edited by the able antiquary, Mr John Gough Nichols, for the *Camden Society Miscellany*, vol. vii. Dean Colet expressly ordered, in the statutes of his school, that all the scholars should attend at the cathedral to hear this sermon, 'with the maisters and serveyors of the scole,' and that each of the children should offer one penny to the youthful prelate. The boy-bishop was even allowed to commence the Mass, and to go on ' up to the more solemn part of the Offertory ' " (Dr Simpson, " Chapters in the History of Old St Paul's," 1881, p. 53). In 1263 some rules were drawn up for the regulation of this function at St Paul's. Care was to be taken lest the liberty of that day should degenerate into licence. The boy-bishop must not, in future, select any of the canons, major or minor, to bear the tapers or the censer, but he must select his ministers from those who sat on the second or third form. The Dean should provide a horse on which the boy-bishop might ride forth to give his benediction to the people, and each residentiary supplied a horse for some other person in the procession. There was feasting throughout the Close. The boy-bishop, attended by two chaplains, two taper-bearers, five clerks and two of the vergers preceding him with wands, supped with one of the canons residentiary. Archbishop Cranmer forbade these processions, Queen Mary restored them, and they were finally abolished by Queen Elizabeth. Much the same description of these ceremonies as observed at Salisbury will be found in Dodsworth's " Historical Account " of that cathedral (1814). At page 190, Dodsworth figures the recumbent effigy of the boy-bishop, discovered, as already mentioned, in 1680. It may still be seen on the north side of the nave. This chorister-bishop probably died during the short period of his episcopal honours. The Treasury of St Paul's contained, in 1245, a mitre for the boy-bishop—of white, embroidered with gold—the gift of John de Belemains, Prebendary of Chiswick in 1225. There was also another mitre for the same personage of small value. It is a little remarkable that one of the boy-bishop's mitres should have been *nullius pretii*, for the City of London was specially devoted to the ceremonial of which he formed a part. The small parish of St Peter Cheap had, in 1431, " ij childes copes for S. Nicholas w^t j myter, j tonycle, j cheseble, and iij feeble aubes for childer, and a crosse for the bysshope, p's xl*s*." A later inventory of 1402 cites " two little staves for the boy-bishop of moderate value." Consult further the statute, *De Officio Puerorum in Festo Sanctorum Innocentium*, printed by the Rev. W. Sparrow Simpson, D.D., in his *Registrum Statutorum et Consuetudinum Ecclesiae Cathedralis Sancti Pauli Londinensis.* 4to., 1873.

A term for a candelabrum or chandelier of burnished brass for holding a number of wax candles, and suspended from the roof of the church by means of a chain. Its manufacture may be said to date, though by no means exclusively, from the Renaissance period. The corresponding mediæval term would be "Corona Lucis" (*q.v.*). The candlesticks, which vary in number according to the size of this *instrumentum*, radiate or "branch" horizontally from the stem, which terminates in a ball. Some of these branches, occasionally called "Spider Chandeliers," were of most elaborate design and workmanship, and when lighted up, presented a most beautiful appearance : others were plainer. Branches varying in size remain in the cathedrals of Canterbury, Chichester, Exeter, Lincoln, Southwark, and Southwell; and in the churches of St Helen, Abingdon, Berks; Barsham, Suffolk, Shorne, Kent; Melton Mowbray, Leicestershire, and many other places. From Drake's "Eboracum," published in 1736, we learn that in winter it was customary to light the choir of York Minster, from All Saints' Day to Candlemas, by means of seven large branches. Three of these handsome *instrumenta* were the gifts of Sir Arthur Ingram in 1638, who also settled £4 per annum on the church for finding them with lights. In addition, a small wax candle was fixed at every other stall. These, with two large tapers upon the altar, were all the light made use of. But on the vigils of particular holy days, the four Greater Dignitaries had each a branch of seven candles placed before them at their stalls. The choir was first lighted with gas in 1824. At Peterborough Cathedral, a fine branch "containing about a dozen and a half of lights" was destroyed by the Puritans in April 1643. There are specimens of branches in certain of Wren's city churches, that in St Nicholas' Cole Abbey (the first church finished after the Great Fire) being considered the finest. At St Paul's, before the introduction of gas into the cathedral in 1822, branches of various sizes were suspended at intervals in the nave, choir, aisles, and transepts. Some of these, renovated, are still in position, and very charming they look. It is to be hoped that the branches of "loud" modern manufacture, now hanging in the choir, and fitted with the electric light, may, sooner or later, give place to others of a design exactly similar to the old ones, and in harmony with the building. At Lichfield is preserved a seven-branched candlestick of brass which stood upon the altar when it was removed into the Lady Chapel during Wyatt's "restorations" in the latter part of the eighteenth century. It bears the inscription, "Jno Cocks fcit. Birmingham, 1812," and figures in old prints and

Branch.

early photographs of the cathedral. It is now in the library. Branches were formerly very numerous, but they have too frequently been disposed of by ignorant and tasteless clergy afflicted with the mediæval mania, and by no less ignorant architects engaged in the " restoration " of churches, and replaced by the slender and vulgar " Gothic " gimcracks sold by advertising " Church ironmongers." The branches which belonged to the mediæval period are fashioned in the same manner. They are still numerous in Germany. An especially beautiful one of this kind, in brass, is in the Catholic Church at Dortmund (see the engraving in Lübke's " Ecclesiastical Art in Germany during the Middle Ages " (p. 175). A similar one, with a figure of the Madonna in the centre, and angels as light-bearers, is in the church at Kempen ; and of the same sort are those in the churches at Calcar and Erkelenz (Rhine Provinces), at Ober-kirchen in Westphalia, and in the cathedral at Ratzeburg. The Oberkirchen example is illustrated by Lübke. Without the statue of the Madonna, but with a somewhat heavily designed stem or centre-piece, is a brass chandelier at Seckau. Besides " coronas " and " branches," even in ancient Christian times candlesticks, candelabra, and light-sticks are mentioned. In the fourth century brass candelabra, inlaid with silver, were presented to churches by Pope Sylvester. The most handsome candlesticks are the seven-armed ones, formed in imitation of the famous Temple candlestick. A noble specimen of this kind in bronze was presented to the minster church of Essen in Westphalia about 1003 by the Abbess Mathilda (see the engraving in Lübke, p. 176). A similar one, adorned with ornaments of the later Romanesque period, is in the Cathedral of Brunswick. Others are in the Church of St Gangolf at Bamberg, the Busdorf-kirche at Paderborn, and the church at Klosterneuburg. In the Church of St John Werben is a five-armed candelabrum, and there are three-armed ones in the cathedral at Xanten, in St John's Church, Luneburg (engraved in King's " Study-Book," vol. i.), and in the cathedral and Madonna Church at Halberstadt. Besides these large candlesticks, there were also *pergulae* (espaliers), *herciae* (harrows), *rastella* (rakes)—that is, candlesticks with a broad upper slab, on which many lights can be brought together by the side of one another, and for which the German name is *kerzstall* (sconce). The three-cornered candelabra (*hercia ad tenebras*) may also be mentioned. There is one of iron in the cathedral at Osnabrück. They were used during the Office of Tenebræ on the Wednesday, Thursday and (Good) Friday of Holy Week, and in such a way that, at the singing of the Psalms, the lights were extinguished one by one in rows (see *sub voce* " Tenebræ). Lastly, there are the simple, but generally very large, candlesticks, made for one very thick taper each, which it was the custom to place before the altar, sometimes in pairs on the steps. Stone candelabra of this kind of the Romanesque period are in the cathedral at Hildesheim (engraved in King's " Study-Book of Mediæval Architecture," vol. ii.) ; others, with the addition of metal parts, in the collegiate church at Königslutter, and the cathedral at Merseburg. Gothic stone candlesticks are in the Church of St Mary-in-the-Meadows, Söest, St John's, Billerbeck, and the cathedral at Havelberg. There is a handsome single candlestick of brass in the church at Schwerte, Dortmund. Another is in the cathedral at Münster. At Nôtre Dame, Mantes, is one of wrought iron. Fastened on the piers and walls were what are termed " wall-lights." They seldom occur, however, among the lights of the Middle Ages. Romanesque examples are in the Church of Fürsten near Munich, and Gothic ones in the Church of St Cunibert, Cologne, and in St Mary's Church, Dortmund. The last-named is illustrated by Lübke (" Eccles. Art in Germ.," p. 182). At Durham Cathedral two of the handsome brass chandeliers or branches in the choir, ordered to be made by Act of Chapter, 20th November 1751, after having been cast out of the church, have happily been restored to their old place. The central and largest one, which for a time served to light Ryton Church, and was then sold to a music hall in Newcastle, was ultimately melted.

Monumental plates of brass, or the mixed metal anciently called latten, inlaid on large slabs of stone, which usually form part of the pavement of the church, and representing in their outline, or by the lines engraved upon them, the figure of the deceased. In many instances in place of a figure there is found an ornamental or foliated cross, with sacred emblems or other devices or insignia. The earliest brass known to exist in England is that of Sir John d'Abernon in the Church of Stoke d'Abernon, near Cobham, Surrey, the date being 1277. On the Continent the oldest is said to be that to Ysowilpe, Bishop of Verden, 1231. It is in the Church of St Andrew, a miserable little building, choked with pews and galleries, situated close to the Cathedral of Verden in Hanover. Consult Boutell's " Monumental Brasses of England " (1849) ; Haines' " Manual of Monumental Brasses " (1861) ; Creeny's " Monumental Brasses on the Continent of Europe " (1883)—a magnificent folio.

Brasses, Sepulchral. Fr. *tombes plates de cuivre ;* Germ. *grabplatten.*

ECCLESIASTICAL TERMS

An arrangement of certain Divine Offices, comprising prayers, hymns, antiphons, psalms and canticles, with readings from the Holy Scriptures and the writings of the Fathers.

Breviary.
Lat.
breviarum ;
Fr. *bréviare ;*
Germ. *brevier.*

Other terms to signify the same arrangement were " Officium Divinum," or " Canonicum " ; " Horæ Canonicæ " ; and sometimes " Cursus." The Breviary or Portiforium of Sarum was arranged from old sources by Osmund, Bishop of Salisbury, and adopted in that diocese in A.D. 1085. Our present Book of Common Prayer is largely a compilation from the Breviary. See further under " Canonical Hours."

An old English term for a spire generally, but mostly used to denote a spire springing from the tower without any intermediate

Broach.

parapet, as at Horsley, Derbyshire. A " broach spire " is an octagonal one, erected on a square base, requiring, therefore, some architectural device to collect its eight sides on the four faces of the tower. Examples : Raunds, Northants ; St Mary, Stamford, Lincs (ancient) ; St Barnabas, Pimlico ; St John Divine, Kennington (modern).

A projection for giving extra strength to the wall, and to resist the thrust of a vault. An arched or flying buttress is one in the

Buttress.

form of an arch for the support of an upper interior wall, by directing the thrust on the exterior outer one. There are flying buttresses of enormous magnitude at the cathedrals of Nôtre Dame, Paris ; Chartres, Rheims, Amiens, Le Mans, Cologne, and on the Continent generally.

A name adopted from the Italian for a bell tower. A campanile is generally attached to the church, but is sometimes unconnected

Campanile.

with it, as at Chichester Cathedral, and is sometimes united merely by a covered passage, as at Lapworth, Warwickshire. There are several examples of detached bell towers still remaining, as at Evesham, Worcestershire ; Berkeley, Gloucestershire ; Walton, Norfolk ; Ledbury, Hereford ; and a very curious one, entirely of timber, with the frame for the bells opening from the ground, at Pembridge, Herefordshire. Old St Paul's had a clochier or bell-tower, which stood at the east end of the church. It contained four very large bells, known as the " Jesus Bells," because they specially belonged to the Jesus Chapel in the crypt of the cathedral. The tower had a spire of wood covered with lead, on the top of which was an image of St Paul. Until 1790 Salisbury Cathedral possessed a fine Early English clochium or belfry which stood a little to the north-west of the building. It appears from early

45

eighteenth-century prints to have been square in form, rose in three stages diminishing in ascent, and was surmounted by a metal spirelet, had walls and buttresses similar to those of the chapter-house, and a single pillar of Purbeck marble in the centre of the lowest storey, to carry the ringing chamber and belfry. Its removal was effected during the " improvements " of James Wyatt " the destructive," under Shute Barrington, who presided over the see from 1782 to 1791. The campanile, tall and square, is a common feature in Italian church architecture. Those at Cremona, Florence, Modena, Verona, and Vicenza are noted examples. At Worcester, until the completion of the present tower in the middle of the fourteenth century, the bells were lodged in the campanile or clochium, an octagonal mass of stonework, ten feet thick, sixty feet high, and sixty feet in diameter at its base. It dated, in all probability, from the time of the rebuilding of the cathedral at the close of the eleventh century, was surmounted by a lead spire rising fifty yards above the stone structure, and was placed so close to the north-eastern transept that there was only space between for processions. Nathaniel Tomkins has left us an account of this interesting clochium in his " Observations on Worcestershire." It was taken down in 1647, and the materials disposed of for £617, 4s. 2d., the principal part of which was given to repair several churches in the county, damaged in the Civil War. It appears to have been a structure of no ordinary importance.

Campanology. The knowledge of the construction and use of bells.

A dignitary in a cathedral or collegiate church. When the monasteries were dissolved in the sixteenth century, the monastic cathedrals were remodelled, a dean and a fixed number of canons being substituted for the prior and monks.

Canon.
Lat.
canonicus ;
Fr. *chanoine ;*
Germ.
domherr.

These are called Cathedrals of the New Foundation, as distinguished from those which, having always been served by secular canons (*q.v.*) remained unaltered in constitution, and are therefore called Cathedrals of the Old Foundation. By the Cathedral Act of 1840 the number of residentiary canons was reduced in many cases to four, and the non-residents were deprived, with some few exceptions, of their emoluments, although they are still called prebendaries (*q.v.*), and retain their stall in the choir, and on certain occasions their voice in the chapter. The appointment of all non-residentiary canons in Cathedrals of the Old Foundation was given by the same Act to the bishop of the diocese ; and he may appoint

ECCLESIASTICAL TERMS

twenty-five honorary canons, with stalls in the New Foundation Cathedrals, and by custom assign them a preaching turn. They have no emoluments and no voice in the chapter, and are quite distinct in origin from the non-resident canons or prebendaries in Cathedrals of the Old Foundation. Before the passing of the Act of 1840, a canon in a Cathedral or Collegiate Church of the New Foundation was styled " prebendary "—*e.g.* as at Canterbury, Durham, Ely, Norwich, Rochester, Worcester, etc. In old accounts of the various coronations, the now so-called " canons " of Westminster are always spoken of as " prebendaries." Consult Jebb's " Choral Service of the Church " (1843) ; Walcott's " Cathedralia " (1865).

Canon is used in the service of the Church to signify that part of the Communion Service, or in the Roman Church the Mass, which follows immediately after the *Sanctus* and *Hosanna* ;
Canon of the corresponding with that part of our service which
Liturgy. begins at the Prayer of Humble Access (" We do not presume," etc.). It is so called as being the fixed rule of the Liturgy, which is never altered. Properly speaking, the Canon ends just before the Lord's Prayer, which is recited aloud ; the Canon being said in a low voice. The *Anaphora* of the Greek Church resembles the Canon of the Latin.

A vocal composition of the strictest kind, the melody of which, though beginning at different times, and in different intervals, is heard continually in all the parts, and the whole so
Canon constructed as to form a perpetual fugue. A canon is
(in music). so called, not, as some think, from the rigorous nature of its construction (one part giving the law to the others), but because, having been *originally* written in a single line, numerals, or other signs, were employed to indicate both the place and harmonic intervals at which each voice was to begin, and so to exhibit the *rule* of its performance. There are various kinds of canons, as the simple, the double, and the triple canon ; the augmented, the diminished, the reversed, and the inverted canon ; the resolved, the unresolved, the finite, and the infinite canon. The English have always excelled in this species of composition, and prizes for its encouragement were for many years awarded by the Catch Club. A list of them from 1766 to 1813 will be found in the preface to Rd. Clark's " Words of Glees," etc. (1814). The words are almost invariably sacred. Many of our composers were wont to introduce canons into their Services, especially with regard to the *Gloria Patri*. Those of Purcell are masterpieces. We also find them in the Services of Orlando Gibbons, Child, Blow, Goldwin, Church,

47

Travers, Boyce, Dupuis, Attwood, Sir J. L. Rogers, E. J. Hopkins, J. L. Hopkins, Ouseley, and Elvey. The *Kyrie* of Attwood's Service in C is a canon 4 in 1, and the *Magnificat* by Chas. Lucas (Gresham Prize Composition, No. 5, 1835) is in canon of various species throughout. The canon, *Non nobis, Domine*, attributed, but on insufficient grounds, to William Byrd, and the "Amen," by Dr Cooke, engraved upon his monument in the cloister of Westminster Abbey, are celebrated. The two collections of "Vocal Canons," by W. Horsley, should be examined.

Certain set hours of prayer, anciently observed by the Universal Church, that all Christians throughout the world might at the same

Canonical Hours.
Lat.
horae canonicae.

time join together to glorify God ; and as Bishop Patrick remarks, " some of them were of opinion that the angelic host, being acquainted with these hours, took that time to join their prayers and praises with those of the Church." The following is the order of the Canonical Hours of the Western Church, which most probably owe their origin to early Eastern formularies :—*Matins*, soon after midnight ; *Lauds*, at daybreak and frequently joined on to Matins ; *Prime*, or first hour, at 6 A.M. ; *Terce* or *Tierce*, or third hour, at 9 A.M. ; *Sext*, or sixth hour, at noon ; *Nones*, or ninth hour, at 3 P.M. ; *Vespers*, or Evening Service, about 6 P.M. ; *Compline*, or final service, at bed-time. All these services have fixed psalms, lessons, antiphons, versicles, hymns, etc. By their means the whole Psalter was recited every week. They were said in parish as well as cathedral and conventual churches, and by the " secular " as well as the " religious " clergy ; but having come to be said in the former case by " accumulation," they were, on the reformation of the service-books, moulded into two services for public use, named after the two principal hours, *Matins* and *Evensong*, the former being constructed from Matins, Lauds, and Prime ; the latter from Vespers and Compline. The Psalter was then distributed to be said through monthly. At the same time, services for the Hours were given for private recitation in the various editions of the " Prymer " (*q.v.*). The Hours are still observed in sisterhoods and other religious houses. At the Westminster Cathedral they are recited daily, accompanied by solemn and beautiful music, and much may be learnt by attendance thereat. The " Divine Office," as the Canonical Hours are collectively called, is said daily as an obligatory duty by all clergy of the Western Church, and by religious throughout the world, and in cathedrals and monastic churches it is publicly sung or recited, though in the former but thinly attended by the laity. It is the daily world-wide prayer of the Church, offered up unceasingly to thank and praise Almighty God, through Christ, the One Mediator, in the Communion of Saints, and thus to obtain mercy and blessing on all mankind. Various reasons have been assigned for the number of these Hours. Some see the original of the number in David's words, " Seven times a day do I praise thee, because of thy righteous judgments " (Ps. cxix. 164). Others say that the Hours are a thanksgiving for the completion of Creation on the seventh day. Another theory connects them, and the idea is a very reverend one, with the acts of Our Lord in His Passion. Thus Dr Neale (" Essays on Liturgiology ") :

> " At *matins* bound, at *prime* reviled,
> Condemned to death at *tierce*,
> Nailed to the Cross at *sext*, at *nones*
> His blessed side they pierce.

> They take Him down at *vesper*-tide,
> In grave at *compline* lay ;
> Who thenceforth bids His Church observe
> The sevenfold hours alway."

At the time of his trial in 1644, Archbishop Laud observed : " They said my prayers were in canonical hours, Hora Sexta, and Hora Nona, etc. I enjoined myself several hours of prayer—that, I hope, is no sin : and if some of them were church-hours, that's no sin neither : *seven times a day will I praise Thee*, was the prophet David's, long before any canonical hours. And among Christians they were in use before papacy got any head. God grant this may be my greatest sin " (" Archbishop Laud's Troubles," etc., p. 314). Some English Churchmen will probably remember the feeling of half-ashamed derision which trickled down them when an Irish archbishop, early in the " sixties" of the last century, "ventured to hope " that in any contemplated alteration of the Matins and Evensong of the Church, the revisers would not reform them upon the pattern of the " Romish Missal." This is exactly as if, *mutatis mutandis*, a Lord of the Admiralty were to get up and " venture to hope " before his brethren that in introducing changes into the fleet, the revisers would not be led to imitate the old rules of castrametation. He could not confound things more entirely distinct than those which the archbishop confounded in this extraordinary slip. The Missal, which is the parent of our " Holy Communion," is a totally distinct office-book from the Breviary, of the offices of which

49

our Matins and Evensong are a judicious abbreviation. At Naumburg in Germany, when Lutheranism was introduced into the city, it was resolved at a meeting of the Princes held in 1553 that the Canonical Hours should, with certain evangelical modifications, be recited in the choir of the cathedral thrice daily—a curious remnant of Catholic usage which was regularly observed until 1807, when it fell into abeyance. An important observation applies to these Services, more beautifully constructed, perhaps, in the Sarum Breviary than they are in that of Rome—viz. that they were never congregational. In their origin, and in their use, they were monastic. The history of the English Church tells of ceaseless endeavours to make them in practice, what they were in theory, the ritual of the whole body of the faithful. But the sevenfold nature of the scheme on which they were formed, and withal their unvernacular shape, forbade the possibility of any such use of them. Our own living Services retain the earlier elements of Psalmody, Scripture, Canticles, Versicles, and Collects, and also deliver these to the people in their own tongue, and in the most ancient form of a twofold daily worship. In the Greek Church, with eight Canonical Hours, prayers are for the most part said three times daily : Matins, Lauds, and Prime, by aggregation, early in the morning ; Terce, Sext, and the Liturgy or Mass, later ; Nones, Vespers, and Compline, by aggregation in the evening. Each of the Hours will be found *verbatim* in the numerous Roman breviaries, and in the reprints of that of Sarum. Consult further " The Seven Hours of the Church of Sarum " (Masters) ; Procter, " History of the Book of Common Prayer " (1856) ; and " A Brief Explanation of the Divine Office and Horarium or Hours of Service in the [Westminster] Cathedral " (Art and Book Co., Westminster). To these should be added " The Day Office of the Church, according to the Kalendar of the Church of England," of which a third edition was published by Walker of Paternoster Row, in 1901. This English version of the Day Hours of the Church is based upon the *Horae Diurnae Breviarii Romani*, the editions of which, published at Mechlin in 1852 and 1862, have mainly been followed in the work of translation. As the book was not intended to have a merely literary value, but for the actual use of the clergy, religious communities, and the faithful of the English Communion, the compiler felt himself at liberty to make any departures from the strict letter of the original which might be needed, the better to adapt it to the practical purpose he had in view. These departures are clearly set forth in the Preface. It may be mentioned that in every instance in which the text of the

ECCLESIASTICAL TERMS

Breviarum Romanum has not been followed, the example of some other Breviary has been sought and scrupulously adhered to ; hence those who use this book may rely upon all that is set out in it being in accordance with some acknowledged precedent.

The 98th Psalm, which was inserted in the Second Prayer-Book of 1552 as an alternative to the *Magnificat (q.v.)*. This was probably done for variety, and still retaining the ancient rule that Psalms and reading of Scripture should be alternated. There are parallel expressions in the *Magnificat* and *Cantate*, which probably led to the selection of the latter as an alternative. It is also supposed that this addition was made to please the Genevan party in the Church, who disliked the use of *Magnificat. Cantate* should not be used on the nineteenth evening of the month, when it occurs in the ordinary course of the Psalms. It had not been sung among the Psalms of Vespers or Compline, but it is appropriate, especially to the season of Epiphany, as a song of praise for the announcement of salvation. At Easter and at times of solemn thanksgiving it may fitly be used, but it should never generally supersede *Magnificat*, which should always have the preference, as being the Gospel, or " Evangelical," canticle. At the same time (1552) *Deus Misereatur* (Ps. lxvii.) was inserted as an alternative to *Nunc dimittis (q.v.)*, and when used should always be preceded by *Cantate*. It should not be used on the twelfth evening of the month when it occurs among the Psalms. When there is service both in the afternoon and evening (*i.e.* first and second Evensong) it seems appropriate to use *Deus Misereatur* in the afternoon, and *Nunc dimittis* in the evening, because the latter formed a part of the ancient Compline, or concluding service of the day. Examples of the *Cantate* and *Deus* are not to be found among the Services of the immediately post-Reformation composers. One of the earliest seems to be that by Dr Child in the key of F, written about the middle of the seventeenth century. During the later Stuart, the whole of the Georgian, and a great part of the Victorian periods, the two Psalms were constantly set. Among the best examples are those of Purcell in B flat, Blow in A major and E minor, Aldrich in A, Croft in E flat, Bishop in D, King in B flat, Hayes in E flat, Shenton in E and E flat, Fussell in A major, Stephens in E flat, Dupuis in E flat and F, Corfe in B flat, Beckwith in C and E flat, Heathcote in B flat, Stevenson in C, E and E flat, Clarke-Whitfeld in D and E major, Camidge in A, Smith in B flat, Attwood in D, Walmisley in F, Bayley in F, Elvey in D, Hopkins in A, Ouseley in C (double choir) and A, Stewart in E flat (double choir), Goss in C,

Cantate Domino.

Torrance in F, Gadsby in D, Prendergast in F, Steggall in C, Roland Rogers in D. At the present day the *Cantate* and *Deus* are never set by our Church composers.

Canted Bay. The architectural term for a bay (*q.v.*) contracted at an angle, to connect a wide with a narrower portion of a church. A most interesting ancient example is the first bay of the choir of Evreux Cathedral, where it is "canted" outwards, it having been found desirable when widening the choir in the fourteenth century not to interfere with the narrower eastern arch of the lantern. Modern examples are to be seen in the churches of St Saviour, Eastbourne; SS. Philip and James, Oxford, and St John Divine, Kennington—all by Street.

Canticle. This literally signifies "song," but it is peculiarly applied to a canonical book of the Old Testament, called in Hebrew the "Song of Songs"—that is, the most excellent of all songs, called also the "Song of Solomon." The word canticle in our Prayer-Book is applied to the *Benedicite*, and was so first used in Edward VI.'s Second Book (1552). But it also denotes all those hymns which are sung after the lessons at Matins and Evensong—viz. *Te Deum, Benedicite, Benedictus, Jubilate, Magnificat, Nunc Dimittis, Cantate Domino*, and *Deus Misereatur*. With the exception of *Te Deum* all are taken from Holy Scripture. The "Service" in C major, for double choir, composed by Sir Frederick Ouseley in 1856, and unpublished, contains a setting of every canticle, as well as the *Venite* or Invitatory Psalm, which was frequently treated as a canticle by many of our earlier composers for the Church, from the Reformation to the reign of Charles I. The same Service is also remarkable as containing the whole of the Communion hymns—*Kyrie, Credo, Sanctus*, and *Gloria*, which at that time (1856) were only beginning to be set.

Canto fermo, or Cantus firmus. (1) The *tenor* or chief melody, originally sung by the tenor voices, afterwards transferred to the treble part, hence called *Canto*. (2) A fragment of plain-song to which counterpoint has been added. (3) Any subject chosen for contrapuntal treatment. Consult Stainer and Barrett's "Dictionary of Musical Terms" (Novello).

Canto figurato, or Cantus figuratus. Florid Church song, in which more than one note of music is sung to a syllable. Generally speaking, Church music in unison may be described as *Canto fermo*, and that in harmony as *Canto figurato*.

ECCLESIASTICAL TERMS

Cantor. (1) Another name for the precentor, a dignitary in cathedrals who leads and directs the choir, etc. (2) A term for a lay singer in the foreign cathedrals.

Cantoris. The side in a cathedral choir on which the cantor or precentor has his stall, usually the north side, opposite to the side of the dean (" Decani "). In musical Services constructed after the antiphonal method, the contractions *Dec.* and *Can.* are used, to denote the passages to be sung by either side. " Full " denotes that both are to take part. Some composers use the direction " Both sides," but this properly applies to " Verse parts " —*i.e.* portions sung by select voices—and as an indication that such portions are to be sung by the select voices both on the *Decani* and *Cantoris* sides. In the " Cathedral Music " of Dr Dupuis, Organist and Composer to the Chapel Royal (1779–1796), the contractions " Dec." and " Sub-Dec." or " Sub." are met with in the Services. The former indicates the side on which the stall of the dean (the Bishop of London) is situated, and the latter that of the sub-dean, who has the general oversight of the chapel and its services. This is the only instance of such antiphonal directions to be found in the whole range of Church music written by composers connected with the Chapel Royal, and primarily intended for use there.

Cappella del Coro. The choir, or chapel of the choir. In St Peter's at Rome, a large chapel with a glazed screen to the north of the north aisle (to speak as if St Peter's orientated rightly) is so designated. Here the ordinary services (Mass, Vespers, and other offices) are daily sung. In St Peter's itself there is absolutely no true choir at all ; the great arm of the cross behind the high altar having no fittings. In fact, the high altar is but rarely used, and by the Pope only ; and the altar at the extreme end of the apse under the papal throne is only occasionally employed. Round the church there are a number of altars, and when any one is used (on occasion, for example, of the festival of the saint in whose honour any one may be dedicated), a temporary choir is formed before it, made by placing longitudinal benches as in a choir ; and one of the great movable organs of the church is wheeled to the spot, and serves as well for a gallery of singers. The Cappella del Coro contains stalls, two organs, and, of course, an altar. The north-west and south-west chapels in our St Paul's may be said to correspond with it in a certain measure.

Capital, or Cap. The head of a column, pilaster, etc. In Classical as well as Mediæval architecture, the orders and styles have each their respective capitals, by means of which such orders and styles may be readily distinguished. Consult the excellent illustrated articles in W. H. Leeds and Talbot Bury's "Rudimentary Architecture" (1848), and in Parker's "Glossary of Terms used in Grecian, Roman, Italian, and Gothic Architecture" (1845).

Caput Jejunii. The head or beginning of the fast : an old name for Ash Wednesday, or the first day of Lent.

Cardinal. (1) A dignitary of the Roman Church, next in rank to the Pope. (2) A title given to two of the minor canons of St Paul's (still retained), probably from their serving at the Chapter or Cardinal—*i.e.* chief—Mass celebrated daily in pre-Reformation times. They had charge of the choir and presented defaulters to the dean on Fridays. They preserved order as rulers of the choir, heard confessions, buried the dead, visited the sick, received the oblations, and weekly taught the Catechism to the choristers. Bishop Compton's "Injunctions" concerning the cardinals (A.D. 1694), subscribed in his handwriting in a document preserved in the Muniment Room of St Paul's, are these: "Cardinales autem videbunt ne quis tempore Divini Officii irreverenter se gerat. Unus è Cardinalibus, Pueros qui in Choro inserviunt, et cantando ministrant, in Catechismo Ecclesiæ Anglicanæ singulis septimanis diligenter institutiunt. Quod si neglexerint, arbitrio Decani et Capituli puniantur." These Injunctions were confirmed in 1813. The offices of senior and junior cardinal are annexed to the second and third minor canonries, the first stall being held by the sub-dean. To other minor canonries in St Paul's are attached the offices of custos or warden, sacrist, succentor, epistoler, gospeller, librarian, and, until 1882, one of the minor canons held the post of Divinity Lecturer. He supplied the place of any prebendary who was unable to keep his preaching turn. For further information respecting the Pauline cardinals consult J. S. Bumpus, "History of English Cathedral Music," p. 119.

Carol. (1) In architecture, a small closet or enclosure to sit and write in. The term is also applied to a window, doubtless a bay window. In the inventories of the Priory of Finchale this word occurs twice in the list of furniture of the Camera, in 1354, and again in 1360. In the "Ancient Rites of Durham," p. 131, we find : "In every window of the cloyster were three pews or carrels ; where every one of the old monks had his *carol* several by himself, to which, having dined, they did resort, and there study their books." (2) In music, a song of praise ; applied to a species of songs (Noëls) sung at Christmastide. It originally meant a song accompanied with dancing. Consult the Introduction (by Rev. S. Baring-Gould) to Rev. R. R. Chope's "Carols for Use in Church" (1875), also W. H. Husk's "Songs of the Nativity" (1866) ; W. Sandys' "Christmas Carols" (1833), and "Carols, English and Foreign," a lecture by Sir John Stainer, delivered at Oxford, 19th November 1890, and printed in *The Musical Times*, December 1901.

Cassock.
Fr. *soutane.*

The under-dress of all orders of the clergy, resembling a long coat, with a single upright collar and confined at the waist by a broad sash called the *cincture.* In the Church of Rome it varies in colour with the dignity of the wearer. Priests wear black ; bishops, purple ; cardinals, scarlet ; and popes, white. In the Church of England black is worn by all the three orders of the clergy. Bishops sometimes wear violet, a colour which signifies rule or authority. A short cassock (popularly called a bishop's apron) is generally worn by bishops and dignitaries in the Church. The seventy-fourth English Canon enjoins that beneficed clergymen, etc., shall not go in public in their doublet and hose, without coats or *cassocks.* In church choirs, cassocks are now almost universally worn in addition to surplices. Amongst the Minutes of Chapter of St Patrick's Cathedral Dublin, 31st May 1676, occurs an order regulating the apparel of the vicars choral. They were admonished not to wear swords in the precincts, and were also to provide themselves with "gowns" against Michaelmas Day, to wear under their surplices. These were, in all probability, cassocks. In many English cathedrals cassocks have been adopted only within comparatively recent years. At St Paul's the boys were so vested for the first time on the Thanksgiving Day, 27th February 1872. Choir-boys' cassocks differ considerably in colour. In addition to black, blue, scarlet, and purple are used. Where there are two sets, scarlet cassocks are generally used for ordinary Sundays and feasts; blue, black, or purple for week-days, Advent, Lent, etc. According to an eminent ritualist, the choristers' cassocks should be ordinarily black ; scarlet in churches which are royal foundations (as now at Westminster Abbey) ; purple in episcopal foundations ; and perhaps blue in churches dedicated in honour of the Blessed Virgin ; but, however sound in theory, this does not seem to be generally adhered to in practice in any part of the Church. At Norwich, until the appointment of Dr Goulburn to the deanery in 1866, the boys wore purple gowns on week-days, and surplices on Saturday evenings, Sundays, Saints' Days, and eves of Saints' Days. In 1866, these gowns were changed to violet cassocks with a crimson girdle. At Lincoln the four "Choristers" wear black gowns with facings of white doeskin over their cassocks, and the remaining boys, or "Burghersh Chanters," surplices, on all occasions. The gowns of the Lincoln "choristers" are probably a remnant of the ancient choral cope. J. D. Chambers ("Divine Worship in the Church of England in the XIII., XIV. and XIX. Centuries") tells us that another name for the cassock was "pelisse." It was the ordinary clerical gown or under garment. It was sometimes of dressed sheeps' or lambs' skin only, sometimes of cloth, serge, or such like material, and lined with fur ; later on the lining of fur was omitted, and it became similar to the modern cassock. It went down to the heels and was confined to the body either by buttons or by a girdle. The colour was usually purple or black, sometimes scarlet ; as with Doctors of Divinity (Rock, "Church of Our Fathers," ii. 20). The minor clergy in the Cotton MS. (Tib. c. viii., 1350) are vested some in purple, some in scarlet cassocks beneath their surplices. The boy with the holy water, ministering to the priest in the Buckland Missal, A.D. 1395, of Sarum Use, has a scarlet cassock with a scarlet hood over his surplice (see the woodcut in Chambers' "Divine Worship," p. 27). By the rule of St Gilbert, A.D. 1139 (Dugdale, *Monast.* vii. 44) and that of St Alban's (Matt. Paris, *Vit. Abbat.* p. 53), the monks wore pellices of lambs' skin. St Thomas of Canterbury wore such a pelisse (Reginald Dunelm, "St Cuthbert," p. 256). St Norbert also, at his ordination, wore "*pellicium agninum*" (*Vitae SS. Junii*, i. 823). A Council at Cologne, A.D. 1260 (Can. ix.), ordered "that the secular clergy should always come to church with a choral pelisse or canonical vest under their surplices, all of which garments were to be drawn down to the heels" (Martene, *Thesaur. Anecdot.* A.D. 1200, iv. 1191). At Worcester, in 1666, "the minor canons would occasionally be seen with 'indecent garments under their surplices,' and were ordered to wear presbyters' gowns or cassocks" (Noake, "History of the Monastery and Cathedral of Worcester," 1866). The Rev. Percy Dearmer ("Parson's Handbook," 4th ed. p. 118) tells us that "the cassock in its English traditional form is double-breasted, *without* buttons down the front, and kept in position by a broad band. The garment that one often sees with buttons all down the front is a *soutane* and not a cassock ; these garments are not convenient to put on, nor to walk in, nor to kneel in. They are a few shillings cheaper than the cassock, and they belong to the clergy of a Church that is not in communion with our own—two reasons which seem a recommendation in some people's eyes. Servers and choristers, as well as clergy, should wear proper cassocks. Now that the civilian's dress is shortened it seems hardly incumbent on the clergy always to wear their cassocks. But on the way to church, in the schools, at confirmations, at clerical meetings, there can be no reasons for ignoring Canon 74, which orders the clergy ' usually ' to wear the cassock, and with it the cap and gown, a beautiful dress." The same Canon says that " in private houses, and in their studies, the said persons ecclesiastical may use any comely and scholar-like apparel." Even the Lutheran clergy of Germany wear their distinctive cap and long gown on the way to church.

Cathedral. The chief church in every diocese, so called because it contains the *cathedra* or chair, the seat or throne of the bishop. The cathedral church is the parish church of the whole diocese (which diocese was commonly called *parochia* in ancient times, till the application of this name to the lesser branches into which it was divided caused it for distinction's sake to be called only by the name of diocese). It was not called the cathedral church till the tenth century, before which the term *ecclesia matrix*, to distinguish it from the ordinary churches, or *ecclesiae dioecesanae*, was used. In cathedrals the bishop is formally enthroned, and in them he holds his ordinations and visitations. The government of each cathedral in England is in the hands of the chapter—*i.e.* the dean and canons residentiary. Each has its own statutes, which the bishop, as visitor, used to vary from time to time with the consent of the whole corporation. Consult the Reports of the Cathedral Commission, 1835, 1854, and 1885 ; Jebb's " Choral Service of the Church " (1843); Walcott's " Cathedralia " (1865), " Traditions and Customs of Cathedrals " (1872), and a paper, " Our Cathedrals," in *The Sacristy*, February 1872.

Cathedrals of the Old Foundation. These cathedrals, which consisted of secular canons, not of monastic or canons regular, are York, St Paul's, Hereford, Lichfield, Salisbury, Exeter, Wells, Lincoln, Chichester, St David's, Bangor, St Asaph, Llandaff. Their statutes and organisation remain substantially unchanged from the pre-Reformation times. All the Irish cathedrals are of the " Old Foundation." Christ Church, Dublin, founded by the Danish King Sitric in 1038 for secular canons, had its constitution changed by Archbishop Laurence O'Toole about 1163 into a priory for regular canons, but in 1541 Henry VIII. restored it to its original state as a Cathedral of the Old Foundation, with a staff consisting of a dean, precentor, chancellor, treasurer, Archdeacon of Dublin, six vicars choral, and choristers. Three years later three prebendal stalls (St Michael, St Michan, and St John) were founded by Archbishop Browne, and after the passing of the Irish Church Act, in 1869, twelve honorary canonries were added on by Act of the Synod.

Thirteen cathedrals in England were remodelled by Henry VIII. at the period of the Reformation. Before that time eight of them had been at the same time monasteries and **Cathedrals** cathedrals; five had been simply monasteries. Of **of the New** these the former were Canterbury, Winchester, Durham, **Foundation.** Ely, Norwich, Worcester, Carlisle, Rochester; while the newly created sees were those of Gloucester, Peterborough, Chester, Oxford, Bristol. Of these churches the abbot was at the head, as in the churches of the Old Foundation the dean presided over the chapter. These new constitutions were apparently modelled on that of the Collegiate and Royal Free Chapel of St George at Windsor, founded some two hundred years before. Two cathedrals, Ripon and Manchester, were transformed from collegiate into cathedral churches in 1836 and 1847, while the sees of St Alban's, Truro, Liverpool, Southwell, Newcastle, Wakefield, Southwark and Birmingham are of still more recent formation. Truro may be described as a cathedral of somewhat mixed character. It is literally of " New Foundation "; it has honorary canons instead of non-residentiary prebendaries, but its residentiary chapter is formed on the model of Cathedrals of the Old Foundation, and its statutes are of a corresponding character. St Alban's has a magnificent history as a monastic church, and Southwell was, up to 1840, a collegiate church, with sixteen prebendaries. Other collegiate chapters, now dissolved, were those of Brecon, Heytesbury, Middleham and Wolverhampton. All had a dean, with a certain number of prebendaries.

Music which has been composed to suit the forms of service (Matins and Evensong) used daily in our cathedrals since the Reformation. It includes settings of the Canticles and **Cathedral** Communion Service, as well as chants and anthems. **Music.** Of its kind, it is the most perfect form of musical service. It is peculiar to this country: there is nothing whatever resembling it on the Continent. As schools for sacred music our cathedrals preserve and diffuse throughout England the love of the most sublime compositions, and nurture also, by a most laborious and expensive instruction, scientific scholars in the knowledge and execution of their harmonies. At the present time, not only are the services at St Paul's, and Westminster Abbey, the Chapel Royal, the provincial cathedrals, and the college chapels of Oxford and Cambridge perfect as specimens of musical art, but as examples of reverent and devout worship ; and, what is more to the purpose, they are thoroughly appreciated as such by vast masses of worshippers, drawn from " all sorts and conditions of men."

The priest who celebrates (or administers) the Holy Communion. At a High Celebration he is assisted by a deacon and sub-deacon, **Celebrant.** or epistoler and gospeller. This was always the custom at St Paul's, even in the darkest days of the Georgian era. The dean or canon - in - residence, and two minor canons were, until 1872, the officiating ministers at the partly choral celebration on Sundays and festivals. At the present day three minor canons officiate exclusively, except for three months in the year (February, June and October), when the celebrant is the Archdeacon of London, canon-in-residence at those periods. In 1820 the chanting of the Ante-Communion Service at St Paul's was discontinued in a summary and singular manner. Hitherto the dean, incompetent to sing, had a minor canon to the eastward of him, at the " north end," who actually sang the service concealed, but Van Mildert, who was dean from 1820 to 1826, and who prided himself on his fine voice, undertook to " say prayers " himself. For the minutiæ of ritual to be observed by the celebrant, deacon and sub-deacon, consult Charles Walker's " Ritual Reason Why " (1866).

Cenotaph. An empty tomb. A memorial to someone buried Gr. Κενοτάφιον. elsewhere.

From the Latin *Thus*, frankincense. A vessel made of brass or silver in which incense is offered. It is usually in the shape of a cup, and carried by three chains, which are attached **Censer, or** to three points around the lower portion of the censer ; **Thurible.** whilst a fourth, connected with them above, being united to the ring or handle which serves for carrying the censer, is used to raise at intervals the upper portion, or perforated covering of the censer, and allows the smoke of the incense to escape. The origin of the use of the censer in religious worship of course dates back to the most remote point in European history, and probably earlier ; and we may fairly conclude that it descended to Christian worship directly from Jewish ritualism. The gifts to the infant Saviour were gold, frankincense, and myrrh. Its use is seen in ancient sculpture, painting, and stained glass. The ship (*navicula*),

59

or " boat," as it is now usually called, was the vessel which contained incense for the supply of the censer, and was so termed from its being very generally made in the form of a ship. A spoon belongs to it, with which the priest takes out the incense, and puts it into the censer. In the earlier times bronze and copper were the materials used for censers, but later they were in brass and silver. Romanesque censers are in the museum at Freising, in the cathedral at Treves (one silver and one of copper-gilt), and in the archiepiscopal museum at Cologne. Lübke (" Ecclesiastical Art in Germany ") illustrates an elaborate twelfth-century censer from Lille, of copper-gilt, with fantastic animals in bold relief, and having on the apex an angel and three smaller figures representing Ananias, Azarias and Misael, in evident allusion to the fiery furnace from the effects of which they were so miraculously preserved. The Church of St Maurice, Münster, possesses a beautiful Early Gothic censer, which in general form yet retains the Romanesque character. The Later Gothic gave to these works a slimmer form, and by furnishing them with supporting piers, pinnacles, and tracery makes them conformable to their system of architecture. We find such censers in the cathedral and the Busdorf church at Paderborn, in the Church of St Alban, Cologne, in the churches at Orsoy and Eltenberg on the Rhine, and one especially rich at Seitenstetten. The last-named is illustrated by Lübke. At Westminster Abbey, in 1388, were : " Turibuli ij magni, ex dono quondam Regis Henrici III. ; continentes in summitate ij parvas campanulas " ; and " Turibulum magnum argenteum deauratum cum ymaginibus in tabernaculis sedentibus ; et dono Dom. Simonis Cardinalis." In 1449 William Bruges, Garter-King-at-Arms, bequeathed to the Church of St George within Stamford, " a peyre of censours of sylver, with a ship of sylver for frankincence, and j spone for the same ship, of sylver." Among the goods of the church at Great Wakering, Essex, which were stolen therefrom in the second year of King Edward VI. (1549) were " ij chaleses p'cell gilt, a senser of sylver & a ship of sylver " ; and at Purleigh, four years later, " a shipp of sylver " (" Inventory of Essex Church Goods," Essex Archæological Society). At St Mary-at-Hill in 1562 were " ij shippis of sylver." In an inventory of the treasury of St Paul's, taken in 1245, are nine censers, some enriched with figures of angels ; two *naviculae* or incense-boats—one of silver-gilt, the other with its *coclear*, or spoon. In the Inventory of 1552 five censers are described, one of them " of silver and parcell gilte with iij libardes [leopards] heddes on the cover with vj windows and pinnacles and iiij chaynes of silver thereunto apperteynynge,"

ECCLESIASTICAL TERMS

and another a " little Sensoure of silver and gilte," the cover in " the forme of an oled churche with wyndows & pinacles with v shorte chaynes of sylver wyre." A third is the great censer used at Whitsuntide, which will be found described *sub voce* " Pentecost." By the Canons of Archbishop Grey and others subsequently, censers were ordered to the provided by the parishioners for the use of the Church. Though disused and discountenanced by the Puritan side, the censer continued partially in use. Thus, the furniture of Bishop Andrewes' Chapel comprised " a triquetral censer, wherein the clerk putteth frankincense at the reading of the first lesson, and the *navicula*, like the keel of a boat, with a half cover and foot, out of which the frankincense is poured." Archbishop Sancroft published a form for the consecration of a censer, which will be found in " Hierugia Anglicana," p. 184. From a paper on Great St Mary's, Cambridge, read before the Cambridge Camden Society, 13th February 1843, by E. Venables, Esq., B.A. (Pembroke College), it appeared that incense was used to perfume that church during all the reign of Queen Elizabeth. Mr Venables, by the way, was afterwards (1867) Precentor of Lincoln. In St Augustine's, Farringdon-within, London, two pounds of frankincense were burnt in the church in 1603 (Malcolm's " Londinium Redivivum, ii. 88). About 1631 George Herbert recommended that " the country parson takes order that the church be swept clean without dust or cobwebs, and at great festivals strewed and stuck with boughs, and perfumed with incense " (" Priest to the Temple," chap. xiii., " The Parson's Church "). Incense was burnt by Dr Cosin in the chapel of St Peter's College, Cambridge, *temp.* Charles I.: " In Peter House there was on the altar a pot, which they usually called the incense pot. . . . A little boat, out of which the frankincense is poured, which Dr Cosins had made use of in Peter House where he burnt incense " (" Canterbury's Doom," pp. 74, 123). In 1683, incense was burnt in St Nicholas', Durham : " For frankincense at the Bishop's coming, 2s 6d." (Surtees' " History and Antiquities of Durham," iv. 52, fol. 1840). In John Evelyn's Diary, under date March 30 (Easter Day), 1684, we find : " The Bishop of Rochester [Dr Turner] preached before the King ; after which his Majesty, accompanied by three of his natural sons, the Dukes of Northumberland, Richmond, and St Albans, went up to the altar ; the three boys entering before the King within the rails at the right hand, and three Bishops on the left—viz. London (who officiated), Durham, and Rochester, with the Sub-dean, Dr Holder. The King kneeling before the altar, making his offering, the Bishops first received, and then

A DICTIONARY OF

his Majesty ; after which he retired to a canopied seat on the right hand. *Note,* there was perfume burnt before the Office began." This would have been at the Chapel Royal, Whitehall. In the coronation procession of George III. in 1761 " appeared the King's Groom of the Vestry in a scarlet dress, holding a perfuming pan, burning perfumes as at previous Coronations" (Thomson's " Coronation of George III.," quoted in the "Book of Fragments," p. 206). For the use of incense at Ely Cathedral until late in the eighteenth century consult T. F. Bumpus, " Cathedrals of England and Wales," vol. i. p. 87. Among post-Reformation bishops who consecrated and blessed censers were Goodman, Laud, and Montagu ; and several others seem to have used them. See also *sub voce* " Incense."

Centry-garth, or Garth. The space within the quadrangle of a cloister, generally laid out with grass and shrubs as a place of sepulture. Examples : Noyon (France), Münster (Germany), Tongres (Belgium) ; Canterbury, Chester, Chichester, Durham, Gloucester, Norwich, Salisbury, Westminster, Wells (in our own country). At Chichester this enclosure is traditionally known as " Paradise," and that at Wells as the " Palm Churchyard," from the yew-tree in its centre, the branches of which, in pre-Reformation times, were carried in procession, in default of the genuine ones, on the Sunday next before Easter.

Ceroferarii. The acolytes who carry the wax tapers in processions, and at the Holy Eucharist. In Old St Paul's, when the bishop on great feasts, at Matins and Vespers, occupied the dean's stall, two acolytes in alb and amice holding lighted tapers stood before him, waiting until he went to cense the altars at *Benedictus* and *Magnificat.* At each corner of the choir stood two boys of the Almonry, or Choristers' School, who acted in turn as taper-bearers.

Chair-organ. An old name given to the " prestant " or choir-organ, from a notion that it formed the seat of the organist when placed behind him. Among English organ-cases that have " chair-organs " are those at the cathedrals of St Paul's, Exeter, Gloucester, Norwich, Chichester, and Lincoln ; those at King's and Trinity Colleges, Cambridge ; New and Magdalen Colleges, Oxford ; St George's Chapel, Windsor ; Eton College ; St Peter's College, Radley. Some of these are ancient. In London such cases are to be seen at St Lawrence, Jewry, and St James's, Piccadilly. Before the unfortunate removal of the organ from the

62

west gallery to a stuffy " chamber," there was one at St Sepulchre's, Holborn. But terrible mischief has been done during the restoration of many of our cathedrals and churches, in the shape of destruction of valuable or interesting organ-cases of Early and Late Renaissance workmanship. Gone for ever are those works of art at Durham, Worcester, Hereford, Wells, Lincoln, Southwell, Canterbury, Winchester, St David's, Chichester, and Salisbury, all of which may be seen represented in old engravings of the interiors of the choirs of those cathedrals. Modern architects and " restorers " have left us nothing of the sort by way of compensation. Instead, we see rows of ugly-looking pipes, often gaudily coloured. In France, the fine seventeenth and early eighteenth century cases have been almost universally preserved with the greatest care, and the chair-organ is an almost invariable appendage. In Germany this feature is not quite so common, but it is to be met with at the Dom, Lubeck ; the Dom, Frankfort ; and the Pfarrkirche, Innspruch. In Spain there are many examples. It may be seen at Odense and Roëskilde in Scandinavia. Consult J. Norbury, " The Box of Whistles, or Notes on Organ Cases at Home and Abroad " (1878) ; also A. G. Hill, " Organ Cases and Organs of the Middle Ages and Renaissance " (1883).

Chalice. The sacramental cup in which the wine is consecrated and from which the people are communicated. Upon the chalice, as was most natural and laudable, every treasure of material and workmanship was lavished. In the year 320, at the great festival held upon the occasion of the body of St Peter being deposited in the Basilica of St Peter, at Rome, the Emperor Constantine and the Empress St Helena presented, amongst other things, three chalices of gold and twenty chalices of silver. At Kremsmünster is the oldest chalice existing in Germany, having been presented by the founder of the church in A.D. 777 ; it is of copper with niello and gold ornaments. The richly decorated chalice of St Remigius, Bishop of Rheims, A.D. 510, formerly in the cathedral, is now in the Imperial Library at Paris. Engravings of both these early chalices are given by Lübke (" Ecclesiastical Art in the Middle Ages," p. 140). One of the finest chalices of the later Romanesque period is in the Church of St Catherine at Osnabrück, completely covered with fine arabesques of pierced filigree work. Still richer is the pontifical chalice presented by Bishop Bernhard (d. 1153) in the Godehard Church, Hildesheim, in silver gilt, with four representations in relief out of the Old Testament, and as many more out of the New, and adorned with precious stones. Other famous chalices of the thirteenth century are in the Nicolai Church, Berlin, the Cloister Church at Zehdenik, in St John's Church, Werben, in the Church of the Holy Apostles, Cologne, and in the museum at Basle. Gothic art altered not only the form, but also the decoration of the cup. Conformably to the law of Gothic architecture the general form became slimmer, but the pictorial decoration was poorer, so that in richness and beauty no Gothic chalice could compare with the best of Romanesque times. Two chalices of this period at the Monastery of Neuburg, are engraved by Lübke. Bingham ("Christian Antiquities," p. 109) mentions that glass was frequently used for chalices at an early date. In the Catacombs at Rome have been found parts of glass cups, enamelled in gold, with subjects which leave no doubt of their having been intended for chalices, but the material was discouraged from fear of accident. An instance is mentioned in the "Legenda Aurea Sanctorum" (ed. Lyons, 1486, fol. cxii.), where, at the Church of St Lawrence, Milan, a deacon was carrying to the altar a crystalline chalice of wonderful beauty, when it slipped from his hands and was broken to fragments ; but the worthy deacon collected the fragments and placed them upon the altar of St Lawrence, and prayed, and the broken chalice was made whole and taken up consolidated. At Westminster Abbey, at the time of the Dissolution, there were amongst other things a golden chalice weighing 14 ounces, and seven chalices of silver and gilt weighing 167 ounces. At St Paul's in 1402 there were sixteen chalices, five of gold, the rest of silver-gilt. These are picturesquely described, with the rest of the contents of the treasury, by Dr Simpson in his book "St Paul's Cathedral and Old City Life" (1894). In the Inventory of 1553, five chalices are mentioned, one of "silver and gilte, the foote vj square with a crucifix Marie and John in the foote and Jesus Christ graven alsoe in the foote, the paten having the ymage of the Trinitie and this scripture graven aboughte the paten 'Benedicamus patrem et filium, etc.'" This weighed 30 ounces. With a few exceptions, the whole of the contents of this magnificent treasury were appropriated by Edward VI.'s rapacious Commissioners. Three of the chalices appear to have been retained. Church plate was so sought after by the Royal Commissioners, and "annexed" for the King's use, that even in 1549 the parish of St Dionis Backchurch, London, had to buy (as appears by the accounts, printed in the "London and Middlesex Archæological Transactions," iv., p. 205) : "ij coppes of sylver and gilt, waying 61 owncys at 7ˢ 4ᵈ tne ownces for the Communyon tabyll, costing xxij*li*. vijs. iiij*d*." Chalices of Elizabethan date are not uncommon in our English churches. They are generally very simple in design, and were, no doubt, given to replace those plundered by the Edwardian Commissioners. When J. P. Malcolm wrote his "Londinium Redivivum," in 1803, he gave a detailed account of the rich service of plate then belonging to St Paul's Cathedral, much of which was presented on the opening of the new choir in 1697. Among it was a "silver-gilt chalice, with the paten, and another of the same materials, embossed with a saint bearing the Agnus Dei, and inscribed ' Bibite ex hoc omnes ; est hic enim Calix Novi Testamenti Sanguine Meo.'" On 22nd December 1810 the sacristy of St Paul's was entered and the whole of the communion plate, valued at £4000 was carried off. The thieves were said to have been occupied some five or six nights upon the work. As violence could not be employed, it took a separate night to obtain a waxen impression of the wards of each lock. At length the booty was reached, and was carried off, it is said, to a house in Little Britain, where the warmest possible reception awaited it. See *The Gentleman's Magazine*, vol. lxxx. pt. ii. p: 655, and the *Annual Register for 1810* (24th December). The place of the stolen plate was supplied by two chalices of copper-gilt, with other vessels of the same material, until 1871, when silver-gilt vessels, including four chalices and patens, a fine flagon, two cruets and a stand, a very noble alms dish, and a pair of candlesticks, all of artistic beauty and value, were offered for the service of the altar by various donors. The revival of Church art in the working of the precious metals for communion plate under the auspices of the Cambridge Camden (afterwards the Ecclesiological) Society should not be forgotten. See the illustrations in " Instrumenta Ecclesiastica" (1847–1850). A paper on altar plate by the distinguished architect, William Burges (printed in *The Ecclesiologist*, August and October 1858), is of great value.. T. H. King in his " Study-Book of Mediæval Architecture and Art " (vol. iii. Pl. VII.) gives drawings of a very interesting chalice which then (1858) was in the collection of Professor Usterlyk of Hanover. The medallions in relief on the foot represent, besides the Sacrifice on the Cross, common to all ancient chalices, and required by the rubric, the typical sacrifices of Abel, Isaac and Melchisedec ; all singularly Byzantine in character. In the same volume (Plates III. and V.) are given detailed drawings of two fine chalices in the cathedral at Osnabrük, and in vol. ii. similar drawings are provided of chalices preserved in the churches of St Gothard and St Maurice, Hildesheim, and there is another of that at Wessel. Mabillon " Voyage des deux Bénédictins " speaks of a remarkable chalice in the Abbey of St Josse-sur-

Mer, near Montreuil, of cast brass, not high, but the cup very large, with two handles bearing the inscription :

" Cum vino mista sit Christi Sanguis et unda
Talibus his sumptis salvatur quisque fidelis."

The section " Chalice and Paten " in Chambers' " Divine Worship " is deserving of careful study.   In it is figured the celebrated Ardagh Chalice (ninth or tenth century), now in the Royal Irish Academy, and made of a mixture of metals, probably zinc and silver, or niello.   Like the chalice described by Mabillon it has two handles, nearly circular, fastened to the sides.

Chalice-veil. A covering of silk, embroidered, and of the colour of the season, used for placing over the chalice and paten when prepared for Mass or Holy Communion, and afterwards.   Walcott (" Sacred Archæology ") mentions that in France it covered the chalice during the Elevation, but not so in England. In the Sarum rite it was also used by the acolyte to wrap the paten in, when held by him at various parts of the service.

Chancel. The eastern part of a church, appropriated to the use of those who officiate in the performance of the services, and separated from the nave and other portions, in which the congregation assemble, by a screen (*cancellus*), from which the name is derived.   The term should, however, be strictly confined to parish churches.   In cathedrals and collegiate churches, where there are choral foundations and daily choral offices, the portion of the church in which those offices are performed is always called the " choir." The choir of a cathedral is constantly written of by newspaper reporters, and also by others, who ought to know better, as the " chancel."

Chancellor.
Lat.
Cancellarius. A dignitary of a Cathedral of the Old Foundation, frequently one of the canons residentiary, as at St Paul's, Lichfield, Lincoln, Chichester, Exeter, and Hereford.   Originally, he had the general care of the literature of the church, and of the preaching, and was the secretary of the chapter.   He was also the superintendent of schools connected with the diocese, and particularly of that for the choristers attached to the cathedral.   He ranks as third of those four dignitaries who take precedence of all other members of the chapter, the other three being the dean, the precentor, and the treasurer.   At Lincoln and Truro, the chancellor has charge of the Scholæ Cancellarii, or Theological Schools for the training of candidates for Holy

ECCLESIASTICAL TERMS

Orders. At St Paul's, until 1885, the chancellorship was a separate dignity; since that time the stall has been held by the second canon residentiary. The Chancellor *of the Church* (the above-named officer) is not to be confounded with the Chancellor of the Diocese, a lawyer. Consult Miss Hackett's "Correspondence and Evidences respecting the Ancient School attached to St Paul's Cathedral" (1832); Walcott's "Cathedralia" (1865); Jebb on the "Choral Service" (1843).

Change Ringing, or changes. The altered melodies produced by varying the order of a peal of bells.

Chant. A short musical composition to which the Psalms (and usually in parish churches the Canticles) are sung, either in unison or four-part harmony. There are two kinds of chants in common use—the Anglican and the Gregorian. Anglican chants are chiefly of two sorts, single and double. A single chant is in two strains, the first of three, and the second of four, bars. A double chant has the length of two, a triple chant of three, and a quadruple chant of four, single ones. Specimens of all forms will be found in the edition of the "Westminster Abbey Chant-Book," published in 1894, and in the St Mary's [Stoke Newington] Chant-Book, edited by C. T. Johnson in 1898—an admirable and comprehensive collection. A Gregorian chant consists of five parts—the intonation, reciting-note, mediation, second reciting-note, and the ending. There are eight Gregorian tones used in chanting, each having an endless variety of mediations and endings.

Chanter, or Chaunter. An old name for the precentor (a minor canon) in cathedrals and collegiate churches of the New Foundation, as Gloucester, Westminster, and Worcester. At New College, Oxford, the principal chaplain (one of ten) was called the chanter. The Rev. E. J. Beckwith, afterwards a minor canon of St Paul's, was "chanter" of New in 1790.

Chantry.
Old Eng.
chauntry. An ecclesiastical benefice or endowment to provide for the chanting of masses. It was very often a testamentary bequest, the testator also directing a chapel to be built, often over the spot where he was buried, in which the Masses were to be celebrated for the especial benefit of the souls of himself and others named in his will; hence the term has come to be sometimes applied to the chapel itself. Chantries are found in various situations, frequently with the tomb of the founder in the middle of them, as at Fyfield, Berks, and are generally enclosed with open screenwork. Some-

times they are external additions to a church, but very often, especially in cathedrals and large churches, they are complete erections within it. Many of those of Late Perpendicular date are most lavishly enriched with mouldings and sculpture in all their parts, and some have been brilliantly painted and gilt. Most of our cathedrals and abbey churches contain specimens of these chapels, as Ely, Lincoln, Wells, Winchester, and St Alban's. With St Paul's, in pre-Reformation times, a large body of men, called chantry priests, was connected. They were bound, not only to say Mass at the special altars to which they were attached, but also to attend in choir, and there to perform such duties as were assigned to them. Chaucer, in the Prologue to the " Canterbury Tales," vv. 509–516, alludes to the eagerness with which some of the country clergy, to the neglect of their own benefices, sought for chantries in St Paul's.

Chapel Royal, St James's Palace. This small chapel, or oratory, situated between the Colour Court and the Ambassadors' Court, St James's Palace, is chiefly interesting from the important place it holds in the annals of English Church music, and for the numerous royal functions which have taken place within its walls. It was not, however, until the reign of Henry VIII. that the duties of the Chapel Royal were performed at St James's Palace, which was first built by that monarch. This spot, now so interesting in British history, was originally occupied by a hospital dedicated to St James, founded by some pious citizens before the Conquest for fourteen leprous maidens, and eight brethren were added afterwards to perform divine service. It was rebuilt in the reign of Henry III. The custody was given to Eton College by a grant of the 28th of Henry VI. It is asserted that the living of Chattisham was given in exchange for it, the college having for that consideration resigned it to Henry VIII., at which time its revenue was valued at £100 per annum. It was surrendered to the king in 1531, who founded on its site the present palace, which Stow, the historian of London, calls " a goodly manor." The chapel, of very little architectural pretensions, is placed just to the west of the picturesque brick gateway, and is distinguished externally by its tall square-headed northern, or altar, window (for the chapel does not orientate) of nine lights. It is oblong in plan, with side galleries, longitudinal pews, the Royal Gallery being at the southern end. The superb ceiling, painted by Holbein in 1540, is described in T. F. Bumpus' " London Churches, Ancient and Modern," p. 194. The organ is in a recess in the middle of the west side. Before 1836, when the chapel was restored by Sir Robert Smirke, it was in a loft on the same side overhanging, and in close proximity to, the altar. The altar window was considerably enlarged at the time of the marriage of Queen Victoria in 1840, and again at that of the Princess Royal in 1858. Various ritual and other ameliorations were made in the building towards the close of the last century. The staff of the chapel consists of a dean, sub-dean, a clerk of the closet, and 3 deputies, 36 chaplains, and 8 honorary chaplains, 4 priests in ordinary, a Master of the Children, 9 gentlemen, and 10 children, or choristers. The office of priest-in-ordinary corresponds with that of minor canon in cathedrals. The gentlemen and children form the choir. The sub-dean is resident chaplain and has the ancient title of Confessor to the Household. He has the general supervision of the chapel and its services. Certain offices, such as " Violist," " Lutenist," and " Tuner of the Regals," are now obsolete. There is now one organist and composer. Formerly there was an organist and composer, and an ordinary organist. The first regular organist seems to have been Dr Christopher Tye (1562). Before that time those of the gentlemen who could do so took it in turn to play. The place of composer was created in 1699, Dr Blow being the first. A second composer's place was added in 1715, when John Weldon was appointed. Each took his month of " waiting." The first organ of which there is any record appears to have been built by Schreider in 1710.. In 1785 it was repaired by a pupil of Samuel Green on the representation of Dr Dupuis, then organist and composer. The pitch was lowered half-a-note, as it used " to strain the voices," and a double swell was added, at a cost of £100. It was again repaired in 1802 for the same sum. In 1819 an entirely new organ was built by Elliott, the old one being removed to the Episcopal Chapel in Long Acre, and again, in 1866, to the chapel of Mercers' Hall, Cheapside. In 1838 another entirely new organ was placed in the chapel. This was built by Hill & Davison. The old one was sent to Milverton, Warwickshire, and thence to Crick, Northants. Thirty years later another entirely new instrument was erected by Hill, the old one being sent to Barrow-in-Furness. This, with sundry improvements, is the organ still in use. From the " Pietas Londinensis," a guide to the hours of service in the London churches, compiled by the Rev. James Paterson, and printed in 1714, we learn that the Holy Sacrament was administered at the Chapel Royal every Sunday at 8, and at noon. The choral services on Sundays and all week-days were at 11 and 5. In 1663 the hours of service were 9 and 4 on Sundays and Holy Days, and 10 and 4 on week-days.

The week-day choral services seem to have been discontinued late in the eighteenth century, the only ones retained being those on Holy Days and on the Wednesdays and Fridays in Lent. The hours of the Sunday services were then altered to noon and 5.30, that at noon consisting of Matins, Litany, Sermon, and Holy Communion, which last was only choral as regarded the *Sanctus* (as an introit) and the responses to the Commandments. The singing of the Creed had been laid aside late in the eighteenth century. Towards the middle of the nineteenth century the morning service was divided, Matins being sung at 10, and the Litany and Communion Service at 12. Within recent years the 10 o'clock service has been transferred to the Marlborough House, formerly the German, Chapel. The 8 o'clock Celebration was kept up, and at this the Duke of Wellington was, for many years, a regular attendant on the first Sunday of every month. On the second Sunday after Easter, 1851, the Rev. A. Cleveland Coxe, afterwards (1864) Bishop of Western New York, knelt to communicate by the Duke's side, and he has given us a touching description of the service in his " Impressions of England in 1851 " (pp. 72–75). During the period at which the service was choral twice daily, it was the custom to have full anthems in the morning and verse or solo anthems in the evening. On Sundays verse anthems were sung at both services. The chapel possesses a large collection of printed and MS. Church music, but of the latter much of value and interest has disappeared. Books of words of the anthems used in the chapel have been published under the direction of Sub-Deans Dolben (1712), Carleton (1736), Pordage (1749), Anselm Bayly (1769), Pearce (1795), Holmes (1826), and Wesley (1856). The book at present in use is the collection published by Novello. The communion plate belonging to the chapel is of the most magnificent and costly description. An excellent woodcut, representing the whole of it, displayed, with the massive candlesticks, on the altar, will be found, in one of the numbers of *The Illustrated London News* during the early part of the year 1858. Although occasionally used in the sixteenth and seventeenth centuries, service was not regularly instituted at the Chapel Royal, St James's, until the beginning of the eighteenth century. For some time it was the guard-room of the Palace. Charles I., who resided at St James's, caused it to be re-fitted as a chapel, and here he attended service on the morning of his execution. Both Pepys and Evelyn, the diarists, make constant reference to the Chapel Royal, but the building almost invariably alluded to is that at the splendid Palace of Whitehall. This no less splendid chapel was consumed by fire, 5th January 1698, and a new

ECCLESIASTICAL TERMS

chapel opened on 9th December of the same year. Dr Blow wrote an anthem, " Lord, remember David," for the occasion. The frontispiece to " Divine Harmony," a set of anthems composed by John Weldon, represents the interior of this chapel during divine service. The Banqueting-House in Whitehall, built by Inigo Jones (1622), was not used as a Chapel Royal until a century later. It was never consecrated, and has for some years been disused as a place of worship. Here on Maundy Thursday the sovereign's eleemosynary bounty was distributed to poor and aged men and women, until the closing of the chapel, when the ceremony was transferred to Westminster Abbey. Formerly the large establishment of clerics and musicians attached to the Chapel Royal belonged to no fixed place, but was bound to attend the sovereign wherever he or she might be resident. Queen Elizabeth, for instance, had a chapel in her palace at Greenwich. It was while " in waiting " here, as one of the gentlemen, that Thomas Tallis died in 1585. He was buried in the old Church of St Alfege, Greenwich, where there existed, until its demolition in 1721, an inscription to his memory, and there were also memorials to Clement Adams, Master of the Children in 1516, and Richard Bowyer, who held the same office in 1548. Of this ambulatory service there are many proofs, and, in later times, George IV., when resident at Brighton, used to command the attendance of a certain number of his choir in the private chapel at the Pavilion. There are other chapels attached to palaces with the title of " Royal " —e.g. St George's, Windsor, the chapels at Hampton Court, Kensington Palace, the Savoy, etc., but when we speak of " The Chapel Royal" that in St James's Palace is always understood. There are private chapels at Windsor Castle and Buckingham Palace. The old German Chapel Royal is that now belonging to Marlborough House. The last occasion on which Queen Victoria attended a Sunday service at the Chapel Royal was 3rd July 1842, the day of her attempted assassination by Bean. The private chapel in Buckingham Palace was then fitted up. At the present day the Chapel Royal is rarely attended by the King. Admission to the noonday service on Sunday is only to be obtained by an order from the Lord Chamberlain. The 5.30 service, and the services held on Holy Days and Wednesdays and Fridays, are open to the public without orders. The services are particularly solemn and devotional, and the impression is heightened by the historical and musical associations of the holy place. This is especially so during the Sunday evening service in the winter months, when the chapel is lighted from end to end with wax tapers, the two lights on the richly appointed altar

71

A DICTIONARY OF

closing the vista in a very charming manner. Consult further " The Old Cheque-Book, or Book of Remembrance of the Chapel Royal," edited by E. F. Rimbault, LL.D., for the Camden Society (1872) ; and " Memorials of St James's Palace," by the Rev. Edgar Sheppard, Sub-Dean (2 vols., 1894). See also *sub voce*, " Children of the Chapel Royal," and " Gentlemen of the Chapel Royal," in the present work.

Chaplain. A person authorised to officiate in the chapels of the sovereign, or in the private oratories of noblemen, or colleges, or public institutions, in the army, navy, etc. The name is derived from *capella* (chapel), the priests who superintend the *capella* being called *capellani*. There are some forty-eight Chaplains to the King, who have preaching turns assigned to them in the Chapel Royal. In the college chapels of Oxford and Cambridge, in the chapel of Winchester College, and in the Cathedral of Christ Church, Oxford, those responsible for the chanting of the daily prayers are designated chaplains, the term corresponding with that of priest vicar or minor canon. At Eton, the corresponding title is Conduct (*Capellanus Conductitius*). At Chester the minor canons were formerly called " Conducts."

Chapter. The governing body or head (*capitulum*) of a cathedral, consisting of the dean, canons, and prebendaries, whereof the dean is chief, " all subordinate to the Bishop, to whom they are assistants in matters relating to the Church, for the better ordering and disposing the things thereof and for confirmation of such leases of the temporalities and offices relating to the bishopric as the bishop from time to time shall happen to make. And they are termed by the canonists *capitulum*, being a kind of *head*, instituted not only to assist the bishop in manner aforesaid, but also anciently to rule and govern the diocese in the time of vacation " (Cod. 56). In Cathedrals of the Old Foundation chapters are of two kinds : the greater and the lesser. The greater chapter consists of all the major canons and prebendaries, whether residentiary or not ; the lesser chapter consists of the dean and residentiaries, who have the management of the chapter property and the ordinary government of the cathedral. The privileges of the greater chapter are now considered to be limited to the election of a bishop, of proctors in convocation, and in some cases they vote on the patronage of the chapter. The new chapters are those eight which were founded or remodelled by Henry VIII. in the place of abbots and monasteries, or priors and monasteries, which were chapters while they stood ; or they are those which were annexed to the five new bishoprics founded by Henry VIII. The

ECCLESIASTICAL TERMS

chapter of a collegiate church is more properly called the *college* : as at Westminster and Windsor, where there is no episcopal see. At Manchester, before the collegiate church was constituted a cathedral (1847), the head of the chapter was styled warden. There may be a chapter without any dean ; as the former chapter of the Collegiate Church of Southwell. In the cathedrals of Llandaff and St David's there used to be no dean, but they are now placed on the same footing as other cathedrals. At St David's until 1840, the precentor was virtually head of the chapter. At Southwark and Truro the bishop is at present dean.

The apartment or hall in which the monks and canons of a monastic establishment, or the dean and canons of cathedral and collegiate churches, meet for the despatch of business relating to the general body of the society. The most elaborate ornament is frequently employed in the architecture of chapter-houses, and the magnificence and richness which many of them display is very striking, as York, Chester, Gloucester, Lichfield, Lincoln, Oxford, Salisbury, Southwell, Wells, Worcester, Westminster, etc. Chapter-houses are of various forms, some oblong, as Oxford, Exeter, Canterbury, Gloucester, Chester ; others octagonal, as York, Wells, Salisbury, Westminster ; or polygonal, as Lichfield, Lincoln, Worcester. Their situation also varies, but they are universally contiguous to the church, and are not generally placed westward of the transepts. They often adjoin the cloisters, through which they are approached from the church, as at Oxford, Salisbury, Worcester, Westminster, Canterbury, Chester. Sometimes they are entered by a passage from the church, as at York, Lichfield, Southwell, Wells. At York the passage to the chapter-house is transcendently beautiful. Old St Paul's had, on the south side of the nave, an exquisite Decorated octagonal chapter-house, standing in the midst of a small cloister. Some portions of both buildings remain. The present chapter-house of St Paul's, on the north side of the church, dates from 1712. Here the Convocation of the Southern Province assembles, before and after the Latin service in the choir of the cathedral, with which a new Convocation invariably opens. Consult "Chapter Houses, their Form and Uses," an interesting paper read before the Wilts Archæological Institute at Salisbury, September 1854, by Henry Clutton, architect, and printed in *The Ecclesiologist*, April 1855. To the chapter-houses polygonal in shape should be added that of Hereford, once the gem of the cathedral, but now only a ruin. It adjoined the south transept. The foundations and fragments

Chapter-house.

which remain show that it was rich Decorated, in shape a decagon, with a projecting buttress at each angle. It was ruined during the Civil War, and much of its stonework was used by Bishop Bisse (d. 1721) and by his successors for the repairs of the episcopal palace. The chapter-house of Durham, when in its original state, up to 1799, was without a rival in the kingdom, both from its architecture and the historic interest of its monuments. It was built during the perfection of the Norman style (1133-1143) by Bishop Galfrid Rufus, and measured 80 by 37 feet. Against the wall in the centre of its semicircular end, stood the ancient Norman chair in which the bishops of Durham had been installed from the earliest period. Bishop Barrington was the last, in 1791. It had a magnificent groined roof, and the pavement was almost formed by the incised slabs and brasses of the early bishops and priors. Here were buried the bones of Aidan, first bishop of Lindisfarne, and of two or three of his successors, which the monks had carried about with them from place to place, till their final settlement at Durham, and of Aldune, first Bishop of Durham, 1018. Afterwards, fourteen prelates—beginning with Edmund in 1042 and ending with Richard Kellawe in 1316—were buried there in their full episcopal robes, and with their croziers. In 1799 it was resolved that this chapter-house was "uncomfortable," and, to remedy this defect, the keystones of the groinings were knocked out, and the whole roof was suffered to fall down, immolating and crushing all the venerable memorials beneath, not even the chair being removed, and no inscription having been copied! Half of the original room was excluded (and thrown into the Dean's garden) by a wall pierced with modern sash windows. Another part was partitioned off as an ante-room. the floor boarded, and the Norman arcading concealed by lath and plaster. In our own day this interesting and unrivalled chapter-house has been restored to something like its pristine beauty under Mr C. Hodgson Fowler, the chapter architect, as a memorial to Bishop Lightfoot (d. 1891); the drawings of it made by John Carter, the antiquary, before the mischief began, proving of great assistance in the recovery of its details. R. W. Billings, in his " Architectural Illustrations and Description of the Cathedral Church at Durham " (1843), gives a " restored view."

At the Restoration (1660) the 30th of January was appointed **Charles I.,** a fast day in commemoration of this event, and a **Martyrdom of.** special form of service was ordered to be used. The observance, however, was abolished by royal order, and the service removed from the Prayer-Book in 1859. On this day, as on Whitsun Even, and the Wednesdays and Fridays in Lent, all the London theatres were compulsorily closed, and concerts of sacred music, called "Oratorios," were given instead at the patent houses, Drury Lane and Covent Garden. This rule seems to have been latterly relaxed, but it was certainly in force in 1830.

Chasuble.
Lat. *casula.*

The eucharistic vestment *par excellence*, and still ordered to be worn by the law of the English Church. The chasuble is adorned with an orphrey of embroidery down the centre, and often with an embroidered edging. It should be made of rich and *pliant* material, such as silk, velvet, or cloth of gold. It was cut of old very much in the shape of a *vesica piscis* (*q.v.*), with a hole for the head in the centre, and fell in graceful folds before and behind. The modern Roman vestment is utterly unlike the old, and extremely heavy and ungainly looking. The **Y**-shaped chasuble of the fourteenth and fifteenth centuries generally had the orphrey on the back arranged in the form of a cross, and filled in with the most delicate embroidery of Scripture subjects. The chasuble represents the seamless vest of Christ : as also the purple garment, after being endued with which He was made to carry His cross. It reminds the priest that he must carry his cross after Christ, and must ever lean on Him as his true support. The colour of the chasuble varies, of course, with the season (see " Liturgical Colours "). Quite one of the first churches in which it was introduced, at the beginning of the Tractarian Revival, was St Thomas', Oxford, during the incumbency of the Rev. Thos. Chamberlain. The Roman Church has altered the chasuble much by cutting it away literally, so as to expose the arms, and leave only a straight piece before and behind. The Greek Church retains it in its primitive shape, under the title of φαινόλιον, or φενώλιον : the old brasses in England also show the same form, some even since the Reformation, and many tombs of bishops in the thirteenth century, and later, show it in a graceful and flowing form. The chasuble was prescribed, under the title of " Vestment," in the rubric of Edward VI.'s First Prayer-Book, to be worn by the priest or bishop when celebrating the Holy Communion. Other terms for this, the " Vestimentum " or principal garment of the priest when celebrating the Holy Mysteries, are Casibula, Penule, Planeta, Infula, πλανήτης πλάνης. When no other explanation is given in the Inventories, that word is used to designate the chasuble. Nevertheless, it is occasionally applied to the stole, dalmatic, tunicle, and even the alb. It derives its Greek name πλανήτης from its flowing dimensions, as it covered all the body from the neck to the feet. The ecclesiastical use of this vestment seems to have been derived from Exodus xxviii. 31, 32, " Thou shalt make the robe of the ephod all of blue, and there shall be a hole in the top of it in the midst thereof. It shall have a binding of woven work round about the whole of it as it were the hole of an habergeon, that it be not rent." This in shape corresponded to the ancient chasuble, which was so large and long that it completely enclosed the arms ; and it was necessary to lift it up at the sides in order to be able to use it. Many of these ancient chasubles were in existence in France in the time of Bocquillot (" Traité historique de la Liturgie," p. 161 ; Paris, 1701), and even of De Vert (1750). Up to the tenth century, and even later, the chasuble worn by a bishop had sometimes a hood which was fastened to it at the back, especially when the bishop walked in processions. Dr Rock, who saw one at Rheims, cites authorities in his " Church of Our Fathers," i. 349. This appears to have been succeeded by, or substituted for, the magnificent humerale or collar worn by bishops. The Greek Church still continues the ancient ample, long and flowing form of the chasuble ; and that this shape lasted in England up to a very late period is proved by numerous MSS. and sepulchral brasses still existing ; for instance, that of St Thomas of Canterbury, at Sens ; and that of Regnobert at Bayeux ; and as represented on the monumental brass of Thomas, Abbot of St Alban's, and on those of Robert de Waldeby, Archbishop of York, and John Waltham, Bishop of Salisbury, in Westminster Abbey. The modern Roman vestment, bitterly and rightly denounced by Pugin, diminished in length and curtailed at the shoulders for the purpose of facilitating the elevation of the Host, bears little resemblance to the graceful and dignified original. The well-known Helston case, decided by Henry Phillpotts, Bishop of Exeter (1831-1869), with the advice of his chancellor, was the first occasion on which the Ornaments Rubric came into dispute in modern times. The judgment was : " It is the duty of the parishioners, by the plain and express Canon Law of England (*Gibson*, 200), to provide the albe, the vestment [chasuble] and the cope. True, it would be a very costly duty, and for that reason most probably Churchwardens have neglected it, and Archdeacons have connived at the neglect. But be this as it may, if the churchwardens of Helston shall perform this duty, at the charge of the parish providing an albe, a vestment, and a cope, as they might in strictness be required to do (*Gibson*, 201), I shall enjoin the Minister, be he who he may, to use them."

ECCLESIASTICAL TERMS

Chevet. The French word for pillow. An architectural term, exclusively French, employed for the eastern extremity of a church, with surrounding chapels. The word is derived from the Latin *caput* (head), and in explanation of this etymology it may be said that the *chevet* of a church in the form of a Latin cross corresponds with that part of the instrument of punishment on which Christ laid or pillowed His head. French ecclesiologists generally use the word *chevet* to denote the east end of a cross church, with a *short* eastern limb, whether square, circular, or polygonal. That portion of Westminster Abbey eastward of the transepts may be truly described as a *chevet*. Consult Adolphe Berty, " Dictionnaire de l'Architecture du Moyen Age " (Paris, 1845).

Chevron. In architecture, an inflected moulding, called also zigzag. The French name for this is *bâtons rompus* (broken sticks). It is characteristic of Norman architecture, but is sometimes found with the pointed arch during the period of transition from the Norman to the Early English.

Children of the Chapel Royal. The name by which the ten (originally eight) singing boys attached to the Chapel Royal, St James's, have been known from the earliest times. The first records concerning them are contained in the " Liber Niger Domus Regis," a MS. *temp.* Edward IV., in which an account is given of the Royal Chapel in the reign of that monarch. They had a " Màster of Songe " to teach them, and they were boarded and educated in the royal palace. For several centuries the " Master of Songe " has been known as " Master of the Children." The ten boys are boarded with him, and now receive an excellent general education. Their residence has not always been in the precincts of the palace, but wherever their master has chosen to fix it. At various periods in the eighteenth century they were lodged in James Street, Westminster, the Sanctuary, Westminster, and the Stable Yard, St James's Palace. From 1817 to 1846 they lived at 7 Adelphi Terrace, Strand, with William Hawes, the then master. With Hawes' successor, the Rev. Thomas Helmore (1846-1886), the boys resided successively at Robert Street, Chelsea, 1 Onslow Square (1851), 6 Cheyne Walk, Chelsea (1854), and 72 St George's Square, Pimlico (1871). They now live in a large house in a healthy situation at Clapham. Their state dress, worn on Sundays and whenever on week-days they attend the Chapel Royal, consists of a scarlet coat (often incorrectly described as a cassock) richly embroidered with gold, cambric or lace bands, lace ruffles, scarlet breeches and black stockings. College caps have, for some years,

77

taken the place of cocked hats, and Oxford shoes are now worn instead of buckled ones. Otherwise the quaint, old-world and gorgeous costume preserves much of its original aspect. The surplice formed part of their dress in chapel until Dr Creighton, Bishop of London, was appointed dean in 1896, when he ordered its discontinuance. Since that period it has not been resumed. At the coronation of George III. surplices were worn, "with scarlet mantles over them." The boys sing on Sundays at the Chapel Royal, St James's, at 12.15 (Litany and Holy Communion) and at 5.30 (Evensong). At 9.45 they sing Matins in the Marlborough House, the old German, Chapel, and when the King is in residence at Buckingham Palace they attend the service held in the private chapel at 11. They also attend at the Chapel Royal, St James's, on all Wednesdays and Fridays at 10.30, and on Saints' Days at 11. As a rule, they sing nowhere else, the exceptions being certain special services at St Paul's and the annual Maundy Service at Westminster Abbey. They have been occasionally requisitioned for services at the openings of organs, consecrations of churches, etc., and at baptisms, marriages, and funerals chorally performed. Their secular engagements include attendance at the periodical meetings of the Madrigal and Western Madrigal Societies, when they supply the treble part. Many distinguished English musicians have held the post of Master of the Children. Usually the master has been appointed from among the gentlemen of the chapel, but occasionally the organist has held the post. The following is a list from the middle of the fifteenth century :—Henry Abyngdon, 1467 ; Gilbert Banistre, 1482 ; Wm. Cornish, 1492 ; Clement Adams, 1516 ; Wm. Crane, 1526 ; Richard Bowyer, 1548 ; Richard Edwards, 1554 ; Wm. Hunnis, 1556 ; Nathaniel Gyles, Mus.D., 1597 ; Thomas Day, 1636 ; " Captain " Henry Cooke, 1661 ; Pelham Humphreys, 1672 ; *John Blow, Mus.D., 1674 ; *William Croft, Mus.D., 1708 ; Bernard Gates, 1727 ; *James Nares, Mus.D., 1757 ; Edmund Ayrton, Mus. D., 1781 ; *John Stafford Smith, 1808 ; William Hawes, 1816 ; Rev. Thomas Helmore, M.A., 1846 ; Rev. H. A. Sherringham, M.A., 1886 ; Claude R. Selfe, B.A., 1892. Those marked * were organists of the chapel. Many of the " Children " educated in this choir have attained eminence as organists and composers ; indeed, like St Paul's and Westminster Abbey, it may be described as the nursery of English musicians. William Hawes, while Master of the Children, made the two senior boys—for reasons best known to himself—do double duty on Sundays by sending them to sing at St Paul's, of which cathedral he was also Master of the

Boys, as well as at their own place of worship. This was easily arranged, as the services at St Paul's were then at 9.45 and 3.15, and those at the Chapel Royal at 12 and 5.30. This made the day's work for these two boys very heavy, and entailed no fewer than four " lightning changes " of costume within the space of eight hours, from the garb of every-day life to the gorgeous scarlet and gold court costume of Charles II.'s period, and *vice versa*. This arrangement ceased with the death of Hawes in 1846.

Chime. (1) To play a tune on bells by means of hammers, or swinging the clappers, the bell remaining unmoved. It is opposed to *ringing*, in which bells are *raised*—that is, swung round. (2) A carillon—*i.e.* a set of bells so arranged as to be played by hand or machinery, such as those at Antwerp, Bruges, Mechlin, Namur, and other places in Belgium.

Chimere. The upper robe of black satin worn by a bishop, to which the lawn sleeves are attached. The name is probably derived from the Italian *zimarra*, which is described as " vesta talare de' sacerdoti e de' chierîci." The sewing of the lawn sleeves to the chimere is a modern innovation. They ought properly to be fastened to the rochet, the linen vestment worn under the chimere. The chimere seems to resemble the garment used by bishops during the Middle Ages, and called *mantelletum*—a sort of cope, with apertures for the arms to pass through.

Choir.
Old Eng.
quire or quere ;
Fr. *chœur* ;
Ital. and
Span. *coro* ;
Germ. *chor*.
That part of the church, eastward of the nave, in which services are celebrated ; also called " chancel," but this term applies to parish churches. When speaking or writing of cathedrals and collegiate churches, which have daily services and choral foundations, it is proper to use the word " choir." The choir is usually separated from the nave by a solid screen of stone, or an open one of wood and metal. In large churches there is generally an aisle at the sides of the choir, which is sometimes continued across the east end of the building, so as to surround it, especially in churches which have polygonal or semicircular terminations, like many of the Continental cathedrals. In England the choir is raised several steps above the nave—necessitated by the crypt beneath—as Canterbury, Rochester, Worcester and Winchester. At Carlisle, Durham, Ely, Hereford, Lichfield, Norwich, Peterborough, Salisbury, Wells, and Westminster, the choir is not raised at all. This was also the case at St Paul's before the alterations of 1871. In strictness the choir does not extend further eastward than the steps leading up to the altar, where the presbytery

or sanctuary begins, but this distinction is by no means adhered to, and the term *choir* is very generally applied to the whole space set apart for the celebration of the services of the Church, including the presbytery (*q.v.*), which is usually marked off by a step called the *gradus presbyterii*. Frequently the ritual choir (where the eastern limb of a cross church is short) includes the transepts and, in some instances, takes in one or more bays of the nave, as at Chichester, Gloucester, Norwich, Peterborough, Tewkesbury, Winchester, and Westminster, and as formerly at Chester and Ely, at which latter, until 1770, it included the octagon. This is also observable at Rheims, Châlons-sur-Marne, Autun, Séez, and several other places in France. The sides of a choir are fitted up with stalls, sometimes returned at the western end. These frequently have canopies of various dates, mostly Decorated. The rows of seats below the stalls are called *subsellae*. In the cathedrals of Spain, the *coro*, or choir, occupying a greater part of the nave, and shut in with lofty, solid screens, is a feature almost universally observable, but one not altogether among the *admiranda* of these vast buildings.

Choral, or Chorale. Another term for a hymn tune, or any piece of metrical psalmody. It is now usually applied to the psalmody of Germany, coeval with that of England in early post-Reformation times. J. Sebastian Bach, fully alive to the beauty of the hymns and tunes of his country, adopted the practice, in which he was followed by his contemporary, Graun, and many years after by Mendelssohn, of including chorales in his numerous sacred works. How magnificently he reharmonised these old tunes, those who have heard his *Christmas Oratorio*, his *St Matthew* " Passion," and his eight-part motett, " Come, Jesu, come," well know. Consult " The Chorale Book for England," compiled and edited by W. Sterndale Bennett, and Otto Goldschmidt (1865). It contains a most interesting and instructive preface.

Choramt. The German name for the capitular office in cathedrals when performed chorally.

Chorus Cantorum. The peculiar arrangement in a church where the ground plan exhibits only a nave and sacrarium ; and the choir is therefore locally in the nave formed by low screens.

Christe Eleison. See *sub voce* " Kyrie Eleison."

Cinquefoil. An ornamental foliation used in the arches of the lights and tracery of windows, panellings, etc., also applied to circles, formed by projecting points or cusps, so arranged that the intervals between them resemble leaves.

ECCLESIASTICAL TERMS

An upper storey or row of windows in a Gothic church, tower, or other erection rising clear above the adjoining parts of the building.

Clere-story or Clear-story. Fr. *clair étage*, *cleristères* ; Ital. *chiaro piano*. In churches it seems to have been adopted as a means of obtaining an increase of light in the body of the building, but the windows are not infrequently so small that they serve this purpose very imperfectly. The term *Clere-story* does not seem to have been generally used by writers on ecclesiastical architecture until early in the last century. In all probability it is a coined word.

A covered ambulatory, forming part of a monastic or collegiate establishment, by the other buildings of which it is surrounded.

Cloister. The cloisters are always contiguous to the church, and are arranged round three or four sides of a quadrangular area, with numerous large windows looking into the quadrangle, which frequently, if not always, were glazed. The walls opposite to these have no openings in them except the doorways communicating with the surrounding buildings. The cloisters were appropriated for the recreation of the inmates of the establishment, who also sometimes used them as places of study, for which purpose they occasionally had cells or stalls on one side, as at Gloucester ; and at Durham there were such cells called Carrols (*q.v.*). The cloisters were frequently used as places of sepulture. They are often richly vaulted in stone, and there is frequently a lavatory in them, and a stone bench along the wall opposite the windows. The largest and finest cloisters in England are those of Gloucester, Norwich, Salisbury, and Worcester. New College, Oxford, has a cloister of extreme beauty, westward of the chapel. Magdalen College, in the same university, has its cloister on the north of the chapel and hall. All these have four ambulatories or walks. At some cathedrals which were never monasteries, the cloisters are small, as Chichester, Wells, and Lincoln, the two first having only three walks. Old St Paul's had a small cloister, in the middle of which stood the polygonal chapter-house. At Salisbury the cloisters are coextensive in length with the nave, and form a perfect square. For a church which never had any monastic establishment in connection with it, they are of extraordinarily noble dimensions. At Winchester College the cloister, one of the most admired features of the place, is south of Wykeham's beautiful chapel. Abroad (except in Italy and Spain) cloisters are not quite so common an appendage. Among the best examples are those at Le Puy in Auverge, Arles, Noyon, Soissons, Tréguier, in France ; St Gall and Zurich in Switzerland ;

A DICTIONARY OF

St Maria in Capitolio (Cologne), Hildesheim, Münster, Laach Maulbronn, Paderborn, Halberstadt, Erfurt, Magdeburgh, Aix-la-Chapelle, Osnabruck, Xanten, Ratisbon, all in Germany ; Liége, Tongres, Nivelles in Belgium ; Burgos and the Convent of the Huelgas near that city, Gerona and Leon in Spain ; the monastery of Belem near Lisbon, Portugal. Cloisters in Italy are too numerous to mention, but those of St Matteo, Gerona, St John Lateran, Rome, the Cathedral and St Zeno, Verona, and those of the Campo Santo at Pisa and the Certosa at Pavia, may be cited as among the best examples. The Cathedrals of Ely, Peterborough and Winchester formerly possessed extensive cloisters in the usual position on the south side of the nave. Those of Ely were destroyed in 1650. The only part remaining is the north-east angle with its magnificent Norman doorway, forming the monks' entrance into the church. The prior's entrance at the north-west angle, in a corresponding style of architecture, is more magnificent still. At Peterborough, the cloisters were destroyed during the Great Rebellion. Winchester is almost entirely destitute of architectural *entourage*. Chapter-house, cloisters, dormitory, and other precincts of a church, which was at once episcopal and monastic, are gone, leaving the south side of the nave bare and naked. Their disappearance is due in a great degree to the atrocities of the Protestant Bishop Horne which, in 1570, exceeded those of Whyttingham, the Dean of Durham. Partly for the sake of the leaden roofs, and partly out of bigotry, this " successor of the apostles " destroyed these, among the most interesting of our monastic buildings. Exeter Cathedral, though never monastic, had (like Old St Paul's) a small cloister on the south side of its nave. This, destroyed during the Civil War, was partly rebuilt by the late Mr Pearson, who formed a Chapter Library over it. At Hereford, another cathedral also never monastic, there was a cloister on the south side of the nave, the east and south walks of which only remain. The western walk was destroyed in the reign of Edward VI., and a room erected on its site for the purposes of the Grammar School. This cloister was called the " Bishop's Cloister," to distinguish it from that belonging to the College of Vicars Choral, which still remains—a long walk of 109 feet of Perpendicular date (*c.* 1474), leading from the quadrangle of the college to the south-east transept of the cathedral, with the oaken beams of its roof very finely carved.

Cœlestis urbs Jerusalem. The Office Hymn for the Feast of the Dedication of a Church, as given in the Roman Vesperale. A recast of *Urbs beata Jerusalem* (" Blessed City,

Heavenly Salem ") in the reformed Roman Breviary. It follows the Capitulum, " Vidi civitatem sanctam Jerusalem novam descendentem de cœlo a Deo, paratam sicut sponsam ornatam viro suo " (Rev. xxi. 2). The plainsong melody is another version of the *Urbs beata Hierusalem* and of the *Angulare fundamentum* (see " Hymns, Ancient and Modern," ed. of 1889, No. 396). It was inserted in the " Hymnal Noted " (1852) as having been the first ancient melody which became popular since the revival of plainsong in the Church of England. It was first sung at the Consecration of the Church of St Barnabas, Pimlico, 11th June 1850, and was used every evening throughout the octave. The translation, beginning :

> " Thou heavenly new Jerusalem ;
> Vision of peace in prophet's dream ! "

was that of the Rev. W. J. Irons. Both words and melody, as appears by an advertisement in *The Musical Times* of August 1850, were printed on a penny leaflet by J. Alfred Novello. Two years later the hymn was inserted in the " Hymnal Noted " as No. 45. The harmonist of the melody is not stated. In all probability it was Helmore, the musical editor, himself. The hymn has long been a feature at the Dedication Festival at St Matthias, Stoke Newington, where each year, since June 1853, it has been sung, not as an office hymn, but as the choir leave the church for the schools, after Evensong. In this respect it is believed that St Matthias now stands unique.

Certain brief and comprehensive prayers which are found in all known liturgies and public devotional offices of the Western Church.

Collects. Liturgiologists have thought that these prayers were so called because they were used in the public congregation or *collection* of the people ; or from the fact of many petitions being here collected together in a brief summary ; or because they comprehend objects of prayer collected out of the Epistles and Gospels. But, whatever may be the origin of the term, it is one of great antiquity. The more usual name in the Latin Church was *orationes collectae*, because the prayers of the bishop and priest, which in any part of the service followed the joint prayers of the deacon and congregation, were both a recollection and recommendation of the prayers of the people. In our Book of Common Prayer the collects occupy the same position in which they occurred in the unreformed offices—viz. after the versicular prayers (*preces*). The Collect for the Day was said at the end of Lauds (*q.v.*), and the

Collect for Grace, and other collects, at the end of Prime (*q.v.*). The Collect for Peace in our Matins is in the Sacramentary of Pope Gelasius, the Collect for Grace is in the Sacramentary of Pope Gregory, and in the Anglo-Saxon Office—both word for word as we now have them. At Evensong, the Collect for Peace is as old as the fifth century, occurring in the Sacramentary of Gelasius, A.D. 494. In the Sarum Breviary it is the fourth collect after the Litany. The Third Collect, for aid against all perils, is also in the Sacramentary of Gelasius, as an evening collect—the place which it occupies in the Sarum Breviary. The collects for the day at Matins and Evensong, and used also in the Communion Service, were, for the most part, translated from the missals in the English Church. Many of them exist in the Sacramentary of Gregory, and therefore date at least from A.D. 590. Some are still older, and are found in the Sacramentary of Gelasius, some may be traced to that of Leo, A.D. 483. Procter ("History of the Book of Common Prayer") tabulates the collects thus : I. Collects substantially retained from ancient liturgies ; II. Collects taken from ancient models, but which have been altered by the compilers or revisers of the Prayer-Book ; III. Table of new collects, composed for the books of 1549, 1552 and 1661 (see pp. 266-268). The Collects for the Sovereign in the Communion Service were composed in 1549. In the Confirmation Service the collect was composed in 1549 from the collect which preceded the laying on of hands in Archbishop Hermann's Order of Confirmation in his " Consultation." In the Order for the Visitation of the Sick, the collect is the original absolution, or reconciliation of a dying penitent, found in the old formularies of the English Church, and in the Sacramentary of Gelasius. In the Order for the Burial of the Dead, the collect was formed from that in the Communion Office at burials in the book of 1549, together with what had been the latter clause of the concluding prayer ; which therefore continued to occupy its original place, closing the service with our Lord's " most sweet and comfortable words." It is not necessary to quote a multitude of writers to show what has always been felt with regard to the collects. " It is," says Canon Bright (" Ancient Collects," p. 198), " the wonderful blending of strength and sweetness in the Collects, which has called forth so much love and admiration, and has made them such a bond of union for pious minds of different times and countries " ; and Lord Macaulay (" History of England," i. p. 160) speaks of " those beautiful Collects which have soothed the griefs of forty generations of Christians." The practice of setting the collects to music for use as anthems has long been common with our Church composers, and it may be said that, as a rule, they lend themselves very well to such treatment ; but they should never be used as introits. Among the most noteworthy are those of Orlando Gibbons (Third Sunday after Epiphany) ; John Travers (Fifteenth Sunday after Trinity) ; J. W. Callcott (Twenty-first Sunday after Trinity) ; Joseph Corfe (Fourth, Sixth, and Twelfth Sundays after Trinity) ; John Marsh (Quinquagesima Sunday) ; Sir John Stevenson (Ninth Sunday after Trinity) ; J. Stafford Smith (Second Sunday after Epiphany) ; Thomas Attwood (The Epiphany, First Sunday after Epiphany, and Twenty-first Sunday after Trinity) ; W. Crotch (Fifth Sunday after Easter) ; T. A. Walmisley (Sunday after Ascension Day) ; W. Horsley (Tenth Sunday after Trinity) ; T. Forbes Walmisley (Fourth Sunday after Trinity) ; Sir George Smart (Collect for Peace at Matins) ; Rev. J. B. Dykes (Nineteenth Sunday after Trinity) ; S. S. Wesley (Seventh Sunday after Trinity) ; Henry Smart (Sunday after Ascension Day, and Twenty-first Sunday after Trinity) ; Sir John Goss (Thirteenth Sunday after Trinity) ; George Benson (First Collect in the Communion Service) ; Rev. Sir. Frederick Ouseley (Sixteenth and Twentieth Sundays after Trinity) ; Sir George Elvey (Second Sunday after Epiphany, and Fifth Sunday after Easter) ; Sir Herbert Oakeley (Sixth and Twenty-third Sundays after Trinity, and St Michael and All Angels) ; W. H. Gladstone (Collect for Aid against all Perils, at Evensong) ; John E. West (The Annunciation of the B.V.M.). The setting of the Collect for the Seventh Sunday after Trinity by William Mason, Precentor of York (1763-1797), had a great vogue, and it is even now popular in some quarters. It will be found appended to many old collections of psalmody. John Garth, organist of a church at Durham, and editor of the English version of Marcello's famous " Psalms," published, in 1794, " Thirty Collects, set to Music for 1, 2, and 3 Voices." This singular work is now scarce. In 1827, the Rev. George Maximilian Slatter, Priest Vicar and Sub-Treasurer of Exeter Cathedral, published " Ten Collects as Anthems " ; and about the same time Charles Smart Evans, one of the Gentlemen of the Chapel Royal, and a clever glee-writer, published at Clementi's the Collects for the First Sunday after Easter and the First Sunday after Trinity as anthems for four voices. These are excellent compositions. The first-named has long been sung at Westminster Abbey. A transcription of it will be found in Vincent Novello's " Cathedral Voluntaries " (1831). Dr S. S. Wesley set the collects for the three first Sundays in Advent as solos ; two for treble voice, and one for bass. These have recently been arranged by Sir Frederick Bridge for a four-part

A DICTIONARY OF

chorus, and published by Novello. After the Collect of the Day has been said, it may be further emphasised in music with by no means unimpressive effect. Many of the settings of the collects above specified may be used irrespective of the day or season to which they belong.

Complete Gothic. That phase of the Pointed style which reached its highest excellence towards the close of the thirteenth century. A term synonymous with "Decorated" and "Middle Pointed."

Compline.
Lat. *completorium;*
Fr. *complies;*
Germ. *complete.*
The last of the canonical hours; the *completion* of the day's services. The Roman order of Compline begins by the hebdomadarius or reader begging the benediction of the Superior—"Jube, domine, benedicere" (Bid, sir, a blessing")—which is thus given: "Noctem quietam, et finem perfectum concedat nobis Dominus omnipotens." ("May the Lord Almighty grant us a quiet night and a perfect end.") The short lesson—1 St Peter v. 8—follows: then "Adjutorium nostrum in nomine Domini" ("Our help is in the name of the Lord"), the Confession and Absolution, and the versicle, "Converte nos, Deus," with its response, "Et averte iram tuam a nobis." Four Psalms—iv., xxxi. to verse 6, xci., cxxxiv.—follow, each with its *Gloria*. According to this order, the antiphon never varies, except in Eastertide, when a thrice-repeated *Alleluia* is instituted. The hymn *Te lucis ante terminum* is also invariable. Then follow a passage of Holy Scripture; the *In manus*; the *Nunc dimittis*; a prayer to ask God's protection through the night; the blessing, and an antiphon, "Salva nos Domine vigilantes" ("Save us, O Lord, waking"). In the Benedictine office three Psalms only are used, and *Nunc dimittis* is not sung. In the Sarum office the officiant, before beginning "O God, make speed" in a loud voice, says, in a somewhat lower tone, "Turn us, O God, our Saviour," to which the rest reply, "And let thine anger cease from us." This is done to ask pardon for whatsoever has been done amiss throughout the day. The Psalms (iv., xxxi. to verse 6, xci., cxxxiv.) are said under one antiphon, and the last two Psalms under one *Gloria*. The hymn, with its versicle and response, and the *Nunc dimittis*, with its antiphon, follow; and the office is concluded with the ninefold *Kyrie Eleison*, the *Pater Noster, Credo*, sundry versicles, the 51st Psalm (on week-days), and the collect, "Lighten our darkness." When chorally rendered, as it may be heard daily at Westminster Cathedral, and in those cathedrals abroad where the daily choral

86

services are kept up, Compline is perhaps the most touching and beautiful of all the canonical hours. In 1874 a form of Compline, or " Order of the Late Evening Service," was drawn up by Canon Liddon for daily use at 8 o'clock in the North-West, and afterwards (1878) in the Crypt, Chapel of St Paul's. It was printed by Novello, the Psalms, hymn, etc., being noted in plain chant. With certain modifications it followed the English office. This late evening service has been discontinued at St. Paul's for some years. The Rev. J. B. Croft's "Simplified Form of Compline in Modern Notation " (1906) is excellent. It follows the simple and sensible form used on Sundays in churches in the dioceses of Western France, notably Rouen.

Composite Order. The last of the five styles or orders of Classical architecture, distinguished by the capitals of its columns, a "composition" of the Ionic and Corinthian (*q.v.*). The order was invented by the Romans. It is of the same proportion as the Corinthian and retains the same general features of detail. There is much of the Composite order in St Paul's and in many of the city churches built by Wren.

Conche. The semicircle formed by the roof of an apse. In Romanesque and Early Gothic times it afforded a field for the fresco-painter, the subject generally employed being the enthroned Saviour or the Madonna. At Gelnhausen, in Germany, it is pierced with small circular windows, a unique arrangement. Consult T. F. Bumpus' "Cathedrals and Churches of North Germany " (1903).

Confessional. Ital. *confessionale*. The recess or seat in which the priest sits to hear the confession of penitents. On the Continent and in Roman churches in this country, confessionals are usually slight wooden erections of modern date, resembling sentry-boxes, enclosed with panelling, having a door in front for the priest to enter, and a latticed window in one or both of the sides for the penitents to speak through. It is not known what kind of confessional was used in this country previous to the Reformation, nor is there anything to be found in any of our churches that can be regarded as evidence of what its nature was (Parker's "Glossary of Architecture," p. 109, and footnote (*e*), 1845). To the prebendal stall, in St Paul's Cathedral, of St Pancratius, or St Pancras, was attached the office of Confessioner or Penitentiary. From 1589 to 1609 this stall was held by the saintly Bishop Andrewes, and " his manner was, especially in Lent, to walk at stated times in one of the aisles of the Cathedral, that if any came to him for spiritual advice and comfort, as some did, though not many, he might impart it to them " (Sir J. Harington " A Brief View of the Church of England to the Year 1608 "). At the Church of Martin-Eglise, near Dieppe, built in the tenth century, there are traces of what was probably a " confessional window " in the north aisle. The Abbé Malais, a former *curé* of the parish, was of opinion that anciently all confessionals were of this plan, and that the penitent, standing outside the church, made his or her confession through this window to the priest within the Church. The Rev. Percy Dearmer, in his " Parson's Handbook " (4th ed., p. 66), tells us that shriving pens were sometimes used in England in old times ; but their shape is not known, and their use was not general ; the clergy usually sat in chairs. The same authority is of opinion that it is better always to hear confessions in the open church, either at a seat or pew by the wall, or in some accessible chapel. To hear confessions in the vestry is certainly a mistake. Among the Add. MSS., 25698, Brit. Mus., is a Flemish miniature of the fifteenth century, showing the interior of a church in Passiontide, with a priest hearing confession, vested in blue-grey cassock and coif (or skull-cap), surplice, black cope, grey almuce on shoulders. The two kneeling men wear a blue lay dress. Over the altar the rood and its attendant figures are veiled in white with red crosses ; the dorsal of the altar is white, with red crosses ; the frontal, superfrontal and orphreys are red with gold fringe. On the altar are two candlesticks. The same is also figured in Dr Rock's " Church of Our Fathers," iii. pt. ii. p. 224 ; and in Chambers' " Divine Worship," p. 94. An article on the Lychnoscope, as used for external confession will be found in *The Ecclesiologist*, February, 1847. Consult also J. T. Micklethwaite, " Some Thoughts on Modern Parish Churches," a paper in *The Sacristy*, ii. 119 (1872).

Congé d'élire. A Norman-French term, signifying *leave to choose*. The king's writ or licence to the Dean and Chapter of the Diocese to choose a bishop in the time of vacancy of the see.

Consistory. From Low Latin *consistorium*, a place of assembly. A word used to denote the Court Christian, or Spiritual Court. In the Church of England, before the Norman Conquest, the ecclesiastical jurisdiction was not separated from the civil ; for the earl and bishop sat in one court—*i.e.* the ancient County Court. William the Conqueror separated the secular from the ecclesiastical courts ; and after that time every bishop had his Consistory Court, in which he tried spiritual causes, either in person or through an official appointed by himself.

ECCLESIASTICAL TERMS

Console.
(Fr.)
A bracket for the support of a canopy, balcony, etc. A term now employed by organ-builders to denote that portion of an organ where the manuals (or keyboard), stop-handles, etc., are placed.

Contra-tenor or Counter-tenor.
The old name for the alto voice. The first movement of Dr Greene's anthem, "Acquaint thyself with God," is an excellent specimen of a counter-tenor solo; see Greene's "Forty Select Anthems" (1743): modern edition by Vincent Novello (1851).

Convocations.
The Provincial Synods of Canterbury and York; ecclesiastical assemblies severally representing the Church in their respective provinces, and, when acting in concert, constituting, in the words of the 139th Canon, "the Sacred Synod of this Nation—the true Church of England by representation." Consult article in Hook's "Church Dictionary," by the Rev. J. Wayland Joyce, also the same writer's "England's Sacred Synods" (1855). The Canterbury Provincial Synod (Upper and Lower Houses) has been for many years summoned to meet first at St Paul's by the Archbishop's mandate. Citations to appear are affixed, some two or three weeks before the appointed day, to the stalls of the dean, archdeacons of London and Middlesex, the canons residentiary, and the prebendaries, who are entitled to vote for proctors, in the choir of the cathedral church. On their assembly the proceedings are as follows :—The members, vested in their proper habiliments, pass from the chapter, or convocation, house in formal procession through the churchyard, and so in by the great west door to the choir. The Litany is sung in Latin by the Bishop of Salisbury, Precentor of the Province, or in his absence by the junior member of the bench. An anthem (in Latin) is then sung by the choir, after which a Latin sermon is preached by a member appointed by the Archbishop. The *Gloria in Excelsis* (also in Latin) concludes the service. The members of the Lower House then retire to one of the side chapels to elect a prolocutor, who, on being presented to the Archbishop at a subsequent session, if approved by him (and there is no instance, so far as this can be ascertained, of disapproval), becomes chairman of the Lower House, and not only there presides, but is the channel of communication between the two Houses, carrying messages from the Upper House to the Lower, and reporting the proceedings of the Lower to the Upper.

Cope.
A large semicircular cloak of silk or other material, stiff with gold and embroidery. It is fastened in front by a clasp or morse, and worn over the alb or surplice by the priest in

89

A DICTIONARY OF

procession, and at solemn Matins and Vespers ; and by the bishop at certain ministrations.   In former times it was assumed
Cope. by the whole adult choral establishment in cathedrals
Lat. *cappa ;* and monastic churches.   It is symbolical of rule, and
Fr. *chape ;* is therefore worn by those who have dignity in the
Germ. church or choir.   It is not a Eucharistic but a choral
chorrock. vestment.   It was, and still is, the most splendid and
Called also profusely adorned of all the vestments.   The orphreys
pallium and are two broad bands reaching from the neck down
pluviale. each side to the bottom ; behind is a hood, originally
designed to be drawn over the head in wet weather, during outdoor processions; hence the term " pluviale."   The utmost skill of the handicraftsman was lavished on the orphreys, as well as on the hood and morse.   The Treasury of St Paul's contained, in 1402, 179 copes, and in the inventory taken in 1552 over 280 are described, besides a large number of chasubles, tunicles, albs, and other vestments.   The rich store recorded in these inventories sets before one a clear and definite view of the wealth contained in the treasury of a great cathedral during the thirteenth, fourteenth, fifteenth and sixteenth centuries.   It is specially observable that many of the ornaments and vestments were the gift of the clergy of the Church.   It is easy for ignorant and vulgar minds to speak of the clergy of the time as extorting from the laity, under the dread of mysterious penalties, the precious gifts and endowments which were so freely given to adorn and beautify God's House ; but at least it must be remembered that the clergy themselves were generous givers, and the records of the treasuries of the cathedrals may be put in evidence.   " It is possible," says Dr Simpson (" St Paul's and Old City Life "), " after the perusal of such inventories, to realize such a scene as Fox, the martyrologist, described, on occasion of the thanksgiving in London for the restoration to health of the King of France in 1536.   There was a grand procession ; the waits [certain minstrels or musical watchmen attached to cities and towns, who paraded an assigned district, sounding the hours at night], and the children of grammar-schools, with their masters and ushers ; the friars and priors with their copes and crosses ; the monks of Westminster, the canons and clergy of St Paul's, the choir of the Cathedral church, the bishops and the abbots.   He estimated the number of ' gay copes ' at 714.   In a like procession, on the Feast of the Conversion of St Paul, in 1555, ' there were fourscore and ten crosses, one hundred and sixty priests and clerkes who had everie one of them copes upon their backs.' "   In 1548 the cope was

90

ordered to be worn by the bishop at ordinations, and by priests when celebrating the Holy Communion. At the coronation of Edward VI. in 1547 "at nine of the clock all Westminster choir was in their copes . . . and the children of the King's Chapel, all in scarlet with surplices and copes upon their backs" (Strype, "Memorials of Cranmer," p. 142, fol. 1694). The same authority tells that at the consecration of Bishops Poynet and Hooper in Lambeth Palace Chapel, "Archbishop Cranmer, having on his mitre and cope, usual in such cases, went into his chapel, handsomely and decently adorned to celebrate the Lord's Supper according to the custom," etc. Copes were enjoined by the Act of Uniformity, and by the rubric, on the accession of Elizabeth in 1558, and at her coronation "they met the bishop that was to perform the ceremony, and all the Chapel [Royal], with three crosses borne before them in their copes, the bishops mitred; and singing as they passed *Salve festa dies*" (Strype's "Annals," p. 29). Copes were worn "upon their surplices" by the bishops attending the obsequies of Henry II. of France in St Paul's Cathedral on 8th and 9th September 1559, and Heylyn ("History of the Reformation," p. 123) states "These Bishops [Parker, etc.] never appearing publickly but in their rochets, nor officiating otherwise than in copes at the holy altar." At the service held in King's College Chapel during the Grand Reception and Entertainment of Queen Elizabeth at Cambridge, 1564, the anthem ended, "the Provost began the *Te Deum*, in English in his cope, which was solemnly sung in prick-song [written music, as opposed to extempore descant], and the organs a playing. After that he began evensong, which also was solemnly sung, every man standing in his cope" (Nichols' "Progresses of Queen Elizabeth," vol. i. pp. 158–164, 4to, 1823). When the same queen returned thanks at St Paul's for the defeat of the Armada, 24th November 1588, she was received at the great west door by the Bishop of London (Aylmer) the dean (Nowell), and fifty other clergymen, habited in superb copes. "At her entrance she kneeled, and pronounced a prayer; then proceeded to her seat, under a canopy in the choir, when the Litany was chanted." At a service held in Westminster Abbey on the occasion of the French ambassadors' conference about the marriage of Prince Charles and Henrietta Maria, in 1624, they "and their great train took up all the stalls, where they continued about half-an-hour, while the quiremen, vested in their rich copes, with their choristers, sang three several anthems with most excellent voices before them, and at their entrance the organ was touched by the best finger of that age—Mr Orlando Gibbons. The Abbey was stuck with flambeaux everywhere, both within and without the quire" (Hacket's "Life of Lord Keeper Williams," pt. i. p. 210). Four years before this, James I. "upon Midlent Sunday, anno 1620, accompanied by the Prince [afterwards King Charles the Martyr] intended to visit St Paul's, and at his entrance into the church was received under a canopy by the dean and canons attired in rich copes, and other ecclesiastical habits. Being by them brought into the quire, he heard with very great reverence and devotion the divine service of the day, most solemnly performed with organs, cornets, and sagbuts, accompanied and intermingled with such excellent voices that seemed rather to enchant than chant" (Heylyn, "Cyprianus Anglicanus," pp. 82, 83). Howe (*Chronicle* cited in Nichol's "Progresses of James I.," vol. iv. p. 601) gives an account of the same ceremony, stating that " the gentlemen of the King's Chapel and the quire of St Paul's were likewise all in rich copes, and so with solemn singing brought the King into the quire, through which he went unto his traverse, which was set up on the south side of the high altar and it being then three of the clock, they began to celebrate divine service, which was solemnly performed with organs, cornets, and sagbuts." "Hierugia Anglicana" (1848) presents us with a lithograph, copied from a print by Hollar in Ashmole's "Ceremonies of the Order of the Garter," representing part of a procession which took place at Windsor on St George' Day in the reign of Charles II. A large number of clergy are depicted as vested in "rich copes of cloth of gold, cloth of bodkin, or most costly embroideries," and the lay clerks and choristers in cassocks and long ample surplices. Copes were worn in many cathedrals, college chapels, and parish churches in the reign of Charles I. Walker ("Sufferings of the Clergy," p. 25) mentions an order in 1643–1644 for selling the copes, surplices, etc., in such places, " to accomplish the blessed reformation so happily begun." At the Restoration (1660) copes were resumed. Bishop Cosin reintroduced them at Durham, at which cathedral they continued to be worn by the dean and prebendaries at the Celebration of the Holy Communion, until late in the eighteenth century. Allusions to these copes (still preserved in the library of the cathedral) are to be found in Ralph Thoresby's "Diary" (1680), Defoe's "Tour through Europe," and elsewhere. They are minutely described by Mr Street in a paper on Mediæval Embroidery, printed in *The Ecclesiologist*, October 1863. "Rich copes" were worn by the dean and prebendaries of Westminster at the funerals of the Duke of Buckingham, 1721 ; the Duke of Marlborough, 1722 ; and the funeral of Queen Caroline, 1737 ; and they have been worn

ECCLESIASTICAL TERMS

by the same dignitaries at all the coronations. At St Paul's, the cope is worn by the dean and canons throughout Matins and High Celebration on all the greater festivals, and also during the processional Litany on certain days. On the greater festivals, also, the celebrant (a minor canon) is vested in cope. These magnificent vestments were first used at the service held on the western steps of the cathedral at the Diamond Jubilee of Queen Victoria, 22nd June 1897. The cope is now the eucharistic vestment of celebrant, deacon, and sub-deacon, at Lichfield. The assertion made by Deans Sampson and Humphries in Queen Elizabeth's reign " that copes were brought in by the Papists " was ably refuted by Archbishop Parker. Cope-stretchers are in use at St Paul's, and Walcott (" Traditions and Customs of Cathedrals," 1872) mentions the existence of ancient ones at York. Innumerable representations of ancient copes may be seen on monumental brasses, in engravings, etc., while many notable Continental examples are photogravured in books treating of vestments and other *instrumenta ecclesiastica*. The multitude of vestments possessed by our great churches before the Reformation can hardly be imagined by us at the present day. It is necessary to look through some of the inventories of their possessions to realise their wealth.

The lightest and most ornamental of the three (or as some say five) orders of Classical architecture. The capital by which the order is distinguished consists of two annular rows of eight **Corinthian** leaves, attached to the bell or campana, with angular **Order.** volutes springing from the caulicoli, supported by leaves on either side. In the centre, between the angular volutes, are two smaller spirals, which also spring from the caulicoli, called helices or urellæ. The sides of the abacus (uppermost division of the capital) are concave, with the exterior range, called the horns, taken off, and often much ornamented. The shaft or column itself is fluted and rests on a base. Ancient examples : the Arch of Adrian at Athens, the Incantada at Salonica, a temple at Jackly, near Mylassa ; the circular temple at Tivoli, the Baths of Diocletian, the Pantheon (Rome), the temples of Jupiter Tonans, Jupiter Stator, etc. Modern examples : nave and choir of St Paul's Cathedral, internally, and lower storey of the building and western portico externally ; Wren's city churches, and others too numerous to mention. Consult W. J. Smith, " Synopsis of Architecture" (1831) ; W. H. Leeds, " Rudimentary Architecture " (1848) ; Rickman's " Styles of Architecture in England " (1848–1862) ; F. C. Penrose, " Principles of Athenian Architecture " (1852).

93

Corona Lucis (Latin).
Eng. *crown of light*; Germ. *kronleuchter*.

A suspended hoop of iron or brass, ornamented in the style of the period of its execution, supporting lanterns and sockets for lamps and candles, which are lighted on occasions of unusual solemnity. Examples: Aix-la-Chapelle Cathedral; Hildesheim Cathedral; Münster Cathedral (German); St Pierre, Louvain; Parish Church of Aerschot (Belgian)—ancient. St Barnabas, Pimlico; St Matthias, Stoke Newington; St Stephen, Westminster; Hereford Cathedral, Christ Church Cathedral, Dublin—modern. In Germany the *corona* frequently takes the form of an image of the Virgin and Child, surrounded by smaller ones representing the Tree of Jesse. This is termed a *Marienleuchter*. There are fine examples at Osnabrück (Westphalia) and Calcar (Rhine Provinces). In the seventh century, and previously, when chancels had not been thrown out eastward, the corona hung above the choir and in front of the altar, as mentioned by Anastasius and other authors, and repeatedly depicted in the Utrecht Psalter. Prudentius (*Cathemeron*, Hymn 5) mentions the corona with lamps. Cahier and Martin ("Mélanges d'Archéologie," iii. 27, etc.) and Viollet-le-Duc ("Mobilier Français, article, "Lampes") delineate a number of these ancient coronæ. They are of two kinds, both circular; one kind containing a quantity of candles in sockets, in one or more rows, as those remaining at Aix-la-Chapelle, Rheims and Toul. The first-named of these is eighteen or twenty feet in circumference, and holds at least one hundred wax lights. At Canterbury, in the twelfth century, a splendid corona of lights hung down in the midst of the choir (*in medio chori*); and at Sarum, in the thirteenth, there was one over the choir. These coronæ, in fact, became a distinguished and noble ornament of the church, and a second was often suspended over the altar, when St Osmund and his successors had prolonged the church eastward. The magnificent brass *corona lucis* presented to the Church of St Matthias, Stoke Newington, in 1855 (designed by Mr Butterfield and executed by Potter), was originally fitted for gas, but upon its restoration, four years ago, sockets for forty wax lights were substituted. When illuminated at festivals this superb work of modern art presents an appearance transcendently beautiful. The Rev. P. Dearmer ("Parson's Handbook," 4th ed. p. 436) tells us that a pretty Mediæval practice was to hang a wooden hoop with candles in it in the midst of the chancel in memory of the Star. This was called the trendle or rowell, and he opines that it is a good way of marking the season. Mr T. Francis Bumpus in his

ECCLESIASTICAL TERMS

"Cathedrals of England and Wales" (vol. iii. p. 267), mentions that among other pious and venerable usages retained at Manchester Cathedral is the following. From Christmas to Epiphany the two beautiful old candelabra, suspended from the arches opening into the procession path behind the high altar, are furnished with tapers, which are lighted during service time. Formerly these were kept burning all day during Christmastide.

Corporal-cloth, or Corporas-cloth.
Ital. corporale.

The linen cloth or napkin spread on the altar at the time of the Eucharistic service. The chalice is placed on the centre of it, and the paten in front of the chalice. When the altar-breads are on the altar, the lower right-hand corner of the corporal should be turned back over them except during the Oblation and Consecration. The burse (or "corporas case," as it used to be called in England) is a kind of pocket, formed of two squares of thick card, covered with silk, and so arranged as to open at the end. In the pocket so formed the corporals are kept when not in use. In texture, colour, and embroidery the burse corresponds with the chalice-veil (a square of silk, used for covering the chalice when empty). It is brought in on the top of the veiled chalice, and when empty during the Celebration stands upright against the retable. St Isidore, of Pelusium, in the beginning of the fifth century, compares the corporal with the clean linen cloth in which St Joseph of Arimathea wrapped the body (*corpus*) of Our Lord.

Corpus Christi, Feast of.
Fr. Fête Dieu.

A festival of the Western Church, instituted by Pope Urban IV. in 1264, and since annually observed throughout the Catholic world on the Thursday next after Trinity Sunday. In the Hereford Missal it is styled *Dies Eucharistiae* —"Eucharist Thursday." In the Sarum rite it was a "Greater Double," or feast of the second class.

This festival has not now a place in our Prayer-Book Calendar, but it is retained in some almanacks, and gives its name to colleges at Oxford and Cambridge. Its object is to commemorate the perpetual presence of Our Lord on the altars of His Church "under the form of bread and wine"—just as Whitsuntide represents the perpetual presence of the Holy Ghost, and Trinity-tide the endless vision of the Godhead in Heaven. The reason for its following these seasons is both because the Church had not leisure worthily to thank God for so great a gift on the actual day of its institution (Maundy Thursday), when she was busied with the Passion of Our Lord; and because the gift commemorated, like that of Pentecost, is promised

95

to the Church to the end of time. It was a pious custom, on these grounds, to consecrate the month of June (in which this festival nearly always fell) to the memory of and thanksgiving for the Blessed Sacrament. The origin of the festival seems to be this : In 1246, Juliana, abbess of the Convent of Cornillon near Liége, having in a vision seen the full moon with a piece out of it, and being told by a voice from heaven that this signified the want of another festival, the aforesaid Pope, who had been a canon of Liége at the time of the " vision," instituted that of Corpus Christi. It was for the Mass of this festival that Thomas of Aquino wrote, about the year 1260, the celebrated sequence, *Lauda Sion Salvatorem*, one of the five which are alone retained in the Revised Roman Missal of 1570. In the same festival Thomas of Aquino, at the request of Pope Urban IV., drew up, in 1263, the office in the Roman Breviary, and probably also that in the Missal. The plainsong melody of the *Lauda Sion* is an extremely noble composition, and is probably coeval with the hymn itself. The words and melody will be found at full length in the beautifully printed " Liber Gradualis," printed at Tournai, 1883, or in any Roman Graduale noted. Among the earliest short polyphonic settings of the *Lauda Sion* is that of Palestrina. Of the numerous settings in cantata form, the most widely known is that by Mendelssohn (*op.* 73, Post. Works, No. 1), who had been invited to compose it for the six-hundredth celebration of Corpus Christi Day at Liége. It was sung for the first time, and under the conductorship of the composer, on 11th June 1846, in St Martin's Church, which, the *Annales Archéologiques* for August of that year inform us, was newly covered with whitey-brown wash by the *curé* expressly for the occasion ! At Seville Cathedral, on the Feast of the Immaculate Conception, the time of the departure of the sun, and in spring, at the time of the sun's return at Corpus Christi, the ten " seises " or choristers dance for half-an-hour in front of the high altar at Benediction. They are attired in the costume of pages of the time of Philip III., wearing plumed hats with dresses of blue plush crossed with white for the Feast of the Conception, and of blue plush covered with red for that of Corpus Christi. While the *Tantum ergo* is sung they stand in two rows facing each other, and then sing an appropriate hymn. At the second strain of the hymn they advance to one another, and then with slow and stately measure, step a sort of minuet, singing the while in two-part harmony. Then the first strain is repeated in the original position. Between the strains are symphonies in which the boys accompany the orchestra on castanets, which they handle with marvellous skill, producing most effective crescendos and diminuendos. At the end, the archbishop, dean, canons, choir-men, and others all group themselves on the altar-steps while the *Tantum ergo* is again sung. At its conclusion the organ peals out, the bells ring, and the veil is drawn before the Host. So far from being frivolous or amusing these dancers of the " seises "are most impressive. The only light in the cathedral is a blaze of candles on the high altar, and single candles at rare intervals throughout the vast building. The traditional music to these dances was arranged by the celebrated Miguel Hilarion Eslava, compiler of the " Liro Sacro-Hispaña," a now enormously scarce collection of Spanish Church music of the sixteenth, seventeenth, eighteenth and nineteenth centuries (10 vols., folio, 1869). A copy is in the Library at St Michael's College, Tenbury. Eslava, who was one of the greatest among modern Spanish composers, was Chapel Master at Seville in 1832, was ordained priest, and in 1844 became Chapel Master to Queen Isabella at Madrid. He died 23rd July 1878, aged 71. Over the doorway of his house, facing the cathedral at Seville, is an inscription to the effect that there he ' compuso immortales obras." Like the celebrated *Miserere* of Allegri, at Rome, no copy was permitted, for a long time, to be taken of the dances played at Seville on the occasions above described. It seems, however, that Mrs Lilly Grove managed, some twenty years ago, to obtain a copy from some nuns at Seville, and she has printed them in her book on Dancing, one of the " Badminton " Series of Sports and Pastimes (Longmans, 1895). The mention of these dances recalls one of Sir Frederick Ouseley's remarkable feats of memory. On one occasion, at Tenbury, he and Dr T. L. Southgate, the distinguished musical critic and writer, were discussing the question of dancing as a part of Church public worship, and Dr Southgate read to Sir Frederick a letter received from a friend in Abyssinia, who told him that there they still danced " before the Lord," as it is recorded David did. " Oh! " said Ouseley, with a smile, " I have seen that much nearer home. In 1851 I went to Spain for a tour, and on a special high day I saw a solemn fandango danced by choir-boys in front of the high altar at Seville ; and this was the music it was danced to." He then went to the piano, and played the movement, a delicate little piece, quite Spanish in tone, with the exception of a peculiar use of the chord of the Italian sixth. Dr Southgate asked him whether that was correct, and expressed astonishment that he should have remembered this piece heard but once, some thirty years ago. " Quite right," replied Ouseley, " I thought that chord would startle you," and

A DICTIONARY OF

then he continued: "If I thoroughly give my mind to receive a piece of music, I generally succeed in mastering and never after forget it."

Cotta. A variety of the surplice (*q.v.*), somewhat shorter than that vestment, and not quite so full, and either entirely wanting in sleeves, or (which is more correct) having short ones reaching to a little below the elbows. The bottom of the cotta and the ends of the sleeves are frequently edged with lace, an ornamentation corresponding with the "apparels" of the alb. Another name for this vestment was "Rocca" (Rochet), an abbreviated surplice or alb, often worn in the choir by the boys and other lay-singers in the thirteenth and fourteenth centuries. It was made without sleeves, so as the more easily to allow the wearer to use his hands and arms in the various offices. "Rochettæ" are named in the Sarum Inventory of 1222 as belonging to the altars of St Paul and All Saints in that Cathedral, and to the parish churches of Ruscombe, Sonning, Hurst, Hull and Horningham. They are also mentioned in the St Paul's Inventories of 1295 (Dugdale's "St Paul's," 381), where there was one belonging to Edmund, Archbishop of Canterbury. By a Constitution of Winchelsea, Archbishop, A.D. 1305 (Lyndewode, Appendix to Constitutions, 35), the parishioners of every church were bound to find three surplices and "one rochet, without sleeves." Lyndewode (*ibid.*), in his gloss on this place, says: "The rochet is without sleeves, and it is ordered for the clerks ministering to the priest, or perhaps for the convenience of the priest in baptizing, that his arms be not embarrassed by the sleeves." J. D. Chambers ("Divine Worship in the Church," 295) figures two cerofers in rochets over cassocks, from an original Flemish painting, *c.* A.D. 1400, attributed to Van Eyck.

Cradle-roof. A pointed or angular roof which is not groined; open-timbered when not ceiled. The nave of Ely exhibited an open-timbered cradle-roof before Messrs Styleman le Strange and T. Gambier Parry undertook its painting—or, to speak more correctly, of the ceiling which was affixed to it for that purpose—1858-1864. St Matthias', Stoke Newington (W. Butterfield, architect, 1853), and St Mary's, Stoke Newington (Sir G. G. Scott, architect, 1858), present us with fine specimens of modern wooden cradle-roofs. The roof at St Matthias' is strongly reminiscent of the now hidden cradle-roof of Ely, as is also that of Romsey Abbey.

ECCLESIASTICAL TERMS

Credence.
Fr. *crédence ;*
Ital.
credenza ;
Germ.
credenztisch.
Called also
the Prothesis
(πρόθεσις).

The small table at the side of the altar at which the Elements are prepared. Its use is partly for convenience, partly out of reverence, so that the altar may be entirely reserved for the actual offering of the Holy Sacrifice, and in order that the Elements may not be placed upon the altar before the Oblation or Offertory. This was a very early custom in the Church, but in many instances the place of the credence-table was supplied by a shelf across the fenestella or niche in which the piscina is placed. This shelf was either of wood or stone, and it is to be found in several of our ancient churches. It is supposed by some authorities to have been used to place the cruets of the altar upon ; for it is frequently too small and narrow to have allowed the Elements to be placed there. The credence, unless the shelf just mentioned served as such, was a thing absolutely unknown in England, both in name and fact. A stone table at St Cross, Winchester, and a wooden table of the time of James I. at Chipping-Warden Church, Northants (illustrated in Parker's " Glossary," p. 115), may have been used as such. Probably the one first mentioned was monumental ; and the word is simply the Italian *credenza* anglicised. In the plan of Bishop Andrewes' Chapel given in " Hierugia Anglicana " (1848) is shown a sier (side) table, south of the altar, on which, before Communion, stood the silver and gilt canister for the wafers, like a wicker basket and lined with laced cambric ; the " Tonne " or flagon ; a basin and ewer, to wash before Consecration and after, and the towel appertaining. See also *sub voce* " Piscina." An able and exhaustive series of articles on this subject will be found in *The Ecclesiologist*, May, June, August, October and December 1847. Consult also J. T. Mickelthwaite, " Some Thoughts on Modern Parish Churches," a paper in *The Sacristy*, ii. 44 (1872).

Credo.

The title in a musical Mass or Communion Service for the Nicene Creed, from the opening words, *Credo in unum Deum.* On this movement many of the greatest composers for the Roman and English Liturgies have lavished their utmost skill. It is frequently the longest and most elaborate portion of the service, and often a veritable sermon in music. Very noble are the settings of the *Credo* in Palestrina's Masses : *Papae Marcelli, Æterna Christi Munera, Brevis, Virtute Magna,* and *Assumpta est Maria ;* in Vittoria's *Vidi speciosam, Trahe me post Te,* and *O quam gloriosum ;* in Vecchi's *Pro Defunctis ;* in Gabrieli's *Pater peccavi ;* in Orlando di Lasso's *Quinque vocum* and *In die tribulationis*—all

A DICTIONARY OF

sixteenth century. Those in the two Masses by Thomas Tallis and in the three by his contemporary William Byrd, are also very fine. One of the Masses of Byrd, that for five voices in D minor, has recently been edited, with English words, by Mr. S. Royle Shore of Birmingham, who remarks in his instructive preface that it is written " with a freedom and a warmth of expression which is wonderfully modern, and at times almost orchestral in feeling." In an equally grand, though, of course, later and more florid, style are the Credos in the masses of Danzi, Lotti, Clari, Jommelli, Leo, and Pergolesi ; Mozart, Haydn, Weber, Schubert, Beethoven, Hummel, Cherubini ; Gounod, Kalliwoda, Dvořák, Silas, Guilmant, and Saint-Saëns, while some of those in the Masses of that indefatigable editor and composer, Vincent Novello, are excellent. That in Bach's great B minor Mass is perhaps the finest of all. Many of the settings of the *Credo* in the " Services " of our own writers have a quiet dignity and devotional expression peculiarly their own. Mention may be made of those of Batten, Byrd, Child, Farrant, Gibbons, Patrick and Tallis (sixteenth and earlier seventeenth centuries) ; Aldrich, Blow, Humphreys, Purcell, and Wise (later seventeenth century) ; Alcock, Samuel Arnold, Cooke, Croft, Dupuis, W, Hayes, Charles King, Nares, and Travers (eighteenth century) ; Clarke-Whitfeld, Stephen Elvey, Rev. G. Heathcote, Sir J. L. Rogers, J. Smith of Dublin, Sir John Stevenson, S. S. Wesley, and T. A. Walmisley (earlier nineteenth century) ; P. Armes, G. B. Arnold, Sir Joseph Barnby, J. Baptiste Calkin, G. J. Elvey, G. M. Garrett, J. L. Hatton, Sir G. A. Macfarren, W. H. Monk, Sir Frederick Ouseley, R. Redhead, Henry Smart, Charles Steggall, E. H. Thorne, and Berthold Tours (mid-nineteenth century) ; Sir Frederick Bridge, Basil Harwood, W. S. Hoyte, Charles Macpherson, Sir George Martin, Ebenezer Prout, B. Luard Selby, Sir John Stainer, Sir C. Villiers Stanford and John E West (later nineteenth century). The student may be left to trace the different styles and their gradual development to something akin to that of the Continental Mass, but preserving, at the same time, all that sobriety so characteristic of the Church music of our best English composers. The earliest notation for the *Credo* in our Liturgy is that of John Merbecke, printed in his " Book of Common Prayer Noted," which closely (1550) followed the publication of Edward VI.'s First Prayer-Book. The music is supposed to be derived from Sarum sources. It may be observed that the usual heading for the Nicene Creed in a musical " Service " is *Credo*, but in the " Cathedral Service " by Sir J. L. Rogers, published in 1839, it appears as *Credo in*

ECCLESIASTICAL TERMS

unum Deum. A few other instances of such a heading might be adduced.

Crockets. Projecting leaves, flowers or bunches of foliage used in Gothic architecture to decorate the angles of spires, canopies, pinnacles, etc. There are fine examples at Southwell Minster, Notts ; at the east end of Lincoln Cathedral ; and on the tomb of Archbishop Gray in York Minster. They were not used until late ¹ ⸱ the Early English style.

Crossing or Crux. A term invented by Dr Whewell (Master of Trinity, Cambridge, 1841-1866) to describe the space between the four arms of a cruciform church. When this is surmounted by a tower open for a considerable distance to the interior, it is styled the "lantern."

Crozier. The pastoral staff of a bishop or mitred abbot, which has the head curled round, something in the manner of a shepherd's crook. The staff of an archbishop is surmounted by a cross. A patriarch or primate has two transverse bars upon his cross ; the Pope has three. The carrying of such a cross before a metropolitan, in any place, was a mark that he claimed jurisdiction there. These insignia were often of the most costly description and elaborate workmanship. Many ancient examples remain. The monumental brass of Robert de Waldeby, Archbishop of York (d. 1397), in the Chapel of St Edmund the King, Westminster Abbey, represents him fully vested and holding his cross. In the Chapel of St Edward the Confessor is the brass of John Waltham, Bishop of Salisbury (d. 1395), on which he is represented as holding his pastoral staff. The chasuble and mitre in which both are vested are of the truly graceful English mediæval shape, and afford a striking contrast to the ugly ultra-montane pontificals of modern Roman Catholic bishops.

Crucifer.
Fr. *porte-croix*. The acolyte who carries the processional cross or crucifix. According to the Old English use the processional cross on all the Sundays in Lent, except the first, was to be of wood painted red, and without the figure of Our Lord, and in Eastertide till the Ascension of crystal or glass. The first pointed to the bloody Passion of our Lord, and His immolation on the wooden altar of the Cross ; the second to the triumph and joy of that holy season in which our Lord's body rose from the tomb, no longer liable to weakness and death, but impassable and glorious, and the cross from an ensign of shame became a standard of victory and rejoicing. At all other times the cross was to be of metal. Many ancient examples of processional

crosses of the last-named material exist on the Continent. In the "Inventarie" of St Paul's taken in 1552 we find "ij cristall crosses with plates of silver at everie joynte ordeinedd for processions." The first instance of the use of the processional cross in England is recorded by the Venerable Bede (*Hist. Eccles.*) when St Augustine marched into Canterbury with his band of missionaries singing hymns, preceded by the figure of the Crucified painted on a tablet. At Sarum in 1222, the Inventory states that there were two staves of silver for carrying crosses in processions. In the latter part of the thirteenth century the processional cross usually had the figure upon it. Thus, at Canterbury, in 1295, were four crosses for processions, "cum patibulis deauratis et gemmis ornatis." At Salisbury in 1222 was a processional cross well gilt, with many stones, and another, for Sundays, covered with silver. Bonneau, "Inventaire du Trésor actuel de la Cathédrale d'Auxerre," 1892, describes, at pp. 148, 149, eight processional crosses. One of these, of Spanish workmanship of the fifteenth century, is phototyped. T. H. King ("Study-Book," vol. iii.) delineates a magnificent example of silver-gilt, at Osnabrück, and P. Clemen ("Kunstdenkmäler," vol. i. p. 76) illustrates one also of silver-gilt, A.D. 1500, in the Katholische Pfarrkirche at Calcar, Rhine Provinces. At the extremities of the arms of the Calcar cross are the Evangelistic symbols in enamel, together with other enrichments. It seems originally to have served as the altar cross as well. There are instances of this in England. Several of our cathedrals are now provided with processional crosses. St Paul's possesses two : one for use at the Greater Festivals ; the other for use on ordinary Sundays, Saturday evenings, and saints' days. Parish churches innumerable have long had processional crosses. One was carried at the Anniversary of the Dedication of St Andrew's, Wells Street, 30th November 1849, as we learn from *The Parish Choir*, No. xlix. "There is no authority," says the Rev. Percy Dearmer, "for fixing a processional cross to one of the choir stalls. Crosses were certainly put away when not in use" ("The Parson's Handbook," 4th ed. 153). From the Inventory of the Parish Church of St Peter Mancroft, Norwich, edited for the Norfolk Architectural Society by Mr Ed. W. H. St John Hope, we learn that the cross stood "in a box made therefor in the further corner in the lower vestry by the jewel chest," and its staff stood "in the corner next the cross."

Cruets.
Lat. *phialae.*   The vessels containing the wine and water to supply the chalice. The "Excerptions" of Ecbright, A.D. 740, say as follows :—"Let the priests of God

always diligently take care that the bread and wine and water (without which Mass cannot be celebrated) be pure and clean ; for if they do otherwise they shall be punished with them who offered to our Lord vinegar mingled with gall, unless penitence relieve them." The *Capitula* of Theodulph, in 994, direct that both the oblation, and the wine and the water that belong to the offering of the Mass-song, be provided and regarded with all purity and diligence and with fear of God, and that nothing be done unchastely or impurely : for there can be no Mass-song without these three things—viz. the oblation, the wine and the water. As the Holy Writ says : *Let the fear of God be with you, and do all that is here with great carefulness.* In the canons of 960 it is ordered that a priest never presume to celebrate Mass unless he hath all thing appertaining to the Housel—viz. a pure oblation, pure wine, and pure water. Woe be to him that begins to celebrate until he have all these. The cruets needed to supply the chalice with wine and water, having an honourable office, though of secondary importance, were more or less costly ; thus, for example, the Earl of Warwick, in 1400, bequeathed to the Chapel of Our Lady of Warwick, with his best censer and a chalice, two cruets of silver-gilt made in the shape of two angels ("Testamenta Vetusta," 154). Sir William Depeden, in 1402, leaves to certain chantries two silver cruets (" Testamenta Eboracensia," i. 295, Surtees Society) ; and Beatrice, Lady de Roos, in 1414, bequeathed to the high altar of the Priory of Wartre, amongst other silver things, ij phialas (*ibid.* p. 378). After the Celebration it was directed that the sacred vessels should be carefully cleansed. The Constitutions of Archbishop Edmund, in 1236, gave the following directions :—" At the celebration of the Mass let not the priest, when he is going to give himself the Host, first kiss It, because he ought not to touch It with his mouth before he receives It. But if, as some do, he takes It off from the paten, let him after Mass cause both the chalice and paten to be rinsed in the water, or else only the chalice, if he did not take It from the paten. Let the priest have near to the altar a very clean cloth, cleanly and decently covered and every way inclosed, to wipe his fingers and lips after receiving the Sacrament of the Altar." In the Inventory of St Paul's *temp.* Henry III., seven *phialae*, or cruets, of silver, are mentioned. Two of these cruets which had belonged to Bishop Eustace de Fauconberge (Bishop of London, 1221-1228, and Treasurer of the Exchequer), had been delivered to William the chaplain, and had been stolen, wherefore they were not to be included in the list. Bishop Andrewes' Chapel had in it in 1634, " the tricanale, a round ball with a screw

cover whereout issue three pipes, and is for the water of mixture."
The cruets are now adjuncts of every properly appointed altar in our
Church where the " Mixed Chalice," as one of the six " points," is in
use. Besides " Phialae," these *instrumenta* of Divine Worship were
termed " Amulae," " Burettes," " Urceoli," and " Gemelliones."
All writers on ritual mention them ; Lanfranc also (*Epist.* xxii. to
John Archbishop of Rouen) and Guillebert, Bishop of Limerick
(A.D. 1091), ordered " every priest to have a crewet (' Ampulla ')
for wine, and another for water." John de Hotham, Bishop of
Ely, A.D. 1336, gave to that church a chalice of gold with two
golden goblets (" Urceoli ") that for wine with a large ruby, and
that for water a beautiful pearl. At Sarum were a pair of crystal
cruets set in silver, and several pairs of silver. Others were
enamelled with figures of vines and other devices ; others were
enamelled and gilt, and some had covers or lids. At Canterbury,
there were four " Urceoli ad vinum et aquam " of crystal, ten
of silver, and many others silver-gilt ; also " Urceoli argentea ad
vinum, olla argentea ad aquam " (Dart, Append. to Hist. of Canterbury Cath.). They are almost always spoken of in pairs, and were
often ornamented with representations of the Marriage at Cana.
Two " Cruetz " in the form of angels were given to serve at the
altar in the Office of the Black Prince at Canterbury. J. D. Chambers (" Divine Worship in England in XIII. and XIV. Centuries ")
gives drawings, by G. Richmond, of cruets worked in intaglio in
the Christian Museum, Rome. In some inventories the cruets
are called " Ampullæ." In that of St Paul's, 1552, we find, " Item,
iij greate Ampulles or cruetts silver and gilte with covers. The
greatest of them having a silver spone in hitt. xx. unc " ; also
" ij cruetts of silver ij w. upon eche of them, on w.[*sic*] used daily."
Three other pairs are inventoried. Dr Rock (" Church of Our
Fathers," iii. 424) gives an account of " The Canterbury Water
and its *Ampul*," with an illustration (p. 428). In an account of the
ecclesiastical vestments, books and furniture in King's College
Chapel, Cambridge, in the fifteenth century, contributed to *The
Ecclesiologist*, October 1859 and February 1860, by the Rev. George
Williams, B.D., Senior Fellow, five pairs of cruets (" fiolae ")
are described ; one pair as " in parcella deauratum cum Scriptura
in medio illarum *Maria* and Jesus," weighing nine ounces.

A vault beneath a building, either entirely or partly under-
Crypt. ground. Crypts are frequent under churches ; they do
not in general extend beyond the limits of the choir
and its aisles, and are often of very much smaller dimensions.

ECCLESIASTICAL TERMS

That of St Paul's, however, is exactly commensurate with the upper church. They were formerly used as chapels, and provided with altars and other fittings requisite for the celebration of religious services. They were also used as places of sepulture. The crypt of St Paul's has been very extensively used as such, but interments there are now rare. It sometimes happens that the crypt of a church is older than any part of the superstructure, as at Gloucester, Ripon, Rochester, Worcester, and York. One of the finest crypts is that under Canterbury Cathedral. In smaller churches good examples may be seen at St Mary-le-Bow; St John, Clerkenwell (London); Hythe, Kent; Repton, Derbyshire; St Peter's in the East, Oxford; Wrexham, Denbighshire; and Wimborne Minster, Dorset.

Cul de Lampe. A species of ornament projecting from the bare space of a wall, and of which the usual design is that of a cone or an inverted pyramid. Culs-de-lampe, rare before the thirteenth century, serve to support a statue or to terminate the foot of a truncated column. The term, one peculiarly French, is sometimes applied to the projecting gallery in which the organ is played, as at Dortmund and Strasburg cathedrals. Berty (" Dictionnaire de l'Architecture du Moyen Age," 1845, p. 121) gives three woodcuts representing these ornaments.

Cusps. The projecting points forming the foliations in Gothic tracery, arches, panels, etc. They came into use during the latter part of the Early English style, at which period they were worked with a leaf, usually a trefoil, at the end. There is a beautiful example in Early Decorated on the organ-screen at Lincoln Cathedral.

Dalmatic. The vestment worn at the Holy Eucharist by the gospeller or deacon. It is so-called because it came from Dalmatia. St Cyprian speaks of it in the fourth century. It is loose, with large sleeves, of the same colour as the chasuble and has an apparelled collar, and apparels before and behind, with an orphrey back and front. Durandus says it signifies bountifulness to the poor. The *tunicle* worn by the epistoler or sub-deacon is similar to the dalmatic, only shorter and smaller.

De Profundis. The 130th Psalm: " Out of the deep "; one of the seven Penitential Psalms appointed by our Church to be sung on Ash Wednesday : Psalms 6, 32, and 38 being sung at Matins Psalm 51 in the Commination Service; and Psalms 102, 130, and 143 at Evensong. In the Church of Rome the *De profundis* is the fourth of the five Psalms chanted at Vespers of the Dead. It is also sung in the Requiem Mass as an anthem or offertory,

105

A DICTIONARY OF

and for this purpose has been more or less elaborately set by various distinguished composers—*e.g.* Palestrina (five voices) in Breitkopf & Härtel's edition of his complete works, vol. ix. ; Clari (four voices, in C minor) in V. Novello's "Fitzwilliam Music," vol. iii., 1825 ; Gluck (four voices, in D minor) in Latrobe's "Sacred Music," vol. iv., 1818 ; Mozart (in C minor, four voices). There is also a fine setting by Gounod (1872) in four movements with orchestral accompaniments, and two English versions, one beginning " From the deep," and a later and revised one, " Out of darkness." Another, by our distinguished countryman, Sir Hubert Parry, is for soprano and bass soli, chorus and orchestra, but neither of these was intended for liturgical use. The Psalm, with English words of course, was set in a very masterly manner by Sir George Martin, organist of St Paul's, for use at the service held in that cathedral on the day of the funeral at Windsor of Queen Victoria, 2nd February 1901. It has since been sung annually at the solemn service held on the first or second Tuesday in Advent, when the *Last Judgment* of Spohr, or the *Requiem* of Brahms is given. The *De profundis* has never formed any portion of the English reformed Office of the Burial of the Dead.

Dean.
Lat. *decanus ;*
Fr. *doyen,*
premier
vicaire ;
Germ. *dechant.*

The first dignitary of a cathedral ; the head of the chapter. In subordination to the bishop he has, according to the statutes of more ancient cathedrals, the cure of souls over the members of the cathedral, and the administration of the corrective discipline of the Church. His stall is the first on the right hand at the entrance of the choir, be the stalls " returned " or otherwise. Except in cathedrals served by monks, the office of dean has existed since 1086. By the Benedictine Rule, c. xxi., the dean in monasteries presided over *ten* monks, hence the derivation from the Greek δεκα (ten). The deans have different degrees of power under the statutes of different cathedrals and collegiate churches. At Westminster he is generally understood to be absolute : at any rate Stanley, who was dean from 1863 to 1881, insisted that he was. Some of the collegiate churches, and also the Welsh cathedrals of Llandaff and St David's, were without deans until 1840, of which Southwell, with a body of sixteen prebendaries, was the chief example. The collegiate foundations of Brecon, Heytesbury, Middleham, and Wolverhampton, now suppressed, had deans, and there are still a few titular " Deans of Peculiars," such as Battle and Bocking, though the Peculiar jurisdictions are abolished. They are mere incumbents, who have kept the title, which is now

106

unmeaning and misleading. The Bishop of London is, as a " Peculiar," Dean of the Province of Canterbury, and he is also Dean of the Chapel Royal. At Lichfield, the dean formerly held the livings of Breewood, Albrighton, and Tatenhall in his gift ; at Exeter he held those of Colyton Raleigh, Braunton, and Bishops Tawton ; at St Paul's, those of Sandon and Lamborne ; at Hereford, those of Allenmore, Clehanger, and Preston-on-Rye. At Lincoln, the dean was one of the four canons residentiary. He was so at St Paul's until 1840, and he also held the prebendal stall of Hoxton. At Christ Church Cathedral, Dublin, until 1846 the dean held a bishopric, usually that of Kildare, *in commendam*. Until 1820 Pretyman Tomline was Dean of St Paul's and Bishop of Lincoln. His successors, Van Mildert (1820–1826), Sumner (1826–1827), and Copleston (1827–1849), were bishops of Llandaff. Though the title is not so universally recognised as with us, the office of dean exists in the constitution of the foreign cathedrals. When the dean is not expressly named in the statutes he is usually the first of the dignitaries, or the senior of the canons, hence the French term *doyen* (elder). In the Eastern Church the head of a cathedral is called the protopapas—*i.e.* archpriest—the title answering to our dean. Consult further Mackenzie Walcott's " Cathedralia " (1865), a work containing, like all the multifarious effusions of the same writer, a vast amount of interesting and useful, but ambiguous, ill-digested, and frequently unreliable information. To the Deans of St Paul's who have held the deanery *in commendam* with bishoprics should be added Joseph Butler, Bishop of Chichester, 1738 ; Thomas Secker, Bishop of Oxford, 1737 ; John Hume, Bishop of Oxford, 1758 ; Frederick Cornwallis, Bishop of Lichfield and Coventry, 1750 ; Thomas Newton, Bishop of Bristol, 1761 ; and Thomas Thurlow, Bishop of Lincoln, 1779. By *commendam* is meant a living *commended* by the Crown to the care of a clergyman until a proper pastor is provided for it. These *commendams* for some time have been seldom if ever granted to any but bishops, who, when their bishoprics were of small value, were, by special dispensation, allowed to hold their previous benefices, which, on their promotion, had devolved into the patronage of the Crown. But by 6 and 7 Will. IV. s. 18, it was enacted that every *commendam* thereafter granted shall be absolutely void.

Their office is of ancient date in the Church of England, long **Deans, Rural.** prior to the Reformation, as it has been throughout Europe. In one of the laws ascribed to Edward the Confessor, the rural dean is called the Dean of the Bishop. Their chief duty is to visit a certain number of parishes and to report their condition to the bishop. Till within the last few years the title of Rural Dean in modern times existed only in name. But now they hold chapters, at which subjects submitted to them by the bishop are discussed, and they present a report annually to the Bishop of the Diocese.

Decagon. A building having ten sides. The magnificent Early English chapter-house of Lincoln is in this form.

Decalogue. The *ten* precepts or commandments, delivered by God to Moses, and by him written on two tables of stone, and delivered to the Hebrews, as the basis and foundation of their religion. The use of the Decalogue in the Communion Service, introduced in the Second Prayer-Book of 1552, is peculiar to the English Church. It is probably derived from the custom of reciting and expounding the commandments at certain intervals, which is so frequently enjoined by the ancient synods, and the bishops of the Church of England, and was perhaps also intended as a warning against the Antinomianism of the age. The translation in our Prayer-Book is that of the Great Bible of 1539–1540. Each commandment is followed by the response, " Lord, have mercy upon us, and incline our hearts to keep this law "—an expansion of the ancient *Kyrie Eleison*, which, with the *Christe Eleison*, was alone in the First Prayer-Book of 1549. The " Responses to the Commandments " form part of every English setting of the Communion Service. In some collections of Church music they are headed " Decalogue Responses " (see Fawcett's " Lyra Ecclesiastica," 1844). In many of our old cathedral MS. books they are often headed " Commandments." The usual term is now *Kyrie Eleèson* or *Kyrie Eleison*. Thomas Weelkes (1600), Matthew Locke (1666), and Thomas Attwood (1831) set the Responses, with the music varied after each commandment. The usual practice is to maintain the same music throughout. It is not uncommon, however, in the services of modern composers to find the *Kyries* with varied music in sets of three. See also *sub voce* " Farse."

Decani. See *sub voce* " Cantoris."

Decorated. A style exhibiting the most complete and perfect development of Gothic architecture, which in the Early English style was not fully matured, and in the Perpendicular began to decline. The most prominent characteristic of this style is to be found in the windows, the tracery of which is always either of geometrical figures, circles, quatrefoils, etc., as in the earlier instances, or flowing in wavy lines, as in the later examples. Exuberance of ornament generally, is another feature. " Decorated " was the nomenclature of this style adopted by Rickman, one of the earliest writers on Gothic architecture; " Second Pointed " was that adopted by the Ecclesiological Society. It is also termed " Middle Pointed " and " Geometrical." The style was adopted in England *c.* 1200–1350. Among the finest examples are the Angel Choir at Lincoln ; the nave and choir, Exeter ; the presbytery, Ely ; the nave and Lady Chapel, Lichfield ; the chapter-house and Lady Chapel, Wells ; the choir, Carlisle ; Merton College Chapel, Oxford ; the choir, Selby Abbey ; Patrington Church, Yorkshire. Good modern examples are St Mary Magdalene, Munster Square (Carpenter, 1852) ; St Matthias', Stoke Newington (Butterfield, 1853) ; St Michael's College, Tenbury (Woodyer, 1856) ; Holy Trinity, Kensington Gore (Bodley) ; Sledmere Church, Yorkshire (Temple Moore) ; St Giles', Cheadle ; St George's, Lambeth, the two last by Pugin. Consult " The Decorated Period," a paper read before the St Paul's Ecclesiological Society, by R. H. Carpenter, F.R.I.B.A., 4th May 1880 (Society's Transactions, i. 21).

Dedications of Churches. On this subject, too lengthy to be discussed here, consult an exhaustive paper read in three sections before the St Paul's Ecclesiological Society, by Charles Browne, M.A., 12th February, 9th May, 13th November 1883 (Society's Transactions, i. 267–293) ; also, for the dedications of the French cathedrals, an article in *The Ecclesiologist*, July 1846.

Deus Misereatur. The Latin name for Psalm lxvii., which may be used after the Second Lesson at Evensong instead of the *Nunc dimittis* ; except on the 12th day of the month, when it occurs among the Psalms. It was first inserted in its present place in the Second Prayer-Book of Edward VI. (1552), but it was familiar in the older services, being the fourth fixed Psalm at Lauds on Sundays. For notable English musical settings as " Services," see *sub voce* " Cantate Domino." It should always follow *Cantate*, as *Nunc dimittis* should follow *Magnificat*.

Diapason (Greek). (1) An octave. (2) Fixed pitch ; normal diapason, a recognised standard of pitch. (3) The most important foundation stops of an organ, termed in other countries more properly " Principal." The diapasons of the old organ builders, John Loosemore, Bernard (Father) Smith, Renatus Harris, Samuel Green, and John Avery, were celebrated. Among moderns, those of Willis, Hill, Lewis, and Schultze (a German of Paulinzelle, Saxony) have a high reputation.

A DICTIONARY OF

An ornament of flowers applied to a plain surface, whether carved or painted. If carved, the flowers are entirely sunk into the work below the general surface ; they are usually square, and placed close to each other, but occasionally other arrangements are used. This kind of decoration was first introduced in the Early English style, in which it was sometimes applied to large spaces. Examples : Westminster Abbey, Chichester Cathedral (Early English) ; chapter-house, Canterbury, St Mary's Chapel, Ely Cathedral, parapet of Beverley Minster (Decorated) ; Lady Chapel, Gloucester Cathedral (Perpendicular). Diaper-work was also executed in the most brilliant colours, combined with gilding ; it was employed in the Decorated as well as in the Perpendicular, and probably also in the Early English, but no examples can be referred to of that period. Excellent modern diaper-work may be seen in the spandrels of the choir arcade of the Church of the Sacred Heart at Wimbledon, and on the apse walls of the Church of St Peter, Dulwich.

Diaper-work, Diapering.
Fr. *diapré ;*
Ital. *diaspro ;*
Germ. *geblümte.*

One of the five " Sequences " or " Proses," retained by the Council of Cologne in 1536 and of Rheims in 1564, but omitted entirely by the revisers of our Liturgy. Formerly they were very numerous (see *sub voce* " Sequence "). The *Dies Irae* follows the Epistle in a Requiem Mass, and its use has been revived in our own Church, in the same place. It was written by Thomas of Celano, a Franciscan friar, about the middle of the twelfth century, and is considered the finest hymn of its kind extant. Sir Walter Scott admired it greatly, and on his deathbed was continually murmuring stanzas from it. It was not admitted as a Sequence for the Dead for some time (sequences as a joyous feature being considered out of place), nor was it ever enjoined as such in the old English office, though the printed missals gave it for those priests who might desire to say it. In the present Roman rite its use is compulsory at Mass on All Souls' Day, and when the corpse is present ; at other times it is optional. Unfortunately, many of the numerous Latin hymns in our books are spoiled in the course of translation—which is indeed an almost impossible process in the case of a Latin hymn—so that it is hardly fair to charge them with being cold and prosaic. One of the greatest of all, the *Dies Irae*, becomes a shadow only of the original, for what Archbishop Trench called " the solemn effect of the triple rhyme, which has been likened to blow following blow of the hammer on the anvil," simply cannot be reproduced in English because we have so few trisyllabic rhymes.

Dies Irae.

110

ECCLESIASTICAL TERMS

Several translators have tried it, and the result is of the baldest, One of the earliest of these translations is that by Wentworth Dillon. 4th Earl of Roscommon (1633–1685). Just before he expired he pronounced with intense fervour two lines of his version :

> " My God, my Father, and my Friend,
> Do not forsake me at my end."

The poet, Richard Crashaw (d. 1650), also made an English version not altogether successful. Undoubtedly one of the best is that made in 1848 by Rev. W. J. Irons, D.D., Vicar of Brompton, afterwards Prebendary of St Paul's and Rector of St Mary, Woolnoth. It was included in the first edition of " Hymns, Ancient and Modern " (1861), and has found a place, with its fine tune by Dr Dykes, in every succeeding edition of the book. The translation by Dean Stanley (" Hymnary," No. 170 ; " Westminster Abbey Hymn-Book," No. 366) is extremely good. The ancient melody was admirably harmonised for the " Hymnal Noted," by Charles Child Spencer (1852), and there is an arrangement by the Rev. H. A. Walker for solo voices and chorus, and in Faux Bourdon, after the French manner of singing it. A magnificent rendering of this world-famed sequence, as printed in the " Hymnal Noted," was given by the Motett Choir at St Martin's Hall, Long Acre, 9th July 1855, " in memory of all who had fallen in the Crimean War." The performance was under the direction of Rev. Thos. Helmore. Every Requiem Mass contains a setting of *Dies Irae*. Among the most celebrated are those by Durante, Gaensbacher, Gossec, Jomelli, Neukomm, Winter (selections from all of which will be found in Latrobe's " Sacred Music," 6 vols., 1806–1825), Mozart, Cherubini (Requiem in C minor and D minor), Verdi, Gounod, and our distinguished countrymen, R. L. de Pearsall and Sir C. Villiers Stanford. The " German Requiem " of Brahms is not a Mass, but a series of choral movements of an elegiac character.

One who holds any preferment to which jurisdiction is annexed. The dignitaries in British cathedrals are, for the most part, the dean, precentor, chancellor, treasurer, and archdeacon. Some-

Dignitary. times the sub-dean and (as at York) the *Succentor Canonicorum* are so called ; and in a few cathedrals in Ireland the provost and sacrist (or treasurer). The only dignitary in Cathedrals of the New (or Henry VIII.'s) Foundation is the dean ; as the archdeacon is not necessarily a member of such chapters. It is a vulgar error to style prebendaries, or canons residentiary, digni-

A DICTIONARY OF

taries. The prebendaries without dignity were styled *canonici* (or *prebendarii*) *simplices*. Consult Jebb on "The Choral Service" (1843).

Diocese. The area of a bishop's jurisdiction. A Province is the area of an archbishop's jurisdiction. Each province contains divers dioceses, or sees of bishops; whereof Canterbury now includes twenty-six, and York nine. Every diocese in England is divided into archdeaconries, each archdeaconry into rural deaneries and every rural deanery into parishes.

Dirge. (1) The Office for the Dead. It derives its name from the opening words of the antiphon, "Dirige in conspectu tuo viam meam" (Ps. v. 9), and was contained in the ancient breviaries, and in the English prymers (*q.v.*). The office was also called the "Placebo" (from the antiphon "Placebo Domino"), or the "Placebo and Dirge." Other names are given to it in the old books, but in the prymers of 1538, 1543, and the King's Prymer, it is called only the "Dirge." The office consisted of two parts, Vespers and Matins; at first it had Vespers only. It is uncertain by whom it was originally composed. By some it is said to date from the Apostolic age, and was added to by Origen; by others it is attributed to St Ambrose or to St Augustine. But on one point all agree : that it is of the highest antiquity, and was used in the earliest ages of the Church. Some of the great Continental writers have set the morning offices of the dead to elaborate music. One of the most celebrated is that by David Perez, Royal Chapel Master at Lisbon, 1752, entitled "Mattutino di Morti." It was written by command of King Joseph Emmanuel, and the full score was published in London, with a portrait of the composer prefixed, by Robert Bremner of the Strand, about 1775. Consult further Maskell's "Monumenta Ritualia Ecclesiæ Anglicanæ," 3 vols., 1846–1847. (2) A piece of music, vocal or instrumental, of a funereal or elegiac character.

Dom. Strictly speaking, this is the German equivalent for "cathedral," but it is apparently applied to the head church of a city or town, whether the seat of a bishop or not.

Domchor. In Germany, the choir or body of singers attached to a cathedral church, consisting of men and boys. At Cologne, Münster, Paderborn, and Ratisbon these choirs are celebrated, and for many years they have kept alive the pure vocal style of Church composition as exemplified in the masses and motetts of Palestrina, Vittoria, Orlando di Lasso, and others. For the domchor of the principal Lutheran church at Berlin Mendelssohn wrote his three famous psalms for double choir, known over

112

here by the titles of " Judge me, O God," " My God, O why hast Thou forsaken me ? " and " Why fiercely rage the heathen ? " The same composer also wrote for this choir a set of six shorter anthems for eight voices apiece. These were afterwards rearranged by the late Dr Steggall for four voices.

Domical Vaulting. Vaulting in which the dome or cupola shape is employed in contradistinction to a waggon-head or an intersecting vault. In Germany it exists in its grandest form in Westphalia. The cathedrals of Minden, Münster, Osnabrück, and Paderborn offer fine instances.

Doom. The ecclesiological term for a representation of the Last Judgment in sculpture, stained glass, or fresco. The subject was a favourite one in the Middle Ages. The most notable examples are these. In sculpture : tympanum of one of the west portals, Bourges Cathedral (Gothic) ; tympanum of the Portail des Libraires, Rouen Cathedral (ditto) ; tympanum of the west portal, Autun Cathedral, Burgundy (Romanesque). In stained glass : tracery of the great east windows at Carlisle Cathedral and Selby Abbey, Yorks. In fresco : wall above the eastern arch of nave in Santa Maria, Toscanella, near Viterbo, Italy ; and the wall above the altar in the Sistine Chapel, Vatican, Rome. The latter was the celebrated work of Michael Angelo, designed in his sixtieth year at the request of Clement VII., and completed in 1541, during the pontificate of Paul III., after a labour of nearly eight years. In order to encourage Michael Angelo in his task, the Pope went in person to his house, accompanied by ten cardinals—an " honour," says Lanzi (" History of Painting "), " unparalleled in the annals of art." Representations of this subject in modern stained glass are the great west windows of St James' Church, Bury St Edmunds, and King's College Chapel, Cambridge. Both windows are by Clayton and Bell. At King's the window is, as many know, one of the largest in England. Further than this, it has a special interest in being the only one of the twenty-five other large windows in the chapel which remained without stained glass until 1879. Moreover, it happens that documentary evidence exists that the subject adopted for the new window (the gift of individual munificence)— viz. the " Last Judgment "—was originally intended as part of the scheme for the entire chapel. Messrs Clayton and Bell, the artists, had the work in hand for some seven or eight years, during which time they had to obtain glass specially made to match the ancient tints, and to study the old glass with much labour and painstaking, so that the new work should be in perfect harmony and tone with

the old, as far as possible. In the early days of the Cambridge
Camden Society there was a theory among ecclesiological under-
graduates that the flood of western light thrown into the chapel
by its plain window was needed for its proper lighting, and improved
rather than detracted from the general effect of the glorious interior.
It is now, however, generally admitted that the effect of the chapel
is much improved by this completion of its original scheme of colour.
An excellent paper on the ancient stained glass in King's Chapel,
by the present Provost, Dr M. R. James, is appended to the historical
and architectural account of the College by C. R. Fay (Scholar)
with illustrations by E. H. New (Dent's series of College Mono-
graphs, 1907). At the Collegiate Church of St Michael and All
Angels, near Tenbury, the stained glass in the great western window
—a noble composition of six lights—represents in the three dexter
lights the Atonement, and in the three sinister ones the Doom.
Although much red and purple is used in this window we do not
for once desiderate white. In the Doom, some flowering on the
robe of Our Lord, and in the Crucifixion the groups of angels in
adoration of the Rood, which is placed within a vesica, are specially
worthy of commendation. This window ranks among the best
works of its artist, John Hardman, and seen during evening service,
under the conditions of a fine sunset, it appears more than ordinarily
magnificent. The tracery of the window was the gift of the Rev. Sir
W. H. Cope, Bart. (one of the oldest friends of the Rev. Sir Frederick
A. Gore Ouseley, the founder of the college), at the time of the
erection of the church, 1854–1856. The stained glass was not
inserted until 1858. As a painting, the Doom was, in ancient times,
at the eastern end of the nave, usually over the chancel arch. The
reason for placing this awful and certain event so conspicuously
before the people is too obvious to need any comment.

Dorian Mode. The now obsolete diatonic minor key of D without a B flat.
The complete "Services" of many of the composers soon after the
Reformation, and until the beginning of the seventeenth century, such as Tallis, Morley, J. Farrant
Strogers, Bevin, Amner, Mundy, Batten and others are entirely in
the Dorian Mode. To us, in the present day, they seem of a
penitential character, but they were not considered so by their composers. The general effect is grand and solemn, and they are eminently suitable for use during Lent, on Fridays, or upon occasions
when the whole of the music is in an elegiac vein. The Dorian Mode
does not seem to have been so extensively employed in anthems,
but Batten's "Deliver us, O Lord" is an excellent example. The

ECCLESIASTICAL TERMS

Credo, as set by Merbecke in his " Book of Common Prayer Noted "
(1550), is in the Dorian Mode, and harmonies—hardly exceeded in
appropriateness since—were added by Charles Child Spencer, one
of our greatest authorities on the old Church modes, and printed in
The Parish Choir of September 1847. A fugue for the organ in the
Dorian Mode, by the Rev. S. S. Greatheed, has been published.
Many of the ancient plainsong hymn melodies are in this mode.

The oldest and simplest of the three orders used by the Greeks,
but ranking as the second of the five orders adopted by the Romans.

Doric Order. The shaft of the column has twenty flutings, which are
separated by a sharp edge and not by a fillet as in
the other orders, and they are less than a semicircle in depth. The
moulding below the abacus of the capital is an ovolo : the architrave of the entablature is surmounted with a plain fillet, called the
tenia, and the frieze is ornamented by flat projections, with three
channels cut in each called triglyphs. Other characteristics are
observable on an examination of good ancient and modern examples.
In the Grecian Doric the column has no base, but in the Roman
there is one, and there are differences in other details of the architrave, frieze, etc. Doric porticos on good models may be seen at
the churches of Brixton (by Porden), West Hackney (by Sir R.
Smirke), and St John, Waterloo Road (by F. Bedford), all built in
the reign of George IV. Consult Leeds' " Rudimentary Architecture "
(1848) ; Smith's " Synopsis of Architecture " (1831) ; Penrose's
" Athenian Architecture " (1852).

A window pierced through a sloping roof, and
Dormer or placed in a small gable which rises on the side of
Dormer- the roof. No examples are found earlier than the
window. fourteenth century. There is a charming Decorated
Ital. *abbaino.* dormer-window at Chapel Cleeve, Somersetshire,
c. 1350.

Hangings at the east end, and sometimes the sides, of the chancel
of a church. The term arises from their being placed at the back
(*dorsum*) of the priests officiating at the altar. They
Dorsal, or were made of tapestry or carpet-work, and frequently
Dossal. embroidered with silks, and gold and silver. The term
Lat. is now generally used for a piece of needlework where
dorsarium, there is no reredos of stone, marble, or wood. In
dorsale ; the " Wills and Inventories of Durham," p. 2, we
Fr. *dossier.* find : " Ornamenta Ranulphi Episcopi (1128)—
' Addidit etiam ornamentis Ecclesiæ magna *dorsalia*
quæ quondam pendebant ex utraque parte chori.' "

A DICTIONARY OF

Double Choir Music. Church music (services, anthems, masses, and motetts) for two distinct choirs, *Decani* and *Cantoris*, of four kinds of voices apiece— *i.e.* treble, alto, tenor and bass. The larger the choir the more effective is this species of writing. As a general rule, it is without organ accompaniment. Among the most noted examples of this sort of writing in English Church music may be mentioned Greene's anthem, "How long wilt Thou forget me?"; Boyce's anthem, "O give thanks"; Samuel Wesley's motetts, "Dixit Dominus" and "In Exitu Israel"; T. A. Walmisley's Evening Service in B flat, and portions of his Commemoration Anthem, "O give thanks"; Sterndale Bennett's motett, "In Thee, O Lord"; part of S. S. Wesley's anthem, "O Lord, Thou art my God," and of Sir John Goss's "Lift up Thine eyes round about"; Sir Frederick Ouseley's Service in C (throughout) and his anthems, "Awake, thou that sleepest," "Blessed be Thou," "O God, wherefore art Thou absent?" "O Saviour of the world," "Thus saith the Lord"; Sir Robert Stewart's Service in E flat; Sir Joseph Barnby's anthem "O Lord God, to whom vengeance belongeth"; two unpublished Evening Services in the keys of C and E and parts of the anthem, "O be joyful in God," by Sir George Elvey; Stainer's anthem for Trinity Sunday, "I saw the Lord"; Dr Pole's setting of the Old Hundredth Psalm; an Evening Service in C and an anthem, "When Israel came out of Egypt," by the late Dr W. B. Gilbert; an Evening Service in C by Dr J. H. Gower; two similar compositions in the keys of A flat and E major, by Dr A. H. Mann; a motett, "Deliver me from mine enemies," by Henry Guy, and a similar composition, "Praise thou the Lord, O my soul" (words from Psalms cxlv. and cxlvi.) by that most talented and distinguished of our few lady composers, Miss Frances Allitsen. This motett has an independent organ accompaniment, and Miss Allitsen has also arranged it for a choir of four voices. By composers of the foreign schools of Church music, double choir writing was much cultivated. Specimens of such are a *Te Deum* in C minor by Giaches de Waert; a *Magnificat* in C by Luca Marenzio; a *Nunc dimittis* in the same key by Giovanni Nanini (all published in Burns' "Ecclesiastical Choir-Book," 1848); Palestrina's masses, *Confitebor Tibi* and *Sine Titulo*; his motetts, *Jubilate Deo, Caro mea vere est cibus, Videntes stellam Magi, Hodie Christus natus est, Surge, Jerusalem illuminare,* and the *Fratres ego* in the music for Holy Week; Leo's *Dixit Dominus*; J. Sebastian Bach's motetts, "Be not afraid," "Come, Jesu, come," "Now shall the grace," "Sing ye to the Lord," "The Spirit also

helpeth us " ; J. Christopher Bach's " I wrestle and pray " and
another, " Blessing, Glory, Wisdom," now usually assigned to him ;
Spohr's " From the deep," and " Jehovah, Lord God of Hosts " ;
the three Psalms written by Mendelssohn for the Domchor at Berlin :
" Judge me, O God," " My God, O why hast Thou forsaken me,"
" Why rage fiercely the heathen " ; Meyerbeer's setting of the
91st Psalm ; and Gounod's Palm Sunday motett, " Lo, the children
of the Hebrews." In oratorio music the great double choruses in
Handel's " Israel in Egypt," " Deborah," " Solomon," etc., and
those of Bach in the St Matthew " Passion " may also come under
this category. There is, of course, a large literature of music for
an eight-part chorus (1st and 2nd treble, 1st and 2nd alto, 1st and 2nd
tenor, 1st and 2nd bass), but not arranged for two *distinct* choirs,
antiphonally. Examples of this sort of writing occur in the anthems
of Gibbons, Purcell, Blow, Croft, and more modern composers, such
as Dr Garrett, Dr C. Harford Lloyd, and Sir Francis Champneys.
The motett " O Thou Most Merciful Jesu " (*O Clementissime Jesu*),
by the last-named, is admirable. Sir Frederick Ouseley's Festival
Service in F (1878) is for eight-part chorus, solo voices, organ and
orchestra.

Dripstone.
Old. Eng.
dropstone.
Called also label, weather - moulding, and water-table. A
projecting tablet or moulding over the heads of
doorways, windows, niches, etc., in Romanesque
and Gothic architecture, either for ornament, or
to throw off the rain. Each style has its characteristic dripstone. See the examples in Parker's " Glossary "
(1851).

**Dublin
Cathedrals,
The Two.**
Dublin is remarkable in having two cathedrals, and the way in
which it came about was this. Dublin was originally
a Danish settlement, and when the Danes were
converted to Christianity they built a rather small
and unpretentious cathedral for themselves, which
they dedicated to the Holy Trinity. In after times this cathedral
became possessed of a very remarkable relic, no less than the
walking staff which had been used by Our Lord ; and this
Baculum Christi, as it was called, was of course a source of great
profit to the establishment, from the offerings of the numerous
pilgrims who came to venerate it. It was carefully treasured up
until the days of the very first post-Reformation archbishop—
Archbishop Browne—who termed it " Nehushtan," and in his
zealous fury burnt it. It seems that while possessed of this staff
the cathedral, which really bore a dedication to the Holy Trinity,

got to be considered as dedicated to Our Lord Himself, and generally went by the name of " Christ Church," although there is no actual and formal dedication in that title. The original dedication is to the Holy Trinity. When the Normans, under Strongbow, came into Ireland, they were not at all satisfied with the small and somewhat unpretentious Cathedral of the Holy Trinity, and they therefore built a very large collegiate church dedicated to the patron saint of Ireland, St Patrick. After they had built this church the Normans were perpetually trying to get transferred to it the status and privileges enjoyed by Holy Trinity or Christ Church. After a century of unceasing negotiations backwards and forwards on this knotty point, in the year 1299 the Pope of that day—Boniface VIII. —issued a bull in which he appointed that Dublin should have two cathedrals, and that for the future the archbishops should be enthroned in the one cathedral and buried in the other. It is impossible to say whether this injunction was exactly carried out, but this was the tenor of the bull. In order to preserve as far as possible the dignity of the smaller cathedral, Christ Church, the dean (Garvey) was appointed Bishop of Kilmore in 1588, and Primate in 1589, still retaining his deanery *in commendam* along with the Primacy. Christ Church was founded by the Danish king, Sitric, in 1038 for secular canons. About 1163, however, Archbishop Lawrence O'Toole changed it from a cathedral into a priory of the Regular Order of Arrosian Canons. In 1541 Henry VIII. restored it to its original foundation as a cathedral, with dean, precentor, chancellor, treasurer, Archdeacon of Dublin, six vicars choral (two clerical and four lay), and four boy choristers. Three years later Archbishop Browne founded three prebendal stalls in the cathedral with the titles of St Michael, St Michan (a Danish saint), and St John. An organist, stipendiary singers and an increased number of choristers were afterwards added as occasion arose. After the passing of the Irish Church Act in 1869, the constitution of the cathedral was somewhat modified, but the ancient chapter was kept compactly together, and twelve new canonries, without emoluments, were added on by an Act of the Synod. St Patrick's, originally a parish church, was erected into a prebendal and collegiate establishment by Archbishop Comyn in 1190. In 1216 King John confirmed its possessions, at the same time enjoining on its members the observance of certain rules, according to the usages of the Church of Sarum. In 1219 this collegiate foundation was elevated into that of a complete cathedral by Henry de Loundres, Comyn's successor, who in the same year granted it a charter. As a Cathedral of the Old Foundation, it was a *beau ideal* one, the staff consisting of dean, precentor, treasurer, chancellor, succentor, archdeacons, twenty-one prebendaries (among whom the Archbishop of Dublin held the stall of Cullen), four minor canons, twelve vicars choral, five of whom were priests and seven laymen, besides choristers. It is interesting to observe that St Patrick's was constituted by its founder, Henry de Loundres, on the model of Salisbury. This prelate was present at the consecration of Salisbury Cathedral by Bishop Poore, in 1225, and it is also worthy of note that, in its general features, and especially in the construction and fenestration of its choir and Lady Chapel, there is in St Patrick's an evident though humble imitation of the church whence its liturgical forms and constitutions were derived. Another interesting feature is that the national cathedral of Ireland is, like Salisbury, homogeneous in style—the Early English prevailing throughout. Both cathedrals owed their restoration late in the last century to individual munificence. Consult further " The Cathedral of the Holy Trinity, commonly called Christ Church Cathedral, Dublin," by the Rev. Edward Seymour, M.A. (precentor), and George Edmund Street (architect of the restoration), 1882; " Some Remarks upon the Bill for Christ Church Cathedral, Dublin," by the Rev. Precentor Seymour (1879) ; " The Cathedral Church of the Holy Trinity, Dublin (Christ Church)—a Description of its Fabric, etc.," by William Butler (1901) ; " Dublin for Archæologists," by Sir Thomas Drew, R.H.A., F.R.I.B.A. (1901) ; " The History and Antiquities of the Collegiate and Cathedral Church of St Patrick, Dublin," by W. Monck Mason (1820) ; " The Cathedral Church of St Patrick," by the Very Rev. J. H. Bernard, Dean of St Patrick's (1904) ; " The National Cathedral of St Patrick, Dublin," by Sir Thomas Drew (1900) ; " Irish Church Composers and the Irish Cathedrals"—two papers read before the Musical Association, 13th February, and 13th March 1900, by J. S. Bumpus. The remarkable relic, the " Baculum Christi " or " Staff of Jesus," alluded to in connection with Christ Church, was a crozier, covered with gold and inlaid with precious stones—one legend connected with it being that it had belonged to St Patrick, having been presented to him by a hermit who had received it from our Blessed Lord ; the more probable account, however, being that of Sir J. Ware, who, on the authority of Giraldus, and the " Black Book of Christ Church " (fourteenth century), and other MSS., says that it was brought to Dublin from Armagh by William Fitz Aldelm and the English. It had been in possession of the church since 1180, and upon it, down to the period of the Reformation, when it was publicly burnt by Archbishop Browne, witnesses were frequently sworn, in presence of the Lord Deputy and Chancellor.

Eagle. A common form of the lectern from which the lessons are read in churches and cathedrals. It has probably some reference to the eagle which is the symbolical companion of St John, in ecclesiastical design. The eagle is frequently employed in foreign churches, generally for the chanting of the service. Sometimes it is used for the reading of the Epistle and Gospel, and there are instances of one being on each side of the choir. There are ancient examples of this kind of lectern in several of our cathedrals and college chapels—*e.g.* Canterbury, York, Winchester, Lincoln, Peterborough, Southwell, and Christ Church Cathedral, Dublin. At Norwich the lectern is in the form of a pelican. Before the Civil War, in 1651, there was in the Cathedral of Waterford a "great standing pelican to support the Bible, a brazen eagle." In the Middle Ages, Durham Cathedral possessed two lecterns, one within the altar-rail, " A goodly fine letteron of brasse, where they sunge the Epistle and the Gospell, with a gilt pellican on the height of it, finely gilded pullinge hir bloud out hir breast to hir young ones, and winges spreade abroade, whereon did lye the book that they singe the epistle and the gosple. It was thought to be the goodlyest lettern of brasse that was in all the countrye." Besides this one " also ther was lowe downe in the Quire another Lettorn of brasse, not so curiously wrought, standing in the midste against the stalls, a marveilous faire one, with an Eagle on the height of it, and her winges spread a broad. Which same stood theire until the year 1650, when the Scots were sent prisoners from Dunbarr fight, and put prisoners into the church, where they burned up all the woodworke, in regard they had no coales allowed them. And there was a fellow, one Brewen, appointed to look to the Scotts, which conveyed this brasse letterne and eagle awaye, and many other things appertayninge to the Church, and sould them for his own gaine " (" Ancient Rites of Durham"). The earliest eagle lectern does not date before 1300. That in St Paul's is the largest and finest in England, measuring 8 ft. 6 in. from the black and white marble pavement of the church to the crest of the bird, the breadth across the wings being 3 ft. 3 in. The maker was Jacob Sutton, and in 1720, £241, 15s. was paid to him for it. The brass fence round it, together with the desk at which two minor canons used to chant the Litany, cost, four years later, £477, 6s. Until 1871 this noble lectern stood in the centre of the choir, but during the alterations in 1871-1872, when the dome was made available for congregational purposes at all services, it was placed somewhat westward of the choir steps. At the same time, the brass fence was not retained in its former position, but was utilised as a low choir-screen. Since 1883, when a new screen was formed out of the original altar-rails, this handsome fence was most reprehensibly stowed away as lumber in the gallery over the south aisle of the nave. Some fifteen years ago the lectern was moved to the north-eastern dome pier. In this side position much of its dignity of effect has been lost ; but for purposes of hearing the situation is, perhaps, more advantageous. There is now a fine eagle lectern at Durham—a replica of that stolen in 1650. Other good modern examples are at Hereford Cathedral, Lichfield Cathedral (where it was the gift of students of the Theological College in 1861), and in the Church of St Matthias, Stoke Newington. See also *sub voce* " Lectern."

The first of the Pointed or Gothic styles of architecture used in this country, after its emancipation from the Romanesque or **Early English.** Norman. "First Pointed" was the nomenclature adopted by the Ecclesiological Society. It is also known as "Lancet" from its narrow and acutely pointed arches and windows. From its Later or Transitional stage, the Decorated was evolved. Examples of this style are countless, but the churches illustrating it are, throughout the land, all worthy of study. The following may, however, be adduced :—Salisbury Cathedral and Beverley Minster throughout ; choirs of Rochester, Southwell and Worcester ; west front, Peterborough ; nave, choir, and transepts, Westminster Abbey ; the Temple Church, eastern portion ; nave, transepts, and St Hugh's Choir, Lincoln ; nave, Wells ; north and south transepts, York ; west front, Ripon ; St Patrick's Cathedral, Dublin ; Glasgow Cathedral—both throughout ; Jesus College Chapel, Cambridge ; Stone Church, Dartford, Kent ; the abbeys of Beaulieu, Jedburgh, Netley, Rivaulx and Whitby, all, alas ! ruined. Modern examples are the churches of St Augustine, Kilburn, and St John, Red Lion Square, as well as Truro Cathedral, all by J. L. Pearson ; St Matthew, City Road (G. G. Scott) ; All Souls', Leeds (G. G. Scott) ; St James, Spanish Place (G. Goldie) ; Church of the Ascension, Malvern Link (W. J. Tapper). The contemporaneous French style is exemplified in large portions of the cathedrals of Bayeux, Bruges, Chartres, Le Mans, Rouen, Soissons, and Tours. Consult "Architecture of the Thirteenth Century," an address delivered before the St Paul's Ecclesiological Society, 21st May 1879, by G. E. Street ; also Sir G. G. Scott's "Gleanings from Westminster Abbey," 1861.

On Easter Day our Church appoints certain anthems to be sung at Matins in place of the *Venite* (Ps. 95). These are selected from

Easter Anthems. 1 Cor. v. 7, 8 ; Rom. vi. 9 ; and 1 Cor. xv. 20, concluding with the *Gloria Patri*. In the Sarum Breviary a short service, introductory to Matins, was ordered for use on Easter Day, after taking the Host and cross from the " Sepulchre " and placing them upon the altar. The office will be found at full length in the Rev. F. Procter's " History of the Book of Common Prayer " (1856). In the First Prayer - Book of 1549 part of this introductory office was retained, but in the revision of 1552 it was omitted, with the exception of the anthems. The first anthem (" Christ our Passover ") was added in 1662. There are six ancient settings of the Easter anthems by Adrian Batten, William Byrd, William (Bishop) Juxon, Edward Tucker, Thomas Wilson, and Michael Wise, all unpublished. Wise was organist of Salisbury Cathedral, and his setting continued for many years in use there on Easter Day (see A. T. Corfe's book of words of anthems, compiled for the use of Salisbury Cathedral, 1830). It is now customary to sing these anthems to the single chant in C by Pelham Humphreys, usually known as the " Grand Chant " ; and also traditionally in some cathedrals as " Common Tune." The Rev. W. H. Havergal's fine arrangement of the " Grand Chant "—a *faux bourdon* in fact with the melody in the tenor—might be used for some of the verses with excellent effect. Havergal arranged the " Grand Chant " in forty different forms. This curious work was published by J. Shepherd, Newgate Street (1867). There is a good modern setting of the Easter anthems by the late Dr John Naylor, organist of York Minster. It was written for use there instead of the *Venite*, during the octave of Easter—an incorrect practice, as the singing of the anthems should be confined to Easter Day itself. It may be proper to mention that these " Anthems " are so called from their being short sentences ; the word " anthems," in this instance, by a peculiar usage, signifying " texts " and not having reference to the way in which they should be " sung " or " said."

Ecclesiology. A branch of art which devotes its energies to the reverent serving and adorning of the church in the best and fittest manner possible. " Antiquarianism " is, in itself, a mere branch of secular learning. For a full account of the origin and progress of the Ecclesiological Society, consult T. F. Bumpus, " London Churches, Ancient and Modern " (1908) ; C. L. Eastlake, " History of the Gothic Revival " (1872).

ECCLESIASTICAL TERMS

Elements. The materials used in the Sacraments, appointed for that purpose by our Lord Himself—" the outward and visible sign of the inward and spiritual grace." Thus, water is the element of baptism, and bread and wine are the elements of the Eucharist.

Ely Con-fession. A setting of the General Confession, some of the clauses of which are in unison, and others in harmony to varied strains. It is so called because arranged and composed by Robert Janes, organist of Ely Cathedral from 1830 to 1866. It is still in use at Ely, and many other churches, and when quietly and reverently sung has a solemn and beautiful effect. Perhaps in all correctness, the Confession should be recited in monotone on a low note, " *humili voce.*" The " Ely Confession " was in use at St Paul's for some years, until 1872. A good arrangement will be found in " The Ferial Responses and Litany," edited by Joseph Barnby (Novello).

Ember Days. These are the Wednesday, Friday, and Saturday after the First Sunday in Lent, the Feast of Pentecost, the 14th of September, and the 13th of December. They are ordered to be observed as days of fasting, in preparation for the following Sundays, which are the stated times of ordination in the Church. The week in which these days fall is called Ember Week, but as Sunday begins the week the Ember Collect is always to be read on the Sunday preceding the Ember Days, not on that which follows them, as is sometimes erroneously done. These days were called " jejunia quatuor temporum "—*i.e.* fasts of the four seasons, whence is derived the German *quatember*, a quarter of a year, or quarter day. The Dutch word is *quatutember* ; the Danish *kvatember*. The old English name of Ember Week was *Ymbren-wuce*. The prefix " Ymb," which also assumed the form " emb " or " embe," cognate with the German " *um* " and Latin " *ambi*," or Greek ἀμφί, means about, around. It was much used in early English, but has died out of our language. " Ren " or " rene " or " ryne " means a course, and so the Ember Weeks (Ymb-ren) would seem to have got the name from coming round periodically. The derivation of the name from " ashes " or " embers," need not be considered. Consult Wheatley, " Common Prayer," c. iv. Append. ; Maskell, " Mon. Rit. Ang. Eccl." i. cxxxv. ; Procter, " Book of Common Prayer," 261 ; Smith, " Dict. Christ. Antiq." ; Hook, " Church Dict."

Entablature. From the mediæval " Tablement." Fr. *entablement* ; Ital. *cornicione* ; Germ. *gebälk*. The superstructure which lies horizontally upon the columns in Classic architecture. It is divided into *architrave*, the part immediately above the column ; *frieze*, the central space ; and *cornice*, the upper projecting mouldings. Each of the orders has its proper entablature. In England the word seems to have been first used by the translator of John Evelyn's book on architecture.

Epiphany, Feast of the. Derived from the Greek compound verb ἐπιφαίνειν, to manifest, or declare. The manifestation of Christ to the Gentiles, commemorated in the Church on the 6th of January. The Epiphany was not originally a distinct festival, but made a part of that of the Nativity of Christ. This was celebrated during twelve days, the first and last of which, according to the custom of the Jews in their feasts, were high or chief days of solemnity, and therefore either of these might be fitly called Epiphany, as that word signifies the appearance of Christ in the world. Those who observed it as a distinct festival from the Nativity did it at first chiefly on account of our Saviour's baptism, and afterwards from the appearing of the star which conducted the wise men of the East to our Saviour. Other reasons were also given—namely, the turning water into wine at Cana, and the feeding of the five thousand —thus " God manifesting Himself by miracles in human nature " (St Augustine, Serm. xxix. *de Tempore*). In the Eastern Church this became one of the days for baptism—" Why is not the day on which Christ was born called Epiphany, but the day on which He was baptised ? Because he was not manifested to all when He was born, but when He was baptised " (St Chrysostom, Homil. xxiv. *de Bapt. Christi*). It was called also the day of light (ἡμέρα τῶν φώτων), baptism being generally called φῶς and φώτισμα. Consult Dr Neale's " Hist. of Holy Eastern Church " ; Bingham, " Orig. Eccles," bk. xx. c. iv. ; Blunt, " Annotated Prayer-Book," p. 83. An interesting custom used to be observed at the Chapel Royal, St James's Palace, on the Feast of the Epiphany. The sovereign proceeded to the altar at the time of the offertory, and made an offering of gold, frankincense, and myrrh, which was laid upon the altar, commemorating the offerings of the Magi. An officer of the royal household now makes the offering in the name of the sovereign. Two anthems have been specially written for use at this function, each to the words of the Collect for the Epiphany—" O God, who by the leading of a star." The first was composed by Dr John Bull, organist of the chapel in 1591, and was originally known as the " Star Anthem." It will be found adapted to other words (Isaiah xxv. 1, 4, 8, 9) in the third volume of Boyce's "Cathedral Music" (1778). The second was composed by Thomas Attwood, and will be found in the collection of his " Cathedral Music," edited in 1851 by his godson and pupil, Thomas Attwood Walmisley. The original MS. score bears date 1814.

Epistoler. The minister who reads the Epistle and acts as sub-deacon, at a Celebration of the Holy Eucharist. In the 24th Canon, and in the Injunctions of Queen Elizabeth, we find that a special reader, entitled an Epistoler, is to read the Epistle in collegiate churches, vested in cope. At St Paul's, the title of Epistoler or Epistler, is attached to one of the minor canonries. At the Chapel Royal one of the gentlemen, or adult singers, was called Pisteler or Epistler. In early times he was in orders. In November 1592 (see "Old Cheque Book of the Chapel Royal," ed. by Dr Rimbault, 1872) "Thomas Morleye [the distinguished Church composer and madrigal writer] was sworne from the Epistler's to the Gospeller's place and waiges." Epistolers are still statutable officers in some Cathedrals of the New Foundation, though in most the institution has fallen into desuetude. By Archbishop Grindal's Injunctions, in 1571, it was required that parish clerks should be able to read the First Lesson and Epistle. In some cathedrals—Lichfield, for example—the First Lesson was assigned to one of the lay vicars choral, and the reading of John Saville (d. 1803) was greatly admired there. A reference is made to this in the Letters of Anna Seward.

Evens. Eves or vigils. The nights or evenings before certain Holy Days of the Church. See *sub voce* " Vigils."

Evensong. The Order for Evening Prayer, called " Evensong " in Edward VI.'s First Book of 1549. It is a judicious abridgment and combination of the offices of Vespers (*i.e.* Evensong) and Compline as used in our Church prior to the Reformation. The sentences, exhortation, confession and absolution were appointed in 1552 to be said before the commencement of the older service, which opened with the Lord's Prayer. This part, however, was not printed until the revision of 1661, although it was given in the office of Matins (*q.v.*). The place of the Little Chapter (*capitulum*) at Vespers was occupied by a chapter from the Old Testament, while our Second Lesson occupies the place of the Little Chapter at Compline. The First Lesson was followed by the *Magnificat*, which was the canticle at Vespers, while the Second Lesson was followed by the *Nunc dimittis*, the canticle at Compline. See also *sub voce* " Cantate Domino " and " Deus Misereatur." The term " Evensong " still occurs in the Tables of Proper Lessons for

Sundays and Holy Days, and Proper Psalms. It is in fact the same as the old word "Vespers"; and only differs from the other authorised expression, "Evening Prayer," in having more special reference to the Psalms and canticles, and the anthems—those holy *songs* which make up so large a portion of the service.

Expectation Week. The ten days after the Ascension are sometimes so called, because they commemorate that anxious period during which the Apostles tarried at Jerusalem, in earnest expectation of the promised gift of the Comforter.

Faburden.
Fr.
faux-bourdon. One of the early systems of harmonising a given portion of plainsong or *canto fermo*; a sort of harmony consisting of thirds and sixths added to a *canto fermo.*

A portable low crossed or folding stool which might be used either to kneel at or sit upon. It is derived "a longo tardico *falden*, plicare; et *stoul*, sedes" (Ducange). It was made **Faldstool, Folding-stool, Faldistory.** Fr. *prie-dieu;* Ital. *faldistorio;* Germ. *schemel*, *krönnungs-schemel.* to fold up in the manner of a camp-stool, and was constructed either of metal or wood, with a rich silk covering. Formerly, when a bishop was required to officiate in any but his own cathedral church where his throne (originally a faldstool) was erected, a similar piece of furniture was placed for him in the choir, and he frequently carried one with him in his journeys. In the Order of Coronation the rubric speaks of a *faldstool* at which the sovereign shall kneel, but this, according to pictures of late coronations, has lost its original shape, and is merely a kneeling-stool. The faldstool is sometimes represented in the illuminations of early MSS. The term is also frequently but erroneously applied to the "Litany-stool," or small low desk at which the Litany is enjoined to be sung. "For her (the Quene) shall be ordeyned, on the left side of the high aulter, a folding stole wherin she shall sit" ("Device for the Coronation of Henry VII.," Rutland Papers, 13). "The Priest goeth forth from out of his seat into the body of the church, and at a low desk before the chancel door called the Fald-stool, kneels, and says or sings the Litany" (Bishop Andrewes' notes, quoted under the frontispiece to Sparrow's "Rationale," 1655). In Langton's Chapel, Winchester Cathedral, is preserved the faldistorium upon which Queen Mary sat at her marriage in the Lady Chapel, on St James's Day, 25th July 1554, to Philip of Spain, when the nobles attendant upon that cheerful monarch wondered at Mass being as solemnly performed at

ECCLESIASTICAL TERMS

Winchester as at Toledo. A woodcut of this faldstool will be found in the " Proceedings of the Archæological Institute at Winchester, September 1845 " (Longmans, 1846).

Fan-tracery Vaulting. A kind of vaulting used in Late Perpendicular work, in which all the ribs that rise from the springing of the vault have the same curve, and diverge equally in every direction, producing an effect something like that of the bones of a fan. It is frequently used over tombs, chantry chapels, and other small erections. Fine examples of fan-tracery roofs are those of Sherborne Abbey, Bath Abbey, St George's Chapel, Windsor, Henry VII.'s Chapel, Westminster Abbey, King's College, Cambridge.

Farse. An addition used before the Reformation, in the vernacular tongue, to the Epistle in Latin, forming an explication or paraphrase of the Latin text, verse by verse, for the benefit of the people. The sub-deacon first repeated each verse of the Epistle or *lectio* in Latin, and two choristers sang the " farse " or explanation. In the Sarum Missal nine " farses " are to be found placed between the *Kyries*, with reference to particular days. This method of placing such sentences was called " farsing," and Henry Bradshaw, the distinguished Cambridge University librarian, did not hesitate to say that it is to these farsings of the *Kyrie* that we owe the Ten Commandments in our present Communion Service. In the musical settings of the *Kyries*, therefore, composers who arrange the *Kyries* in sets of three are only following the original form, and are keeping in mind the ancient order. Consult J. Baden Powell, " Choralia," p. 108 ; Wordsworth, " Breviarum Sarum," vol. iii. Append. II. p. lxxxix.

Fenestriform Tracery. Tracery arranged in the form of a window, but not glazed. It is of frequent occurrence in a shallow form in the Westphalian church towers of the fourteenth and fifteenth centuries.

Feretory. A bier, or coffin ; tomb, or shrine. Parker (" Glossary of Architecture ") is of opinion that this term seems more properly to belong to the portable shrines in which the reliques of saints were carried about in processions, but was also applied to the fixed shrines or tombs in which their bodies were deposited. In the " Ancient Rites of Durham " (p. 77) we find : " Hugh, Bishop of Durham, having finished the chapel called the Galiley, caused a *Feretory* of gold and silver to be made, wherein were deposited the bones of Venerable Bede, translated and removed from St Cuthbert's Shrine."

127

A DICTIONARY OF

Ferial. Non-festal ; as ferial-use—music for use on ordinary (or week) days (*feriae*), especially with regard to the responses and Litany. Consult Jebb, " Choral Responses and Litanies of the United Church of England and Ireland " (2 vols., 1847–1857) ; an invaluable publication.

Figured-bass. A convenient species of musical shorthand. A bass stave having the accompanying chords suggested by certain numbers and other signs above and below the notes. The original printed copies of the scores of Croft, Greene, Boyce, Arnold, Nares, Dupuis, and many other old cathedral writers, have not the separate accompaniment for the organ with which we are now so familiar, the only guide to the player being this figured-bass line underneath the vocal score. " Playing from figured-bass " is an accomplishment acquired only after much study, and especially by those who have passed their noviciate in a cathedral. John Stafford Smith, in his volume of anthems, 1793, was the first to supply a thin accompaniment (treble and bass lines only) in addition to a figured-bass. He was also one of the first, if not the first, to discard the alto and tenor C clefs in the score. The editions and original compositions of Vincent Novello were the first to have a regular accompaniment for a keyed instrument, compressed from the vocal score.

Finial. In architecture, the flower or foliage terminating a pinnacle (*q.v.*).

First Pointed. The Ecclesiological Society's nomenclature for the Early English style. English and French examples have been adduced under " Early English," but the following analagous Continental specimens may be cited as supplementary : nave of Paderborn Cathedral ; western door, Naumburg Cathedral ; western apses, Bamberg Cathedral and St Sebald's, Nuremberg ; the Cistercian Church at Riddagshausen, near Brunswick (German) ; choir, St Martin, Ypres ; choir aisles, St Gudule, Brussels ; Church of Nôtre Dame de Pamèle, Oudenarde (Belgian) ; St Andrea, Vercelli (Italian) ; parts of Trondjhem Cathedral (Norwegian).

Fish. The representation of a fish as a symbol of our Lord is of frequent occurrence, and its import seems to be satisfactorily explained, as taken from the word ΙΧΘΥΣ, the initials of the words " Ἰησοῦς Χριστὸς Θεοῦ Υἱὸς Σωτήρ " (Jesus Christ, the Son of God, the Saviour). Among the paving tiles at the Abbey Church, Great Malvern, is one ornamented with the fish, enclosed in the pointed ellipse, to which the name Vesica Piscis (*q.v.*) has, on no very sufficient authority, been assigned. Parker (" Glossary of

Architecture ") quotes a very remarkable instance of the use of this symbol, introduced in so grotesque a manner as to be bordering on irreverence. It occurs on the seal of Aberdeen Cathedral, whereon is represented the Nativity, with the Blessed Virgin and her husband watching the manger at Bethlehem, behind which are seen the heads of horned cattle ; instead of the Infant Saviour, however, a fish is lying upon the manger. The character of this seal would fix its date at about 1250. Consult Cordiner's " Remarkable Ruins " (1788). By the early Christians the fish was regarded as the symbol of death.

Flagon. A vessel used to contain the wine, before and at the Consecration in the Holy Eucharist. In the marginal rubric in the Prayer of Consecration the priest is ordered " to lay his hand upon every vessel (be it chalice or flagon) in which there is any wine to be consecrated," but in the same prayer he is told to take the cup only in his hands ; and the rubric before the form of administering the cup stands thus, " the minister that delivereth the cup." The distinction, then, between the flagon and the cup or chalice is, that the latter is the vessel in which the consecrated wine is administered ; the flagon that in which some of the wine is placed for consecration, if there be more than one vessel used.

Flamboyant. A term applied by the ecclesiologists of France and Germany to the style of architecture contemporary in that country with the Perpendicular or Third Pointed of England, from the flame-like wavings of its tracery. It ought rather to be regarded as a vitiated Decorated rather than a distinct style, though some of its characteristics are peculiar, and it seldom possesses the purity or boldness of earlier ages. In rich works the intricacy and redundancy of the ornaments are often truly marvellous. Examples : transepts, Beauvais Cathedral ; churches of Caudebec, Harfleur, and St Ouen, Rouen, Normandy ; west front, Tours Cathedral (French) ; churches at Görlitz and Zwickau, Saxony ; St Lambert, Münster ; rood-loft in the Dom, Halberstadt (German).

Flèche. The French architectural term for a spirelet or small spire. It is usually of stone, or of wood covered with slate or lead, and placed on the roof, sometimes at the intersection of the nave, choir and transepts in a cross church. There are fine examples at Amiens, Rheims, Nôtre Dame and Ste Chappelle, Paris ; the Cathedral, Dijon ; and the Chapel of the Hôtel Dieu, Beaune. Modern English examples are those at St Ninian's Cathedral, Perth (W. Butterfield, 1850) ; Holy Trinity, Winchester (Henry Woodyer, 1854) ; Exeter College Chapel, Oxford (Sir G. G.

Scott, 1858) ; St Andrew, Westminster (Sir G. G. Scott, 1855) ; St Cuthbert, Earl's Court (Roumieu Gough, 1888). Consult the articles "Flèche" in Berty, "Dictionnaire de l'Architecture du Moyen Age" (1845), and Viollet le Duc, "Dictionnaire Raisonée de l'Architecture Française" (10 vols., 1858–1872).

The authority always quoted in evidence that at an early period it was customary to set flowers upon altars is the famous work of St Augustine the Great, "De Civitate Dei." It **Floral Decora-** narrates that a certain man went to the shrine of St **tion of Altars** Stephen, and prayed earnestly for Martial, his father-**and Churches.** in-law, a pagan, then lying on his deathbed ; and when he departed he took from the altar the first flower that came to hand, and put it, for it was now night, at the head of his father-in-law, who was asleep, and who, by its silent instrumentality, was converted, and sought baptism. From the fact of flowers being thus mentioned in connection with one individual, and but once, we can only draw the inference that it was not the general practice to employ them for the decoration of altars. They are not represented in any very ancient work of art ; perhaps the earliest is a painting, dated 1573, by Sebastian Vraux, where vases for flowers are represented ; and where we read of them in parish accounts they are only for strewing or general decorations of the church, for garlands for the choir on Corpus Christi Day, and the festival of the patron. At all events, it seems quite clear that they were not, at an early date, set upon the altar itself, but on the gradine or shelf. The practice of decorating altars with flowers placed upon the shelf can be scarcely said to prevail anywhere except in England. In France, the sanctuary is very usually decorated with cut flowers and plants in pots, and wreaths of evergreens (frequently artificial), at the commencement, and more or less during the period, of the "Month of Mary" (May), but the origin of that festivity is quite modern ; while in Italy, with its wealth of flowers, we seldom or never see used for the purpose any but tawdry artificial plants and flowers, fit in every way for ornaments of a second-rate music-hall. If not used for the adornment of the altar, there can be no doubt that the practice of decorating the church with flowers and branches of trees is of great antiquity. To an ecclesiologist the sight of an altar bristling with candles and crowded with flower-pots and bouquets, till it looks like a stall at Covent Garden Market, is not a pleasing one. It is little less offensive than an altar covered with a lot of useless plate, like a sideboard—a fashion which seems to reach its climax at St George's Chapel, Windsor, on the occasion of a state wedding. But there can be no doubt that a reasonable number of extra lights, and vases of cut flowers, tastefully arranged, are a very beautiful and appropriate decoration for the altar on festivals. The fault here, as in nearly all our modern art, is, that men will mistake means for ends : they forget that they are decking the altar, and think only of putting candles and flowers upon it, and consequently imagine that the more they put on the better they succeed. It would be well if every altar had a definite scheme for its decoration, which should be constantly adhered to, the choice of flowers alone being left to the discretion of the decorators. Although there is not much to be said from an archæological point of view for flowers as a decoration for the altar, they seem to possess an inherent or natural appropriateness, as being in honour of Him who is the Rose of Sharon and the Lily of the Valley, besides being an offering of the most lovely works of God's creation, and no practical or tangible reason has ever been urged against them. For the decoration of churches and altars W. A. Barrett's work, " Flowers and Festivals " (1868), will afford some useful hints, and two excellent papers by the Rev. H. L. (afterwards Bishop) Jenner, printed in *The Ecclesiologist*, December 1846 and March 1847, should certainly be consulted. The Rev. P. Dearmer ("Parson's Handbook," 4th ed. p. 97) has some sensible remarks on this subject, which are well worthy of perusal.

Foil. In architecture, a leaf-shaped form produced by adding cusps to the curved outline of a window-head or circle forming its tracery.

Font. The vessel which contains the consecrated water to be used in Holy Baptism. The font is generally placed near the west door to show that Baptism is the gate by which we enter into the fold of Christ's Church. Ancient fonts were always large enough to allow of the immersion of infants, the hollow basin usually being about a foot or rather more in depth, and from one and a half to two feet in diameter. The age of a church may frequently be told by means of its font. Churches in the Perpendicular style, but of original Norman foundation, frequently retain their Norman fonts, for when a church was rebuilt the font was, as a rule, scrupulously preserved. There are a few fonts of Norman date made of lead, but with such exceptions the common material for them is stone or marble lined with lead. The curious leaden font at Childrey Church, Berks, is figured in Lyson's " Magna Britannia," vol. i. Fonts should always be provided with a drain through which the water can be allowed to escape after use, and also with a cover. Of Norman fonts, among the finest examples are those at

Winchester and Lincoln cathedrals ; West Meon, Hants ; Fincham, Norfolk ; Newenden, Kent ; and Iffley, Oxon. By a constitution of Edmund, Archbishop of Canterbury, 1236, fonts were required to be covered and locked ; at that period the covers are likely, in general, to have been little more than flat movable lids, but they were afterwards often highly ornamented, and were sometimes carried up to a very considerable height in the form of spires, and enriched with a variety of little buttresses, pinnacles, and other decorations, as at Thaxted, Essex ; Ewelme, Oxon ; Sudbury (St Gregory's), Suffolk ; Fosdyke, Lincolnshire ; Ufford, Suffolk ; Ticehurst, Sussex ; and Walsingham, Norfolk. A beautiful German example is in the Church of St Catherine at Brandenburg. There is a fine modern example of a spiral font canopy at St Michael's Collegiate Church, Tenbury, where the north transept forms the baptistery. The ancient canopies were sometimes richly painted, gilt, and emblazoned. There are modern examples of such at Worcester Cathedral, and in the Church of St Alban, Holborn. The earlier Norman fonts were usually either round or square. Latterly they became octagonal, a form which was also very common in the Early English, and it is sometimes difficult to decide to which of these styles a font belongs, especially when devoid of ornament. Early English fonts were also very often circular, and sometimes square ; when of the latter form they are not unfrequently supported on a central stem, with four small shafts under the corners, as in the Norman, and of which there is an example at Shere, Surrey. In the Decorated and Perpendicular styles they are usually octagonal, but in all other respects the forms and the modes of adapting the stem and applying the ornaments vary to an extent which it is impossible to describe. At Heckington, Lincolnshire, and Rolvenden, Kent, there are fonts hexagonal in shape. Canterbury Cathedral possesses a beautiful font of Jacobean workmanship, which originally stood on the north side of the nave, as represented in the view in Dart's " Canterbury " (1726). In Dean Horne's time (1781–1790) it was relegated to the old lavatory, opening out of the north-east transept, but late in the last century it was restored to its proper place. It was presented in 1636 by Warner, Bishop of Rochester, at that time a prebendary of Canterbury, and consecrated by Bancroft, Bishop of Oxford. It is an admirable specimen of ecclesiastical art of a period when latent ideas of religious splendour were beginning to revive the works which had been wantonly destroyed by the early Reformers. On this account, therefore, it is not surprising to learn that it met with very rough usage at the hands of that " minister of God's Worde," Richard

ECCLESIASTICAL TERMS

Culmer, and his despicable crew during the Great Rebellion. Somner, the historian of Canterbury, "enquired with great diligence for all the scattered pieces, bought them up at his own charge, kept them safe till the King's return, and delivered them to that worthy Bishop, who re-edified his font, and made it a new beauty of holiness, giving Mr Somner the great honour to have a daughter of his first baptized in it." Ely Cathedral possessed an exquisite font of Later Renaissance workmanship, the money for the erection of which was willed by Dean Spencer in 1693. It was surmounted by a representation of the Baptism of Christ, above which hovered the Holy Dove. Until early in the last century it stood within the third bay on the south side of the nave, when it disappeared, its place being taken by a font in pseudo-Norman, totally uninteresting, cold, lifeless, and now standing in the south-west transept. Steps should be taken to recover the font of 1693, and replace it in its original position. It will be found finely engraved in Bentham's "History and Antiquities of the Church of Ely" (1771). The remarks of Precentor Millers, in his description of the Cathedral Church of Ely (1834). anent this font, and the "unsuitability" of its style, are not worthy of consideration for a single moment. Like a good many other people at that time the worthy precentor could not rid himself of the idea that everything else than "Gothic" was profane, being utterly without knowledge of the fact that excellent English Renaissance work is seen to lend itself to reverent and artistic treatment. This "Gothic" fever of the "twenties" and "thirties" resulted in the miserable organ-cases, choir-stalls, and other furniture with which certain of our cathedrals, and so many of our churches, were disfigured at this time—namely, just before the rise of the Ecclesiological Movement. The city churches built by Wren present us with many fine examples of fonts ; these are generally in marble, adorned with cherubim and other enrichments, some of them having small canopies of wood. Round that in the Church of St Martin, Ludgate, runs the palindromical inscription or anagram : NIΨON ANOMHMA MH MONAN OΨIN, which in English reads thus : "Wash the guilt, not the face only." Another reading is " Wash the whole body, not the face only." This inscription is also to be found on the font at Sandbach, Cheshire ; Harlow, Essex ; Dulwich College Chapel, and elsewhere. The font in Rufford Church, Lancashire, is mentioned by Jeremy Taylor as bearing this palindrome. On the *bénitier* in the church of the Petits Pères at Paris the Latin equivalent is given in addition, *Ablue peccata, non solum faciem.* The large plain font introduced by Wren into St Paul's Cathedral was moved some twelve years ago from its symbolical and proper position within the second bay on the south side of the nave, to the space vacated by the Wellington Monument in the south-west chapel, originally the Consistory Court. Since that portion of the building has been converted into the Chapel of the Order of St Michael and George the font has been moved to the western aisle of the south transept. The Gothic revival has given us some fonts of remarkable beauty, and originality of design. Those in the cathedrals of Lichfield and Llandaff, and Boston Church, Lincolnshire, are notable. The Church of St Mary, Stoke Newington, was equipped in 1858 by its architect, Sir G. G. Scott, with a circular font having figures of angels from the chisel of the younger Westmacott. That in the neighbouring Church of St Matthias—an octagonal bowl of black marble, supported on a stone cylinder, with four small shafts of serpentine grouped around it—was the gift of children attending the church. The design was entrusted by Mr Butterfield, the architect of the church, to Mr (afterwards the Rev. William) Lowder, brother of " Father " Lowder, of St Peter's, London Docks. Consult further, F. A. Paley's " Illustrations of Baptismal Fonts " (1844) ; Francis Bond's " Fonts and Font Covers." The celebrated brazen font in the Dom, Hildesheim, Hanover, is a splendid example of the occasional departure of the ancients from their usual practice of employing stone in the construction of this *instrumentum*. Even wood has been employed, but less often than metal. The rule of the Church does not prescribe stone, but only that the material shall be suitable for the purpose. The font must be made *de lapide vel de aliâ materiâ congruâ et honestâ videlicet quae sit* SOLIDA, DURABILIS *et* FORTIS, *ac acquae infusae* RETENTIVA. There is one instance of a font made entirely of wood ; this is at St Michael's Evenechtyd, in Denbighshire. It is hewn out of a solid block. In England there are several of lead. In Westphalia, Hanover, and other parts of Northern Europe, bronze fonts are comparatively common. Fine specimens are to be found at Frankfort-on-the-Oder, Münster, Brunswick, Wurtzburg, Halberstadt, Liége, Brussels, Louvain and Hal. The finest of all is unquestionably the one at Hildesheim, dating *c.* 1260. It is fully described by T. Francis Bumpus in his " Cathedrals and Churches of the Rhine and North Germany " (pp. 260–262) ; while T. H. King in his " Study-Book of Mediæval Architecture," vol. ii. (1857), devotes four plates to its illustration. In the Stadtkirche at Wittenberg, Saxony, is another remarkable font of bronze, the work of Hermann Visscher, 1557. It is admirably figured by L. Puttrich in his " Denkmale der Bau-

ECCLESIASTICAL TERMS

kunst des Mittelalters in Sachsen," vol. ii. (1844). The same writer also figures and describes the fine octagonal stone font in the Church of St Severus at Erfurt, which has a lofty spiral canopy of rich tabernacle work, thirty feet high, sustaining a figure of the Virgin and Child. It is a remarkable example of interpenetration or stump tracery, and dates from 1467. The beautiful spiral font canopy at Durham, erected by Cosin, soon after his elevation to the see in 1660, coeval with the choir-stalls, and curious from its admixture of Gothic and Renaissance detail, replaced a cover "opening like a four-quartered globe, with St John baptizing our Saviour, and the four Evangelists curiously done and richly painted within the globe, all about so artificially wrought and carved with such variety of joyner's work as makes all the beholders thereof to admire" (Raine's "Guide to Durham," p. 15). This canopy was destroyed (together with the ancient choir-stalls erected in the fifteenth century by Prior Wessington) by the Scots during their imprisonment in the cathedral after the battle of Dunbar in 1650. The designer of Bishop Cosin's canopy and stall-work was James Clement, a Durhamian. Unfortunately much of his work (including the stately organ-screen and returned stalls) was destroyed or mutilated in 1847, when a redistribution of the choral fittings took place under Anthony Salvin, the architect employed by Dean Waddington and his chapter, and who, a few years later, was let loose upon Wells Cathedral, where, perhaps, he did still greater mischief. Bishop Cosin's fine canopy at Durham was cast aside by Salvin, who put up a pseudo-Norman font of his own, replacing the handsome white marble basin erected in 1663. However, in the course of some ameliorations (1870–1876) under the direction of Mr C. Hodgson Fowler, the present distinguished surveyor to the fabric, when, as far as circumstances would permit, the interesting post-Restoration choral fittings were brought back to their original state, the canopy was replaced in its former position at the western end of the nave, where it may still be seen. At Billingham Church, Co. Durham, the Early English font has a tall richly carved Elizabethan cover. It is figured in R. W. Billings' "Architecture of the County of Durham," 1846. The Norman font of Beverley Minster has a good canopy of Renaissance work, adorned with cherubim, foliage, etc., and at its summit is the Holy Dove. Camille Enlart ("Manuel d'Archéologie Française," 1902) figures fine examples of baptismal fonts at Lanmeur (Finisterre) ; at Vermand (Aisne), early twelfth century ; at Nogent-l'Artaud (Seine-et Marne), middle of thirteenth century ; and at Escœuilles (Pas-de-

Calais), fifteenth century. All these, being of early date, have no canopies. Enlart also gives specimens of the *bénitier*, or holy-water stoup, at Brantôme (Dordogne) ; at Nôtre Dame, Châlons-sur-Marne, middle of twelfth century ; at Mézières (Ardennes), in marble ; and at Saint-Jean-aux Bois (Oise), *c.* 1200. Font canopies are either suspended from the roof by a counterweight, or a portion of the tabernacle work is made to open on the side. Pugin's fonts in his churches, St Mary's, Derby ; St Chad's, Birmingham, and St Giles's, Cheadle, have canopies copied from ancient examples. The statement, on page 133, that the font in St Paul's was designed by Wren, is found to be incorrect. It was the work of Francis Bird, who executed much carving for Wren. In the " Items of Expenditure " it is called the " new marble font," and £354, 13s. 10d. was paid for it on 31st December 1726. Wren had then been dead three years. It originally had a cover which has, for some years, been removed, and which is now preserved in the crypt. This font was either an afterthought, or it may have taken the place of a temporary one, if the word " new " in the Items of Expenditure is to be taken in its literal sense. Until 2nd February 1875 the font in St Paul's had never been used. On that day, Bishop Claughton (Canon-in-Residence) baptised in it his grandchild, Francis William Douglas (Dr Simpson's " Miscellaneous [MS.] Notes on St Paul's," in the Cathedral Library). Since that time the Sacrament of Baptism has been administered frequently in St Paul's. Fonts unprovided with canopies should always have a wooden cover secured by a lock, to prevent the baptismal water, and indeed the whole interior when empty, from profanation. Some sad cases have occurred from lack of this precaution.

Fratery, or Frater-house. The refectory or hall of a monastic establishment. The fine Perpendicular fratery of Carlisle Cathedral, restored by G. E. Street in 1880, is now used as a chapter-house and library.

Friday. This day of the week was, both in the Greek Church and Latin, a litany or humiliation day, in memory of our Lord's Passion : and is so kept in ours. It is set apart as our weekly fast for our share in the death of Christ, and its gloom is only dispersed if Christmas Day happens to fall thereon. As Friday is a weekly memorial of our Lord's Death, so Sunday is set apart as a weekly memorial of His Resurrection. In many of our cathedrals it has long been the custom for the organ to be silent throughout Friday in non-festal seasons. The choral services thus performed at St Paul's and Westminster Abbey are very solemn and

ECCLESIASTICAL TERMS

affecting, and on these occasions some of the greatest masterpieces of choral music, in the shape of services and anthems, are to be heard.

A word the literal meaning of which signifies " the seat of peace."

Frith-stool, or Freed-stool. The frith-stool was a seat or chair, generally of stone, placed near the altar in some of our old churches, and was, when perilous times rendered it absolutely necessary, considered the last and most sacred refuge for those who claimed the privilege of sanctuary within it, and for the violation of which the severest punishment was inflicted. Examples exist at Hexham Abbey, Northumberland, and Beverley Minster, Yorks. Knockers on church doors have frequently served the purpose of a frith-stool, and, as an instance, when Durham Cathedral enjoyed the right of being a sanctuary, anyone flying for protection, and laying hold of the knocker on the north door of the cathedral, was accounted safe. A knocker, probably used for this purpose, is still extant on the west door of Noyon Cathedral, France.

Frontal. Lat. antependium. The covering for the front of an altar. This should always be used, because it is ordered in the 82nd Canon of 1603. Altars with carved or painted fronts are of very modern introduction in this country,; they are not such " as were in this Church of England in the second year of King Edward the Sixth," and the best of them are far less decent than properly, though it be plainly, vested altars. The frontal should cover only the front of the altar, for there is a rule of old standing, and a very good one, that there is nothing on the top except white linen. Nevertheless, a super-frontal is almost invariably used. Good taste, and the literal obedience to the rubric, equally require that the frontal shall be hung freely, and not be nailed to a rod or stretched on a frame. The colour, of course, would vary, according to the sequence observed. Abroad we meet with frontals of three kinds : (1) of precious metals, adorned with enamels and gold ; (2) of wood —painted, gilt, embossed, and sometimes set with crystals ; (3) of cloth-of-gold, velvet, or silk, embroidered, and occasionally enriched with pearls. Of frontals in precious metals there is an example, dated 1019, in the Musée de Cluny, Paris, which was formerly at Basle. Another is in the Church of San Ambrogio at Milan. In the Chapel of St James, in the Duomo of Pistoja, is a magnificent specimen, dated 1316, with wings dated respectively 1347 and 1361. The whole is of silver, the frontal measuring 6 ft. 7 ins., and the sides

3 ft. 5 ins., all by 3 ft. 6 ins. high.   Major Heales, **F.S.A.**, in a paper,
" The Adjuncts, Furniture and Ornaments of the Altar," read before
the St Paul's Ecclesiological Society, 17th March 1881, cites examples of magnificent frontals at Monza Cathedral, St Mark's,
Venice, Salerno Cathedral, Tournay Cathedral, St Patroclus, Söest,
etc.   In a chapel out of the cloister of Sta Maria Novella, Florence
(built 1325), is one which the Rev. Benjamin Webb (" Continental
Ecclesiology," p. 328) considered the most beautiful he had ever seen,
On cloth-of-gold is embroidered the Coronation of the Blessed Virgin,
and on either side six apostles under canopies, the super-frontal
also being embroidered in subjects.   Very little research would be
needed to refer to glorious frontals of gold and silver enriched with
precious gems and enamels, formerly existing in this as well as other
countries.   The changes of sentiment which took possession of
Europe in the middle of the sixteenth century led to the destruction
of most of them, and the barbarous taste of the Renaissance period,
and the still viler and more barbarous perceptions of the eighteenth
century, caused yet greater destruction ;   and one cannot wonder
that frontals dating earlier than the sixteenth century are extremely
rare.   Good old vestments, such as copes and chasubles, are scarce,
(especially if unmutilated), though examples may be found in the
treasuries of many cathedrals in France and Germany ; but frontals
are much rarer.   The number which the cathedrals and larger
churches possessed was very great : at Salisbury there were some
fifty, and at Durham there would appear to have been seventy-two.
Many frontals are described in the Inventory of St Paul's, 1552.
One is described as " a hanginge of blewe silke with the Crucifix,
Mary and John in the myddes, goodlye wroughte " ;   another as
" an hanginge of redd and pretie bawdkin with a Crucifix Mary and
John with flowers " ;   a third as " a fronte richelie sett with perells
with the Sonn and the Moone and thedds of the twelve Apostells " ;
a fourth as " an hanginge of white damaske powderedd, with the
holye gost richelie made with nedellworke in the myddes with
curetines of white Sarcenett."   But this " Inventarie of the Plate,
Jewells, Copes, Vestments, Tunacles, Albes, Bells, and other Ornaments appertayninge to the Cathedral Church of Sayncte Paul in
London in 1552," signed by the truly " reforming," Dean May, and
the three residentiaries William Ermsysted, Gabriel Dunne, and
Gilbert Bourne, all seized and sold by the King's Commissioners,
is sad reading.   Many of these frontals, as well as copes, after
having been sold and dispersed, found their way into private
houses, where they were used as table-cloths and coverings for beds !

ECCLESIASTICAL TERMS

At the parish church of Chipping Barnet, the Edwardian Commissioners found " xj alter clothes, bettar and worse " : of which they left for the church (with unusual liberality) two of the best and two of the worst. In England, the frontal was one of those things which it was the duty of the parishioners to provide for the celebration of divine worship, as specified in the Canons and Constitutions of the Archdioceses of Canterbury and York in 1250, 1281, and 1305. At the coronation of Queen Victoria, 28th June 1838, following the ancient practice, she, being at the steps of the altar, made her first oblation, which was a pall or altar-cloth of gold, delivered by an officer of the wardrobe to the Lord Chamberlain, and by him, kneeling, to her Majesty; the pall to be reverently laid by the Archbishop upon the altar. Many of our churches now possess superb sets of frontals, In certain cases these have been designed by distinguished architects, such as Street and Bodley. Perhaps one of the most elaborate frontals worked in modern times is that used at St Paul's on the great festivals of the Church. The design, by Mr John Medland, F.R.I.B.A., is in thorough keeping with the architecture of the cathedral. Ir consists of three large panels, the centre one containing a representation of Our Lord in glory, seated on a rainbow and surrounded by adoring angels. The subject of the panel on the left is the Martyrdom of St Stephen, with the figure of St Paul standing conspicuously forward as a witness consenting to his death. The right-hand panel shows the Apostle in fetters preaching before Agrippa and Bernice. The spaces between these subjects are occupied by large figures of the four archangels standing under canopies, and bearing their emblems—St Michael, for instance, being clad in armour and weighing souls. The super-frontal is embroidered with half figures of adoring angels, with some beautiful scrollwork, in crimson embroidery, dividing one group from the other. The whole work is 11 ft. in length, and is in solid embroidery, in the stitches used in the ancient Church needlework. This frontal, the gift of Miss Noyes, was executed at the East Grinstead School of Embroidery. It was first used on Trinity Sunday, 1888. The red and gold frontal in use at the same cathedral on the Feasts of Martyrs and at the Feast of Pentecost was designed by the late Mr G. F. Bodley about the year 1863. Another very beautiful frontal in St Paul's is that used at certain seasons for the altar in the North-West, or St Dunstan's, Chapel. It is woven throughout of rich silk damask of Sarum blue, into which are brocaded various symbolic devices. The central piece consists of a wreath of thorns encircling a pelican tearing her breast for her young, around whom she stretches her

A DICTIONARY OF

protecting wings. Within the circle are the words : IHΣOUΣ XPΣ. The orphreys are composed of the eucharistic symbols of the vine and wheat. The super-frontal is rich in symbols of the four states of Life, Birth, Death, and Resurrection. Life is shown as the pelican giving her life for her young.; Birth by the Holy Dove hovering between the heavens and the waters ; Death by the fish, that symbol of Christ that marked the resting-place of early Christians ; and Resurrection by the Lamb triumphant, supporting the Cross, and surrounded by Easter blossoms, while rays of light stream forth from a sun, in the centre of which is shown a chalice. Many other symbols are also to be found in it, as no ornament has been introduced which is not fraught with some religious meaning. This frontal was designed by Mr Edmund Hunter, and executed at his weaving works at Haslemere. In 1863 Mr G. E. Street read a valuable paper on Mediæval Embroidery before the Durham Architectural Society, which was printed in *The Ecclesiologist* (New Series, No. cxxii.). It is deserving of the most careful study, for he was an authority of high repute on the subject. He cites examples of several magnificent mediæval altar-frontals at Berne, and one at the Collegiate Church at Manresa in Catalonia, 10 ft. 9 ins. in length, which, he opined, was the most exquisite work of its age (*c.* A.D. 1400).

A composition for voices, or instruments, in which one part, beginning with a short melody, called the Subject, is followed in succession by the other parts with the same melody, then called the Answer, and in the same intervals. It thus resembles, as it were, a flight or pursuit. Fugue differs from canon only in being less rigid in its construction. In each, the leading part gives the law to the rest, but in the course of a fugue it is allowable to introduce episodes and new subjects, which are excluded from canon, this latter being, in its nature, a *perpetual* fugue. A fugue is generally brought to a close by a pedal-point and coda. Many of the anthems and other choral works of our cathedral writers contain fugues of great ingenuity and learning. The great organ fugues of J. Sebastian Bach continue to excite our wonder and admiration the oftener we hear them interpreted by our most eminent performers. Certain of our old cathedral organists were adepts in the playing of extemporaneous fugues on given subjects—*e.g.* Dr J. C. Beckwith (Norwich, 1808–1809), John M. W. Young (Lincoln, 1850–1895), Dr S. S. Wesley (successively of Hereford and Exeter Cathedrals, Leeds Parish Church, Winchester and Gloucester Cathedrals (d. 1876), and Dr G. B. Arnold (Winchester, 1865–1902). Professor T. A. Walmisley, Sir

Fugue.
Lat. *fuga,*
"a flight."

ECCLESIASTICAL TERMS

Herbert Oakeley, Sir Robert Stewart, and Sir Frederick Ouseley, were highly accomplished extempore fuguists. The art seems now almost a lost one. Consult Cherubini, "Course of Counterpoint and Fugue" (1837) ; R. L. de Pearsall, "Analysis of a Fugue" (1849) ; Jas. Higgs, "Fugue" (1878) ; Ouseley, "Treatise on Counterpoint, Canon, and Fugue" (1869) ; Prout, "Fugue and Fugal Analysis."

Full Anthem. An anthem in which there is neither solo nor verse. We have, in our cathedral music, a very large repertory of such anthems by composers of all schools from the Reformation to the present day. Many of the choruses from the verse and solo anthems of Croft, Greene, Boyce, and others make excellent short full anthems for morning use in cathedrals.

Full Service. A setting of the morning and evening canticles, designed to be sung antiphonally throughout by all the voices on the *Decani* and *Cantoris* sides of the choir, with occasional passages marked "Full," in which both sides are to join. Such services have no verse or solo portions. Most of the earlier services are in this style, one brought to perfection by Dr Boyce (1760) in his settings of the *Te Deum* and *Jubilate* in the major keys of A and C. The same composer's "Verse Service" in A is a model of that species of writing.

Galilee. A porch or chapel at the entrance of a church. The term also appears sometimes to be applied to the nave, or at least to the western portion of it, and in some churches there are indications of the west end of the nave having been parted off from the rest, either by a step in the floor, a division in the architecture, or some other line of demarcation. The Galilee porch is traditionally supposed to be connected with some purposes of discipline, and to have borrowed its name from the words of the angel at the sepulchre to the women, "Go your way, tell his disciples and Peter that he goeth before you into Galilee : there shall ye see him, as he said unto you" (St Mark xvi. 7). The Galilee at Lincoln Cathedral is a porch on the west side of the south-west transept. At Ely it is a porch at the west end of the nave. At Durham a large chapel projecting from the west front is called the Galilee. The name is thus accounted for by Precentor Millers in his "Description of the Cathedral Church of Ely" (1834) : "As Galilee, bordering on the Gentiles, was the most remote part of the Holy Land from the holy city of Jerusalem, so was this part of the building, most distant from the sanctuary, occupied by those unhappy persons, who, during their exclusion from the mysteries, were reputed scarcely, if at all, better than heathens." St Stephen's

Chapel, Westminster, formerly had a Galilee—a kind of vestibule or ante-chapel at the west end. The great narthexes or open porches in France, such as those at Autun, Beaune, Nôtre Dame at Dijon, Paray le Monial, Tournus, and Vezelay, correspond in some measure with our Galilee. One of the finest was at the Abbey Church of Cluny, destroyed early in the last century. In Italy, one of the most wonderful of these narthexes is that of the cathedral at Casale Monferrato. Consult T. F. Bumpus, "Glories of France" (1901), and "Cathedrals and Churches of Northern Italy" (1907). James Wyatt, during his devastations at Durham in 1796, had actually stripped the lead off the Galilee, designing to make on the site a carriage-way for the prebendaries to drive straight to their houses, when, most opportunely, the Dean (Lord Cornwallis), who had driven in all haste from Lichfield, opposed. Dean Cornwallis has had the credit of saving the Galilee, but it was through John Carter, the antiquary and architectural draughtsman, having drawn attention to the contemplated destruction of that building at a meeting of the Society of Antiquaries that the Dean, who had sanctioned the removal, became alarmed by the expression of opinion against the scheme and stopped it. In 1828 the Galilee was only redeemed from being a lumber-room, to provide for Sunday evening services from Easter to Michaelmas.

Gargoyle, or Gurgoyle. A projecting spout used in Gothic architecture to throw the water from the gutter of a building off the wall. Sometimes they are perfectly plain, but are oftener carved into figures or animals, which are frequently grotesque. These are very commonly represented with open mouths, from which the water issues, but in many cases it is conveyed through a leaden spout, either above or below the stone figure. Excellent examples are at Merton College Chapel, Oxford, *c.* 1277. See the woodcut in Parker's "Hand-book for Visitors to Oxford" (1858), p. 44.

Garth. See *sub voce* "Cloister-garth."

Gentleman of the Chapel Royal. The term for an adult singer in the Chapel Royal, St James's Palace, the office corresponding with that of lay vicar or lay clerk in cathedral and collegiate foundations. In the early part of the reign of Henry VIII. the gentlemen of the Chapel Royal were thirty-two in number. In 1800 there were sixteen. The number is now reduced to nine. One of them has usually held the post of Master of the Children. Their dress in chapel is a surplice and a scarlet cassock. Their attendance is technically termed "waiting." The senior gentleman was formerly known as "Father of the Chapel Royal," and, by a not very laudable custom, was excused attendance. At the coronation of James II., 23rd April 1685, Dr Child, then one of the organists of the chapel, walked in the procession as "Father," wearing his academical robes. He was then in his seventy-ninth year.

Geometrical Decorated. The earlier phase of the Complete Gothic period as distinguished from the Later or "Flowing" one. It refers more particularly to window tracery.

"Glory be to God on high." One of the doxologies of the Church, sometimes called the Angelic Hymn, because the first part of it was sung by the angels at the birth of Our Lord.

Gloria in Excelsis. This first part is found in the Liturgies of St James and St Chrysostom. The latter portion is ascribed to Telesphorus, Bishop of Rome, c. A.D. 137 ; though there is no evidence that he did more than order its use in the Liturgy, if even that. It is used by both the Greek and Latin Church, but in the former, except among the Nestorians, as part of a morning canticle, not in the Holy Eucharist. In the Roman Mass it follows the *Kyrie Eleison* at the beginning of the service. The First Prayer-Book of Edward VI. retained it in the same position, but at the revision of the book in 1552 it was removed to its present, and far more appropriate, place at the end of the service. When choral Communion was abolished, not long after the Reformation, the *Gloria* dropped out of use as part of a "Service," the only music provided being that for the *Kyrie* and *Credo*. Its revival amongst us is due to the re-establishment of choral Celebrations at the time of the Oxford Movement, and its setting is now, of course, general. There are, however, a few detached examples (sometimes with the *Sanctus*) to be found among the works of Child, Blow, Humphreys, Dean Aldrich, Rev. Tobias Langdon, Jeremiah Clark, Weldon, Croft, and Charles King—a period ranging from the Restoration to the year 1748. During the later Tudor and early Stuart periods it was the custom to have a second anthem after the sermon in the morning service. Bishop Andrewes, in a sermon preached before James I. at Whitehall on Christmas Day, 1610, speaks of the angel's sermon, and after that the hymn " Glory be to God on high." The circumstance of the existence of some settings of the *Gloria in Excelsis* by John Amner, Edmund Hooper, Henry Loosemore, Thomas Tomkins, and a few others of the period, point to the possibility of the hymn being sung, as a second anthem, after the sermon, instead of in its proper place in the Holy Eucharist, of which the sermon is only a part. The complete Services of Thomas Tallis (early post-Reformation) and Adrian Batten (c. 1620) contain the whole of the Communion hymns. It is also noted at full length by Merbecke in his musical edition of Edward VI.'s First Book. With these exceptions the remarks already made on musical settings of the *Credo* will apply equally to the *Gloria in Excelsis*. Consult J. S. Bumpus, " Music of the Litany and Holy Communion," a series of papers contributed to *Musical News*, 2nd March, 27th April, 4th, 11th, 18th, 25th May, 1st June 1901. The *Gloria in Excelsis* invariably closes the Latin service held at St Paul's on the opening of a new Convocation. On the last occasion the setting in Byrd's five-part Mass was used. Until sixty years ago our repertory of English Church music was not so rich as it ought to have been in music for the entire service of the Holy Communion, though the pious and skilful labours of the Rev. Sir F. A. Gore Ouseley led the way in diminishing this lack, so emphatically a reproach to the past apathy of our Church on the subject. Out of thirteen cathedral Services in Dr Boyce's famous collection only *one*—that by our earliest post-Reformation composer, Tallis—has any music provided for the *Gloria in Excelsis*. Three of these were supplemented in the collection published by Sir Frederick Ouseley in 1853—" Cathedral Services by English Masters " —viz. *Aldrich in G*, by a *Gloria in Excelsis* from the pen of the same composer, the famous Dean of Christ Church, Oxford, musician, architect and logician ; *Gibbons in F*, by one cleverly arranged from other parts of the same Service by John Foster, then organist of St Andrew's, Wells Street ; while a third, *Rogers in D*, is supplied with a composition in excellent keeping with the rest of the Service by Sir Frederick Ouseley himself. Seven of Ouseley's own Services are provided with music for this hymn—namely, those in A major, B minor, C major (double choir), C major (4 voices), E major, E flat and F major, and they were among the first by a modern composer to be so provided. The present writer possesses a *Gloria in Excelsis* in completion of Dr Nares's well-known Service in F. It is arranged from portions of the Morning Service, but on the printed score the names of arranger and publisher are not stated. Dr Langdon Colborne, organist of Hereford Cathedral (1877–1889), arranged a *Gloria* to complete S. S. Wesley's Communion Service in E, adapting it to certain passages in the *Te Deum* belonging to the same Service. This has not been printed. For the history and theology of the *Gloria in Excelsis* consult an admirable article in *The Church Quarterly Review*, No. xli. (October 1885).

Good Friday. The day annually set apart to commemorate the death of Our Lord. It received its name from the blessed effects of our Saviour's sufferings, in obtaining eternal redemption for us. It has been observed from the first ages of Christianity; and in every church the history of Christ's Passion was read. This is fitly taken from St John's Gospel, because he was present at the Crucifixion; and from his example we may learn not to be ashamed or afraid of the Cross of Christ. "The Epistle," says Procter ("Book of Common Prayer"), "shows the insufficiency of Jewish sacrifices, and urges that they typified the one oblation of the Saviour, who made full satisfaction for the sins of the whole world: the collects contain expressions of boundless charity, praying that the effects of His death may be as universal as the design of it." The proper Psalms were selected at the last revision: they were all composed for times of great distress, and most of them belong mystically to the sufferings of our Saviour; especially the 22nd, of which several passages were literally fulfilled by the events of the Crucifixion. All, except the 69th, had occurred in the ancient Matin offices. The first Morning Lesson relates Abraham's readiness to offer up his son Isaac, which has always been regarded as a type of the sacrifice of the Son of God: and the first Evening Lesson contains the clearest prophecy of that sacrifice. The "Three Hours' Agony," a devotion now almost universallyobserved on Good Friday, is not a liturgical service, but arose from the need of an exercise to enable the faithful to spend the actual hours during which the Lord of Glory hung on the Cross in devout meditation and prayer. Such devotions are common on the Continent, and are expressly provided for in Edward VI.'s Acts of Uniformity, " provided they do not let or hinder the course of public worship." The order of this service is as follows:—Matins having been sung at 9 A.M., at which hour it is believed that the scourging at the pillar took place, and the altar service and " Reproaches " (q.v.) being concluded about noon, when He was nailed to the Cross, the clergyman who is to conduct the devotion ascends the pulpit, and begins by a collect, or the invocation of the Blessed Trinity. The prayers and hymns that follow are intermingled with short addresses on the Seven Words spoken by our Lord from the Cross, and are so arranged as to keep the mind fixed without weariness on His agony and death, and to conclude at 3 P.M., at which hour He gave up the ghost. That divine composition of Haydn " The Last Words of the Redeemer," or " Passion," had its origin in the devotion of the Three Hours. In the preface to the full score of the work, published by Breitkopf and Härtel at Leipzig in 1801, the great composer himself observes: " It is about fifteen years ago, since I was applied to by a clergyman in Cadiz, who requested me to write instrumental music to the Seven Words of Jesus on the Cross. It was then customary every year during Lent to perform an oratorio in the Cathedral at Cadiz, the effect of which the following arrangements contributed not a little to heighten. The walls, windows, and columns of the church were hung with black cloth, and only one large lamp hanging in the centre, lighted the solemn and religious gloom. At noon all the doors were closed, and the music began. After a prelude suited to the occasion, the Bishop ascended the pulpit, pronounced one of the Seven Words, which was succeeded by reflections upon it. As soon as these were finished, he descended from the pulpit, and fell on his knees before the altar. This pause was filled by music. The Bishop ascended and descended again a second, a third time, and so on, and each time the orchestra filled up the intervals in the discourse. My composition must be judged on a consideration of these circumstances. The task of writing seven *Adagios*, each of which was to last about ten minutes, to preserve a connection between them, without wearying the hearers, was none of the lightest ; and I soon found that I could not confine myself within the limits of the time prescribed. The music was originally without text and was printed in that form. It was only at a later period that I was induced to annex the [Latin and Italian] text." It is said that Haydn considered this " the very best of all his works." There is more than one English adaptation of the Italian text. That published with Novello's octavo edition is by the Rev. H. Clementi-Smith, sometime precentor of Manchester Cathedral. The work concludes with a representation of the earthquake (Il Terremoto " L'Uom Dio morì "). It should be observed that the name " Good Friday " is peculiar to the Church of England. In France the day is called " Vendredi Saint " ; in Germany, " Der Charfreytag." In the Breviary the heading for the day's offices is " Feria VI. in Parasceve." Holy Friday, or Friday in Holy Week, was its most general appellation : also παρασκευή—ἡμέρα τοῦ σταυροῦ —*dies dominicæ passionis*—σωτηρία—*dies absolutionis*. Among the rites practised in England on Good Friday was the ceremony of blessing cramp-rings by the king, which were supposed to prevent the falling-sickness. The form used on these occasions is printed in Maskell's " Monumenta Ritualia Ecclesiæ Anglicanæ," iii. pp. 335 *sqq*.

The custom of singing an ascription of praise before and after the reading of the Gospel in the Holy Communion is one derived from the Sarum Missal. This ascription was enjoined by Edward VI.'s First Prayer-Book ; and, though the rubric directing it has been twice

Gospel Doxology and Thanksgiving.

omitted, yet the custom has been maintained, and, in such a case, as Dr Bisse observes, " the voice of custom is the voice of law " (" Rationale on Cathedral Worship or Choir Service," 1720). In 1873, Convocation agreed to recommend the reinsertion of the rubric. The use of these ascriptions was enjoined in Laud's Scottish Liturgy of 1637. The direction in the Prayer-Book of 1549 runs thus : " Immediately after the Epistle ended, the priest, or one appoynted to reade the Gospell, shall saie, *The holy Gospel written in the   Chapter of*   . The clearkes and people shall answere GLORY BE TO THEE, O LORDE." It subsequently became the custom to sing a similar ascription when the Gospel was concluded, the form being *Thanks be to Thee, O Lord*, or *Thanks be to Thee, O Lord, for this Thy Holy Gospel*. Merbecke provided no music for this ascription, but Lowe (" Short Directions," etc., 1661) says : " When the Epistle is done and the Gospell named, the Quire sings, *Glory be to thee, O Lord*, as is here set down." In the " Review " of his " Short Directions " (1664), the same authority observes : " When the Epistle is done and the Gospell named, the quire sings, *Glory be to Thee, O Lord*, either of the two formes here set downe ; which will serve to the Key of any Service, as the Organist shall apply it." This evidently intimates that the Ascription was to be transposed into the key of the Service used. The two forms are given in four-part harmony. The first is in monotone ; the second an adaptation of the chant as printed by Boyce and others for the Athanasian Creed in their editions of Tallis's Service. The same directions were given by Playford in 1674. Clifford, in the matter prefatory to his anthem-book of 1664, says : " After the Epistle the heavenly ejaculation, *Glory be to Thee, O Lord*." Soon after the Restoration it became the custom with composers to set this ascription to their own music. We find it so treated in the Services, Rogers in D, E minor, F and G ; Bryan in G ; Ferrabosco in A minor, D minor and E minor ; Loosemore in D minor ; W. King in B flat ; Portman in F ; Ramsey in F ; Hawkins in A and G. Some of these Services are unpublished. We do not meet with it in any of the Services of Child, Humphreys, Blow, Purcell, Aldrich, Wise, Creyghton, Croft, King, or Travers, but later on in the Georgian period its setting appears to have been revived, and we find it in the Services of W. Hayes in E flat, P. Hayes in F, Highmore Skeats in C, Jackson of Exeter in C, E, E flat, and F, and Clarke Whitfeld in E. It also occurs in the Cathedral Service by Sir John Rogers which appeared in 1839, as well as in that by J. L. Hatton, 1855. Nearly all the principal Services composed during the last forty years contain not only the *Gloria Tibi* before, but also the *Gratias Tibi* after, the reading of the Gospel, and set, like the earlier examples, to original music. The tendency, however, at the present day, is to use the form given by Lowe, and as provided in the "Cathedral Prayer-Book" and other modern choral manuals. The late Gerard F. Cobb, in the preface to his Service in G (Novello, 1883), offers some remarks on these ascriptions, which are well worth reading. There is extant a somewhat elaborate setting by Thomas Attwood, in the key of A, of the words "Thanks be to Thee, O Lord, for this Thy Holy Gospel." It was composed expressly for St Paul's (of which cathedral Attwood was organist) about 1825, and was, for many years afterwards constantly sung there. Goss, Attwood's pupil and his successor at St Paul's, set the same words, but in a less extended and elaborate form. His music will be found in Mercer's "Church Psalter and Hymn-Book." In the Roman Missal the ascription "Gloria Tibi, Domine" is sung after the Gospel is named. In the Greek Liturgy, the form is Δόξα σοι, κύριε, δόξα σοι.

Gradual. The term for the few verses of Holy Scripture sung at High Mass after the reading of the Epistle. It is followed by the *Alleluia* with its verse, or in penitential seasons by the *Tract*. On certain occasions the *Sequence* (*q.v.*) is sung after the *Alleluia* or *Tract*. These liturgical chants (*Gradual* and *Alleluia*) are both of considerable antiquity. The book containing these pieces of music was called the Gradale or Graduale ; which term was afterwards extended, and included the introit, tract, offertorium, and Communion. It is to be distinguished from the Antiphoner, the latter belonging to the service of the Hours, the former to the Mass.

Grill. A high open fence, or railing, of metal, in any part of a church. There are ancient examples of various dates at Amiens Cathedral, Sens Cathedral, St Ouen, Rouen (French) ; the cathedrals of Burgos, Seville, and Toledo (Spanish) ; the cathedrals of Orvieto and Perugia, the Certosa at Pavia, and the Chapel of the Palazza Publico, Siena (Italian) ; Lincoln Cathedral, St Paul's Cathedral ; St Editha, Tamworth ; St Mary Redcliffe, Bristol ; All Saints', Derby ; Chichester Cathedral ; St Alban's, Holborn ; St Andrew's, Wells Street ; St Michael's College, Tenbury ; Christ Church Cathedral, Dublin—the five last modern. Those who visit the Abbey of St Ived at Braisne, near Soissons, a characteristic specimen of the purest French Gothic, should not fail to observe the fine specimen of wrought-iron railing, coeval with the church, 1216. Details are figured by T. H. King in his "Study

ECCLESIASTICAL TERMS

Book of Mediæval Architecture and Art," vol. i. Pl. VI. (1857). Puttrich ("Denkmale der Baukunst des Mittelalters in Sachsen," 1844) engraves the notable grill between the nave and the choii of the Dom at Erfurt, as well as some other examples in the Marien-Kirche at Mühlhausen. At Ulm, the ironwork round the font and at the entrance of the choir is very fine. Details are figured by King in his "Study-Book," vol. iv.

Grisaille. A term applied to that kind of stained glass in which geometrical or floral patterns are employed in lieu of single figures or groups, and the tone of which is, or should be, a greyish-white. The "Five Sisters" window in the north transept of York Minster is a fine example. There are some remains at Salisbury Cathedral. The introduction of *grisaille* was one of the beauties of the Early English style.

Groin. In architecture, the curved line made by the meeting of the surfaces of two vaults, or portions of vaults, which intersect. The "Groining-rib" is a bar of masonry or moulding, projecting beyond the general surface of a vault, to mark its intersection, or subdivide its surface, and to add strength.

Hagioscope. From the Greek ἅγιος, sacred, holy, and σκοπη, a view. Frequently and more familiarly termed a "squint." An opening through the wall of a church in an oblique direction, for the purpose of enabling persons in the transepts or aisles to see the Elevation of the Host at the high altar. The usual situations of these openings is on one or both sides of the chancel arch, and there is frequently a projection, like a low buttress, on the outside across the angle to cover this opening. These openings are common enough in England, though they have been often plastered over, or sometimes boarded at the two ends; in other cases filled up with bricks. Examples: Mayor's Chapel, Bristol; Haseley, Oxon; Minster Lovell, Oxon; Chipping Norton, Oxon; Fifield, Oxon; St John's, Winchester; Bridgewater, Somerset, where there is a series of these openings through three successive walls, following the same oblique line, to enable a person standing in the porch to see the high altar; West Pennard, Somersetshire; Little Malvern, Worcestershire. In the neighbourhood of Tenby, South Wales, they are particularly abundant. In the case of Bridgewater Church it seems to have been for the use of the attendant who had to ring the sanctus-bell at the time of the Elevation of the Host.

Hall Church. One in which the aisles are uniform in height with the nave; an unclerestoried church on a very

149

A DICTIONARY OF

lofty scale, a type almost exclusively German. Examples: St Mary-in-the-Meadows, Söest; St Elizabeth's, Marburg; Paderborn Cathedral.

A name taken from the monastery to denote the priest for the *week* (ἑβδομα) who sang the daily High Mass and began the Hours.

Hebdoma-darius, or Septanéer. In old St Paul's this was the duty of each of the twelve minor canons in weekly rotation. The word " Hebdomadarius " is still inscribed on the Book of Common Prayer used by the minor canon chanting the service. He was also known as the " Reader." At Lichfield, one of the four priest vicars on weekly duty as chanter is still called "Hebdomadary Priest." At Louvaine the treasurer was perpetual hebdomadary. At Hereford he gave leave of absence to vicars. The hebdomadary inflicted discipline on the bare back of a delinquent deacon or sub-deacon; a priest had to ask pardon on the morrow in chapter. Edward Phillips in his " New World of Words, or a General Dictionary " (1658) thus defines hebdomadarius: " The Ebdomadary or Weeks-man, an Officer in Cathedral Churches." In grammar schools the master who took duty for a week was styled " Hebdomadarius."

Herse, Hearce, or Hearse. A portcullis, so called from its resemblance to a framework termed *hercia*, fashioned like a harrow, whereon lighted candles were placed at the obsequies of distinguished persons. Also a frame set over the coffin of a person deceased, and covered with a pall. This was usually of light woodwork, and appears, in many instances, to have been part of the furniture of the church, to be used upon occasion. There is a brass frame of a similar kind over the effigy of Richard, Earl of Warwick, in the Beauchamp Chapel, St Mary's, Warwick. This is called a *herse* in the contract for the tomb. There is also one of iron over an ancient tomb in Bedell Church, Yorkshire. See also *sub voce* " Bier."

High Service, or High Prayers. A traditional name at St Paul's Cathedral for Matins and Evensong when the festival responses of Tallis are sung, accompanied (as they *always* should be) by the organ. The term is also in use at St Michael's College, Tenbury, and probably elsewhere. At both places " High Service " is the rule on all the Greater Festivals and their eves —*e.g.* Christmas, Epiphany, Easter Day, Ascension Day, Whitsunday, and throughout the octaves of those festivals. At St Paul's " High Service " is also the rule on the Feast of the Conversion of St Paul, on its eve, and throughout its octave; on the

ECCLESIASTICAL TERMS

Feast of the Purification, and on that of the Annunciation. At all other seasons the ferial use for the responses, based on Merbecke, is the rule. In some cathedrals Tallis' responses are sung on ferial days without the organ—a most incorrect usage. They should be reserved for the Greater Festivals.

Holy Week. The week before Easter. Called also the " Great Week," and the " Indulgence Week " from the great absolution at Easter. Holy Week is often incorrectly called " Passion Week," which is that following the Fifth Sunday in Lent or " Passion Sunday." The German name for Holy Week is " Charwoche."

Hosanna. **Gr. ὡσαννά,** " Save, we pray." At the Feast of Tabernacles, when the great *Hallel* (the six Psalms, from the 113th to the 118th, deriving their name from the first word of the first Psalm in the series) was chanted by the priests, the multitude joined in at intervals, shouting " Hosanna," as they waved branches of willow or palm ; and the seventh and greatest day of the feast was distinguished as the great Hosanna day. According to Rabbi Elias Levita, the Jews call the willow branches which they carry at the feast " Hosannas," because they sing " Hosanna," shaking them everywhere. Grotius observes that the feasts of the Jews did not only signify their going out of Egypt, the memory of which they celebrated, but also the expectation of the Messias : and that still on the day when they carry those branches they wish to celebrate that feast at the coming of the Messias ; from whence he concludes that the people carrying those branches before our Saviour showed their joy, acknowledging Him to be the Messias. Consult Lightfoot, " Temple Service," xvi. 2 ; Smith's " Dictionary of the Bible," *s.v.* " Hosanna " is a portion of the *Sanctus* in the Mass. The words " Glory be to Thee, O Lord Most High," in the *Sanctus* of our Communion Service are a free translation of " Osanna in Excelsis." In the First Prayer-Book of 1549, the words of the *Sanctus* and *Benedictus* (immediately following) ran thus : " Holy, Holy, Holy, Lord God of Hosts : heaven and earth are full of Thy glory : Osannah in the highest. Blessed is he that cometh in the Name of the Lord : Glory to Thee, O Lord in the highest " ; and they were so noted by Merbecke. In 1552 the words of the *Sanctus* were altered to their present form, and the *Benedictus* omitted.

A recent writer on (Roman) Catholic Church music states that the magnificent six-part anthem " Hosanna to the Son of David," by Orlando Gibbons is an adaptation of the Palm Sunday antiphon, "Hosanna Filio David." There is, however, no evidence to prove this assertion. Without doubt Gibbons set it to English words at the outset. He did not compose for the Latin rite, as did his great contemporary William Byrd.

The Blessed Eucharist. Johnson derives it from the Gothic *hunsa*, a sacrifice, which is probably derived from a root signifying to kill. The Rev. H. J. Todd, sometime (1786–1816)

Housel. minor canon of Canterbury, remarks, in his emenda-
Saxon, *husel.* tions to Johnson's Dictionary, on the verb to " housel," that an old lexicography defines it specially, " to administer the Communion to one who lieth on his deathbed." It was, perhaps, in later times, more generally used in this sense : still it was often employed, as we find from Chaucer, and writers as late as the time of Henry VIII., as in Saxon times, to signify absolutely the receiving of the Eucharist. From this comes the word " Housel-ling Cloth "—a cloth extended before the communicants to catch any fragment of the consecrated bread. This houselling cloth is ordered in the Coronation Office, and it is to be held by two bishops. Early in the last century it was always used at the royal chapels, and there are churches in which its use survives. It is generally employed on the Continent, where the altar-rails are covered with a white cloth. In Germany it is frequently relieved with a text worked in red stitch, as at St Patroclus, Söest. Queen Elizabeth, at " the Princelye comminge of her Majestie to the Holy Communion" in the Chapel Royal at St James's on Easter Day, 1593, had " a moste princely lynned clothe layd on her cushion pillowe, and borne at the foure ends by the noble Erle of Herefford, the Erle of Essex, the Erle of Worcester, and the Erle of Oxford : the side of the sayd clothe her Majestie toke up in her hande, and therewith toke the ffoote of the golden and nowe sacred cuppe, and with like holy reverend attention to the sacramentaon words, did drinke of the same most devoutly " (" Old Cheque Book, or Book of Remembrance of the Chapel Royal," p. 151). Anent the houselling cloth, a letter appeared in *The Ecclesiologist* of February 1859, signed " W. S.," the initials of William Scott, a learned ecclesiologist, for many years the well-known incumbent of Christ Church, Hoxton. He observes : " Did you never notice a practice common, and in my days of rustic experience universal, in the country, for women always to carry their Prayer-Books wrapped in a white handkerchief to church ? London female servants as a rule carry, or rather used to carry, for they are getting too fine now-a-days, their Prayer-Books in their white handkerchief, Prayer-Book and white handkerchief was the use of Sunday. On week-days and in their best, there was no dis-

play of this white handkerchief; on Sundays it was the rule. It was the outward sign of church-going. I have long *suspected* that this invariable and anomalous white kerchief was the old houselling cloth: and I remember that in conversation this suspicion of mine was pronounced by you to be at least a probable guess. I have just got proof of it. I was called upon to-day [the Epiphany] in an official capacity to administer Communion to a considerable number of old almsfolks in a church in the very heart of the city of London, the very last place where one would expect to find this old ritual tradition observed. One poor old woman, from Bristol, who communicated, when she knelt at the altar-steps, deliberately spread her white—or rather yellow-white—pocket-handkerchief all along the rails before communicating. I wish some of your country readers would, when they see the Sunday pocket-handkerchief, investigate this subject, and inquire whether in any place any knowledge of its meaning, or traces of this practice survive." Those who know their Dickens will probably remember the description he gives, in one of his delightful "Uncommercial Traveller" Sketches, of a journey citywards in an omnibus to visit churches on a Sunday morning, in which he says: "We have put down a fierce-eyed spare old woman, whose slate-coloured gown smells of herbs, and who walked up Aldersgate Street to some chapel, where she comforts herself with brimstone doctrine, I warrant, and also a stouter and sweeter old lady, with a pretty large prayer-book in an unfolded pocket-handkerchief, who got out at a corner of a court near Stationers' Hall, and who, I think, must go to church there, because she is the widow of some deceased old Company's beadle."

Iconostasis. In Greek churches, the high solid screen between the sacrarium and the choir, on which the icons, or pictures, are fixed. Examples: Church of Kostroma, Russia (ancient); Greek Church, Moscow Road, Bayswater (modern). In early times the Iconostasis was apparently of much the same nature as our own rood-screens; for Eusebius (x. 4) calls it δίκτνα ἀπόξύλου, wooden nets. But afterwards it assumed its present shape of a solid erection. The rood-doors were called the "Holy Gates." On the right side, on entering, was invariably figured Our Lord: on the left the Mother of God: other saints were represented in any position that the piety or taste of the architect might suggest. But some principal saint (ἐικὼν στασιδίου τοῦ ἡγουμένου) was so placed as to be very conspicuous from the seat occupied (if a monastic church) by the Hegumen; (if a cathedral) by the Bishop:

the easternmost—viz. on the south side of the choir. Before the "Holy Gates" hung a curtain, embroidered with the image of St Michael, brandishing his sword, as if to "keep the way of" this second "Tree of Life" from irreverent access.

Imitation. In music, the technical term for a studied resemblance of melody between the several passages of the harmonical parts of a composition : a likeness in which only the motion, or the general figure formed by the notes, is imitated, without preserving the exactness in the corresponding intervals, by the rigorous rules of fugue and canon. A fine example of the "imitative" or "fugato" style, throughout, is the Morning and Evening Service in D major by Dr Child, organist of the Chapel Royal, Whitehall, and St George's Chapel, Windsor (d. 169$\frac{6}{7}$). It will be found in Boyce's "Cathedral Music," vol. iii. p. 691 (Novello's edition of 1849), and is said to have been written by Child to puzzle his choir-men, who had previously ridiculed some of his music on account of its simplicity. Charles I. greatly admired this Service, as we learn from Playford's "Brief Introduction to the Skill of Music," and would frequently command its performance at the Chapel Royal. It is called by Tudway and other old writers "Dr Child's Sharp Service." In many places the melody closely resembles that of the more simply constructed and better-known service in D by Benjamin Rogers, a contemporary of Child.

Incense. "Among all the symbolical Rites of the Church, none is more ancient, scriptural, catholic, beautiful, significant, and impressive than the use of Incense." So wrote Robert Brett in his "Churchman's Guide to Faith and Piety" (1862). Appointed by God to be used in His service, it not only formed an important part of the Jewish ritual, but has also continued, according to prophecy, to be used at the Holy Sacrifice, in every branch of the Christian Church, from the earliest ages, even to the present day. Incense is spoken of in many parts of Holy Scripture. Malachi prophesied that in the worship of the Gentiles " *In every place incense shall be offered* unto My name ; and *a pure offering*"—indicating that it should be offered with the " pure offering " of the Eucharist. So, accordingly, it is prescribed in every ancient Liturgy and has been in perpetual use throughout every branch of the Eastern Church, as well as the Western. In our own Sarum office-books it is prescribed at certain parts of the Eucharistic office. Many examples of its use in the English Church *since the Reformation* might be adduced. It was while Zacharias was burning the *incense, and the whole multitude of the people were praying without,* that the angel appeared to Zacharias. The wise men offered frankincense to the Infant Saviour. Burning incense is full of symbolic meaning : 1st, It indicates that the altar is holy to the Lord, and that all should be consumed in His service. 2nd, It signifies those fervent prayers, which, like the smoke of the incense arising from the burning coals, ascend from the heart of the Christian kindled by the love of God. 3rd, It is symbolical of the prayers of the saints—" the golden vials full of odours, which are the prayers of the saints " (Rev. v. 8). It also represents the angel before the throne—" The smoke of the incense, which came up with the prayers of the saints, ascended before God out of the angel's hand " (Rev. viii). " What, therefore " (continues Robert Brett), " Almighty God has prescribed for His worship on earth, and permits before His throne in heaven, must be acceptable and pleasing to Him, and ought to be so to all His faithful people." It is strange beyond all comprehension how churchmen could have so neglected a rite which has such abundant Scripture testimony, as well as the sanction of all antiquity, and of every branch of the Universal Church. Among the first London churches where incense was introduced were St Mary Magdalene's, Munster Square (in procession on Easter Day, 1859), and St Matthias', Stoke Newington (at the funeral of Robert Brett's daughter, Maria, April 1864). Since then its use has become more general, notwithstanding " law " and " prohibitions " and the withdrawal of the light of the episcopal countenance. At a High Celebration, incense is used at the Introit, reading of the Gospel, Offertory, and Consecration. At " Solemn Matins " it is offered at the *Benedictus* and at " Solemn Evensong " at the *Magnificat*, in honour of the Incarnation, which is especially celebrated in these, the Gospel, or " Evangelical," Canticles. It is also used in processions. At funerals it is used in recognition of the Communion of Saints—the truth, that is, that the departed are not severed from the Church on earth, but that they still hold communion with her, being the objects of her *intercession* (of which incense is the type), and also interceding for her. For the same reason the body is incensed, as also to show our reverence for that which was the temple of the Holy Ghost (1 Cor. vi. 19) ; which was illuminated and regenerated in Holy Baptism, was fed on Christ in the Eucharist, and which some day will be raised again, being awakened (as our trust is) to a joyful resurrection. Consult Atchley, " History of the Use of Incense in Divine Worship " (Longmans, 1909) ; " Hierugia Anglicana " (1848). See also *sub voce* " Censer " in this work.

Stone or alabaster slabs, with figures engraved upon them, used as sepulchral memorials, and called in France *tombes plates de pierre.*

Incised or Engraved Slabs. In England incised slabs do not appear ever to have existed in great number, the prevalent fashion being to use the brass, shaped to the form of the figure, and embedded in a cavity in the slab, whereby the cost of the tomb was much less than that of the French or Flemish brasses, which usually were formed of large sheets of metal, covering the entire surface of the slab. The long article on Incised Slabs in Parker's "Glossary of Architecture" is admirable and exhaustive, and should be consulted.

Intonation. (1) The method of reciting the prayers and other portions of the choral service. The only one sanctioned by the Church; hallowed by its origin and its antiquity, and which renders a voice of moderate power distinctly audible in the largest congregations; thus making the service of God different from common ordinary conversation. (2) The notes which precede the reciting note in a Gregorian chant. In the Mass and Communion Service the opening words of the *Credo* and *Gloria in Excelsis* have their proper "Intonations" for the celebrant. In our cathedral music, many of the *Te Deums*, by composers from the time of Tallis, soon after the Reformation, to that of Dr Boyce in the middle of the eighteenth century, are provided with an intonation for the officiating minor canon or priest vicar. Such intonations are marked "Priest." For the various intonations, English and foreign, consult Jebb, "Choral Responses and Litanies" (2 vols. 1847–1857); J. Baden Powell, "Choralia" (1901); "Notes on Ceremonial" (1882); Haberl, "Magister Choralis" (Ratisbon, 1864).

Intrados. The inner surface of an arch, which in early German Gothic work was often an undeveloped smooth, flat surface, answering to the pier surface from which it arose. There is a good example in the nave of Münster Cathedral, Westphalia.

Introit. One or more verses, mostly from the Psalms, sung at the entrance (*ad introitum*) of the clergy into the sanctuary for the celebration of Mass or Holy Communion. It is sung as an act of preparation for the service which follows. So the Psalmist advises: "Let us come before His presence with thanksgiving, and show ourselves glad in Him *with Psalms*" (Ps. xcv. 2). The Introit, like the Collect, Epistle, and Gospel varies with the season. An introit proper consists of two parts—the *antiphon* or

ECCLESIASTICAL TERMS

anthem, and the *Psalm*. When plainsong is used, the antiphon is sung in one of the modes, entire, before or after the Psalm, which follows to the corresponding tone. The *Gloria Patri* is always added, except in funeral Celebrations, and from the 5th Sunday in Lent till Easter. Prefixed to the collects, epistles and gospels in the Book of 1549, is an introit for every Sunday and Holy Day throughout the year, a Psalm being invariably selected. These Introit-Psalms were ill chosen, and their removal from the Book of 1552 and subsequent revisions was no loss. Merbecke gives the first verse of Psalm i. noted to the 8th Tone, 1st Ending, by way of specimen, adding this direction: " And forth with ye Introite, as is Appointed for the day." The Rev. Thomas Helmore, in his " Brief Directory of Plain-song " (1850) reprints the table of Introits from the Book of 1549, while the Rev. J. Baden Powell, in his valuable hand-book, " Choralia," gives a list from the Sarum Missal. In our old English use the introit was more usually termed the " Office " (*Officium*). This *Officium* consisted of an antiphon (sung through) ; a verse of a Psalm ; the antiphon repeated ; the *Gloria Patri* throughout, and then the antiphon for the third time. It was to take the place of this *Officium* that the table of Psalms was given in Edward VI.'s First Book, and called " Introits," but with very much less significance as to the day and intention of the service. The old Sarum *Officium* is frequently far more appropriate. It must be remembered that every Eucharist of old had, not only its introit, but also its gradual, alleluia or tract, offertory, and Communion—selected Scriptures appropriate to the day or season (independent of the Epistle and Gospel) which poured a flood of Scripture light upon the devotions of the day. It is much to be regretted that the framers of our Prayer-Book rejected the Sarum *Officium*. With the disappearance of the Edwardian introits, in 1552, no directions were given as to the manner in which the Communion Service was to be ushered in. In cathedrals it became the custom for a solemn voluntary to be played upon the organ while the clergy walked to the altar. This, as we learn from the preface to Clifford's " Divine Services and Anthems," published in 1664, prevailed at St Paul's at the time of the Restoration. Not long afterwards it became very general to sing the *Sanctus* as an introit, between the Litany and Communion Service, and this was the custom within memory. This use of the *Sanctus* was incorrect certainly, as it was left unsung in its proper place in the service, but the effect was undoubtedly solemn. A short anthem has now taken the place of the *Sanctus*, where the introit proper is not used. A collect, set anthemwise,

157

should *never* be used as an introit. At St Andrew's, Wells Street, a hymn has long been sung in this place. Books of introits have been published, from time to time, for use in our Church, which ought to satisfy the demands of the advocates of either plain-song or Anglican (harmonised) music. Among the former may be mentioned those of Charles Child Spencer (1847), Richard Redhead (1853 and 1869), W. H. Monk—as a companion to " Hymns Ancient and Modern " (1864), A. H. Brown (1885) ; while among the latter may be cited those of Sir George Macfarren—fifty-two, all of his own composition (1866), Rev. Walter Hook—thirty-one, by various sterling composers then living (1867) ; C. J. Viner (1896). The last-named (consisting of contributions by living composers) follows Sarum use most closely, as regards the selection of the words, the Psalm being set to plain-song. In Macfarren's collection the texts were selected by Dr E. G. Monk from Holy Scripture and the Book of Common Prayer, but in this, and also in Hook's collection, there are no Psalms. A useful series of short anthems by various modern writers, begun in 1890, and still flourishing, contains many compositions eminently useful as introits. This is published by Novello, the original editors being Sir John Stainer and the Rev. W. Russell. The Sarum " Offices," or Introits, for the Sundays and Festivals throughout the year, have been published by the Plain-song and Mediæval Music Society.

Invitatory. Some text of Scripture, or short versicle, inviting the people to offer their praise and adoration to God. St Cyril speaks of an invitatory Psalm being sung before the celebration of the Holy Mysteries (" Catech. Myst." v., n. 17), but the word was generally used for a short versicle sung before the *Venite* (Ps. xcv.), repeated after every second verse, and intended to furnish a keynote to the whole service, by indicating to the congregation the doctrine which they were more especially to keep in mind at that particular season. In the Prayer-Book of 1549 these invitatories were omitted, probably because the *Venite* is itself of a sufficiently invitatory character. They broke the continuity of the Psalm in a senseless manner. The versicle, however, immediately preceding the *Venite*, " Praise ye the Lord," with its response, " The Lord's name be praised," may be considered as an unalterable invitatory.

Invocation. (1) The opening of the Litany, containing the invocation of each person of the Godhead, severally, and of the Blessed Trinity in Unity. This distinction is made in the margin of Nichols' " Illustrations of the Book of Common

ECCLESIASTICAL TERMS

Prayer" (1710). (2) The words, " In the Name of the Father, and of the Son, and of the Holy Ghost," used instead of a collect, by many preachers, before beginning the sermon. The general formula, " And now to God the Father," etc., used at the end of a sermon, is termed the " Ascription."

Ionic Order. The second of the Greek, and the third of the Roman, orders of architecture. Its most distinguishing feature is the capital, which is ornamented with four spiral projections called volutes, placed flat on the front and back of the columns, supported by an enriched ovolo (a moulding whose profile is the quadrant of a circle) leaving the two opposite sides to form what is called a balustre. The details in Greek and Roman Ionic vary somewhat. The shaft is sometimes plain and sometimes fluted. The best examples of the Ionic order are the Temples of Minerva Polias and Erectheus in the Acropolis, the (now destroyed) temple on the bank of the Illisus and the Aqueduct of Hadrian, all at Athens; the temples of Apollo Didymeus at Miletus, Minerva Polias at Priene, and Bacchus at Teos; and the temple of Fortuna Virilis at Rome. Good modern Ionic may be seen in the portico of the Church of St Pancras, Euston Road (W. & H. W. Inwood, architects, 1822), copied from the Temple of Erectheus. Consult W. J. Smith, " Synopsis of the Origin and Progress of Architecture" (1831); F. C. Penrose, " Principles of Athenian Architecture" (1852).

Ite Missa est. The concluding words of the Mass (" Go, the Mass is over ") from whence the name of that service (Mass) is derived. The words are sung by the deacon with elaborate inflections, the choir responding *Deo gratias*. Haberl (" Magister Choralis," Ratisbon, 1864, p. 84) gives six different forms of the *Ite Missa est*. 1. Vom Charsamstag bis zum weissen Sonntag [*i.e.* from Easter Eve to the First Sunday after Easter] exclusive. 2. In Festis solemnibus. 3. De apostolis et in Festis duplicibus. 4. In Missis Beatæ Mariæ. 5. In Dominicis infra annum, in fest. semidupl., et infra Octavas, quæ non sunt Beatæ Mariæ. 6. In Festis Simplicibus, et Feriis temp. Paschali. On Sundays in Advent and Lent is chanted *Benedicamus Domino*, with the response, *Deo gratias*, and at Masses of the Dead, *Requiescant in pace*, with the response, " Amen." Various other forms will be found in all missals musically noted. The Sarum form was " Go, you are dismissed." In Masses for the Dead it was " May they rest in peace. Amen." In the Ambrosian rite the *Ite missa est* is not sung.

A DICTIONARY OF

Jah. A form of the name Jehovah, which occurs in Psalm lxviii. 4—" Praise him in his name JAH, and rejoice before him."

Jesse, or Tree of Jesse.
Fr. *arbre de Jesse;*
Lat. *radix Jesse* (Root of Jesse).

A favourite mediæval representation of the genealogy of Christ, in which the different persons forming the descent are placed on scrolls of foliage branching out of each other, intended to represent a tree. It was a frequent subject for sculpture, painting, and embroidery. At Dorchester Abbey Church, Oxon, it is curiously formed in the stonework of one of the chancel windows. At Christ Church, Hants, it is carved in stone on the reredos of the altar. At Chartres Cathedral it is to be found in a painted window at the west end of the nave. It may be also seen at Rouen Cathedral, and many other churches, both in France and England. At St George's, Hanover Square, the glass in the east window, originally belonging to a religious house at Mechlin, and inserted in its present position about 1843, has some of the attributes of a " Jesse Window." It is fully described in T. F. Bumpus' " London Churches, Ancient and Modern," ii. 41. 42. The Jesse (east) window of Winchester College Chapel formed the subject of a poem by Robert Lowth, Bishop of London (1777–1787), written when a Winchester scholar. It will be found in Pearch's collection of poems, published at the close of the eighteenth century. Parker (" Glossary of Architecture," 1845) mentions an example in stained glass at Llanrhaidr yn Kinmerch, Denbighshire, with the date, 1553. In the cathedral at Osnabrück is a hanging " Radix Jesse," the centre being formed by an image of the Virgin and Child within a vesica. The scrolls and foliage are of wrought-iron, as are also the six elegant branches for lights which surround the base. The figures are of wood. A drawing of this will be found in T. H. King's " Study-Book of Mediæval Architecture and Art," vol. iii., 1858. Tournay Cathedral possesses an altar-frontal embroidered with the Tree of Jesse. Representations of this subject in modern stained glass may be seen in the following churches, and by the annexed artists :—East window, St Paul's, Bow Common, London (Powell) ; East window Solihull Church, Warwickshire (C. E. Kempe) ; East window, St Paul's, Brighton (Hardman) ; West window, Doncaster Parish Church (Ward and Hughes) ; West window, All Saints', Margaret Street (Gibbs) ; East window, St George's, Lambeth (Wailes) ; East window, St Paul's, Knightsbridge (Lavers and Barraud); West window, Durham Cathedral; North transept rose, Truro Cathedral ; North transept lancets, Lichfield

ECCLESIASTICAL TERMS

Cathedral; all by Clayton and Bell. In 1245 the Treasury of St Paul's Cathedral contained a chasuble which the King had presented at the dedication of the church, embroidered with the Tree of Jesse.

Jubé. The French term for the rood-loft, derived from the formula, *Jube domine benedicere*, prefacing the singing of the Gospel which in mediæval times took place here. The German equivalent is "Lettner," derived from the Latin word "Lectorium," because, on the desuetude of the ambons (*q.v.*) the Epistle and Gospel were read from it. Hence our terms "Lectern" or "Lettern." Upon the screen stood, and, in some parts of Germany still stands, the Crucifix, with the figures of SS. Mary and John, hence the term, "Rood-screen." Examples: Albi; Arques; St Florentin—these two are Renaissance; La Madeleine, Troyes; St Marie de l'Épine, near Chalons (French); Halberstadt; Meissen; Naumberg—(1) Romanesque, (2) Early Pointed (German); Canterbury, Exeter, Lincoln, Ripon, St David's, Southwell, York (English). The screen in St George's Chapel, Windsor, is of commendable Third Pointed for the period of its erection (1789).

Jubilate Deo. Psalm c. ("O be joyful in God, all ye lands"). One of the Psalms appointed to be used after the Second Lesson at Matins. It had been sung among the Psalms of Lauds in the old offices; and the only difference between its present and former positions is, that it was formerly sung before the Lesson, and is now sung after it. It is an appropriate song of praise for creation and providence, and has been most commonly used; but it is scarcely fitted for a penitential season; and, indeed, from the history of its appointment, and the words of the rubric, it appears that *Benedictus* (*q.v.*) should be used, "except when that shall happen to be read in the chapter for the day, or for the Gospel on St John Baptist's Day." *Jubilate*, however, inviting all nations to praise God, harmonises with the season of Epiphany, and is always ordered, with *Te Deum*, on the occasion of a solemn thanksgiving. It was added at the revision of the Prayer-Book in 1552. Although *Jubilate* must have come into use so soon afterwards, we find *Benedictus* universally favoured by those composers who wrote for the earliest reformed service, and there are instances of its composition down to the time of Charles II., after which *Jubilate* became the favoured canticle. In 1874 the use of the *Benedictus* at St Paul's on all days but Wednesday and Friday created a demand for its setting by many of our modern writers, and *Jubilate* again retired into the background, but at the present day composers include settings of both in their complete Services. In the Services of

A DICTIONARY OF

Attwood in A, B flat, C, D, and F ; in those of Professor Walmisley in B flat, C, and F ; in that of E. J. Hopkins in A ; in that of S. S. Wesley in E, and in that of Henry Smart in F, the *Jubilate* is admirably set. One of the earliest instances of a post-Reformation setting of *Jubilate* is that by John Farrant in the Dorian Mode, given by Sir Frederick Ouseley in his volume, " Cathedral Services by English Masters " (Novello, 1853). Handel wrote his famous *Jubilate* in the key of D, for the celebration of the Peace of Utrecht. It was first performed (preceded by a *Te Deum* in the same key) at St Paul's Cathedral, 7th July 1713. Queen Anne, though too ill to be present at the first performance of these compositions, heard them afterwards, in the Chapel Royal, St James's, and rewarded Handel with a pension of £200 per annum for life. During the next thirty years they were performed at St Paul's, alternately with Purcell's *Te Deum* and *Jubilate*, for the benefit of the Sons of the Clergy. This honour they enjoyed till 1743, when Handel's *Dettingen Te Deum* caused all other works of the kind to be laid aside ; and for this reason alone they are now almost forgotten, even in the land of their birth. To the various settings of the *Jubilate* already mentioned may be added those in the Services of Dr Rogers, Dr Child, Dr Blow, Henry Purcell, Dean Aldrich, Dr Croft, Charles King, John Travers, William Raylton, Dr Boyce, Dr Cooke, Dr Dupuis, Dr Arnold, Sir John Stevenson, Dr Clarke-Whitfeld, Archdeacon Heathcote, Dr Camidge, Sir George Smart, Rev. W. H. Havergal, Sir George Elvey, James Turle, Dr J. L. Hopkins, Sir George Macfarren, the Rev. Lord O'Neill, Dr John Smith (Dublin), Dr W. B. Gilbert, Dr Garrett, J. Baptiste Calkin, Sir Frederick Ouseley, Sir Herbert Oakeley, Sir Robert Stewart, Sir Joseph Barnby, Sir C. Villiers Stanford, Sir Frederick Bridge, and Mr John E. West. The *Jubilate* written by Mendelssohn for our cathedral service, in 1847, should not be forgotten.

Key-stone.   In architecture, the central stone, or " voussoir " (wedge-shaped stone), at the top of an arch ; the last which is placed in its position to complete the construction of an arch. The bosses (*q.v.*) in vaulted ceilings are also sometimes called "keys."

Kyrie Eleeson or Eleison.
Gr.
Κύριε ἐλέησον ;
Eng. " Lord, have mercy."
A form of supplication frequently used in the services of the Church. It is found in all the ancient liturgies, being repeated before, sometimes after, certain prayers. It was customary to say it thrice, as it was addressed to the Father, Son, and Holy Ghost. For this reason, in the Western Church, the second invocation was changed to " Christe

162

Eleison," but this was never used in the Eastern Church. This form of supplication was in early times known by the name of the Lesser Litany. The Ambrosian Rite of Milan recites the *Kyrie* three times—viz. after the *Gloria in Excelsis*, after the Gospel, and at the end of the Mass—but in the eleventh century it was sung nine times (see *sub voce* " Farse "). In the Salisbury Portiforium (*q.v.*), as in the other " Uses " of the English Church, it was untranslated. It was threefold before the Lord's Prayer at Lauds, though ninefold at Prime. In the First Prayer-Book of Edward VI. (1549), according to the Use of Sarum, the Collect for Purity in the Communion Service was followed by the introit, and then came the *Kyrie* nine times. In our present Prayer-Book the Greek words are translated, and generally precede the Lord's Prayer, but not when that prayer is used in the Eucharistic office. For it is to the *prayer* what the " Gloria Patri " is to the *praise* of the whole office ; a prayer setting forth the tone, and fixing the object of all the rest, and being addressed to the Holy Trinity. In a musical Mass the *Kyrie Eleison* is invariably one of the most elaborate parts of the service. In our own service *Kyrie* is the heading for the Responses to the Commandments (see *sub voce* " Decalogue "). By some composers it is ignorantly termed "Miserere." See some examples in Arnold's " Cathedral Music " (1790), and in the collection appended to B. St J. B. Joule's Chant-Book (Novello, 1882). It is singular that in the Mechlin office-books noted, the *Kyries* in the third set are sometimes directed to be sung twice, and a fresh notation is given for the *last Kyrie* : thus, like the Litany, having addressed each person separately, offering the last petition to the Holy Trinity—a symbolic arrangement still more clearly marked, perhaps, in our *tenth Kyrie.*

Lady Chapel. A chapel dedicated to the Blessed Virgin, called Our Lady, which, from the thirteenth century to the time of the Reformation, was attached to large churches. It was generally placed eastward of the high altar, often forming a projection from the main building, but was sometimes in other situations. At Ely it is a distinct building attached to the north-east corner of the north transept. At Rochester it is on the west side of the south transept ; at Oxford on the north side of the choir ; at Bristol on the north side of the north aisle of the choir ; at Durham at the west end of the nave, where it is usually known as the Galilee. The Lady Chapel is generally an addition to churches which are of earlier date than the thirteenth century. Henry VII.'s Chapel is the Lady Chapel of Westminster Abbey.

The name for an acutely pointed window of one opening, peculiar to the Early Pure Gothic period. Lancets are frequently found arranged in groups of three (triplet) and of five (quintuplet). Examples of lancet windows may be seen at St Patrick's Cathedral, Dublin ; Salisbury Cathedral ; the Temple Church, London ; Southwell Minster ; Lincoln Cathedral ; Glasgow Cathedral. The east end of Ely Cathedral presents us with two ranges of lancets, the upper quintuplet, the lower triplet ; that of Worcester has also two ranges (restorations), but both quintuplet ; while the beautiful Early English chancel of Chetwode Church, Bucks, has a quintuplet at the east end, and a triplet on both north and south sides. Modern examples of lancets may be met with in Truro Cathedral and many of the churches built by the late J. L. Pearson. In French Gothic the lancet window is represented in the apsidal chapels of the cathedrals of Auxerre, Le Mans, Soissons, Séez, Tours, and Troyes. At Laon Cathedral, where there is one of the few square east ends in France, we find a triplet of lancets under a rose window.

Lancet.

Lancet Style. A generic name for the Early Pure Gothic. Explained under " Early English."

In Italian or modern architecture a small structure on the top of a dome, or in other similar situations, for the purpose of admitting light, or for ornament, of which that on the octagon at Ely and those on the domes of St Paul's Cathedral and the Radcliffe Library at Oxford may be cited as examples. In Gothic architecture the term is sometimes applied to louvres (turrets) on the roofs of halls, etc., but it usually signifies a tower, which has the whole height, or a considerable portion of the interior, open to view from the ground, and is lighted by an upper tier of windows. Over the centre of cross churches lantern towers of this kind are common, as at Canterbury, York, Durham, Ely, Lincoln ; the cathedrals of Coutances, Evreux, Rouen (Normandy) and the Church of St Ouen, Rouen. The same name is also given to the light open erections often placed on the top of lofty towers, as at St Helen's, York ; Boston, Lincolnshire ; Fotheringhay, and Lowick, Northants. The tower of St Dunstan's, Fleet Street (James Shaw, architect, 1831–1833), affords a good modern example of a " lantern."

Lantern.

Latten.
Fr. *laiton ;*
Ital. *ottone ;*
Germ. *messing.*
A mixed metal of brass and copper, of which many articles of church furniture were composed. The monumental brasses so common in our churches are mentioned as being of latten. In " The Ancient Rites of Durham," p. 20, we find : " The finest and most curious candlestick metal, or *latten* metal, glistering like gold."

ECCLESIASTICAL TERMS

Lauda Sion. See *sub voce* " Corpus Christi."

Lauds. One of the offices of the canonical hours. It was formerly sung just before dawn, so as God might be praised (lauded) at the earliest moment for the coming day. In the Roman Breviary it consists of the *Pater Noster, Ave Maria* (omitted when said continuously after Matins), five Psalms (the third is always the 63rd, and the fifth is always the 148th), a short chapter of Holy Scripture, a hymn, with versicle of Holy Scripture, the canticle of Zacharias (*Benedictus*), the Collect of the Day, and an antiphon of the Blessed Virgin, according to the season. This night office was, and is still in many places, sung during the night. It is now allowed to be celebrated (with Matins) by "anticipation," on the evening before. The office of Lauds, as in the Sarum Breviary, will be found detailed, together with Matins, Prime, Vespers and Compline, in Procter's "History of the Book of Common Prayer." The student will thus be able to compare the Sarum office with that of Rome.

Lay Clerk. A title borne by the adult singers in Cathedrals of the New (or Henry VIII.'s) Foundation, as distinguished from that of lay vicar in those of the Old Foundation. They do not form a corporation like the lay vicars, but are mere stipendiary singers, in some cases having a common estate given to them subsequently to their foundation, besides their statutable payments from the chapter. They vary in number from twelve to six. Before the Civil War (*temp.* Charles I.) the numbers were in many cases much larger. At Westminster Abbey (though modelled on the New Foundation) the title is " lay vicar." In the college chapels of Oxford and Cambridge which have choral foundations the title is, as in the New Cathedrals, " lay clerk." At St Andrew's, Wells Street, where there has been a daily choral service since its consecration in January 1847, the adult members of the choir are denominated " lay clerks." This is also the title at St Michael's College, Tenbury, where full cathedral service, in its best and purest form, is celebrated twice daily.

Lean-to Roofed Aisle. One whose roof is formed in a single slope, with the top resting against the wall of the nave below the clerestory.

Lectern, or Lettern. Fr. *lutrin ;* Ital. *leggio ;* Germ. *singepult, lesepult.* A word often ignorantly spelt " lecturn." The desk or stand on which the larger books used in the services of the Roman Catholic Church are placed. Since the Reformation it has been employed to hold the Bible. The principal lectern stood in the midst of the choir, but there were sometimes others in different places. They were occasionally made of stone or marble, and fixed, but were usually of wood or brass, and movable. They were also often covered with needlework, embroidered in the same manner as the hangings of the altar. Of wooden lecterns, ancient examples remain at Bury and Ramsey, Hunts; Detling, Lenham, and Swanscombe, Kent; Newport, Essex; Hanstead, Suffolk; Wednesbury, Staffordshire; Aldowry, Bucks; Lingfield, Surrey; Astbury, Cheshire; St Thomas's, Exeter (formerly in the cathedral). The oldest of these is at Bury (early twelfth century). The specimens of mediæval brass lecterns are not so numerous as those of wood, but they may be seen at King's College, Cambridge, Eton College, Merton College, Oxford, St George's Chapel, Windsor, Norwich Cathedral, Christ Church Cathedral, Dublin, Peterborough Cathedral, and Southwell Minster. The three last are in the form of an eagle, with the wings extended to receive the Sacred Volume. At Norwich the figure takes the form of a pelican. Mediæval lecterns were usually made with two flat sloping sides or desks for the choir-books, and are styled " coped lecterns." Renaissance examples of brass are the lecterns at Canterbury, Exeter, Lincoln, and York—all eagles. At Wells is a magnificent coped " brazen deske with God's Holy Worde thereon," given by Dr Robert Creyghton, Dean and afterwards Bishop of Wells, "upon his return from fifteen years' exile with our Soverayne Lord King Charles yᵉ Second, 1660 "—so runs the inscription thereon. The good dean would be little pleased to see it now, as we have, expelled by his successors from its legitimate place in the choir. The fine eagle lectern at St Paul's has already been noticed, *s.v.* " Eagle." Its predecessor was a coped one of wood, still preserved, but relegated to the gallery over the south aisle of the nave. It is an interesting relic of post-Restoration ritual arrangement, and should be placed, for use, in the north-west chapel or in one of the other chapels of the cathedral, and not put out of sight as so much lumber. There are fine coped lecterns of brass at St Andrew's, Wells Street (1847), All Saints', Margaret Street (1859)—both designed by W. Butterfield—and at Westminster Abbey (1848). The last is an exact counterpart of that at St George's, Windsor. Before their restoration the cathedrals of St Asaph, Carlisle, Durham, Ely, Gloucester, Lichfield, Oxford, Rochester, and Salisbury were without lecterns, but these—all eagles—have since been supplied. St George's Cathedral, Southwark, contains a fine brass eagle, designed by Pugin, the architect of the building (1848). The eagle lecterns at Nôtre Dame, Paris (given by Napoleon I.), and Chartres are large and noteworthy. In Germany, where the churches have retained

ECCLESIASTICAL TERMS

their mediæval *instrumenta*, the lectern is commonly met with. As a rule it is of cast-bronze. A three-sided stand, surmounted with pierced supporting arches and piers, bears the eagle, which, on its back and extended wings, offers a place on which to lay the book. There are such lecterns at the churches of St Mary and St Reinhold, Dortmund, and at Aix-la-Chapelle Cathedral. The last is engraved by Lübke (" Eccles. Art in Germ.," p. 207). At Nôtre Dame des Victoires, Brussels, and at St Remi, Rheims, are single sloping desks of iron with plain pedestals. In Italy the lecterns are commonly of wood, cope-shaped, the pedestal resting on a large square base. At Canterbury, until 1847, when a litany-desk was for the first time placed in the choir, the lectern was improperly used for the Litany, the lessons being read from his stall by the minor canon or the prebendary-in-residence. The Lesson Books used in the Church, before the Reformation, were exceedingly heavy, and would have taxed the strength of any ordinary man if held up before the face of the reader for even a brief space of time. Lecterns, or book-rests, were indispensable ; and accordingly we find that, when the Lessons were not read from the Pulpitum or Ambo, desks or lecterns were necessary in the choir. It will be as well to distinguish between the supports, or Eagles, which were used by the Gospeller and Epistoler in the Presbytery, and the Lectricia, which stood below in the choir. " The Churches of St Clement, St Lorenzo and St Pancras at Rome, have two Ambones besides Lectricium, the Gospel Ambo being much higher and larger than the other. At Sarum, York, Hereford and Exeter, in the thirteenth century, the Pulpitum was single in the centre of the west end of the choir. In the upper portion was an eagle, from whence on Sundays and Festivals the Gospel was read ; lower down in it was a desk or lectern, facing towards the choir, whence the Epistle was read on Sundays. Besides these, there were Lectricia in the choir for the Lessons, Epistles, etc., on Ferials. It was the union of the two Ambones by a beam or gallery thrown across this entrance to the choir above them, whereon was placed the great Cross, or Crucifix, which ultimately resulted in what in England is called the Roodloft or Screen, and in France the *Jubé*, from the ' Jube domine benedicere ' before the Lesson "—J. D. Chambers, " Divine Worship in England in the XIII. and XIV. Centuries," 1877. A Ferial Gospel Lectern, or " Evangelistarium " (twelfth or thirteenth century) is figured by Viollet-le-Duc, in his " Dictionnaire Raisonné de Mobilier Français," vol. i., 1865. It may be added that when, in 1859, by the munificence of Chancellor Harrington, the nave of

A DICTIONARY OF

Exeter Cathedral was seated with chairs to accommodate a Sunday afternoon congregation numbering some 1200, and new seats were provided for the dean and chapter, the priest and lay vicars, the boys of the choir, etc., a lectern of simple design was provided, approached by a sort of half Ambo, so as not to obstruct the passage up the church, and by this arrangement the reader is enabled to throw his voice over the vast assembly to the end of the nave, while he stands " conspectu omnium." The lectern in the choir being also raised on the fourth step from the entrance, places the reader in a commanding position for the reading of the Lessons on all occasions (as on week-days and Sunday mornings) when Divine Worship takes place in the choir. At Rochester, in the thirteenth century, was a red and gold cloth for the Lectorium (*Reggist.* Roffense, 240) ; at Sarum, 1222, one cloth for the Eagle, a linen cloth embroidered with gold for the Pulpitum on Greater Feasts, a linen cloth for the Lectern on week-days. These veils were long and beautiful. The fine bronze Adlerpult (eagle-desk) in the Maxkirche at Düsseldorf, 1449, is figured by Paul Clemen in his " Kunstdenkmäler der Rheinprovinz," iii. 52. Many fine lecterns of brass which once adorned our churches have been sold at various times by rapacious churchwardens. That, for instance, in the church, of St Martin, Leicester, was sold in 1569 for the paltry sum of £4, 18s. " Receyved of Mr. Morres for the Egle, iiij^{li} xviij^{s} " (Churchwardens' Accounts). The Church of St Mary-le-Port, Bristol, contains a fine brass lectern, weighing 692 lbs., which had been given to the cathedral in 1693 by the sub-dean, George Williamson, and which was sold by Dean Layard in 1812 for about £27. It was bought by a Mr William Ady, and given to the Church of St Mary-le-Port on condition that it should remain there for ever. The Rev. R. L. Caley, Precentor of Bristol from 1838 until his death in 1861, a good and earnest churchman, several times endeavoured to regain for the cathedral the lectern given to St Mary-le-Port ; but in vain, owing to the conditions under which it was presented to that church. The eagle lectern now in Bristol Cathedral forms a memorial to Precentor Caley.

From the Anglo-Saxon " lich," a corpse, and " geat," gate. A wooden shed over the entrance of a churchyard, beneath which the bearers sometimes paused when bringing a corpse for interment. The term is also used in some parts of the country for the path by which a corpse is usually conveyed to the church. There are examples at Birstall, Yorks ; Bromsgrove, Worcestershire ; Garsington, Oxfordshire ; Lenham and Becken-

Lich-gate,
Lych-gate, or
Corpse-gate.
Germ.
leichengang.

ham, Kent; Beckingham, Lincs; Bray, Berks; Bockleton, near Tenbury, Worcestershire. They are in general use in Wales, Cornwall, Herefordshire, and Monmouthshire, and are there usually of stone, but most of them are modern and plain. In Herefordshire,[§] and probably in some other counties, they are called Scallage or Scallenge Gates. The lich-gate is referred to as the " church stile " in the first rubric of the Burial Office in the Prayer-Books of 1549 and 1552—" The Priest meeting the corpse at the Church stile, shall say," etc. Within recent years the lich-gate has been erected as an entrance to many of our churchyards and cemeteries. Some of these are of very picturesque design.

The two altar-lights, which are authorised by law to be used at the Celebration of the Holy Communion, signify the light of faith

Lights. revealed in the two Covenants, and symbolise the twofold nature of Christ, and are also, as set forth in the injunctions of Edward VI., " For the signification that Christ is the very true light of the world." Unlighted altar candles are a miserable, meaningless sham, the absurdity of which did not escape the scorn of the old Puritans, who observed, " the candles on our altars, most nonsensically, stand unlighted, to signify what ? the darkness of our noddles." For the history and use of lights in the English Church at Holy Communion, Evensong, etc., consult Strypes' " Annals of the Reformation " ; Wheatley on the Book of Common Prayer ; Nichols and Procter on ditto ; Maskells' " Monumenta Ritualia " ; Smith's " Dictionary of Christian Antiquities " ; Walcott's " Sacred Archæology " ; Dearmer's " Parson's Handbook." The last-named may now be pronounced our standard authority. See also *sub voce* " Altar Lights."

The stone or beam covering a doorway or window-head, and often used in conjunction with an arch, the space between them

Lintel. being styled the tympanum, which, in Continental Gothic, served as a field for sculpture or painting. Sometimes this space is pierced for a window and glazed. The tympanum is rarely found after the Early English period amongst ourselves, but continued in use on the Continent to the close of the Gothic epoch. In Germany particularly it was carried to exaggerated dimensions.

Litany.
Gr. Λιτανεία ;
Lat. *litania*
and *letania*.
Supplication or prayer; called in Latin also Rogation, " Litania quæ Latine rogatio dicitur, inde et Rogationes " (*Ordo Romanus*). The old English rubric for this important part of the service was very minute, and ran, " The Litany, preceded by the fifteen Gradual

Psalms, is to be said for all the people of God, after Terce (*q.v.*) in the week-days of Lent, from the first Monday after the first Sunday, to Wednesday before Easter inclusive. But besides this, on every Wednesday and Friday in Lent (*i.e.* from and after the Monday succeeding the first Sunday, up to Maundy Thursday) there is a procession after None (*q.v.*) and before the Mass to one side altar of the church (unless a Feast of Nine Lessons intervene, which supersedes it), of the priests and their ministers in Albs without the Cross ; and after saying the petitions given in the Proper of the Time, in returning, two clerks of the Second Form, without changing their vestments, say the Litany, as far as Holy Mary, pray before the Altar, and then proceeding, going round the Presbytery, until it is finished at the step of the choir, with Note [plain chant]. On these occasions, however, it is said no farther than ' All ye Saints ! ' On Holy Saturday, the Vigil of Easter, after None, and after the Benediction of the [Paschal] Candle, the officiating Priest stands at the Altar, and having kissed it sits down. His two Ministers remain standing with two wax tapers on wands, at each corner of the Altar, until the Septiform Litany is finished ; the Lessons are then read, and then the Septiform Litany proceeds, which is said by seven boys in surplices in the middle of the choir. In the meanwhile the Priest puts off his Chasuble, and puts on his red Cope, and stands before the Altar until the Litany is finished. When this is ended, the Quinqueform Litany is said in like manner by five Deacons of the Second Form ,in the midst of the choir, in surplices, and when they come to ' Holy Mary, pray,' the procession proceeds to the Fonts for the benediction of them. In these two Litanies the Petitions, ' O Father of Heaven,' or ' O Son,' or 'O Redeemer,' or ' O Holy Spirit,' or ' O Holy Trinity,' are not said." On Monday in Rogation Week after None, " the usual procession takes place from the Cathedral to some church in the city ; in the end of which, preceded by the seven Penitential Psalms, is said the full Litany, with the Petitions and Collects, without Note, unless it is a festival, when it is otherwise." On Tuesday and Wednesday in Rogation Week the same took place. Besides these, litanies were chanted at other times : as for favourable weather, etc. In the latter years of Henry VIII., reformed opinions were making steady progress. A great event was the order (1540) to set up the English Bible in the churches, where it might be read by the people, although it was not yet in the public service. Ten years later it was proposed in Convocation that certain Church books—" missals, antiphoners, and portiuses (breviaries) "—should be examined and corrected.

ECCLESIASTICAL TERMS

A new edition of the Sarum Breviary—" Portiforium secundum usum Sarum noviter impressum, et a plurimis purgatum mendis, etc.," was issued at the same time, and printed in London by Edward Whitchurch, the House of Bishops deciding that its use should be observed throughout the province of Canterbury (see J. Wayland Joyce, " England's Sacred Synods," 404). It was also ordered that " every Sunday and Holy Day throughout the year, the curate of every parish church, after the *Te Deum* and *Magnificat* should openly read to the people one chapter of the New Testament in English, without exposition ; and when the New Testament was read to begin the Old." Thus, the first step was taken towards liturgical reformation by introducing the reading of Scripture in English into the public service of the Church, and this was done by the authority of the bishops in Convocation, who had also received the proposal to correct the service-books. Thus the way was prepared for the further substitution of English for Latin in the prayers. The first change in this respect was made in the Litany. This form of petition, used in solemn procession, particularly at Rogation-tide and on week-days during Lent, as already mentioned, had been in the hands of the people in the vernacular, certainly for 150 years ; but in 1544 it was revised by Archbishop Cranmer, who, besides the old litanies of the English Church, had also before him the Litany formed from the same ancient model, which had been prepared by Melancthon and Bucer, for Hermann, Archbishop of Cologne, in 1543. The chief alteration consisted in the omission of the long list of names of saints, which had gradually been inserted into the Western litanies ; although Cranmer still retained three clauses, in which the prayers of the Blessed Virgin, the angels, and the patriarchs, prophets, and apostles, martyrs, confessors, and virgins were desired. With this exception our English Litany was set forth for public use by command of Henry VIII. (11th June 1544), in its present form, and very nearly in its present words. It was intended to be a distinct office, and was then put forth as a separate book, and noted in plain chant. It has always been attached, in its non-processional use, to the service of Holy Communion. The Injunctions of Edward VI. (1547) ordered it to be said " immediately before high mass." A rubric in the Book of 1549 ordered it to be said on Wednesdays and Fridays, and to be followed by the first part of the Communion Office. In 1552 it was placed where it now stands, with the rubric directing it to be said " upon Sundays, Wednesdays, and Fridays, and at other times when it shall be commanded by the Ordinary." The Injunctions of Elizabeth (1559)

171

renew the direction that the Litany should be said "immediately before the Communion of the Sacrament." The Litany was first printed by T. Berthelet, the royal printer, 15th May 1544, in a work, " An Exhortacion unto Praier thought mete by the Kynges Majestie, and his clergie to be read, etc. Also a Litanie, with Suffrages, to be sayd or sung, etc." Heylyn (" Ecclesia Restaurata") tells us that the Litany was first sung in English in St Paul's Cathedral, 18th September 1547, "between the choir and the high altar, the singers kneeling half on one side and half on the other." That the Litany was both translated and set to plain chant by Cranmer is probable ; but it is not certain, as Burney, the musical historian (1776), concludes from a letter in the State-Paper Office, and given by Collier in his " Ecclesiastical History." The letter, in fact, is dated a year after the Litany in question was published, and refers to it as being already set forth in English with notes ; which notes, or similar ones, Cranmer recommends for the new " procession " which, at the request of the King, he had prepared, and to which, by way of experiment, he had adapted the old music. This new " procession " was possibly an altered translation of some of those included under the head of processions " pro variis necessitatibus publicis " ; and, as such, was only complementary to, and to be used along with, the Litany already published. Whatever it was, Strype, in his " Memoir of Cranmer," says he was unable to discover a copy of it. The music to which this Litany was noted follows the Sarum Use very closely, and is that now commonly known as Cranmer's or the Ferial Litany. Dr Jebb, in the second volume of his " Choral Responses and Litanies " (1857), gave an exact reprint, except as to pagination, of the first English Litany. It was made from a very rare and undated copy in the library of Brazenose College, Oxford. He also gave many interesting notes on other copies he had examined and collated, together with examples of the sources of the notation (Gallican, Roman, and Sarum) of the English Litany of 1544. A glance at these examples will show how the authorities differ, and how difficult it is to constitute a standard. It is evident that Cranmer, or whoever arranged the first English Litany, simplified it very much, adapting all the clauses to the tune of the invocation. In June 1544 the Litany was republished by T. Grafton, for Berthelet, with harmonies in five parts, " according to the notes used in the King's Chapel." This was followed in 1560 by an arrangement by Robert Stone, one of the Gentlemen of the Chapel Royal, and printed in Day's " Service-Book," the first collection of polyphonic Church music (services and anthems) published after the Reformation. A

ECCLESIASTICAL TERMS

copy of this now excessively scarce book is in the library of the Dean and Chapter of Westminster (for a full description of its contents consult J. S. Bumpus, " History of English Cathedral Music," pp. 14–17, 561). The tenor part coincides with the plain chant of 1544. This arrangement was followed by Edward Lowe (" Directions for the Performance of Cathedral Service," 1661–1664) and John Playford (" Introduction to the Skill of Music," 1674–1730). Towards the end of the sixteenth century came the famous harmonies of Tallis, or, as some think, Byrd, forming an embroidery, as it were, to the plain chant. To these harmonisations, perhaps, it is mostly owing that the chant to the Litany has been used in a more entire and unmutilated state, down to these days, than any other part of the plainsong. It should be observed that Tallis' Litany ends at the Lord's Prayer, and it was so printed by Barnard (" Selected Church Music," 1641) and Boyce (" Cathedral Music," 1760). The " Suffrages " in the latter part have been arranged and harmonised (chiefly from responses in the Morning Service) by various composers and editors, such as Dean Aldrich, c. 1700 ; Archdeacon Heathcote, c. 1800 ; Rev. John Finlayson, c. 1840 ; and Robert Janes, c. 1850. The arrangement by John Bishop of Cheltenham in his beautifully printed edition of Tallis' Service (1844) was followed by Thomas Oliphant in his folio edition of 1845, and it has since been adopted in the octavo copy recently edited for Novello by Sir George Martin, organist of St Paul's Cathedral. At Lichfield, whenever Tallis' Litany is sung, the latter suffrages follow the ferial use, a not very commendable practice. From the time of Tallis to the close of the seventeenth century, settings of the Litany were produced by numerous composers. Ample material for the study of such is afforded by the specimens given in Jebb's two exhaustive volumes. Here we find Tallis' Litany in a variety of forms ; also litanies by Wm. Byrd, Adrian Batten, Thomas Tomkins, Robert Ramsey, Richard Ayleward, Henry Molle, Henry Loosemore, William King, and Thomas Wanless—all fine, solemn pieces of ecclesiastical harmony, and printed at full length, with copious notes, explanatory of the source whence each was derived. The litanies of Richard Ayleward (in D major), Henry Loosemore (in D minor), and William King (in B flat) formed parts of complete Services written by those composers. The Latin Litany of Tallis, with the latter suffrages by Aldrich, was sung to the organ at St Mary's, Oxford, before the University on the first day of Act Term, and on the day preceding each of the others. It used also to be formerly chanted on Saturdays during Lent, the stated congregation

being the determining bachelors. Its Lenten use seems to have
been discontinued in 1822, about which time, also, the chanting by
the two chaplains was also given up. Dr Crotch printed an organ
copy of this Latin Litany in both editions of his " Psalm Tunes,"
1803 and 1807. Many of the settings of the English Litany, as printed
by Jebb, have long been obsolete. Those, however, by Loosemore,
King, and Wanless have recently been revived, though the last-named
has been sung at York, with a short period of disuse, since its composition. They were introduced at Lichfield by the Rev. W. St
George Patterson (from 1845 to 1890 sub-chanter of that cathedral)
soon after his appointment, and sung in weekly rotation, together
with the litanies of Cranmer and Tallis, thus forming a cycle of
five. Excellent modern editions of the litanies of Loosemore, King,
and Wanless were prepared in 1902 by Mr J. B. Lott, Mus.B.,
organist of Lichfield, and published by Novello. Each has a short
but interesting explanatory preface. Dr Alcock, organist of the
Chapel Royal, has also written about them in *The Musical Times* of
February 1910. Some of the earlier settings given by Jebb, especially those of Ayleward, Byrd, and Molle, as well as Loosemore's
Latin Litany in G minor, equally deserve republication in an inex-
pensive form. Samuel Wesley (d. 1837) wrote a fine setting of the
Litany in the key of G major, which was occasionally sung at St
Paul's during Thomas Attwood's organistship of that cathedral
(1797–1838). A florid Litany composed by John Soaper, one of the
vicars choral of St Paul's during the end of the eighteenth century,
continued " a great favourite " at St George's Chapel, Windsor,
until the appointment as organist, in 1835, of G. J. Elvey, who
summarily banished it in favour of that of Tallis. Unisonal settings
of the Litany, printed by Jebb, as in common or ferial use in 1857,
were those of the cathedrals of Salisbury, Lincoln, and Winchester,
and that of New College, Oxford. The harmonised ones were those
of Canterbury, St Paul's, Westminster, Bristol, and Norwich.
Except that of Bristol all agreed substantially in following the
plain tune of the Litany of 1544. In the harmonised ones the voice
parts varied in every case. Three litanies from the Mechlin " Processionale Parvum " (where they are assigned in order to the three
Rogation Days) were edited in 1881 by J. W. Doran and W. Spenser
Nottingham (Novello). The music of the first, down to the Lord's
Prayer, agrees for the most part with the Use of Sarum, fragments
of which have come down to us through Merbecke, Tallis, Barnard
and others, and the various traditionary uses of our cathedrals.
These might be fitly used on the three days for which they were

primarily intended, or on Fridays in ferial seasons, and perhaps throughout Lent, in churches where a severe and archaic style of music is cultivated. They are, of course unisonal, but organ harmonies are provided. There is also a very beautiful and solemn arrangement of the Litany to the 3rd Gregorian Tone by W. Spenser Nottingham, eminently fitted for use during Holy Week. A Latin version of the Ferial Litany was edited, in 1886 (primarily for use at the service opening Convocation at St Paul's), by Sir John Stainer and the Rev. W. Russell, and printed by Novello. In certain of our cathedrals a dual performance of the Litany is traditional, that is, as regards the minister's part. Thus at York the petitions are chanted by two of the priest vicars choral; at Durham, Hereford, and Norwich by two minor canons; at Exeter and Lichfield by a priest vicar and a lay vicar, and at Lincoln by two lay vicars. At Chichester, in 1700, the Litany was sung by two lay vicars, and at the reopening of the cathedral after its restoration, 14th November 1867, by two priest vicars, but neither custom now obtains there. At the enthronement of Archbishop Sumner in Canterbury Cathedral, 28th April 1848, Tallis' Litany was sung by the Rev. Joshua Stratton, precentor, and the Rev. G. P. Marriott, one of the minor canons. At the Dedication Festival of St Andrew's, Wells Street, 30th November 1849, the Litany was sung by the Rev. James Murray, incumbent of the church, and the Rev. Thomas Helmore, Master of the Children of the Chapel Royal, both kneeling upon the lowest step of the chancel. At St Paul's, the ancient custom of two minor canons chanting the Litany was discontinued about the year 1874. The five-part Litany of Tallis is now sung in procession at St Paul's on the Monday and Tuesday of Rogation Week, on the Feast of the Conversion of St Paul, on St Andrew's Day, and at other stated times, with magnificent effect. The invocations and petitions are chanted by four minor canons, and responded to by the full choir. Starting from the high altar, in front of which the invocations are sung, stationary, the procession moves down the south choir aisle, across the dome, and so on to the extreme west end of the cathedral. Then, advancing up the nave, the choir is reached as the *Agnus Dei* (perhaps the most touching part of the composition) is chanted. The ancient outdoor Rogation procession has, very laudably, been revived in many parishes, both in London and the country. In that of St Matthias', Stoke Newington, Loosemore's setting is sung, and the same composition precedes the High Celebration on Sundays in Advent and Lent. The Litany forms part of the Coronation Service, as also in the Ordering of Priests and Deacons, and the

Consecration of Bishops. For the sources (verbal) of our Litany consult Karslake, " Litany of the English Church " (1876).

Litany-desk. A convenient, though not correct, term for this piece of church furniture is " Faldstool," whose true import has already been explained. The Sarum " Processional " orders the litany-desk to stand between the stalls and the altar, in accordance with the Jewish practice of " weeping between the porch and the altar " (Joel ii. 17). This would seem to refer more particularly to cathedrals, and to churches with large chancels. Its usual position in cathedrals is now in the midst of the choir, as at Canterbury, Carlisle, Durham (where it was presented by Bishop Cosin, 1662), Exeter, Lincoln, Peterborough, Truro, Worcester, and York. At Bristol, Chester, Hereford, Lichfield, and Salisbury it is placed a little westward of the open choir-screen. At Lincoln it stands upon a spot where an inscription, *Cantate hic*, marks the place occupied in pre-Reformation times by the Rulers of the Choir. At St Paul's, its position has been more than once shifted. Until 1871 it was just eastward of the great eagle lectern in the centre of the choir. At the time of the redistribution of the choral fittings in 1871–1872 it was placed immediately in front of the low screen fencing off the dome from the choir. Within recent years it has been removed to the western part of the choir itself, but it is not a fixture, being placed there only when required—a great mistake. A litany-desk should always form part of the permanent fittings of a choir. At the Collegiate Church of St Michael, Tenbury, the litany-desk, covered with needlework varying in colour with the season, is placed between the *decani* and *cantoris* choir-stalls, thus following general cathedral usage. In parish churches the desk is usually at the eastern end of the nave. Some ancient litany-desks still remain. In the eighteenth century many were cast aside, like the lecterns. There is one at Jesus College, Cambridge, which was found amongst some lumber at the time of the restoration of the chapel in 1848–1849. That at Durham is coeval with Bishop Cosin's stallwork of 1662. Westminster Abbey is still without its litany-desk. Perhaps the finest and most iconographically correct litany-desk made in modern times is to be seen at St Andrew's, Wells Street. It was the gift of an anonymous donor in 1867, and designed by the distinguished architect, William Burges. Of unusual beauty are the carvings in walnut of " Zacharias, the son of Barachias," offering incense ; of the prophet Joel, and of SS. Andrew, Michael, and George, with figures of angels swinging censers. In front is the legend, *Libera nos, Domine*, with the date of the year inlaid in maple

ECCLESIASTICAL TERMS

wood on the walnut, the surface of the desk itself being inlaid with the emblems of the Passion. The idea embodied is, of course, that the litany-desk in Christian art represents, in a manner, the " altar of incense " in the Temple. A full description of this desk will be found in *The Ecclesiologist*, February 1868. The issue of the following August contains a photograph. At some churches it is customary on Litany days to cover the desk with a violet hanging, with the words " JESU, MERCY " embroidered thereon.

Those who follow the course of the Church's worship welcome all appropriate aids to joining in it intelligently. It would be a serious loss if the church itself should always present **Liturgical** the same uniform appearance ; and it is a correspond-**Colours.** ing help when the alternation of fast and festival is made visible to the eye. It would be unnatural, for example, if, in passing from Holy Week to Easter, no difference were made in the outward appearance of the church and the vestures of the ministers. It is with the view to making such reasonable difference that, from remote times, the employment of various liturgical colours has been adopted. Such a custom was in use in the English Church in the second year of the reign of Edward VI. (see Rev. Vernon Staley, " The Catholic Religion," 1904). For the altar-frontals and vestments of the clergy the following sequence of liturgical colours has English pre-Reformation precedent :—

Advent, *violet*, or *blue of subdued hue*.
Christmas to the octave of Epiphany, *white*.
Epiphany to Septuagesima, *green*.
Septuagesima to Ash Wednesday, *violet*, or *blue of subdued hue*.
Lent (first four weeks), *violet* or *subdued blue*, or *white linen*.
Passion and Holy Weeks, *violet* or *red*.
Good Friday, *black*.
Eastertide, *white*.
Ascensiontide, *white*.
Whitsuntide, *red*.
Trinity Sunday and six following days, *white*.
Trinity Season to Advent, *green*.
Ember Days, Rogation Days, and Vigils, *violet* or *subdued blue*.
Feasts of the Blessed Virgin, St John Evangelist, St John Baptist, Michaelmas, All Saints', Virgins, *white*.
Apostles (except St John Evangelist), Evangelists, Martyrs, Holy Innocents, *red*.
Confessors, *yellow* (*saffron*) or *green*.
Dedication of a church, *white*.

177

A DICTIONARY OF

Feast of patron saint, *colour of the saint.*

Baptism, confirmation, marriage, churching, ordination, consecration of bishop or archbishop, *white.*

Funerals and memorials of departed, *black.*

The vestments of the clergy and vestings of the altar are *white* on all the great festivals of Our Lord, of the Blessed Virgin, and of all saints who did not suffer martyrdom : white being the colour appropriated to joy and signifying purity. *Red* is used on the feasts of martyrs, typifying that they shed their blood for the testimony of Jesus ; and at Whitsuntide, when the Holy Ghost descended in the likeness of tongues of fire. *Violet* is the penitential colour, and so used in Advent, Lent, on vigils, etc. *Green* is the ordinary colour for days that are neither feasts nor fasts, as being the pervading colour of nature. The use of *black* on Good Friday and at funerals is self-explanatory. The ancient Use of the Diocese of Sarum prescribed *red* for all Sundays throughout the year, except from Easter to Pentecost, unless a festival superseded the Sunday services. The same colour served for Ash Wednesday, Good Friday, Maundy Thursday, and Easter and Whitsun Eves. *White* was employed throughout Eastertide (*i.e.* from Easter to Whitsun Eve), whether the service were of Sunday, of a saint's day, or of the feria, with the exception of the Invention of the Cross (3rd May). *Yellow* was employed for the feasts of confessors ; *blue* was used indifferently with *green* as the ferial colour ; and *brown* or *grey* with *violet* for penitential times. In this rite, *red* was used in a twofold aspect ; as a solemnly penitential colour (hence its use on Ash Wednesday and the last three days of Holy Week), and as an ordinary dominical or Sunday colour ; in the first case in order to connect all our penitence with the Passion of Christ, teaching us to mourn for our sins, not merely because they have injured us, but chiefly because they " have crucified the Son of God afresh " ; in the second, because Sunday is the weekly feast of Him who is the King of Martyrs. It served also for Whitsuntide, the feasts of martyrs, and of the Cross, for the reason given above. *Yellow* or *saffron* is symbolical of the " robe of glory " with which those who have confessed the name of Jesus are clothed. *Blue,* the colour of the firmament, was employed for the week-days after Trinity, the season which represents the everlasting rest that remaineth to the people of God ; and thence came to be used for the similar days after Epiphany. *Brown* and *grey,* as expressive of the " sack cloth " of mourning and penitence, were assigned for week-day use in penitential seasons. Amidst much that is obscure concerning the colours of the vestments

178

ECCLESIASTICAL TERMS

anciently used in England, it is clear that several of the cathedrals and abbeys had certain colours of their own, differing one from the other, perhaps influenced by the heraldic colours of their armorial bearings. Certainly the inventories of church goods, made by the orders of Henry VIII., show that colours not recognised in any known sequence, including parti-coloured vestments, were in use in many places. Attempts had been made to introduce the Roman sequence, or something like it, notably by Bishop Grandisson of Exeter and Bishop Clifford of London. Grandisson, in his Ordinal, A.D. 1337, gives a table of colours, which he says " follows the custom of the Court of Rome " ("juxta morem Curiæ Romanæ "), and which is in fact the Roman sequence with slight modifications. Nearly in the same words is the table of colours given in the Pontifical of Clifford, Bishop of London from 1406 to 1426. Such publications as these had, no doubt, an extended influence, and help to account for the violet and green vestments which are shown by the inventories to have been in use in the sixteenth century, the violet vestments being fairly numerous. Clifford's sequence was drawn up when the Roman tendency was beginning to exercise an influence. Grandisson pressed his on Exeter successfully, but not so Clifford, St Paul's having its own peculiar ceremonial use, while accepting the Sarum Breviary " in cantando et legendo "—that is to say, St Paul's was English to the backbone. At Soissons, in France, a peculiar and perhaps unique use is found. In this diocese green vestments are put on immediately after None (*q.v.*) and continued through offices of Easter Eve up to the vigil of Pentecost, including even the procession on St Mark's Day and the Rogations. " Of the use of this colour," says Dr J. Wickham Legg (" Comparison of the Liturgical Colours "), " a canon of Soissons gave two explanations —one natural ; the other mystical. The natural reason is, that in the sixteenth century the Protestants destroyed all the precious vestments except the green ones. The mystical reason is the hope which our Lord's Resurrection gives to the human race. The first of these reasons is destroyed by finding that in a manuscript Soissons ritual, of date before the sixteenth century, the bishop, deacons, and archdeacons are directed to wear green during the ceremonies of Easter Eve, and the reason given is : ' Viror namque vestimentorum redemptionem nostram approprinquante jam die ressurectionis vivere designat.' As to mystical reasons, it is not hard to manufacture such in abundance. We may say that as the festival is celebrated on this side of the equator in the spring, when all nature is bursting into a fresh life, green is especially symbolical of the

179

Resurrection." Dr Legg quotes as his authority Martene, " de Antiquis Ecclesiæ Ritibus," lib. iv. cap. xxiv. Antiq. Rit. Eccl. Suesson. Dr Legg's paper, " A Comparison of the Liturgical Colours in certain Gallican and Anglican Uses, with those of Rome and Milan," and one by the Rev. J. Baden Powell, " The English Liturgical Colours," both read before the St Paul's Ecclesiological Soicety in 1880 and 1881, and printed in the first volume of the Society's " Transactions," may be perused with pleasure and profit. A paper, " The Sarum Colours," by E. C. Channer, B.A., printed in *The Sacristy*, February 1872, is also of interest, and on the same subject the Rev. Percy Dearmer's " Parson's Handbook," c. iii., should by all means be consulted. Many of us can remember how, in numbers of our churches, red was the covering for the altar throughout the year, except in Lent, when it was black. In all probability this was a lingering tradition of the Sarum red for ordinary Sundays. While the saintly Dr Hamilton was Bishop of Salisbury (1856–1869) it is related that his custom was to present a red altar-cloth to every new church which he consecrated, or to an old one at whose reopening after restoration he preached. It was formerly the custom at St Paul's and Westminster Abbey to cover the altar, pulpit, etc., with black cloth during the season of Lent. At St Paul's the curtains of the dean's stall and that of the canon-in-residence, together with those of the stall and throne of the Bishop of London, were black. Since 1891 St Paul's has possessed an altar-frontal of black and ash-colour, *cinericius*. This is used only on Good Friday, and at obsequies, either actual or memorial, of eminent persons. On these occasions the carpet of the sanctuary is black, and on Good Friday, for the past two or three years, the altar cross has been veiled in crape. On the death of the sovereign it was usual to drape churches with black cloth and mourning devices, more or less expensive according to the wealth and loyalty of the parishioners, which fittings after having hung the proper time became the property of the vicar or rector. In the case of rich city of London parishes the cloth employed was of considerable value. This custom seems to have been generally observed for the last time on the death of William IV. in June 1837.

Low Sunday. The octave of Easter, and so called because a kind of second but lower celebration of the great feast.

Lychnoscope. A word used by the Rev. Benjamin Webb and other early ecclesiologists, in default of a better one, to denote a hagioscope (*q.v.*) that does not seem connected with an altar ; common in England, but only hypothetically introduced into foreign ecclesiology.

ECCLESIASTICAL TERMS

Maestro di Cappella (Ital.). Choirmaster, leader, or conductor in a Germ. *capellmeister*. cathedral church or royal chapel.

Magnificat. The Psalm uttered by the Blessed Virgin upon her visit to St Elizabeth, after the angel had made known to her that she should be the mother of Our Lord, and appointed to be sung "in English" after the First Lesson at Evening Prayer. Its place in the old offices was at Vespers, when it was immediately preceded by five Psalms, the Capitulum (or short chapter) and the office hymn. It has been sung as long as the office can be traced in the Western Church. Being one of the canticles extracted from the Gospel of St Luke it is styled "Evangelical," and as such should always be preferred to the alternative provided in the Books of 1552 and 1662, *Cantate Domino*. Thus inserted it occupies a most significant place in our service. After reading the Old Testament we have this Song of Mary, testifying to the fulfilment of God's promises of mercy to the fathers. The music to which it is sung in our Church ranges from the severest plainsong to the most elaborate choral treatment with organ and orchestral accompaniment. All our cathedral writers have included it in their "Services," from Tye and Tallis downwards. Merbecke, in his "Book of Common Prayer Noted," sets it to the 1st Gregorian Tone. Innumerable instances of the *Magnificat* set service-wise are to be found among the works of the writers for that "other great Church." Thirty-five of such pieces, for four, five, six, and eight voices, by Palestrina, including the celebrated *Magnificat Octo Tonorum*, are given in Breitkopf and Härtel's splendid edition of his complete works (vol. xxvii.). In some of these *Magnificats* the verses are set alternately in *canto fermo* and *canto figurato*. Specimens of this style may be also seen in Burns' "Ecclesiastical Choir-Book" (1848) which contains likewise a noble setting by Luca Marenzio (eight voices). *Magnificats* for four voices by Ludovicus Viadana and Antonio Lotti—distinguished masters of the sixteenth and seventeenth centuries are published by Messrs Breitkopf and Härtel. Eslava's now enormously scarce collection, "Lira Sacro-Hispaña," contains *Magnificats* by many distinguished composers of the various Spanish schools. The *Magnificat* in C of Mozart has been adapted to English words for the use of St Andrew's, Wells Street, as well as a similar composition in G by Batti, an Italian writer. These are usually followed by the settings of the *Nunc dimittis* by Thomas Attwood (Mozart's favourite and only English pupil), and Benjamin Cooke. The Rev. Thomas Helmore published effective settings of the *Magnificat*, with English words, arranged for alternate plain and figurate singing, from Orlando di Lasso, as given in the third volume of " Musica Divina," published at Ratisbon under the editorship of Carl Proske, 1859. These Continental settings for alternate verses in *canto fermo* and *canto figurato* probably suggested the " chanting services " of the Ely organists, James Hawkins (1682), Thomas Kempton (1729), and Richard Langdon (1777). The library at St Peter's, or Peterhouse, College, Cambridge, contains *Magnificats* to Latin words by Robert Fayrefax, John Taverner, and other celebrated English pre-Reformation writers. Consult the Rev. John Jebb's catalogue of this valuable MS. collection (1861), also Henry Davey's " History of English Music." In Day's " Service-Book " (1565) there is an Evening Service for four voices (*Magnificat* and *Nunc dimittis*) by William Whitbroke, Warden of the College of Minor Canons of St Paul's in 1560. It is interesting to note that the *Magnificat* begins on the words " and my spirit hath rejoiced," indicating that the first hemistich was intoned by the precentor or succentor, a custom observable in the *Magnificats* of the unreformed service. Of this there appears no trace in subsequent settings of the canticle. The custom, however, of giving the opening words to the priest in the *Te Deum* and *Credo* was pretty generally observed, as may be seen in the Services of many of the composers of the seventeenth and eighteenth centuries. The settings of *Magnificat* contained in Eslava's " Lira Sacro-Hispana " (10 vols., 1869) are by Ramos, Ribera and Torrentes (sixteenth century) ; Heredia (*super 8 Tonos*) and Vargas, both seventeenth century ; and Doyagüe (nineteenth century). In the same collection there is a *Nunc Dimittis* by Fr. Andrevi (nineteenth century). Mozart's *Magnificat* forms part of his " Vesperæ de Dominica " (No. 1), published by C. F. Peters, Leipzig and Berlin. The five Psalms of Sunday Vespers—*Dixit Dominus* ; *Confitebor* ; *Beatus vir* ; *Laudate pueri* ; and *Laudate Dominum*, are elaborately set, like anthems. Examples of such settings of the same Psalms by earlier composers will be found in Proske's " Musica Divina."

Maîtrise. (1) The French term for the choristers' school attached to a cathedral. (2) A school in which descant (the forerunner of modern counterpoint and harmony) was taught. Another name is " Psallette." In the French cathedrals the high altar, or altar of the choir, is called the Maître-Autel.

Majesty. A sculptured or painted figure of Our Lord seated, enthroned, and crowned, and generally in the act of benediction. A favourite subject for the semi-dome of an apse or the tympanum of a doorway. The Majesty in the apse of St Paul's is executed in mosaic.

Manilia. A metal vessel from which water for the lavation of the hands was poured through a long spout. It was usually made in some fantastic shape, such as a lion, a horse, a dove, a hen. A manilia formed as a siren is to be seen in the Church of St John, Herford. Westphalia, and one as a lion in the Church of Berghausen. Lübke ("Ecclesiastical Art in Germany," p. 153) engraves the first-named. Probably the use of the manilia was confined to the larger and wealthier of the cathedrals and monasteries.

Maniple.
Lat.
manipulus. Sometimes called *Phanon* and *Sudarium*. Originally a narrow strip of linen as wide as a stole, and about two and a half feet long, suspended from the left arm of the celebrant, deacon, and sub-deacon, and used for wiping the hands (*manus*) and for other cleanly purposes. Gradually it received embellishments; it was bordered by a fringe and decorated with needlework. In the eleventh century it was given to the sub-deacons as the badge of their order. The maniple was not retained among the ecclesiastical vestments of the English Church, but its use has been revived. At St Michael's College, Tenbury, it serves for wiping the rim of the chalice during the administration of the Holy Communion, a practice introduced by the Rev. W. J. E. Bennett in the early days of St Paul's, Knightsbridge and St Barnabas', Pimlico.

Männerchor. The gallery formed in the nave of a German church immediately over the arches opening to the aisles. It is set apart for the male portion of the congregation. The usage on which it depended was, however, local, and it rarely makes its appearance out of North-Western Germany or after the middle of the thirteenth century. See also *sub voce* "Triforium."

Matins. From the Latin *matutina*, which means appertaining to the morning. The ancient name for early morning prayers, which were sung or said in religious houses soon after midnight. "At midnight I will rise to give thanks unto thee, because of thy righteous judgments" (Ps. cxix. 62). So Dugdale ("Monast. Ang." vi. 679), "Ante auroram vel ex ortu aurorae." This, the first of the canonical hours, stood thus in the Sarum Portiforium or Breviary :—In Nomine, Paternoster, Ave Maria, Domine labia, Deus in adjutorium, Gloria Patri, Alleluia, or Laus Tibi, Invitatory, Venite, 12 or 18 Psalms with Antiphons (sung in three nocturns), and Gloria after certain Psalms, Benedictions, and three or nine Lections with antiphons, Te Deum. In the revision of the Roman Breviary by Cardinal Quignonez the office stood thus: Paternoster, Ave Maria, Confiteor, Absolutio, Domine labia, Deus in adjutorium, Gloria Patri, Alleluia, or Laus Tibi, Invitatory, Venite, 3 Psalms with Gloria after each, Paternoster, Benediction and First Lection from the Old Testament, Benediction, Second Lection (New Testament), Benediction, Homily, Te Deum, or Psalm li. Lauds, the next office, was frequently joined on to Matins. The Sarum order was: 5 Psalms, among them the *Jubilate* and *Benedicite*, the Little Chapter (*Capitulum*), office hymn, *Benedictus*, Collect of the Day, petitions, and the Collect for Peace. The Roman arrangement has been given *s.v.* "Lauds." The next morning office was "Prime," said at 6 A.M. (hence *prima hora*, the first hour), or at least soon after sunrise. According to the Use of Sarum it comprised: Paternoster, Ave Maria, Deus in Adjutorium hymn, 3 to 9 Psalms, the Athanasian Creed (*Symbolum Athanasii*), Capitulum, Kyrie Eleison, Paternoster, Credo, versicular petitions, Confiteor, Absolutio, Collect for Grace, Benedicamus Domino, Deo Gratias. The same office in the Roman Breviary consists of the Paternoster, Ave Maria, Apostles' Creed, hymn, 3 or more Psalms, the last two being the first portion of the 118th (in our Prayer-Book the 119th), Athanasian Creed (on Sundays only), Capitulum, versicles, Collects for Grace and Peace, the Martyrology of the day—viz. a short list of all the saints and martyrs throughout the world commemorated on that day, followed by prayers to consecrate one's thoughts, words, and deeds of the day to God, concluding with a short passage of Scripture and a blessing. On a comparison of our Morning Service with the offices of Matins, Lauds, and Prime, it will be seen that it is a judicious abridgment of the three. It may be divided into three principal parts. First, the introduction, which extends from the beginning of the office to the end of the Lord's Prayer; secondly, the psalmody and lessons, which extend to the end of the Apostles' Creed; and thirdly, the prayers and collects, which occupy the remainder of the service. The use of the double "t" in the word "Matins," as in the calendar, and as frequently to be met with elsewhere, is probably derived from the custom of doubling the last letter of an abbreviation in Latin. Thus *Matutina* (*hora*) was written *Matt*: and so we get "Mattins." In the Greek Church τὸ μεσονύκτιον is still the word used for Matins. The three or nine Lections read in the Nocturns of Matins were generally very short; some consisting only of a few verses of Scripture; and some being short extracts from Expositions or Homilies of the Fathers, or Lives of the Saints. Hence, although the Lessons were numerous, but little Scripture was read; and that small portion was interrupted by antiphons. It was a most important change that was introduced in 1549 into this part of the Public Service; for not only was the quantity of Scripture increased that was actually read, but the reading was made intelligible by being continuous; while the appointment of two chapters, one from the Old and one from the New Testament, was a return to primitive custom. Thus Cassian (*Inst. Cœnob.* ii. 6): " quibus [psalmis] lectiones geminas adjungentes, id est, unam veteris, et aliam novi Testamenti. . . ." In the mediæval lection system, it was the Old *or* New Testament that was read; not both on the same day (see Freeman, " Principles of Divine Service," 344).

Maundy Thursday
(Dies Mandati). The Thursday in Holy Week, on which day Our Lord gave His new Commandment or *mandatum* (St John xiii. 34), and on which the Sacrament of the Holy Eucharist was instituted. It was therefore called also *Dies Cœna Domini, Dies Natalis Eucharistiae, Dies mysteriorum, Dies natalis Calicis,* etc. On this day the candidates for Baptism publicly rehearsed the Creed, and penitents were reconciled. The very early ceremony of washing the feet of twelve or thirteen poor men was confined to bishops and other great ecclesiastical and secular personages. Archbishop Cranmer practised and defended the custom. Queen Elizabeth kept it up, herself washing and kissing the feet of as many poor persons as corresponded with her age. This was in imitation of the action of Our Lord. The Pope does the same on Maundy Thursday at the present day. In the "Hierugia Anglicana" (p. 282) an account is given of the ceremonial of washing the feet of the poor by Queen Elizabeth. The Hanoverian sovereigns deputed the office to the royal almoners, who soon dropped the washing (1737), but retained the custom of giving alms, food and clothing. Money is now given in lieu of the two last-named. This quaint ceremony was formerly performed at the Chapel Royal, Whitehall, but since the closing of that building as a place of worship (1891) it has been transferred to Westminster Abbey. A vestige of the old ceremony of washing is retained in this service, the Almoner and his assistant being girded with long linen towels during the distribution. The order of service used on this occasion is given by Blunt in his " Annotated Prayer-Book." Psalm xci. has since been substituted for Psalm xli.. Four anthems, varied each year, are sung in the course of the service. In the Sarum Missal the rubric runs: " Post

prandium conveniant clerici ad ecclesiam, ad altaria abluenda ; et ad mandatum faciendum ; et ad completorium dicendum." While the *mandatum, pedilavium*, or feet-washing took place, the antiphon " Mandatum novum do vobis," followed by certain psalms and antiphons, was sung. From the first word of the first antiphon the name Maundy is derived ; certainly not (as some have thought) from the Saxon, " maunds," the baskets which contained the royal gift. More novel practices of the Roman Church on Maundy Thursday are the consecration of the chrism for the following year ; the *praesanctificatio*, or consecration of the Host for Good Friday ; the extinction of all the tapers, and removal of the ornaments from the altar ; the communion of the priests, and the excommunication of all heretics. Formerly, at Magdalen College, Oxford, the President washed the feet of seven choristers on Maundy Thursday. Among the College disbursements in 1531 we find : " Sol. Dno Presidi in Cena Domini pro Chorustis lavando eorum pedes, vii^d " ; and again in 1535 : " Sol. Septem Chorustis, quorum pedes lavabantur a Dno Preside in cena Domini. vii^d." (Bloxam, " Magdalen College Register," i. Preface vii., 1853). Dr Rimbault (" Old Cheque Book of the Chapel Royal," 112–121) gives a list of " Certayne benevolence yearelie from the Lord Almoner to the Gentlemen of the Chappell on Maundye Thursdaye," from 1580 until early in the eighteenth century. The Holy Eucharist should be sung with much solemnity on this its birthday. At St Paul's, the organ, silent throughout Holy Week until the first Evensong of Easter, is used at the choral Celebration (following Matins) on this day—a custom instituted in 1881. A setting for the *Kyrie, Credo, Sanctus* and *Gloria* of a festal character is usually selected.

Maytinantes, or Matutinales. Clerks who sang at the night services and matins.

Mensa (Latin). Eng. *table*. The upper slab of an altar, whether of stone or wood. Ancient altar-slabs have usually five rude crosses cut in them, which mark the places anointed by the bishop at the consecration. The reproduction of these crosses on unanointed altars is unmeaning.

Mid-Lent Sunday. Fr. *Mi-Carême*. The fourth Sunday in Lent. It was anciently known as *Dominica Refectionis*, or Refreshment Sunday, probably from the subject of the Gospel—the feeding of the five thousand in the wilderness. Others attribute the name to the fact that on this Sunday above others in Lent certain festivities have been allowed, as at the Mi-Carême in France, and the benediction of the Golden Rose by the Pope at Rome. Brand ("Popular Antiquities") tells us that it was an old custom in England to feast on rich cakes, etc., on this Sunday; and it was also usual to visit the mother church of the diocese, and to make offerings at the high altar, whence it was called "Mothering Sunday." Presents also were in many places made by children to their parents, which often took the form of what were called "Mothering Cakes." On the fourth Sunday in Lent the Church makes a kind of pause in her penitential exercises, saying, as it were, with the Psalmist, "Though I walk in the midst of trouble, yet shalt thou refresh me" (Ps. cxxxviii. 7). In both the Roman and Sarum missals the opening words of the introit were " Lætare Jerusalem, et conventum facite omnes, qui diligitis eam " (" Rejoice ye with Jerusalem, and be glad with her, all ye that love her "). From this circumstance the Sunday received the title of " Lætare " in the calendar. It was usual to employ dalmatics richly embroidered in gold, and to use dalmatics of *rose*-colour, yet further to symbolise the temporary change from sorrow to joy. " Thou hast put off my sackcloth, and girded me with gladness " (Ps. xxx. 11). " The desert shall rejoice and blossom as the rose: it shall blossom abundantly, and rejoice even with joy and singing " (Isa. xxxv. 1, 2). In Advent and Lent the deacon and sub-deacon laid aside the dalmatic and tunicle, as being festal garments, and ministered in the *planeta*, or folded chasuble, or in their albs. On the Third Sunday in Advent, and the Fourth Sunday in Lent the dalmatic and tunicle were resumed for the day only. The reason assigned is, that Advent is a time partly of sorrow and partly of joy, and in the lesson for the Third Sunday the joyous element predominates (as it does also in the Epistle for the Fourth Sunday). The reason why this was done on the Fourth Sunday in Lent is that assigned above.

Middle Pointed. The Ecclesiological Society's nomenclature for that period of Gothic which flourished, roughly speaking, from *c.* 1270–1350. See *sub voce* " Decorated."

Minor Canons (*Canonici Minores*). Priests in cathedrals, not members of either the great or small chapters, who are responsible for performing the service, but who, as a rule, have no preaching turn assigned to them in the ancient rota. In most of the Cathedrals of the Old Foundation they are called priest vicars choral, and with the lay vicars choral (singing men) form, in some cases, a corporation. In the Old Cathedrals one of the minor canons is called succentor or sub-chanter, and acts as the precentor's deputy.

In the New Cathedrals (Henry VIII.'s foundation) a minor canon is invariably "chanter" or precentor, the office of precentor not existing among the dignitaries. The qualifications for the office of minor canon are a fine voice, a knowledge of Church music, and an irreproachable life. At St Paul's, whenever a vacancy occurred in the college of twelve minor canons, the Fellows were privileged to nominate two candidates, whom they presented to the dean and chapter, one of whom that body was required to elect. The person so chosen was admitted to a year's probation. If his conduct was approved of, the dean and chapter instituted. The election is now entirely with the chapter. Their original dress in choir consisted of a white surplice, black copes with cowls, and almuces of Calabrian fur, lined with minever. A statute issued by the dean and chapter in 1364 states that they excel in honour and dignity all chaplains in the cathedral, that they officiate at the high altar in the stead of the greater canons, and that they are to wear almuces of fur after the manner of the greater canons, instead of almuces of black cloth, such as chaplains wore. They had lands belonging to them, *jure ecclesiae*, and let those belonging to their corporation by a common seal. Until the time of Dean Milman (1849) they had no stalls assigned to them in choir, their places being in the sub-stalls, level with the vicars choral, and behind the choristers, or boys of the Almonry School. The twelve minor canons of St Paul's formerly constituted an important part of the choir. Until early in the last century many of them were resident in St Paul's College, in the immediate neighbourhood of the cathedral, and, with the sub-dean at their head, were in daily attendance. They were bound to take their several parts, counter-tenor, tenor, or bass, in all the services and anthems, like the vicars choral, and they took their turn in singing the solos and " verses " allotted to them. The numerical strength of the adult choir of St Paul's was thus the same as at the present day, the difference being that twelve were priests and six laymen. Now the choir is composed exclusively of eighteen laymen, all accomplished singers, and zealous in their calling. This ancient and honourable body, incorporated under the title of the Warden and College of Minor Canons by King Richard II. in 1394, but dating back to the remote days of the foundation of the cathedral itself, possessing the royal charter and seal, and endowed with lands, became, in 1875, the subject of parliamentary legislation. The objects of the " St Paul's Cathedral, London, Minor Canonries Act," were to bring the constitution of the corporation of minor canons into accordance with the Cathedral Act of 1840 (see " The English

ECCLESIASTICAL TERMS

Cathedral Service—its Origin, its Decline, and its Designed Extinction," by Professor Edward Taylor, 1845), and thus to place beyond dispute the legal character of the tenure of their stalls, by those minor canons who had been appointed after the year 1840 ; to define the duties of the minor canons more explicitly in accordance with modern requirements ; to equalise their incomes, and raise them in all cases to a sufficient amount ; to prohibit their holding benefices, minor canonries at Westminster and Windsor, and the office of priest of the Chapel Royal, as many of them had hitherto done ; and to make provision for their retirement after the age of fifty-five. Such legislation was rendered necessary by the reduction of the number of minor canons from twelve to six, in accordance with the Act of 1840. At the present time the corporation consists of seven minor canons, of whom two were appointed under the old system, and five under the new. The 1st, 2nd, 3rd, 4th, 5th, 6th, 7th, 8th, 9th, and 11th minor canonries have lapsed. The holder of the 10th stall is the Rev. W. J. Hall, who was appointed in 1862, and that of the 12th the Rev. J. H. Coward, whose appointment dates back to the year 1846. (Consult " Observations upon the question ' Whether further powers of revising from time to time statutes of capitular bodies should be granted, etc.' "—a letter addressed by the Rev. W. H. Milman to the Ecclesiastical Commissioners, 21st January 1880, printed in the Appendix to the Commissioners' Report on St Paul's Cathedral, 1883.) Those minor canons appointed under the Act of 1875 who have resigned their stalls in consequence of their having exceeded the age limit are styled " honorary minor canons," and take occasional duty. The following offices were attached to some of the stalls : sub-dean (1st stall), senior cardinal (2nd stall), junior cardinal (3rd stall), epistoler, gospeller, sacrist, librarian, succentor, warden, pitanciary, divinity lecturer, and occasionally almoner. Certain of these offices are retained. Consult " The Charter and Statutes of the College of the Minor Canons in St Paul's Cathedral, London," communicated to the Society of Antiquaries by the Rev. W. Sparrow Simpson, M.A., F.S.A., 1871, and printed in *Archæologia*, vol. xliii. pp. 165–200. The number of minor canons in the English cathedrals varies considerably. Before the Cathedral Act of 1840 the number in the New Cathedrals was larger. Thus, for instance, at Norwich there were eight ; there are now only three. The Act crippled the choirs, of which the minor canons formed an important part. At Norwich every minor canon was a singer, and gave his daily attendance and assistance in the choir (consult Professor Taylor's book, *ut supra*, p. 30). At St George's

Chapel, Windsor, the choir consisted originally (besides the chorister-boys) of eighteen adult members—eleven lay clerks and seven minor canons, but in his reply to the Ecclesiastical Commissioners in 1852, the organist, Dr Elvey, observed that the latter members had long ceased to take any part in the choral service beyond chanting the prayers. At Hereford, up to 1840, the twelve adult singers were all clergymen—*i.e.* vicars choral—and there are several instances in the seventeenth and eighteenth centuries of the organist of the same cathedral having been in Holy Orders. Among the abuses of certain cathedrals in a lax age was the appointment to minor canonries of men incompetent to sing. This was for a long time the case at Chester, Ely, Christ Church, Oxford, and Rochester. It was likewise so at the colleges of King's and Trinity, Cambridge, and Eton, where those responsible for the chanting of the service are styled conduct chaplains (*capellani conductitii*). This was in direct violation of the cathedral and college statutes which, one and all, concur in setting forth that the minor canons and chaplains are to be " skilled in singing." It is hardly necessary to observe that this abuse has long been rectified. At Christ Church Cathedral, Oxford, the minor canons are termed chaplains (*capellani chori*), the foundation being partly cathedral and partly collegiate. At Manchester, before the creation of the collegiate church into the cathedral of the new diocese in 1847, the two minor canons were styled chaplains. At St Patrick's Cathedral, Dublin, the four minor canons are quite distinct from the priest or " clerical " vicars choral. We must look abroad for a similar constitution ; the only two instances that can be called to mind are the eight *moindres chanoines* of Rouen, and the petty canons of Toledo. Consult further the section " Petty Canons, Vicars Choral, and other Ministers of the Church," in Mackenzie E. C. Walcott's " Cathedralia " (1865)—a work which contains an immense amount of information on the constitution, corporate rights, internal discipline, and uses of capitular bodies, such as has probably never been got together before. The arrangement, how-ever, is not lucid ; and never did a book cry so loudly for an index. Impressions in wax of the ancient silver seals of the College of Minor Canons of St Paul's may be seen under the glass case in the Library of the Cathedral. They are also figured by Dr Simpson in his " Charter and Statutes of the College of Minor Canons in St Paul's Cathedral " (p. 18). The common seal represents a full-length figure of St Paul, bearing in his right hand a book and in his left a sword with the point downwards, surrounded by the legend, s' : COË : COLLĪĪ : XII : MINOR : CANŌICOR : ECCLĪE : S̄CĪ : PAVLI :

ECCLESIASTICAL TERMS

LOND.' The private seal exhibits two swords saltire-wise, in chief the head of St Paul, in base a clasped book ; in the remaining quarters the letters 𝕸 and 𝕮 ; the whole surrounded by a circle with octo-foiled cuspings, and the legend, s' CO'E COLL XII MINOR CANONIC' ī ECCL S PL' AD CAVSAS. For many years past these two seals have been used as seal and counterseal. At page 35 of his "Charter and Statutes," Dr Simpson prints the form of prayer used "at the Installment of a Member of the Minor Canons," and Miss Hackett in her "Popular Account of St Paul's Cathedral" (21st edition, p. 90) gives a list of the founders of the stalls, together with the names of their then (1834) incumbents : Revs. Dr Henry Fly (Sub-Dean), H. J. Knapp (Senior Cardinal), Christopher Packe (Junior Cardinal), R. H. Barham (Epistoler), W. J. Hall (Gospeller), Dr J. W. Vivian (Warden and Sacrist), James Lupton, J. T. Bennett, R. C. Packman (Librarian), R. Shutte, J. V. Povah and E. G. A. Beckwith (Succentor). The arrangement of having an "appearer," as well as a "reader" or "hebdomadary," was made among the minor canons on 1st January 1867, the "appearer" to read the Lessons, and the juniors still to be responsible for the Lessons on Litany Days and Holy Days (Dr Simpson's "Miscellaneous MS. Notes on St Paul's," preserved in the Cathedral Library). On 29th December 1863 the service was chanted by a minor canon (Rev. B. M. Cowie) from his own stall, for the first time. In 1860, the time of the alterations in the choir, the "hebdomadary," or "reader," chanted from the easternmost stall on the north side. Before that his place was in the sub-stalls, with the other minor canons and the vicars choral, and where he was provided with a slightly raised desk. Since the last redistribution of the choral fittings (1872) the "hebdomadary" has chanted from a raised desk, immediately westward of the vicars and assistant vicars choral. There are two such desks, one on the *Decani* side, the other, facing it, on the *Cantoris* side ; the "reader" chanting from the desk on whichever side of the choir his stall may be, and the minor canon on duty for the Lessons and Litany occupying his own stall. On 6th December 1875 the minor canons agreed to a rota of duty in which each man took four weeks' duty consecutively. Formerly they had taken a week at a time. Hence the term "Hebdomadarius" for the "Reader," or minor canon on weekly (hebdomadal) duty. On 6th March 1875 the minor canons (all appointed under the old system) agreed to surrender their estates to the Ecclesiastical Commissioners for a fixed money payment (Dr Simpson's MS. Notes). The two first minor canons appointed under the new system (see p. 188) were the Rev. Henry Cary Shuttleworth and the Rev. William Russell. Now that the services at St Paul's have so greatly increased in number, there being on an average four daily, the seven minor canons arrange weekly duty by means of a fixed rota.

Minster. A word signifying, in its true sense, the church of a monastery, or one to which a monastery has been attached, but it has come to be applied to a cathedral, as Lincoln, Southwell, and York, none of which were ever monastic establishments. Beverley, although originally a college of secular canons, is termed a "minster." It has now only the status of a parish church.

Miserere. The projecting bracket on the under side of the seats of stalls in churches. These, when perfect, are fixed with hinges so that they may be turned up, and when this is done the projection of the "miserere" is sufficient, without actually forming a seat, to afford very considerable rest to anyone leaning upon it. They were allowed in pre-Reformation times as a relief to the infirm during the long services that were required to be performed by the ecclesiastics in a standing posture. They are always more or less ornamented with carvings of leaves, small figures, animals, etc., which are generally very boldly cut, and frequently grotesque. Examples are to be found in almost all churches which retain any of the ancient stalls. The oldest is in Henry VII.'s Chapel at Westminster, where there is one in the style of the thirteenth century.

Miserere. The Latin title of the 51st Psalm ("Have mercy upon me, O God"). It occurs in our Psalter on the 10th morning of the month, and is one of the seven Penitential Psalms distributed among the services of Ash Wednesday. As a Penitential Psalm its place is in the Commination Service, and it is ordered to be said by "the priest and clerks [*i.e.* choir-men] kneeling." In the Latin rite the *Miserere* occurs in the office of Tenebræ (*q.v.*). The Psalm has been set in alternate verses, for officiant and choir, by many of the great Continental masters, including Palestrina, Josquin des Près, Allegri, Bai, Lotti, Leo, Pergolesi, Jommelli, Gluck, Sarti, Michael Haydn, Hasse, Basili, and Eslava. That of Allegri (1638), set alternately for a four-part and five-part, and at last for a nine-part choir, has long been considered the most celebrated. Until 1771 it was unknown in this country, when it was published, together with the *Miserere* of Bai, the *Improperia* or "Reproaches," and some other pieces of Palestrina, by Robert

ECCLESIASTICAL TERMS

Bremner of the Strand, under the editorship of Dr Burney. Vincent Novello subsequently reprinted it in his " Music for Holy Week " (1841), since which time there have been several editions. That by Sir George Martin, as sung at St Paul's Cathedral after Evensong on every Friday in Lent, is good, and has English words. Sir John Stainer's arrangement of the *Miserere* to the "Tonus Regalis," used at St Paul's on Ash Wednesday and at the special service on Tuesday in Holy Week, when Bach's great "Passion" (St Matthew) is performed, is exceedingly fine and effective. There is a simpler arrangement by Richard Redhead suitable for parish choirs. Dr John Alcock, one of the vicars choral of Lichfield Cathedral from 1749 to 1806, and until 1766 organist, composed an extremely fine setting of the *Miserere*, with the Latin words, in the key of A minor, the verses being set alternately for four solo voices and chorus, instead of for priest and choir, like the Italian and other foreign *Misereres*. It was written in 1756 but not published until 1771. In the Sarum Breviary the *Miserere* closes the office of Terce, and, on week-days, that of Compline.

Missa Sicca.
Lit. "Dry Mass."

A term used in the Roman Church to imply the ordinary part of the office without the canon, there being neither consecration nor Communion ; equivalent to our " Altar Service," " Ante-Communion," or " Table Prayers "—*i.e.* when the Communion Service is said only as far as the offertory and prayer for the Church Militant ; customary in many churches on Good Friday, when it is immediately followed by the Reproaches (*q.v.*).

Missal.

The office-book of the Western Church, containing the whole Liturgy, the fixed " Ordinary " and " Canon " of the Mass, with the changeable introits, collects, epistles, gospels, etc. In the ancient English Church the several parts of divine service were arranged in distinct books. Thus the collects and the invariable portion of the Mass formed the book called the " Sacramentary." The lessons from the Old and New Testaments constituted the " Lectionary," and the gospels made another volume, with the title of " Evangelistarium." About the eleventh or twelfth century it was found convenient, generally, to unite these books under the name of the Complete or Plenary *Missal*, or Book of Missæ. Of this description were almost all the liturgical books of the Western churches, and the arrangement is still preserved in our own. There was considerable variation in the missals of different dioceses, those of the Anglican

193

branch being known by the names of the Sarum Use, Hereford Use, York Use, Bangor Use, etc. Our Prayer-Book may be said to be founded on the Sarum Use. The Roman Missal was not used by Romanists in this country till 1740, when the Jesuits would not permit any other. Before that the Sarum Use continued to be followed, and, in forsaking this, Romanists in England surrendered the last link of connection with the old National Church. A good reprint of the Sarum Missal is that known as the "Burntisland Edition," published by C. J. Stewart, King William Street, Strand, 1861. Of this, the Rev. Benjamin Webb, for many years the distinguished vicar of St Andrew's, Wells Street, and Dr A. P. Forbes, Bishop of Brechin, were among the editors. The Roman Rite is now used throughout all the Roman Catholic countries of the Continent, except in the archdiocese of Lyons, where the Romano-Lyons Rite (differing slightly from the Roman) is used, and in numerous churches in the province of Milan, where the Ambrosian Liturgy still serves some million souls. Certain of the religious orders (*e.g.* Dominicans and Carthusians) follow their own rites, and exceptional local rites are used in one or two places in the Peninsula. In the foreign cathedrals there is usually a Chapter High Mass every day, and as it is mostly sung to simple liturgical music it may be easily followed (see Athelstan Riley, "Guide to High Mass Abroad," 1908). In France, during the reign of Napoleon III., the abolition of the old Diocesan Uses (which though wrecked in the cataclysm of the Great Revolution, partially revived under Napoleon I. and the Bourbons) gave much offence. The Gallican Church was always in a great degree independent of the see of Rome, and had its own separate uses, such as the sequence of colours, manner of conducting the ceremonial, office-books, music, and so forth, differing considerably from the Roman ones, and not derived from them but from one independent source common to both, the tradition of the early Church of the Apostles. Between 1855 and 1860 the Roman Church succeeded in depriving the Gallican Church of this privilege, both ritually and liturgically, but the change was not effected without much opposition, many dioceses clinging with the greatest affection to their venerable uses, and insisting on a retention of a certain amount of *proprium Sanctorum*, as may be seen by a study of the *Paroissiens* (the term corresponding with our Book of Common Prayer) in use in the various dioceses. All these local uses were no doubt a mine of interest to the liturgiologist and the ritualist, but they must have been very inconvenient to those who had the practical working of them. English Churchmen attending High Mass in France will do well to provide themselves with Mr Athelstan Riley's "Guide to High Mass Abroad" (Mowbray, 3rd edit., 1908). It is intended for the use of those members of the Church of England travelling on the Continent of Europe, who, from their inability to follow the celebration of the Eucharist in its Latin form, must often find themselves deprived of any opportunity of liturgical worship.

The episcopal coronet. Originally the word meant first a girdle, and secondly a head-dress, and is mentioned by heathen writers as worn by women as well as men (Virg. *Æn.* ix. 616 ; **Mitre.** Eurip. *Bacch.* 833). It is derived probably from the Gr. μίτρα. same root as μίτος, a thread, and would primarily signify anything to be bound on the person. The Septuagint gives μίτρα and also κιδάρις, for the cap worn by the high priest mentioned in Exodus and elsewhere. But it is a question whether the use of the mitre is of extreme antiquity. Some even assign its introduction to the tenth century. Bona, however (Rer. Lit. i. c. xxiv.), while admitting the possibility of the fact, shows that *some* ornament of the head was worn from the earliest ages. The earliest mitres were very low and simple, being not more than from three to six inches in elevation, and they thus continued till the end of the thirteenth century. In the fourteenth century they gradually increased in height to a foot or more, and became more superbly enriched ; their contours also presented a degree of convexity by which they were distinguished from the older mitres. During the Middle Ages there were three kinds of mitres in use among the English bishops : one covered with gems and precious stones, and with gold or silver plates ; the second made of white damask studded with small pearls, and ornamented with gold threads ; the third, called simplex, made of damasked silk or white linen. It is generally considered that the mitre is cloven in the midst, like the "tongues of fire" which fell upon the Apostles (Acts ii. 3), to show that the wearer is a successor of the Apostles, and shares with them in the Pentecostal gift. But Pope Innocent III., alluding to the horn shape, gave another signification : "Mitra pontificis scientiam utriusque testamenti significat ; nam duo cornua duo sunt testamenta," etc. Until lately, mitres have fallen into desuetude in England, even at coronations. They were worn, however, at the coronations of Edward VI. and Queen Elizabeth. Dr Milner's assertion ("Hierurgia Anglicana," p. 89) that they were worn at the coronation of George III. is incorrect, and this mistake is followed by Walcott ("Sacred Archæology," p. 383). In the detailed accounts of that ceremony—*e.g.* that in the *Annual Register* for 1761, the bishops are described as carrying their square caps, and putting them on when the lay peers assumed their coronets. This disuse of the mitre seems to date only from the eighteenth century. We learn from "Hierugia Anglicana" that mitres and staves of silver-gilt were carried at the funerals of Juxon, Duppa, Frewen, Cosin, Wren, Trelawny, and Lindsay (1724) ; mitres only at the burials of Monk and Ferne. The mitres of Morley and Mews are preserved at Winchester Cathedral. The effigy of Bishop Hacket in the south choir aisle of Lichfield Cathedral represents him with his mitre on his head, and his pastoral staff in his left hand. The effigy of Bishop Creyghton, in the cloisters of Wells Cathedral, subsequent to the Restoration, has mitre and pastoral staff. In Drake's "Eboracum" (1736) are figured the monuments of Archbishop Sterne, d. 1683 ; Archbishop Dolben, d. 1686 ; Archbishop Lamplugh, d. 1691 ; and Archbishop Sharpe, d. 1713. All these prelates are represented with mitres on their heads. This most essential part of the episcopal dress is strangely omitted in the effigy of Dr Creighton, late Bishop of London, in the south choir aisle of St Paul's. The small mitre, as worn by many of our English bishops at the present day, the design copied from mediæval brasses, tombs, etc., is far more graceful and becoming than the huge, ugly, bulbous shape assumed by the bishops of the Roman Communion. The treasury of the cathedral at Halberstadt contains a fine collection of ancient mitres. In some of the cathedrals of Italy the canons wear mitres, as well as other epis-copal insignia.

Monogram, The Sacred. The name of our Lord in short. The original form was the X intersected by the P, the two first letters of χριστος. Later on the X was turned into the Egyptian T, the P being still kept on the top ; and this was called the Taw-cross. Afterwards, the letter P began to be disused, and the X was retained only in the form of a Latin or Greek cross. The letters A and Ω, the Beginning and the Ending (Rev. i. 8), are often displayed with the cross, or used by themselves. To this monogram St Clement of Alexandria and Tertullian allude. Later monograms were the I.H.C. and the I.H.S., being the first three letters of the Holy Name. Under one of the three great East windows of Milan Cathedral, a marble tablet is let into the wall with this monogram and inscription :

ECCLESIASTICAL TERMS

Chrisnom Sancti Ambrosii

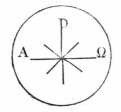

Circulus hic summi continet Nomina Regis
Quem sine principio et sine fine vides
Principium cum fine tibi denotat A Ω.

This inscription may be translated :—" The Christian signature of St Ambrose. This little circle contains the Names of the greatest King, which thou seest (is) without beginning and without end. The (name) Alpha and Omega denotes to thee the beginning with the end." The circle is the emblem of heaven and eternity ; hence many Christian figures are constructed on its principles in design. The A and Ω at the extremities of the transverse arm denote Alpha and Omega. The upright or vertical bar is used to denote the first letter in the Holy Name, Iesus. The St Andrew's cross X will also be made out ; it is often in Christian symbolism that we come across these two devices in one, thus ⳩ stands for the first three letters of the Messianic name of the Son of God, C.H.R., or in Greek letters, XP. Therefore the whole is " Jesus Christ, Alpha and Omega, the first and the last." The straight lines form an eight-pointed star, which is supposed to be emblematic of the eight beatitudes (St Matt. v.). Some suppose this to be a Gnostic monument. It is hardly necessary to observe that St Ambrose was Bishop of Milan.

Monstrance. A transparent pyx (*q.v.*) in which the Blessed Sacrament is carried in solemn processions, and exposed on the altar. It is derived from the Latin *monstrare* (to show), as it was in these vessels that the Holy Eucharist was first visibly exposed to the adoration of the faithful in processions, benedictions, and on other solemn occasions. The use of the monstrance is not very ancient, but as the solemn procession of Corpus Christi is not older than the early part of the fourteenth century, and as the Blessed Sacrament was originally carried in a covered pyx without procession, it is not probable that monstrances were introduced before the end of the fourteenth, or generally used till the fifteenth, century. It was also called an *ostensorium* ; the standing pyx was often identical with it. Walcott ("Sacred Archæology") refers to Acts of the Council of Cologne, in 1452, leading to the inference that the Holy Sacrament had previously been usually carried in a closed ciborium. Such would also appear from the fact that by far the greater number of the ancient existing examples date from the second half of the fifteenth and the sixteenth and subsequent centuries. Pugin ("Glossary of Ecclesiastical Ornament," 1859) mentions an example extant as early as the beginning of the fifteenth century. The usual form of the modern monstrance is that of a radiated sun, with a crystal pyx in the centre—a style which came in with the seventeenth century. Ancient monstrances were made in the shape of images, crosses, angels bearing a crystal pyx surmounted by a cross, a large tube of crystal fixed in a metal foot, etc., the whole enriched by tabernacle work and pinnacles. They were almost invariably of the costliest description, and made a vehicle for the art of the jeweller in its most *recherché* form. Among the contents of the treasury of Westminster Abbey, in 1388, was "Tabernaculum vetus, cum costis, de berillo cum ymaginibus in eisdem depictis, ornatum argento, pro Corpore Christi antiquitus, in eodem ponendo" ("London and Middlesex Transactions," v. 431.) Lübke ("Eccles. Art in Germ.") illustrates a magnificent example of a monstrance from Klosterneuberg ; and Clemen ("Kunstdenkmäler der Rheinprovinz") gives two from Nieukirk and Straelen. See also *sub voce* "Tabernacle."

Morrow Mass. The old English term for the daily Mass said for the repose of the souls of faithful departed and benefactors. Such a Mass was among the several said daily in old St Paul's. The treasury of the cathedral contained, in 1402, a black frontal for the high altar, exhibiting figures of Our Lord, with SS. Mary and John on either side ; and in the inventory taken in 1552 "an hanginge for the high altar of black damask" is mentioned, doubtless intended for use at this Mass.

Morse. The clasp or brooch of a cope. These were, and still are, often magnificently wrought. At St Paul's that of Alardus de Burnham, the dean in 1215, was of pure gold, with an amethyst in the centre, a sapphire and a cornelian on either side, together with other stones large and small. That of Peter of Blois, Archdeacon of London, was set with a sardonyx in the midst, surrounded with pearls. That of Richard, Archdeacon of Colchester, contained a representation of the Majesty with four figures in the angles. The morse of Cynthius Romanus, prebendary of Rugmere in 1220, contained a figure of St Paul between two angels, while that of William de Sancta Maria, Bishop of London in 1200, was of pure gold, set with a sapphire and two cornelians, with other sapphires and precious stones.

In Church music a short piece of music, more or less elaborate, of which the subject is taken from the Psalms or other portions of Scripture. The derivation is from the Italian *mottetto*, **Motett.** a little word or sentence ; originally signifying a short epigram in verse, and afterwards applied as now defined, as the words of the motett properly consist of a short sentence from Holy Scripture. By some it is supposed that the word is a diminutive form of the Italian *moto*, signifying movement, the earliest compositions of this class being in one movement, full, without solo parts, and generally short. Our present English anthem is an evolution of the motett of the Latin Church, and of our own in pre-Reformation times. The anthems of our earliest composers after the Reformation were almost invariably short, as are those given in Day's " Service-Book " (1560 and 1565). First and foremost of course stand the motetts of Palestrina. Breitkopf and Härtel's monumental edition of his works (33 volumes) contains over four hundred of these compositions for four, five, six, eight, and twelve voices, of varying dimensions, and replete with the most artistic work, the purest harmony, and the noblest melody. The collections of Bodenshatz (1603), Alfieri (1841–1845), Proske (1853–1863), Commer (1857), Eslava (1869), Pedrell (1900), together with Vincent Novello's " Fitzwilliam Music " (1825), the Motett Society's publications (1842), and Burns' "Ecclesiastical Choir-Book" (1848), afford ample material for the study of the motetts of the greatest masters of the sixteenth and seventeenth centuries—Italian, Spanish, Flemish, and German. In Italy, in the middle of the seventeenth century, the composition of the motett attained its perfection. In the magnificent library formed by the Rev. Sir F. A. Gore Ouseley at St Michael's College, Tenbury, is a manuscript volume in score containing compositions of this period, for two, three, and four voices, by Abbatini, Antonelli, Benevoli, Bicilli, Carpani, Carissimi, Cechelli, Durante, Fabri, Florido, Foggia, Giovannoni, Gratiani, Margarini, Mazzochi, Medesimo, Santucci, and Tarditi. This fine volume bears date " Rome, 1650." Among motetts by the great German writers of the eighteenth century, those of J. Sebastian Bach stand pre-eminent ; notably the set of six mostly for double choir, edited by Dr Steggall, with English words by W. Bartholomew ; originally published by Ewer, and since reprinted by Novello. The fine collection of Church music compiled by John Barnard, one of the minor canons of St Paul's (1641), and printed in ten separate part books, contains a number of our earliest English anthems in the short motett form. In 1841 a body was formed in London for the revival of sacred music in general, and for the study of that of the great masters preceding the seventeenth century in particular. This, called the Motett Society, was founded by William Dyce, R.A. The members were exclusively churchmen, and a choir met weekly for the practice and study of these compositions, seven or eight public performances being given each season. The publications of the society comprised three volumes of services, masses, motetts, and anthems, in the pure vocal style, by the great masters of the English, Flemish, Italian, and Spanish schools. These were edited by Dr Rimbault. Consult further, J. S. Bumpus' " History of English Cathedral Music " (T. Werner Laurie, 1908). The motett was at first written for voices alone. Subsequently, the term was applied somewhat differently. The motetts of Sebastian Bach were intended to be sung with organ accompaniment. This is pointed out by the late Professor Prout in his book, " Applied Forms " (1895). His authority is Spitta, who clearly shows in his great work on Bach that there can be little doubt that the performance of these celebrated works by an unaccompanied choir is not in conformity with the composer's intentions. Indeed, in one motett, " Der Geist hilft uns'rer Schwachheit auf " (" The Spirit also helpeth us "), orchestral parts exist in the composer's handwriting. A special feature of the motett is that the instrumental accompaniment doubled the voices, and was only *obbligato* in most exceptional cases. With more modern motetts, however, free orchestral accompaniments are sometimes to be found, as, for instance, in the three celebrated ones by Mozart, and in Haydn's " Insanæ et vanæ curæ," an adaptation of the chorus, " Im Augenblick verschwindet," in the oratorio, " Tobias' Heimkehr " or " Il Ritorno di Tobia," and well known in our choirs as an anthem beginning, " Distracted with care and anguish," or by the other adaptation, " The arm of the Lord," made by William Gardiner of Leicester for his *pasticcio* " Judah." Again, Mendelssohn's " Three Motetts for Female Voices," Op. 39, have an organ accompaniment which is in many places independent of the voices.

Moulding. A general term applied to all the varieties of outline or contour given to the angles of the various subordinate parts and features of buildings, whether projections or

ECCLESIASTICAL TERMS

cavities, such as cornices, capitals, bases, door and window jambs and heads, etc. Both the Classical orders and the Gothic styles have their peculiar mouldings, by which such orders and styles may be distinguished, and the diversities in the proportions and arrangements of these mouldings are very great. Consult the admirably illustrated article " Moulding " in Parker's " Glossary of Architecture " (1845).

Mullion.
Old Eng.
monion,
monyal.

The division between the lights of windows, screens, etc., in Gothic architecture. Mullions are scarcely ever found of earlier date than the Early English style, for though windows are not unfrequently used in couplets, and sometimes in triplets in Norman work, they are almost invariably separated by small shafts, or by piers too massive to be called mullions. Early English windows are often separated by piers (as at Wimborne Minster), but in many instances they are placed so close together that the divisions become real mullions, and from the date of the introduction of tracery they are universal. In Bailey's " History of the Tower," Appendix, vol. i. p. xviii. we find an account of " Reparations done within the Kyng's Tower of London," *temp.* Henry VIII., and the statement :—" The olde monyalls of them (the wyndowes) new stopped wᵗ tymber " ; and in the Articles of Enquiry of Richard Montague, Bishop of Chichester, 1638 : " Are the lights and windows of your church and chancell clear, not dammed up, well *monioned,* well glased, and kept clean ? "

Music Table.

A species of lectern, with three sides, round which the choir were placed. There was one in the middle of Bishop Andrewes' chapel, as appears by the plan given in " Hierugia Anglicana " (1848).

Mynchery.

The Saxon name for a nunnery. Nuns were sometimes called "mynches," from the Anglo-Saxon *minicene.* The word is still retained and applied to the ruins of such buildings in some parts of the country, as the mynchery at Littlemore, near Oxford. It is supposed by some that the word is a corruption of ministere, or minster.

Nave.

The portion of the church in which the congregation assists during the celebration of Divine Service. It extends from the west end to the transept or choir. The derivation of the word " Nave " has been a matter of dispute. Some derive it from the Greek ναός, a temple ; others from the Latin *navis,* a ship (a figure often used with reference to the Church), since the nave resembles the hull of a ship turned upside

201

down ; and refer both this term and ναός also to the ancient Phœnicians, whose original temples were said to be their vessels thus reversed. The longest Gothic nave in the world is that of St Alban's Cathedral (over 300 feet) ; the next is that of Winchester (some 275 feet). No foreign naves, except St Peter's and St Paul's, at Rome, Bologna and Milan, approach those of our cathedrals. But many of them exceed ours both in height and width considerably, having often two aisles on either side (Antwerp has three). Chichester is our only four-aisled cathedral nave, but a few churches have them, such as Kendal, St Michael's, Coventry, St Mary Magdalene's, Taunton, and St Helen's, Abingdon. The word " aisle " is derived from the French, and signifies wing or side, and can be only applied with propriety to the lateral portions of the building. " Middle aisle " is a contradiction of terms ; " side aisle " becomes tautology. In the ancient arrangement of the faithful, the men were placed in the upper part of the nave, and the women behind, at the lower end ; but by the custom of later times, the women were placed on the Gospel (or north) side, and the men on the Epistle (or south) side. This rule has been observed in many churches built since the rise of the Tractarian and Ecclesiological movements ; notably St John's, Harlow, St Matthias', Stoke Newington, St Mary Magdalene, Munster Square, St Andrew's, Wells Street, St Barnabas', Pimlico, and All Saints', Margaret Street. In some of these churches the order is reversed. At Hereford Cathedral, and many old country churches, the separation of the sexes in public worship has long been observed. An article on this subject in *The Ecclesiologist*, February 1846, should be consulted.

Newel.
Fr. *noyau d'escalier ;*
Germ. *spindel.*

The central column round which the steps of a circular staircase wind. In the north of England it is sometimes continued above the steps leading up to the vaulting of the roof, and supports a series of ribs which radiate from it, as at Carlisle Cathedral. Newel staircases are employed in all church towers where they are required — Mediæval, Renaissance or modern. There is one in the spacious library of St Paul's Cathedral, forming a communication from the floor to the light gallery which runs round the building. At St Michael's College, Tenbury, there is a newel staircase in a picturesque turret jutting out from the main building of the college at its western end, giving access to the dormitories and other ἀνώγεω.

ECCLESIASTICAL TERMS

Nocturns
(nocturnae horae ; nocturnae vigiliae).
Services held during the night. Anciently the night was divided, in religious houses, into three parts, at each of which certain psalms were said ; Lauds following at dawn. All the Psalms were thus appointed to be sung weekly. But there was great neglect. To this reference is made in the preface to the First Prayer-Book of Edward VI. (1549), " notwithstanding that the ancient Fathers have divided the Psalms into seven portions, whereof every one was called a nocturn ; now of late time a few of them have been said, and the rest utterly omitted." From twelve to eighteen Psalms had alone been sung in the nocturns of Matins. Since 1549 the whole Psalter has been taken in order every month, instead of fixed Psalms for each of the canonical hours throughout the week. The Psalter thus became more generally known by the whole of it being used in turn in the Sunday services. The version used in the Psalter is the old translation of the Bible—that of Tyndale and Coverdale (1535) and Rogers (1537) —which was revised by Cranmer (1539), and published in a large volume, and placed in the churches with the royal sanction. The other portions of Scripture in the Prayer-Book were taken at the revision in 1661 from the translation of 1611. But, happily, the old Psalter was not altered : the choirs were accustomed to it ; and its language was considered to be more smooth and fit for chanting. For Basil's account of the nocturnal service in his church (St Basil, Op. III. 311. " Epist. ad Clericos Neocæsar," p. 450, ed. Bened., Paris, 1839) see " Procter on the Book of Common Prayer," p. 215.

Nones.
One of the " Lesser " canonical hours. The service held at three o'clock in the afternoon, at the ninth hour (*nona hora*), the hour at which Our Lord yielded up the ghost on the Cross. Where the evening offices are said by accumulation it precedes Vespers, which, in the Continental cathedrals, are usually fixed at 3, and in some places as early as 2 o'clock, or 2.30, as at Nôtre Dame, Paris; Beauvais; Rheims, etc. It consists of Pater Noster, Ave Mara, Deus in adjutoriuim, the hymn *Rerum Deus*, verses 129 to 176 of the 119th Psalm (118 in the Roman Psalter) with antiphons, a short chapter of Holy Scripture, scriptural versicles and the collect of the day. The antiphons and versicles vary with the season.

Norman Architecture.
Fr. architecture romane.
The style introduced into this country at the time of the Conquest by the Normans, in 1066. " Norman " was the nomenclature adopted by Rickman, one of the first writers on Gothic architecture in the early part of the last century. The Cambridge Camden (afterwards Ecclesiological) Society's term was " Romanesque."

A DICTIONARY OF

The chief characteristics of this style, erroneously termed by eighteenth - century architectural writers "Saxon," were very thick walls without buttresses, semicircular arches, supported by massive columns with rather a regular capital and base. The style was modified and continued in use till about the beginning of the twelfth century. The pillars, at first very massive, subsequently became much lighter ; they were sometimes channelled or moulded in zigzag or spiral lines. Spires and pinnacles were not used, but there are some turrets of rather later date which have conical tops, as at the west end of Rochester Cathedral, and in Normandy several small church towers have steep pyramidical stone roofs, the forerunners of spires. In its later stages the details of the style became much enriched, and the ornaments used are much too numerous and too variable to be particularised. Examples of English and foreign Romanesque (or Norman) might be multiplied *ad infinitum*, but the following may serve. The cathedrals of Chichester, Durham, Norwich, Peterborough and Christ Church, Oxford; St Alban's Cathedral (nave), St David's Cathedral (nave), Ely Cathedral (nave), Rochester Cathedral (nave), Hereford Cathedral (choir and arcade of nave), Gloucester Cathedral (nave), Southwell Minster (nave), Bristol Cathedral (passage to chapter-house), Winchester Cathedral (transepts), Worcester Cathedral (crypt), Christ Church Cathedral, Dublin (transepts) ; Romsey Abbey ; Selby Abbey (nave), St Bartholomew, Smithfield ; Christ Church Priory, Hants (nave) ; St Peter-in-the-East, Oxford ; St John's Chapel, Tower of London ; Barfreston Church, Kent ; Iffley Church, Oxon ; Steyning and Clymping Churches, Sussex ; Stukeley Church, Hunts ; Kilpęck Church, Herefordshire. *France* : Abbaye aux Hommes (St Étienne) and Abbaye aux Dames (La Trinité), Caen ; St George, Bocherville, near Rouen ; St Rémi, Rheims ; Nôtre Dame, Clermont Ferrand ; crypt of St Eutrope, Saintes. *Belgium* : Nave, Tournai Cathedral ; St Vincent, Soignies. *Germany* : Churches of the Holy Apostles and St Maria in Capitolio, Cologne ; Spires Cathedral ; the minster at Bonn ; the abbey at Laach ; St Patroclus, Söest ; Neuwerks Kirche, Goslar ; St Blasius, Brunswick ; Bamberg Cathedral ; the Premonstratensian Church, Jerichow ; St Jacobus, Ratisbon. *Italy* : St Ambrogio, Milan ; St Michele, Pavia ; the Cathedral, Parma ; St Zeno, Verona ; St Stephano, Bologna. *Norway* : The cathedrals at Lund and Ribe ; churches of Kallundborg, Röeskilde, Gamle Akers, Soro, Ringsted, and the transepts of the Cathedral, Trondjhem. *Switzerland* : The cathedrals, Zurich, and Basle ; the monastery, St Gall. The

Norman style has not been very successfully imitated by modern architects. Perhaps one of the most pleasing examples is the church at Bonchurch, Isle of Wight, E. B. Ferrey, architect, 1848.

Nunc Dimittis. The Song of Simeon (St Luke ii. 29). The canticle which follows the Second Lesson at Evensong in our service. After reading the chapter from the Gospels or the Apostolical Epistles, and thus beholding how the promises were fulfilled in the propagation of the Gospel among the Gentiles, we express our readiness to receive that Gospel for ourselves, in the song of the aged Simeon, and our faith that by so doing we shall have peace in our death, of which every night brings a type in sleep. In the old offices the Canticle was sung in that of Compline, and it is still so placed in the Roman Breviary (see *sub voce* Compline). It is preceded by the office hymn, *Te lucis ante terminum* ("Before the ending of the day"). It is possible that the "Middle Voluntary," still kept up in some churches after the Second Lesson, is a lingering tradition of the division of the offices of Vespers and Compline. The more usual place, however, for the "Middle Voluntary" seems to have been after the Psalms. This was so at St Paul's in 1664, as we gather from the "Brief Direction for the Understanding of that part of the Divine Service performed with the Organ at St Paul's Cathedral on Sundays, etc," prefixed to the "Divine Services and Anthems," the now excessively rare black-letter duodecimo, published by the Rev. James Clifford, one of the minor canons, and sometime succentor of St Paul's. The observations made on the music for the *Magnificat* will apply equally to that for the *Nunc dimittis*.

O Sapientia. "O Wisdom." The opening words of the first of seven antiphons to the *Magnificat* formerly sung between 16th December and Christmas Eve. Each is founded on some title of our Lord derived from Holy Scripture. As we approach Christmas, the great festival of the Incarnation, our thoughts are to be directed to that wonderful event; and with that view the antiphons to the *Magnificat*, which is *par excellence* the hymn of the Incarnation, are so arranged as to bring before us the different titles or attributes under which our Lord is referred to in the Old Testament; and the first of these, that for the 16th December (17th in the Roman calendar), runs in the Latin thus: "O Sapientia, quæ ex ore Altissimi prodiisti, attingens a fine usque ad finem, fortiter suaviterque disponens omnia, Veni ad docendum nos viam prudentiæ." Thus identifying Our Lord with the "Wisdom" of the Old, and the Λόγος of the New, Testament. The other antiphons respectively began : (2) "O Adonai," (3) "O Radix Jesse," (4) "O Clavis David," (5) "O Oriens Splendor," (6) "O Rex Gentium," (7) "O Emmanuel." They were commonly called "the O's." An eighth, "O Virgo Virginum," is not generally received. The ancient melodies for these antiphons are given (from the Sarum Antiphonary) by Mr G. J. Tredaway, organist to the Duke of Newcastle at Clumber, Notts, in his "Vade Mecum for Church Choirs" (1895)—an invaluable publication. They are also to be found in Charles Child Spencer's "Short Anthems and Introits" (1847), and in the collection of introits musically edited by W. H. Monk for the compilers of "Hymns, Ancient and Modern" (1864). There are settings of the "O's" in four-part harmony by Sir Frederick Ouseley and Dr Philip Armes, both unpublished. These, like a set published by Sir John Stainer in 1896, were intended as short anthems, for use on the days immediately preceding Christmas. All three sets contain much beautiful music. In some of our churches these antiphons are sung to the traditional plainsong melodies, and in their proper place—*i.e.* before and after the *Magnificat*. At St Matthias', Stoke Newington, they have been so used for many years. The title of the first antiphon, "O Sapientia," is still preserved in our calendar on 16th December. The late Mr Charles Brown, in his exhaustive paper on the Dedications of Churches, read before the St Paul's Ecclesiological Society in 1883, observed : "I recollect that when the Ritual Commission was sitting [1867], a friend of mine who was being examined before the Commission, was asked by a bishop, who was one of the Commissioners, 'And pray, sir, what do you do on the black-letter saints' days ? For instance, what sort of service do you have on *O Sapientia* ?' To which my friend, greatly startled, replied : 'Oh, my lord, my lord ! O Sapientia is not a saint, it is an antiphon.' Now, Mr Nugee—for I may as well give my friend's name —was undoubtedly right when he said that 'O Sapientia' was an antiphon ; but whether he was equally right when he said that it was not a saint, may perhaps be questioned. Under this title we have a church dedicated, which is one of the most noteworthy in Europe. When the Emperor Constantine had transferred his capital from Rome to the city of Byzantium, which was renamed after him *Constantinople*, he set to work to build in it a church which should be worthy to be the cathedral of the new seat of government ; and this church, which he did not live to complete, he dedicated to The Divine Wisdom, ' H Ἁγία Σοφία, or as it is Latinised, *Sancta Sophia*, and which is well known to us as *Saint Sophia*. When Mahomet II. captured Constantinople, Saint Sophia was converted into a mosque

ECCLESIASTICAL TERMS

for the performance of the Mahometan rites. But notwithstanding the change, the ancient structure remains practically intact to the present day ; for although all signs and symbols of the Christian religion have been, as far as possible, obliterated, they have only been covered with plaster ; and although the old church remains to our times as the principal mosque of the Mahometan religion, yet it needs but for the plaster and other accretions to be removed from its walls, so as to bring to light the glorious mosaics with which it is studded all over, and it will once more start into life, ready for use as a Christian church, so soon as Constantinople passes into Christian hands, to serve once more, let us hope, as the seat of a Christian bishop's throne. So that if it had occurred to the Bishop of Gloucester and Bristol (for I do not know why I need keep back the names) to have replied to Mr Nugee's ' Oh, my lord ! O Sapientia is not a saint.'—' Then pray, sir, how about Saint Sophia ? ' he would have scored one against the examinee." The " Seven O's " were called in old French " les Oleries de devant Noël." Dean Goulburn (Collects, etc., i. 141) proposed that during the eight days before Christmas these antiphons should be sung instead of the *Venite*, like the Easter anthems, but their proper, and only, place is before the *Magnificat*, as may be seen by consulting any *Vesperale*. These " Greater Antiphons " seem to be still a popular devotion among Roman Catholics, and it may be observed that they are still printed in the *Cæleste Palmetum*. In France, in the eighteenth century, they formed materials for homilies, a volume of which, " Réflexions sur les O de l'Avent, en forme d'Homélies," was printed at Paris in 1784. In the " Liber Familiaris Clericorum," printed at Venice by Liechtenstern in 1550 (a sort of *Manuale* or *Agenda*), an office for asking any special grace begins with the Psalm, *Confitemini Domino*, followed by the seven greater antiphons, and ends with the collect, *Festina, Domine*. Mr Everard Green, in his paper, " On the Words ' O Sapientia ' in the Kalendar " (*Archæologia*, xlix. 1., 1885) brings forward a mass of valuable and interesting information on the subject, and shows us, *inter alia*, that the antiphons were sung on Ember Days, and that in Alcuin's time, " O Key of David " was sung on Whitsun Day at Vespers. Besides, a Vatican MS. interpolates the antiphons with the psalm *Beati Immaculati* as part of an office for the Veneration of the Cross. The view that these antiphons were therefore sung on Good Friday is strengthened by the fact that to the older offices for the Veneration of the Cross on Good Friday, printed by Thomasius and Martene, the *Beati Immaculati* is very often assigned. It would seem, therefore, that the

207

A DICTIONARY OF

use of the greater antiphons in early times was much more widely spread than at present over the Church's year. It also appears that they were often more in number than seven. At Rome, for instance, in the twelfth century they were sung at Lauds, and began on the feast of St Nicholas (6th December). If one were sung for every day, they must have been eighteen in number. Sicardus, a writer of the end of the twelfth and beginning of the thirteenth centuries, tells us that some churches in his time sang twelve antiphons in commemoration of the twelve prophets, others nine, including " O Virgo " and " O Gabriel," but he thinks that seven was the right number. It is to be wished that Mr Green, who has given us in his paper a short account of the Feast of the " Expectation," had also told us more of the festivals and ceremonies which announce to us the coming of Christmas. We know that the " Expectation" on December 18th was once the Feast of the Annunciation, called by the Spaniards *nuestra Señora de la O,* not, as Mr Green inclines to think, from the Greater Antiphons, of which there are no traces in the Mozarabic Breviary, but because at the end of the Vespers of the feast all in choir exclaimed " O," to show the desire of the Fathers in limbus, and of the angels in Heaven, for the coming of the Saviour. At least, this is the opinion of Leslie, expressed in the notes to the Mozarabic Missal. Like this is the custom at Angers during the week before Christmas ; all in choir calling out after Lauds, for some twelve or fifteen times, *O Noel, O Noel.* The Advent Ember Wednesday was kept in white vestments, the service speaking of the Incarnation, while the Gospel " Missus est Angelus " was sung with impressive ceremonies. At Milan, the Sunday before Christmas is kept in like manner ; white vestments are worn, and a solemn commemoration of the Incarnation is made. St Joseph's Day, which seems always to accompany the Annunciation and now to cause it to be almost forgotten—a French church is crowded on 19th March and empty on 25th March—was recommended by Gerson to the Chapter of Chartres to be kept on 12th December, and Thursday in the Advent Ember week was chosen by Claude de Vert for St Joseph in the reformed breviary of the great Abbey of Cluny.

The place of the Greater Antiphons is often taken in the English service by the hymn, " O come, O come, Emmanuel," which is nothing but a versification of five of the antiphons, taking the last first. The Latin hymn, " Veni, veni, Emmanuel," was published by Daniel in 1844 (*Thesaur. Hymnolog.* ii. 336, Appendix). At p. viii. of the preface he says that the Hymns in the Appendix are of the

ECCLESIASTICAL TERMS

Middle Ages, but that the use of them in Offices is uncertain. It seems a pity that we can trace nothing more definite of the history of this hymn. There is a hymn for the " Expectation " in Arwalus, in which the first words of each antiphon are brought into the verses :

> " O lumen æternum Patris,
> O dux Adonai, maxime
> Defensor, O Jesseia
> Virente radix germine.

> " O clavis, et Davidicæ
> Sublime sceptrum regiæ,
> O sol sub ortu, gentium
> O rector, O Emmanuel
> Veni."

At the south end of the crypt under the dormitory at Durham was the Common House wherein " did the master thereof keep his *O Sapientia,* once in the year—viz. betwixt Martinmas and Christmas, a solemn banquet that the Prior and Convent did use at that time of the year only, when their banquet was of figs and raisins, ale and cakes, and thereof no superfluity or excess, but a scholastical and moderate congratulation among themselves " (Rites of Durham, p. 75).

Obiit, or Obit. An office performed at funerals when the corpse was in the church before it was buried ; it afterwards came to be performed on the anniversary of the death of a benefactor. Thus in many of our colleges the obiit, or anniversary of the death of the founder, is piously observed. The Obiit Sundays at St George's Chapel, Windsor, were formerly celebrated with great magnificence, and are to a certain degree still. They take place on the next Sunday to every quarter day, in commemoration of departed benefactors of the Order of the Garter. A special service is appointed, the Psalms being xxi., cxlvi., cxlvii. ; the lessons, Ecclesiasticus xliv. and Hebrews xi. The proper Collect of the Day is always used, the Epistle and Gospel being changed for Deut. xxxiii. and St John v. 24-30. The Holy Communion is ordered to be celebrated with choral *Sanctus* and *Gloria*, and two special prayers, or rather thanksgivings, for departed benefactors, are said immediately before the blessing. The office for this and other "Obiits" will be found at full length in Blunt's "Annotated Prayer-Book," ii. 302. The fine anthem " O give thanks " (Ps. cvi. 1 ; Ps. cxii. 6 ; Ps. cvi. 46) was composed by Professor Walmisley for the

Commemoration of Benefactors at Trinity College, Cambridge, 27th October 1834.

Certain feasts are kept up for eight days ; the eighth day is the octave day, the intermediate days being "within the octave."

Octaves. Octaves are observed to add greater dignity to the festivals. Thus, Easter has been observed with an octave from the earliest times. Also (as Durandus says), as significant of the future glory of the saint whose day is being observed, the day itself commemorating the event (as Christmas, Our Lord's birth), the octave day its future consummation, when we shall reap the full fruition. Sometimes the octave commemorates a distinct event, as the octave of Christmas is observed as the Feast of Our Lord's Circumcision, wherein He *completed* His humiliation by taking upon Him the yoke of the law ; the octave of Whitsun Day as Trinity Sunday, because the *end* of the Holy Spirit's outpouring on the Church is to lead us to the beatific vision of the Eternal Three in One. Sometimes a feast has an octave, not only because of its dignity but because of the many mysteries celebrated thereon. Thus, Epiphany commemorates not only Our Lord's Manifestation, but also His Baptism, and His first miracle at the marriage of Cana (see Charles Walker, "The Ritual Reason Why"). Our five great festivals, Christmas, Easter, Ascension Day, Whitsun Day, and Trinity Sunday have each a proper preface in the Communion Service, ordered (except the last) to be said on the "seven days" after, thus showing that the framers of our Prayer-Book intended a *daily* Celebration. These proper prefaces are five out of ten which occurred in the Roman and English Missals. The last of these, in honour of the Virgin Mary, was added by Pope Urban, 1095. That for Christmas Day was composed in 1549. That for Easter is as old as the Sacramentary of Pope Gelasius. The preface for Ascension Day was probably composed by Gregory the Great. That for Whitsun Day was composed in 1549, the form in the Missal containing a very short and imperfect allusion to the great event which is commemorated on this day. The Trinity Sunday preface dates from the time of Gelasius. The octave of the dedication or anniversary of the consecration of a church should always be observed by special services. These festivals at such churches as the Parish Church, Leeds, St Barnabas', Pimlico, St Andrew's, Wells Street, St Matthias' Stoke Newington, St Michael's College, Tenbury, and All Saints', Margaret Street, have long been famous, the music being of the highest order, and sermons delivered by many of the most celebrated preachers and learned divines of the day.

ECCLESIASTICAL TERMS

The one hymn—and one only—appointed to be sung at each of the canonical hours, and bearing distinctly upon the services **Office Hymn.** of the day. In the ordinary ferial service they commemorate the order of the Creation, except that for Saturday at Evensong, which is a prayer to the Holy Trinity for light. In the Sarum Breviary the various seasons have proper hymns commemorating the mystery therein celebrated. Thus, the Advent, Christmas, Epiphany, Ascension, and Whitsun seasons, have each proper office hymns for Matins and Evensong. So has Eastertide, with an additional one for Saturdays at Evensong. There are also proper hymns for Trinity Sunday, St Stephen, Holy Innocents, the Invention and Exaltation of the Cross, St John Baptist, St Mary Magdalene, the Transfiguration and Holy Name of Jesus, St Michael, and All Saints' Day ; and for the feasts of Apostles and Evangelists in and out of Eastertide, of one and of many Martyrs, of Confessors, of Virgins, of Holy Women, and of the Blessed Virgin Mary. These hymns are distinguished thus : The ferial hymns throughout the week in the Epiphany and Trinity seasons are called the " Ordinary of the Season " : those for the other seasons are the " Proper of the Season." Similarly, the hymns common to all saints of any class, as martyrs, virgins, etc., are the " Common of the Saints " ; those appointed especially for any saint form the " Proper of Saints." When the Reformers drew up the Prayer-Book which we now use, they did not sit down and spin a new one out of their own heads. They took the Sarum and other English breviaries and translated the new Prayer-Book out of the various offices contained therein, and admirably well they did their work. But there was one part which they did not translate ; and that was the hymns. Cranmer and others tried more than once, but they could not succeed ; and they had wisdom enough to know that they were not successful. They only put one translation in the Prayer-Book, the hymn " Come, Holy Ghost, Eternal God," in the Ordination Service. They left it as their wish, however, that others might arise in the English Church who should be able to translate the hymns which they left untranslated. But as years went on their wish was neglected. Men, such as Sternhold and Hopkins, and Tate and Brady, put the Psalms into verse, and sang *them* by way of hymns : forgetting that the Psalms are best to be sung in a very different way—namely, by chanting them. Whittingham, the notorious puritanical Dean of Durham (1563–1579), even turned the Creed, Lord's Prayer, and Commandments into rhyme, and superseded the use of the choral service in his cathedral by these and other monstrous impertinencies. At last people saw that hymns were wanted. But instead of going back to the ancient hymns of the English Church, of which there was so rich and varied a treasury, they wrote new ones, and so a great number of " collections," that had no authority, came into the Church. Indeed, it may be said that at one time almost every church had its own " selection." In the " Hymnal Noted," the first part of which was published in 1852, and the second in 1858, the wish of the English Reformers was carried out. The old hymns of the English Church were translated here, just as the old prayers of the English Church are translated in the Prayer-Book ; and they were given to the traditional plain-song melodies, which was also the wish of the Reformers. These hymns were not written by any one man, nor at any one time. They are offerings, cast into the treasury of the Church, slowly, and at different periods, during the space of a thousand years. The writers of most of them are unknown. Of those whom we do know, some are amongst the greatest saints that God has raised up in the Church. The hymns themselves, being so different from those to which we are chiefly accustomed, will perhaps, at first sight, seem strange and cold. But the more they are studied the more their value will be seen and felt. In them we find Evangelical truth combined with Apostolic fervour. They all, with one heart and voice, and in much the same words, proclaim the grand and unvarying theme— Glory to God and to the Lamb. Many of our most distinguished liturgiologists have been engaged from time to time on the translation of these ancient hymns of the Church ; among them the Rev. J. M. Neale, one of the greatest men that the English, or indeed any other, Church can boast of in modern times. " Hymns, Ancient and Modern " contains a larger selection of these translations than any other book. Here and there, along the course of the seventeenth and eighteenth centuries, isolated attempts were made to translate some choice Latin hymns. Crashaw, Bishop Cosin, Drummond, Dryden, and Lord Roscommon had each contributed one or two ; but Dr Mant, Rector of Bishopsgate, and afterwards (1823) Bishop of Down and Connor, went a step further, and, taking the Roman Breviary, translated, with few exceptions, all that it contained. The ice thus broken, Mant's leading was followed with much zeal by Isaac Williams (who did the same with the Paris Breviary), by Copeland, Dr Chandler, Dr Pusey, Rev. E. Caswall, Rev. W. B. Heathcote, Dr Irons, Dr Bright, the Rev. Francis Pott, Mr D. T. Morgan, and last, but by no means least, Dr Neale, already mentioned ; so that there have been produced almost as many Anglo-

Latin as new and original English hymns during the last three quarters of a century. Due honour must therefore be given to Bishop Mant, as the pioneer of those who have given us in the vernacular these divine office hymns, which, in their Latin originals, have through ages been, and still continue to be, to countless saintly souls, the joy and consolation of their earthly pilgrimage. A glance at any foreign Breviary with musical notation, and at the musical edition of the " Hymnal Noted," will show the order and arrangement of the office hymns. In the compilation of the " Hymnal Noted," the Rev. Thomas Helmore, the musical editor, had the co-operation (as regards the harmonisation of the ancient melodies) of such authorities on plainsong and the old Church modes as the Rev. S. S. Greatheed, Rev. H. L. Jenner, and Edward Cruse, the first-named, apparently, having the lion's share in the undertaking. The harmonies of Sir Henry Bishop were used for the melody of the *O beata beatorum*, the morning hymn for the festivals of martyrs ; and it may be interesting to mention that those for the hymns, *Quando noctis medium* (Sunday morning hymn), *Magnae Deus potentiae* (Thursday evening hymn), *Jam Christus astra ascenderat* (evening hymn for Whitsunday), and *Haec rite mundi gaudia* (hymn for festivals of holy women), were entrusted by Mr Helmore to his distinguished pupil, Arthur Sullivan, then (1857) one of the children of the Chapel Royal. An interesting account of the origin of the " Hymnal Noted " is given by Frederick Helmore in the " Memoir " of his brother the Rev. Thomas Helmore, published by Masters in 1891. Where the office hymn is now adopted in our Church its proper place is before *Benedictus* at matins, and before *Magnificat* at evensong. In churches where anthems are not sung, its place is generally after the Third Collect. The Sarum Breviary directs it to be used before *Benedictus* at Lauds, and before *Magnificat* at Vespers. But every office of the canonical hours has its office hymn. In the Roman Breviary it follows *Venite* at Matins, and precedes *Benedictus* at Lauds. At Prime, Terce, Sext, and None it precedes the Psalms, and at Vespers *Magnificat* ; while at Compline it comes before the Little Chapter (*Capitulum*) and *Nunc dimittis*. " The Hymner," edited by the Rev. G. H. Palmer for the Plainsong and Mediæval Music Society, contains translations of all the Hymns, save two, from the Sarum Breviary. Nearly one half are by Dr J. M. Neale. The remainder are by the Rev. M. J. Blacker, J. D. Chambers, W. J. Copeland, Dr Littledale, Rev. J. W. Doran, Rev. T. A. Lacey, Rev. W. J. Blew and others.

When a church is built, care should be taken that the faithful face the east while at prayer. Such has been the practice of the **Orientation of Churches.** Church from the earliest period, and very few are the examples of any deviation from this rule. The chancel should consequently be turned towards the east, and all the altars in the church should be so placed that the celebrant, while officiating, looks towards the same quarter. An inspection of a plan of an old cruciform church would readily show how strictly this principle was adhered to in the arrangement of the various altars, whether in the transepts, extremities of aisles, or lateral chapels of apses. Independently of all Christians turning towards the same point being a beautiful figure of the unity of the Church, those learned writers, Durandus, Gavantus, and Bona, have adduced the following reasons for this rule :—(1) That the Apostles turned towards the east while at prayer. (2) That the Holy Spirit descended on them from the east at Pentecost. (3) That we should all turn towards the Holy Land, where Our Lord was born. (4) That as Our Lord was the great Light of the World, we should turn towards the brightest quarter of the world, as a figure of His glory. (5) That as Our Lord was crucified looking towards the west, the roods, placed in the same position, face the faithful. (6) That the star appeared in the east to the three wise men at the birth of Our Lord. (7) To distinguish the faithful from infidels or heretics, who, being without faith or unity, turn in any direction. (8) That, according to the traditional belief of the Church, Our Lord will come from the east to judge the living and the dead. But independent of these mystical and pious reasons, the ancient and canonical position is the most judicious. As A. Welby Pugin ("Present State of Ecclesiastical Architecture in England," 1843) well observes, "How beautifully do the rays of the rising sun, streaming through the brilliant eastern windows of the choir or chancel, darting their warm and cheerful light to the very extremity of the nave, correspond with the hymn appointed to be sung at Prime, *Jam lucis orto sidere*, etc. Thus, as the day advances, from the whole southern side a flood of light is poured into the building, gradually passing off towards evening, till all the glories of a setting sun immediately opposite the western window light up the nave with glowing tints, the rich effect being much increased by the partial obscurity of the choir end at the time. Now this beautiful passage of light from sunrise to sunset, with all its striking and sublime effects, is utterly lost in a church placed in any other than the ancient position." In short, there are both mystical and natural reasons for adhering to

ECCLESIASTICAL TERMS

antiquity in this practice, a departure from which can only be justified under the most urgent necessity. It must be admitted that, in modern times, architects, and those who have had the care of the planning and erection of our churches have, on the whole, been diligent in preserving orientation. Sir Christopher Wren, when he rebuilt the city churches after the Great Fire, was scrupulous in this respect. The Church of St Edmund the King and Martyr, Lombard Street, is the only city church of his that does not orientate, the space of ground from east to west not having been sufficient properly to allow of this. Three other exceptions are St George's, Bloomsbury (N.Hawksmoor, architect, *temp.* George I.); St Botolph's, Aldgate (George Dance, architect, 1744), and St Dunstan's, Fleet Street (James Shaw, architect, 1833). French and German architects were equally careful in the matter of orientation, but this was not invariably the rule in Italy. The turning of the choir to the east at the singing of the *Gloria Patri* is a very ancient custom, and observed in many of our churches. At Manchester Cathedral it has never been dropped. It is a solemn act of adoration to the Holy Trinity, whose praises are especially set forth in this doxology. For the same reason the people incline their heads at the first clause. At the recitation of the Creeds we turn towards the east, because such was the attitude used in all the more solemn parts of the service, and as signifying that a right faith, like every good and perfect gift, cometh down from the Father of Lights, and must be sought from Him by diligent prayer. It was one of the articles exhibited against William Beale, Master of St John's College, Cambridge, 1641, " that he commanded the Deans of the said College to severely punish according to the expressed infliction, who would not likewise convert their faces towards the east at ' Glory be to the Father,' etc., and many times in Divine Service, so that he did luxuriously introduce Popish innovations." An editorial note in " Hierugia Anglicana," p. 366, mentions that " this custom was observed till of late [1848], at Exeter Cathedral, and also that adoration towards the altar is still practised there by the Bishop and Clergy." At Christ Church Cathedral, Oxford, and at Durham Cathedral, the dean and canons, on leaving the choir, make a low obeisance to the altar ; a custom which has never been dropped at either place. John Noake in his " Monastery and Cathedral of Worcester " (Longman & Co., 1866) mentions that in the latter part of the seventeenth century it was ordered that the schoolmaster should see to the King's Scholars going into church reverently two by two, " doing their reverence towards the east, and the like when they pass out." One, Story, in his " Journal," 1687 (p. 4), says " I went diligently to the public worship, especially to the Cathedral of Carlisle, where in time of public prayer we used all, male and female, as soon as that creed called the Apostles' Creed began to be said, to turn our faces towards the east, and when the name of Jesus was mentioned we all as one bowed and kneeled towards the altar-table as they call it, where stood a couple of Common Prayer-books in folio, one at each side of the table, and over them, painted upon the wall, I H S, signifying Jesus." Samuel Pepys, in his Diary, 26th February 1666, records his attendance at choral matins in St George's Chapel, Windsor, when there was "great bowing by all the people, the poor Knights in particularly to the Altar."

Orphreys. The embroidered bands or strips of lace, or other material, on a chasuble, cope, dalmatic, altar-frontal, etc. The greatest skill of the artist in needlework was, and still is, lavished on these orphreys.

Our Lady. The old English designation of the Blessed Virgin Mary. The term is retained in our Calendar of Proper Lessons.

Pain Béni. In French cathedrals and churches a cake or loaf is brought in at the Offertory on Sundays, often with considerable pomp. This is blessed, and the pieces, *pain béni*, handed round to the congregation in baskets. It is the custom for each person to take a piece and make the sign of the cross with it before eating it. Additional pieces are sometimes taken home for those members of the family who are unable to be present. It is a custom peculiar to the Gallican Church.

Pall. (1) A piece of millboard, six to eight inches square, covered with linen and embroidered with a cross and border on the upper side, used to place over the surface of the chalice at certain portions of the Mass. Probably it would be a very difficult task to show at all conclusively what the article was until a modern date. Walcott (" Sacred Archæology ") states it to be another name for the corporal (*q.v*) ; as also for the linen cloth covering the mensa ; and in our own Coronation Service it is spoken of as of gold. Archbishop Gray's Constitution, in 1250, enumerates, amongst the articles which it was the duty of the parishioners to provide for their church, *tribus thuellis et corporalia.* (2) The covering for the coffin at the Office of the Burial of the Dead. It is a vexed question among ritualists as to the proper colour to be employed in funeral obsequies. All are, however, agreed that all unnecessary gloominess should be avoided, and that the arrangements should be such as speak of Christian hope, and not of the despair of sorrow as they that have no hope. For this end the pall should be of a more cheerful hue than black, generally violet, with a red cross, or with a white cross for young persons. In an office-book of the fifteenth century, executed by French artists, now in the Egerton Collection of the British Museum, a choir of monks singing the *dirige* or dirge is well represented. The bier is covered with a red pall charged with a gold cross. The same subject is illustrated again on another page of the MS., the bier being covered with a blue pall and red cross. A latter-day custom, one of omission, is the non-use of funeral palls, a shift of the modern undertaker, eager to display his tawdry coffin bedizened with vulgarities in brass, which he denominates " furniture." One cannot imagine anything more unseemly than this growing and all but universal practice of carrying a naked coffin through the street, a practice no one would have committed a generation ago. Mr W. Sancroft Randall, in a paper " Ceremonial and Offices connected with the Burial of the Dead," read before the Guild of All Souls, observes : " I well remember, when a boy, being much struck by the sight of a poor person's funeral in the country, whose relations were too poor to hire the customary black velvet pall from the village store, and so they supplied the void by covering the coffin with a clean white sheet, and thus in procession it was carried to the church." In many churches a pall of the proper colour is now kept exclusively for use at the burial of those dying in the parish.

Parclose. A screen, generally of stone and solid, built across the north and south arches of the crossing to serve as a backing for the choir-stalls, where the eastern limb is not of sufficient length to contain them. In Spain these are termed *rejas*. In Germany there is usually a door at the eastern extremity of this screen for entrance to the choir, and the side facing the transept is enriched with arcading, filled in some instances with sculpture, in others with painting. In Germany we find examples of such an arrangement at the cathedrals of Limberg, Münster, Naumberg, and Treves ; St Michael, Hildesheim ; and St Mary, Halberstadt. Elsewhere the term comprehends an enclosure, screen or railing, such as may be used to protect a tomb, to separate a chapel from the main body of a church, to form the front of a gallery, or for other similar purposes. " The carpenters do covenant to make and set up finely and workmanly a *parclose* of timber about an organloft ordained to stand over the west dore of the said chapell "

(Contract for Beauchamp Chapel at Warwick, 1450). " I will that the roof of that Chapel be raised, the walls enhanced, the windows made with strong ironwork, with a quire and *perclose*" (Will of Walter, Lord Mountjoy, 1474, in "Testamenta Vetusta," vol i.). The richly sculptured parcloses at the back of the stalls at Amiens, Chartres, and Nôtre Dame, Paris, are celebrated.

One that has full possession of all the rectorial rights of a parochial church. He is called parson (*persona*) because by his person the

Parson
(*Persona*
ecclesiae).

Church, which is an invisible body, is in his parish represented. He sustains, in the eye of the law, the person of the Church, in any action touching the same. The term " Persona " is applied in ancient cathedral and collegiate statutes to those who held particular offices, not necessarily of dignity or of jurisdiction, but involving personal responsibility and strict residence. In England at the Cathedrals of the Old Foundation—St Asaph, Bangor, Chichester, St David's, Exeter, Hereford, Lichfield, Lincoln, Llandaff, St Paul's, Salisbury, Wells, and York—the dignitaries, as the dean, precentor, chancellor, treasurer, etc.—were called *Personae Principales*, or *Privilegiatae*, as having each a peculiar office, connected with the service of the Church. At St Paul's the five archdeacons of London, Middlesex, Essex, Colchester and St Alban's were included in this title, though incorrectly. By the Hereford Statutes, the bishop, dean, precentor, treasurer, and chancellor are *personae in dignitatibus constitutae*. In foreign churches the inferior cathedral clergy are called *personats*.

The word parvise is the Anglo-Norman form of the Low Latin *parvisum*. Some derive it from the Latin *pervius*, open to passengers,

Parvise, or
Parvis.
Germ. *vorhof*.

while others consider that is a corruption of the Italian " paradisa," an open space in front of a church. The Latin *paradisus* means a garden, and the open spaces before some Italian churches were laid out as such.

Παράδεισος was a word applied sometimes by the Greeks to a court. In Germany—as for instance at Münster, Paderborn and Herford—the great spaces before the southern doors were called "paradises." It appears that " paradise " was also a name given to a study, as in the descriptions of old houses, "Great and Little Paradise" frequently occur. Doubtless the room over the porch of so many English churches formed a study for the parish priest, or for itinerant priests, who served rural churches, or said masses for the dead. Perhaps they may also have been used by "watchers," or as a muniment-room, or as a school, and in some cases

as a library. The French use the term for the open space at the
west end of a cathedral or large church, or a similar space at the end
of either transept. The area at the west front of Nôtre Dame,
Paris, is known as the " Parvis Nôtre Dame." The Court of the
Hundred and other law courts were formerly held in the *parvis*.
Gervase, in his description of Canterbury Cathedral, speaking of the
south porch, says that all the differences of the hundreds were there
determined as in the King's Court. Dugdale mentions the " Pervyse
of Pawles." The custom of teaching children in the porch is of very
early origin. It is distinctly mentioned by Matthew Paris in the
time of Henry III. The examination at Oxford, properly called
Responsions but in university slang known as " smalls," owes this
last appellation to the expression *in parviso*, which has been
erroneously attributed to the word *parvus*, small, but in reality
has reference to the parvise or porch of St Mary's, the University
Church, which was formerly used for the examinations.

From very early times this name has been given to the Fifth
Sunday in Lent—the Sunday but one before Good Friday—because
on that day Our Lord began to speak openly to His
disciples of His coming sufferings and bitter death.
It was called *Dominica Passionis*, and an Anglo-Saxon
homily for the Fifth Sunday in Lent begins by stating
that from that day until Easter the time is designated *Christ's
Passiontide* (Alfric's " Homilies," ii. 224). The Collect is taken
from the Sacramentary of Pope Gregory. It is a prayer of God's
people that He would (1) govern and (2) preserve then both in
body and soul. The Latin original connects the " government "
with the body, and the " preservation " with the soul : " *Ut, te
largiente, regatur in corpore, et, te servante, custodiatur in mente.*" The
Epistle refers to our Lord's Passion (Heb. ix. 11-15) ; the Gospel
to the rejection of Him by " His own," which leads up to, and pre-
pares us for, His final rejection (see Evan Daniel on the Prayer-
Book ; Blunt's " Household Theology "). In the Missal the introit
proper for the Sunday was *Judica me, Deus*, " Judge me, O God,"
or " Give sentence with me, O God " (Ps. xliii.), and Sir Frederick
Ouseley was careful to remember this when composing his introit,
assigned to this Sunday in the Rev. Walter Hook's collection (1867).
The hymn at Vespers until Wednesday in Holy Week was *Vexilla
Regis* (" The Royal Banners forward go "), widely known by its
grand plainsong melody (see " Hymnal Noted," 1852, p. 89). Before the first Vespers of this Fifth Sunday in Lent, it was customary
to veil crosses and pictures throughout the churches. They remained

**Passion
Sunday.**

covered till the celebration of the Easter Festival. This veiling has been revived in many of our churches. Purple veils are the Roman use ; white, with red crosses, to call attention to the spotless but bloody Passion of Our Lord, the English.

Pastoral Staff. See *sub voce* " Crozier."

Paten. A small plate of gold or silver-gilt on which the sacred bread in the Eucharist is laid for consecration, and from which the people are communicated. The ancient patens are simply thin pieces of metal slightly hollowed, containing a shallow octofoil, or sexfoil, or even a quatrefoil, beaten down in the middle. In the centre is generally an engraving of the Agnus Dei, or some other subject, within a circle, but occasionally we find an enamel. It would appear, however, that this excessive plainness of decoration did not obtain anciently. De Caumont ("Abécédaire de l'Architecture," p. 52) tells us that the paten of Suger at St Denis (A.D. 962) was made of porphyry with sundry gold dolphins in the centre, the whole surrounded by a most elaborate border of gold filigree, enamels and gems, as also that of St Goslin, now in the cathedral at Nancy. The very beautiful paten presented by Minor Canon Simpson to St Paul's Cathedral in 1871 measures eight inches in diameter ; the centre is quite plain, the edge being engraved with wheat and grapes and enriched with six medallions—the symbols of the Passion—to correspond with the equally beautiful chalice presented by the same pious and munificent donor. A pair of patens, stolen with the rest of the cathedral eucharistic plate in December, 1810, bore the inscription : *Benedixit, fregit, dedit ; accipite, comedite ; hoc est Corpus Meum.* Another paten, forming a covering for the chalice, had upon it a representation of the Agnus Dei.

Pax. A small tablet, having on it a representation of the Crucifixion, or some other Christian symbol, offered to the congregation to be kissed at the *Pax tecum* during the celebration of Mass. It was usually of silver or other metal, with a handle at the back, but was occasionally of other materials ; sometimes it was enamelled and set with precious stones. It was introduced when the primitive kiss of peace, which used to circulate throughout the Christian assemblies, was discontinued on account of some appearance of scandal which had grown out of it. Its introduction is attributed to the Franciscans (Bona, *Rer. Lit.*, ii. c. xvi.). In England it is mentioned at York in 1250. It is called the " asser ad pacem " in a Council of Oxford, 1287. In " The Inventairie of the Plate, Jewells, Copes, Vestements, Tunacles, Albes, Bells, and

ECCLESIASTICAL TERMS

other Ornaments appertayninge to the Cathedrall Churche of Sayncte Paule in London, 1552," printed in *The Ecclesiologist* (1856), p. 197, and reprinted by J. Orlebar Payne, 1893, from a document in the Public Record Office, a pax is described as " with the ymage of the Crucifix and of Marie and John all gylte with the Sonn alsoe and the Moone, the backsyde whereof crymssin velvett." Another had the " ymage of our Ladie sett aboughte with x greate stones the backside whereof is grene velvett." There is a pax of silver-gilt at New College, Oxford, *temp.* Henry IV. ; and Archbishop Chicheley gave one of glass to All Souls' College. At Durham the embossed cover of the book of the Epistles and Gospels served as the pax.

Pediment.
Ital.
frontispizio.

The triangular termination used in Classical architecture at the ends of buildings, over porticos, etc., corresponding to a gable in mediæval architecture. It is much less acute at the top than a gable.

Pelican.

The representation of this bird vulning herself, as expressed heraldically, occurs not unfrequently as a sacred emblem among the ornaments of churches. A beautiful specimen is preserved at Ufford, Suffolk, at the summit of the elaborately carved spire of wood which forms the canopy of the font ; and another occurs over the font at North Walsham, Norfolk. The import of this symbol is thus explained in the *Ortus Vocabulorum*, compiled early in the fifteenth century : " Fertur, si verum est, eam occidere natos suos, eosque per trie-duum lugere, deinde seipsum vulnerare, et aspersione sui sanguinis vivos facere filios suos. Versus,

> Ut pellicanus fit matris sanguine sanus,
> Sic nos sanati sumus omnes sanguine nati,

id est, Christi " (Parker's " Gloss. Arch." p. 276). The lectern was occasionally made in the form of a pelican, instead of that of an eagle, a specimen of which is to be seen at Norwich Cathedral ; and previous to the Reformation there was another at Durham as appears from the " Ancient Rites " of that church. At the church of St Michael, Cornhill, there is a vigorous representation of the pelican in her piety feeding her young and standing upon a nest. This group, formerly over the altarpiece, and removed to a recess under the west window during the alterations in 1860-1867, is attributed to Grinling Gibbons, but is replete with a true mediæval character and quaintness. The emblem is more than once introduced into the carvings in Wren's city churches. It appears on the font-cover of St Martin's, Ludgate. In Dr Neale's translation of the eucharistic hymn, *Adoro te devote*, the sixth stanza begins thus :

> " Pelican of Mercy, Jesu, Lord and God,
> Cleanse me, wretched sinner, in Thy precious Blood."

Pentecost.
From
πεντηκοστος.
the fiftieth.

A solemn festival of the Jews, so called because it was celebrated fifty days after the Feast of the Passover (Lev. xxiii. 15, 16). It corresponds with the Christian Whitsuntide, which in the Roman Church is still called by the same name, all the following Sundays until Advent being termed " after Pentecost," not " after Trinity," as with us. A curious and beautiful custom was observed in old St Paul's at Whitsuntide. William Lambarde, an able antiquary (b. 1536, d. 1601), tells us in his " Topographical Dictionary " : " I myself being a child, once saw in Paul's Church at London at a feast of Whitsuntide, when the coming down of the Holy Ghost was set forth by a white pigeon that was let to fly out of a hole that is yet to be seen in the midst of the roof of the great aisle, and by a long censer which, descending out of the same place almost to the very ground, was swung up and down to such a length that it reached at one sweep almost to the west gate of the church, and with the other to the choir stairs of the same, breathing out over the whole Church and company a most pleasant perfume of such sweet things as burned therein." The censer used in this ceremony was that described in the Inventory of the Ornaments of St Paul's, taken in 1552, as " a greate large Sensoure all silver with many windowes and batillments usedd to sense withall in the Penticoste weeke in the bodie of the Chirche of Pawles at the Procession tyme." It weighed no less than 158 ounces 3 quarters. Bishop Pilkington also alludes to the practice, " in the midst alley [nave] was a long censer, reaching from the roof to the ground, as though the Holy Ghost came in there, censing down in likeness of a dove." According to the *Liber Albus* (p. 26), compiled in 1419 by John Carpenter and Richard Whittington, edited and translated by Mr H. T. Riley, it appears that on Monday in the Feast of Pentecost, " before dinner and between 9 and 10 of the clock, it was the custom for the Mayor, Aldermen, and Sheriffs, arrayed in their suits, to meet in the Church of St Peter upon Cornhulle, as also those of the livery of the Sheriffs, as well as of the Mayor. From which place the Rectors of London heading the procession, those who were of the Sheriffs' livery followed, and next to them, preceding the Mayor, those who were of his livery ; after whom came the Mayor, with the Recorder and Aldermen in order of precedence, the procession passing through Chepe to the Churchyard of St Paul's. Entering this on the north side, they were there met in procession by the officials of that Church ; and then passing out by the South side of the churchyard and through the Close of Watling Strete, they entered the Church by the Great Door on the West side. Which done, they came to a stand in the Nave while the Hymn *Veni Creator* was chanted by the Vicars to the music of the Organ in alternate verses, an angel meanwhile censing from above. This ended, the Mayor and Aldermen, ascending to the Altar, made their offerings, after which they returned each to his home." The angel was, in all probability, an acolyte or other official of the church arrayed as such. This was by no means an uncommon practice on great occasions and public ceremonials. In the centre of the nave roof at Norwich is a circular opening, and the Sacrists' Rolls contain an entry for letting a man habited as an angel down from the roof with a thurible to cense the rood (Didron, *Annal. Archæolog.* xi. 12, 15). In 1170, at Lichfield, "clouds formed with vast quantities of incense, were made to fill the church with perfume," and probably, as in some places, had lighted tow mingled with them to represent the descent of fiery tongues. Doves were loosed, whilst one, as if hovering, was suspended from the roof.

Perpendicular Style. The last of the styles of Gothic architecture which flourished in this country. The nomenclature adopted by the Cambridge Camden (afterwards the Ecclesiological) Society was "Third Pointed." It arose gradually from the Decorated during the latter part of the fourteenth century, and continued till the middle of the sixteenth. The term "Perpendicular," as adopted by Rickman, Parker and others, is derived from the arrangement of the tracery, which consists of perpendicular lines, and forms one of its most striking features. A leading characteristic of the style, and one which prevails throughout its continuance, is the square arrangement of the mouldings over the heads of doorways, creating a spandrel on each side above the arch, which is usually ornamented with tracery, foliage, or a shield. Another peculiarity is the constant use of transoms crossing the mullions at right angles, and in large windows these are occasionally repeated several times. Panelling is used most abundantly on walls, both internally and externally, and also on vaulting. At the commencement of the style the arches were of good elevation, but subsequently they became much flattened. The roofs of this style (especially in Norfolk) are mostly of a high pitch, and have a magnificent effect, the spaces between the timbers being filled with tracery, and the beams arched, moulded, and ornamented in various ways. That the Perpendicular exhibits a decline in art it is idle to deny, but this epoch of architecture has given us a glorious assemblage of buildings, as may be seen from the following examples :—Canterbury Cathedral (nave), Winchester Cathedral (nave) ; York Minster (choir, presbytery, and Lady Chapel) ; Eton College Chapel ; Winchester College Chapel ; New and Magdalen College Chapels, Oxford ; King's College Chapel, Cambridge ; Henry VII.'s Chapel, Westminster Abbey ; St George's Chapel, Windsor ; Gloucester Cathedral (choir) ; the parish churches of Cirencester ; Louth ; St Mary Redcliffe, Bristol ; St Peter Mancroft, Norwich ; St Michael and Holy Trinity, Coventry ; the towers of the cathedrals of Canterbury and Gloucester ; of Magdalen College, Oxford ; of the churches of St Stephen, Bristol ; Wrington ; St Cuthbert, Wells ; Glastonbury ; North Petherton ; Huish Episcopi ; Kingsbury and Bishop's Lydiard, all in Somersetshire ; of Chipping Camden, Oxon ; Probus, Cornwall ; Wrexham, Denbigh, and the Huntingdonshire St Neot's. To the Perpendicular period we owe the graceful choir-stalls of Beverley, Carlisle, Chester, Lincoln, Manchester, and Ripon, as well as the splendid timber roofs, screens and bench-ends of those east and west Anglian churches that are, one may say, veritable lanterns for the display of stained glass which by the middle of the fifteenth century had reached its acme. Nor must those towering altarpieces that so grandly close the vistas of Winchester, St Alban's, Christ Church Priory, St Saviour's, Southwark, and All Souls' Chapel, Oxford, be overlooked. Good examples of revived Middle Pointed are St Andrew's, Wells Street (1847) ; Hornsey (new) Parish Church ; St Mary's, Portsea ; St Barnabas', Dulwich ; and St Cyprian's, Marylebone. Consult " The Architecture of the Perpendicular Period," a paper read before the St Paul's Ecclesiological Society, by J. D. Sedding, 27th May 1880. Printed in the Society's Transactions, i. 31.

Perpeyn Wall. A word probably derived from the old French " Parpaigne " or " Parpeine." A pier, buttress, or other support, projecting from a wall to sustain a beam, roof, etc. There is a fine Early English example at Lincoln Cathedral. Consult the article " Perpent-stone," in Parker's " Glossary of Architecture."

Pie. A table and rule in the old English offices, showing in a technical way how to find out the service which was to be read on each day, which, consisting of numerous particulars by the intermixing the several offices which sometimes fell in together to be read, made it difficult to be understood. As to the meaning of the name, which was called the " Pie " by the clergy before the Reformation, it was called by the Greeks Πιναξ, the index ; for that word signifies, metaphorically, a painted table or picture, and the indexes or tables of books being formed into square figures resembling pictures or painted tables hung up in a frame, these likewise were called πινακες, or being marked only with the first letters of the word πι, " Pies." This was probably the origin of the term ; but these tables being made with initial letters of red, and likewise some other remarkable letters or words thereof being of the same colour, it was thought that the table was called " Pie " from the parti-coloured letters whereof it consisted ; and from this account, when they put it into Latin, they called it " pica." Thus, in former times, some of the friars, from their parti-coloured habits, were called " pies." Afterwards, when printing came into use, those letters which were of a moderate size, not so big as the large text hand in the MSS., but were of the bigness only of those in the comments and tables, were called " pica " letters (see Nichols' " Commentary on the Book of Common Prayer," 1710). The instructions for the use of the " pie " were given in a very confused manner, and Maskell (*Mon. Rit.*, " Dissert. on Service-Books ") observes that it was not possible for the same service to occur on the same Sunday of the year twice running. The confusion in the " Pie," or order of services, was one of the difficulties which the framers of our Prayer-Book had to grapple with (see preface to the Prayer-Book, " Concerning the Service of the Church ").

Pier. The solid mass between doors, windows, and other openings in buildings ; the support of a bridge on which the arches rest. The name is often, but incorrectly, given to the pillars in Romanesque and Gothic architecture. See also under " Respond."

Pinnacle. A small turret, usually tapering towards the top, much used in Gothic architecture as a termination to buttresses, etc. It is also very frequently employed on the corners of towers, on tops of gables, parapets, and other elevated situations. It consists of a shaft and top, the latter generally in the form of a small spire, surmounted with a finial (*q.v.*) and often crocketed at the angles. In the Norman style pinnacles were not used, though there exist a few small turrets of later date, with pointed terminations, which appear to be their prototypes, as at the west end of Rochester Cathedral, and the north transept of the Church of St

Etienne at Caen. In the Early English style they are not very abundant, but at the west front of Wells Cathedral there are some beautiful specimens, surrounded by small shafts of blue stone. At the east end of Battle Church, Sussex, is a fine example, perfectly plain. In the Decorated style they are very numerous, being most usually square, and in a few instances octagonal, hexagonal, and pentagonal. In the Perpendicular style they do not differ much from the Decorated. They sometimes terminate in the figure of an animal holding a vane or some other device.

Piscina. A recess in the wall, on the south side of the altar, intended to receive and carry away the rinsings. It has a shallow basin in the cill, with a drain, and in the fourteenth century there were often two such basins and drains, one being presumably for the rinsings of the chalice, and one for those of the celebrant's hands. The drain is carried in the substance of the wall into the ground beneath. Very often the piscina had a shelf across it, half way up, which is supposed to have served as a credence, but its extreme narrowness militates against the presumption ; the still existing shelf is often of wood, though of very early, and probably original, date. In Northern Europe an altar invariably had its piscina, and where one exists it offers sure evidence that an altar once existed in close proximity ; but in Southern Europe such a thing is more rare. On the other hand, the credence, unless the shelf just mentioned served as such, was a thing absolutely unknown here, both in name and in fact. A stone table at St Cross, Winchester, is sometimes referred to as an English example, but probably the structure was monumental ; and the word is simply the Italian *credenza* anglicised. Ancient examples of the piscina exist all over England. The pedestal of a piscina of Norman date was discovered among some rubbish at Tollerton Church, near Nottingham, early in the last century. Parker (" Glossary of Architecture ") mentions that the drains of the piscinas in the chapels which surround the choir of Nôtre Dame, Paris, on the south side, were then (1844) remarkable as terminating externally in gargoyles, with their apertures several feet above the soil, in place of the usual drains communicating directly through the wall or floor into the earth. Other terms for the Piscina were *Lavacrum, Lavatorium, Locus reliquiarium* and *sacrarium*. The last-named was adopted by the Ecclesiological Society in its early Cambridge days for the sanctuary, or space within the altar rails, but the mistake was rectified when it was discovered that *sacrarium* meant the *piscina*. Piscina is the Θαλασσίδιον of the Greek liturgists. As previously mentioned, the most ancient piscinæ had (what is most complete and reverent) two basins, as may be seen by those at Salisbury and Lincoln Cathedrals, and at the Cathedral of Séez in Normandy ; one for the ablution of the hands at the *Lavabo,* and the other for the ablutions of the chalice. The old rubric respecting the *Lavabo* is as follows :— " Eat ad Piscinam dicens Lavabo : reversus dicit In spiritu humilitatis, etc." This is found in many ancient missals. When the rubric for the priest to receive the ablutions of the chalice became generally observed, the second basin was disused, and the later piscinæ have one basin only. In the Cotton MS., Tiberius I., British Museum, *temp.* St Osmund, directions are given to the clergy (*fol.* 101) in the Provincial Council by the Bishop, " Let a place be prepared in the Sacristy or hard by the Altar, where the water may be poured out wherewith the sacred vessels are washed ; and let there also a clean vessel be placed with water, wherein the Priest may wash his hands after Communion." Dr Rock (" Church of Our Fathers," i. 167) says that the priest washed his hands always, at least almost everywhere, in the piscina. The rubric was " Deinde lavet in sacrario ; postea dicat Communionem et Postcommunionem." The words " Lavate puras manus " are written over some piscinæ, notably at Great Cressingham, Norfolk. Viollet-le-Duc (" Dictionnaire Raisonné de l'Architecture Française," vii. 195) figures the interesting thirteenth-century double piscina at Séez, and J. D. Chambers (" Divine Worship in England," p. 12) the double piscina, together with its ground plan, at St Stephen's Church, near St Alban's. There is a beautiful Early English double piscina, richly carved with dog-tooth, at Castor, Northamptonshire. In T. H. King's " Study-Book of Mediæval Architecture " (vol. i.) will be found drawings of two single piscinæ, exactly similar in design, in chapels of the choir at Semur, Burgundy. Each has its narrow fenestella or shelf. Camille Enlart (" Manuel d'Archéologie Française," 1902) figures interesting piscinæ at Druyes (Yonne), twelfth century ; at St Thibaud (Côte-d'Or), thirteenth century ; at Rédon (Ille-et-Vilaine), fourteenth century, and a fine double piscina in the principal apse of the Cathedral at Famagusta, Cyprus, *c.* 1310. In Greek churches the piscina is situated immediately under the altar : it is called χονὶ, χονεῖον, or more frequently θαλασσίδιον, " The place of the sea." Its position and name are not improbably derived from the account (3 [1] Kings, xviii. 32) of the altar and trench made by Elijah ; where the Septuagint explains " trench " by θάλασσα. In the same way, the great laver which stood in the court of the Temple, upon oxen of brass, is in our own translation called the "Sea" (3 [1] Kings, vii., 23). In the great Church of the Holy Wisdom at Constantinople, it was richly ornamented with precious stones. This practice never seems to have obtained in the Western Church. The Piscina is not often met with in modern churches. When there is one it is usually to be found in the sacristy. The Church of St John Baptist, Holland Road, Kensington, however, posessses two—both in their proper position on the south side ; one serving for the High Altar, the other for that in the Lady Chapel. The architect of this fine Early English church was the late James Brooks. *The Ecclesiologist*, vol. viii., contains an important article on the uses of piscinas.

Plain-song. The most ancient species of Church music. The kind of music used from time immemorial in the worship of the ancient Jewish Church, as well as among all the churches of Christendom throughout the world. It is a well-known form of musical accent, recitation, and simple melody. There are eight principal modes, tones, or scales in use, called the Gregorian Tones ; the first, third, fifth, and seventh of which were arranged by St Ambrose, in the fourth century, and are termed authentic ; the plagal, or collateral scales of a lower range—viz. the second, fourth, sixth, and eighth, were added by St Gregory the Great, in the sixth century. In plain-song the stave consists of four lines only, and the characters used are three in number, the long, ▐, the breve, ▄, and the semi-breve, ◆. Two clefs are employed, the Ut or Do clef, and the Fa or F clef, which may be placed on any one of the four lines, as required, to keep the melody within the range of the stave. Consult the article "Plain-song," by the Rev. Thomas Helmore in Stainer and Barrett's "Dictionary of Musical Terms," and the "Primer," by the same author (Novello) ; also the numerous foreign treatises of Alfieri, La Feillé, Clement, Janssen, Lambillotte, and, in the English, the instruction-books of Lambert, Benz, Charles Child Spencer and Burgess. The publications of the Plainsong and Mediæval Music Society are of great value, and the Rev. J. B. Croft, priest-organist of St Matthew's, Westminster, now, indubitably, one of our greatest authorities, has written on the subject of plain-song.

Plate Tracery. That kind of solid tracery which appears as if formed by piercing a flat surface with ornamental patterns. Examples of such tracery may be seen at Lincoln Cathedral (north-west transept), St John's Church, Winchester (south aisle), St Michael's College, Tenbury (windows in cloister), St Columba's, Haggerston, and St John's, Finsbury Park, London ; Chartres Cathedral (transept roses), Münster Cathedral (western transept).

Plinth. The solid square under the base of a column, pedestal, etc.

Podium. A continuous pedestal or basement ; also a dwarf wall used as a substructure for columns. At St Paul's the semicircular erection, with steps on either side, projecting from the south transept into the street is termed a podium. Within recent years a narrow footpath has been made round its base. Formerly this podium was a source of danger to pedestrians.

Pointed. The emphatically Christian architecture, commonly called Gothic, characterised chiefly by the pointed arch, and contrasting in almost every particular with the round-arch architecture from which it was developed. This style may be subdivided into three periods: First or Early Pointed, Second or Middle Pointed, and Third or Late Pointed (the Flamboyant of the Continent, the Perpendicular of England), emphasising respectively its growth, full development, and decline. This series is most clearly marked in England, and should be borne in mind in order to understand Foreign Pointed, in which the same succession as really, though less systematically and less apparently, ran its course.

Polyphony. Music in many parts, as opposed to " Homophony," unison of voices or instruments of the same character.

Poma. Hollow metal balls, so contrived as to be filled with burning charcoal or hot water, that the celebrant during the intervals of Mass might warm his hands, and thus the more readily hold the sacred vessels in times of frost and cold. This convenient instrument was also called *calefactorium, calepungnus,* and *scutum.* In the inventory of St Paul's Cathedral, *temp.* Henry III., three poma are mentioned—one of silver and white metal, another of silver-gilt—the first adorned with figures of animals and bunches of grapes, the third with representations of the months.

Poppy-head. An elevated ornament often used on the tops of the upright ends, or elbows, which terminate stalls, benches, etc., in churches. They are sometimes cut merely into plain *fleurs de lis,* or other simple forms (a good example is at Merrow, Surrey), but are frequently carved with leaves, like finials, and in rich work are sculptured into animals and figures. No examples are known to exist of earlier date than the Decorated style, and but few so early. Of Perpendicular date specimens are to be found in very numerous churches, especially in the cathedrals and old abbey churches. In the contract for the Beauchamp Chapel, Warwick, 1450, we find " a pair of Desks of timber, *Poppies*, seats, sils, planks, etc." ; and from an old account published by Thomas Hearne, in the appendix to the History of Glastonbury : " Memord, comenawntyd and agreid wyth Comell Clerke, for the makyng off the dextis in the liberary [of Christ Church, Oxford] to the summe off xvi after the maner and forme as they be in Magdaleyn college, except the *popie heedes* off the seites." *The Ecclesiologist*, June 1846, contains an exhaustive illustrated article on poppy-heads.

Portiforium. Another name used in England for the Breviary, or Book of Canonical Hours. It was also called Portfory, Porteau, Portuary, Portuis, Porthuasse, Porthoos.

Post Communions, The. In the First Prayer Book (1549) are given sixteen passages of Scripture, following the *Agnus Dei* in the Communion Service, " to be said or sung every day one, after the Holy Communion." The rubric runs, " When the Communion is ended, then shall the Clerks sing the post Communion." These texts seem to have been designed to correspond with the ancient portions of the plain-song, still known as the Communio, in all books of Latin ritual music. " While the priest administers the Sacrament of the Holy Communion to the people, the choir sing an antiphon, which is therefore called the *Communio* "—*i.e.* the Communion Anthem (Clément, " Methode Complète de Plain-Chant." Paris, 1854). These Post Communions were noted in their entirety by Merbecke, like the Offertory Sentences. The 1st, " If any man will follow Me," is adapted from the music of an antiphon for Vespers within the Octave of Corpus Christi. The 6th, " Behold, thou art made whole," is to the music of antiphons for the Sixth Sunday after Epiphany and the Fourteenth Sunday after Pentecost. It seems to have been the subject of Byrd's Mass for five voices (recently edited, with English words, by Mr S. Royle Shore). The same music, however, with slight alterations, is set to several antiphons occurring in services for the Sundays after Pentecost. Of the 7th, " If ye shall continue in My Word," the original music occurs in the Roman Antiphonarium on the Feast of the Annunciation, to the words, *Gabriel angelus locutus est Mariae*. The music of the 8th, " He that hath My Commandments," and of the 10th, " If God be on our side," is of frequent occurrence in the old choral books, and forms the subject of Palestrina's beautiful motett, *Veni, Sponsa Christi*. Of the 11th, " Who shall lay anything to the charge of God's chosen ? " the music occurs in the Roman Vesperal, in the

ECCLESIASTICAL TERMS

antiphon to the *Magnificat* for Shrove Tuesday. That of the 12th, " The night is passed, and the day is at hand," is from the antiphon to the *Magnificat* at Vespers on the Fourth Sunday after Pentecost, beginning, *Praeceptor, per totam noctem laborantes* (see W. Dyce's " Book of Common Prayer, with Plain-Tune," 1844). At the revision of 1552, these Post Communions were omitted, never (like the Introits) to reappear. None of these sentences of Scripture bear any resemblance to the passages now sung as " Post Communions." Likewise the " Post Communions " given in the Sarum Missal for every Sunday and Holy Day are totally different from those in the Book of 1549.

A clergyman attached to a Cathedral of the Old Foundation or to a collegiate church, who formerly enjoyed a *prebend* (Lat. *prae-benda*, a stipend) in consideration of his officiating at **Prebendary.** stated times in the church. By the Cathedral Act of 1840 most of the prebendal stalls have been deprived of their endowments, but the holders of them are still called prebendaries. A modern title (as at Lincoln) is honorary canon. In the New Foundation Cathedrals, before 1840, the canons, of whom there were from twelve to eight, and then reduced to six or four, were called " prebendaries." Thus, at coronations, the canons of Westminster were mentioned always as " prebendaries." At Christ Church, Oxford, however—a Cathedral of the New Foundation—" canon " has *always* been the title. In 1840, a number of " honorary canons " were added to the staff of Cathedrals of the New Foundation. These stalls, like those of the prebendaries in the Old Cathedrals, are always in the gift of the bishop of the diocese. When separate endowments were attached to stalls the incumbents were called prebendaries (*Canonici Prebendali*). Canon and prebendary were one man, the canonry being his spiritual right to a stall in the chapter, his prebend was a temporal endowment. Prebendary is an honourable name from its antiquity, but must become an *anachronism* except under a system of re-endowment. Out of the revenues of the suppressed prebends of St Paul's, C. J. Blomfield, while Bishop of London (1828–1856), endowed ten new churches in Bethnal Green. One of the prebendal stalls has been re-endowed—that of Cantler's or Kentish Town—and it now serves as a provision for the Diocesan Inspector of Schools. So much has, at various times, been written about chapters and prebendal residence that it seems worth while to unearth a joke on the subject from Chambers' " Biographical Illustrations of Worcestershire " (1820), p. 470 : The Rev. Wm. Hughes was a minor canon of Worcester Cathedral for fifty years and died in 1798. The dean having complained to him that he was greatly annoyed by rats, Mr Hughes replied : "Make prebendaries of them, Mr Dean ; you will only see them once a year." Formerly, at St Paul's, when a prebendary "read himself in" to his stall, he read the lessons and the whole of the prayers, in place of the two minor canons on duty. This was on the Sunday afternoon following the day of his installation.

The leader of a choir. The only precentors now recognised by the English Church are those of cathedral and collegiate churches.

Precentor.
Lat.
praecentor,
cantor, caput
scholae;
Span. *capiscol*
(same as Lat.
caput scholae),
armarius,
primicerio;
Fr. *préchantre,*
grand chantre;
Germ.
vorsänger.

There is no mention of this office before the fourth century ; then it appears that in many churches one singer, the precentor, or "pronunciator," recited the first half of a verse and the people took up the rest. Afterwards the office was considered very important, and the holder invested with great dignity. The precentor in almost all the Cathedrals of the Old Foundation in England, and very generally on the Continent, was the first dignitary in the chapter after the dean. In some few instances the archdeacon preceded him. In the choir his stall is opposite that of the dean—viz. the first on the left hand on entering. His side is called *Cantoris*, the side of the *Cantor*, as the other *Decani*, the side of the dean. The office of precentor was instituted at Exeter *c.* 1080 ; at Salisbury in 1091 ; at Chichester, 1115 ; at Wells *c.* 1135 ; at St David's, 1224 ; at Hereford *c.* 1195 ; at Lichfield, 1130 ; at Lincoln, 1097 ; at York, 1090 ; and at St Paul's in the reign of King John. The duties of this dignitary were multifarious. He had to direct the divine offices as regards the chant ; to select candidates to supply choral vacancies ; to provide and keep the choir books in good condition ; to table the weekly rota of duty ; to choose and present a succentor, or deputy, when necessary ; to instal the dean and canons, and assign stalls to the prebendaries ; to superintend the training of the choristers, not only as regards their morals and choral instruction, but also their food and clothing. On great festivals he "ruled the choir," when two canons, robed in the red soutane (cassock), were the chanters, whom he followed up and down the choir, regulating the offices and overseeing the service in rochet and cope, holding a staff in his hand. He further observed that all the choir sang with proper modulation, and that various and proper chants according to the day and feast were used. He gave the note to the celebrant at the altar, distributed the copes, regulated processions, and having presented offenders to the chapter left correction to them. In the Inventory of St Paul's, 1552, the precentor's staff is thus described :—" Item, a staffe all silver and parcell gylte with muche fyne worke ; in the hedd whereof ar the ymages of ower Ladie and Pawle. This staffe hath iiij. partes to be joynedd together with vices. lxxxix. unc." Again, " A staffe of yverie for the chaunter of the queere with a hedd and a crosse of birall wrought with goldsmith work with vij joyntes sylver and gylte besides the picke and the bosse." Two others are also described, probably those used by the choir rulers. A fine example of a precentor's staff is figured in Dr Lee's " Glossary of Ecclesiastical and Liturgical Terms " (1876). The special business of the precentor, as his name implies, was to take a personal care of the music of the church, which forms so prominent a feature in the cathedral system. No one at all conversant with that most difficult and important art, choral music, but must know that its conduct requires not only the skill of a musician, but the knowledge and discretion of a ritualist and divine. When these have been combined the most salutary results have followed. In most cathedrals the revenues of the precentor's office have been taken away and its dignity and status lowered. Since the Reformation holders of the stall have, until within recent years, possessed no qualifications of a practical nature. Rare cases are those of Creyghton (Wells, 1674–1733) ; Mason (York, 1763–1797), after a fashion ; Ouseley (Hereford, 1855–1889) ; Allott (Armagh, 1852) ; Seymour (Christ Church, Dublin, 1876–1883) ; Rowden (Chichester, 1859–1863) ; Walcott (Chichester, 1863–1880). During the last few years there has been a more general attempt to revive the musical responsibilities of the precentor, as at Hereford, Lincoln, St Paul's, Salisbury, Southwark, and Truro. At Salisbury, however, in 1843, Walter Kerr Hamilton (afterwards bishop) and in 1856 his successor, W. Beadon Heathcote, son of Gilbert Heathcote, the very musical Archdeacon of Winchester (d. 1829), gave much attention during their precentorships to the regulation of the choir, and the ordering of suitable chants, services, and anthems. At Lichfield in 1856 the precentor, John Hutchinson, was active, and there he initiated those diocesan choral festivals now so universal throughout the country. As soon as a precentor became non-resident, or thought music beneath his dignity, or found it beyond his skill, he relegated his duties in choir to a deputy with the title of succentor or sub-chanter (q.v.). Thus, at St Paul's, in 1812, we find the precentor, the Rev. Herbert Randolph, who was in receipt of a large income, delegating his authority over the choir to the Rev.

A DICTIONARY OF

E. J. Beckwith, one of the minor canons, at the annual magnificent stipend of £6, 13s. 4d. ! From 1819 until his death in 1886 (a period of sixty-seven years) the Rev. Charles Almeric Belli was precentor of St Paul's without performing one particle of the duties of his office, beyond appointing his deputy and preaching an occasional sermon. In the New Foundation Cathedrals the precentor, not being found among the dignitaries, is always a minor canon. His old title was "chanter" or "chaunter." The office has always been regarded as an important and responsible one, and of late years at Bristol, Canterbury, Chester, Durham, Ely, Gloucester, Norwich, Peterborough, Ripon, Rochester, Winchester, Worcester, and at Westminster Abbey the precentor has frequently been a man of some note—no pun being intended. In certain of the Old Cathedrals the precentorship has always been united to a canonry—*e.g.* Lichfield and Lincoln. At St Paul's this has been the case since 1886. In some of our large and important parish churches, where there are elaborate musical services, the senior curate is sometimes styled precentor. Thus we speak of the precentor of Leeds, the precentor of Wigan, etc. Consult further, J. S. Bumpus, "Organists and Composers of St Paul's Cathedral," (1891); Miss Hackett, "Letters to the Bishop of London, the Dean of St Paul's, the Precentor and other Dignitaries of that Church" (1811–1814); Jebb, "The Choral Service of the Church" (1843); Seymour, "The Cathedral System" (1870); Walcott, "Cathedralia," 1865.

Preces. The Latin word for prayers; but it is often applied in a technical sense to the shorter sentences, as versicles and suffrages, which are said in the way of verse and response. The longer prayers were called "Orationes," and were in fact equivalent to our collects. "The distinction," says Dean Hook ("Church Dict."), "is given by St Cyprian, who speaks of the 'preces' as a 'litany.'" In the English service the term is limited to those versicles (with the *Gloria Patri*), immediately preceding the Psalms, beginning "O Lord, open Thou our lips," and those after the Creed. Thus we speak of the preces as musical compositions, such as the "Preces and Responses of Tallis," and so on. Consult Jebb, "Choral Service of the Church" (1843) and the same author's "Choral Responses and Litanies of the Church of England" (1847-1857). In the old offices the preces were said daily at Prime and Compline, and also at Lauds and Vespers on week-days. Our versicles after the Creed appear to have come from the selection used in the Cathedral of Salisbury, in the form of "Bidding the Bedes" :—

ECCLESIASTICAL TERMS

Ostende nobis, Domine, misericordiam tuam.
Sacerdotes tui induantur justiciam.
Domine, salvum fac regem.
Salvos fac servos tuos et ancillas tuas.
Salvum fac populum tuum, Domine, et benedic hæreditati tuæ.
Domine, fiat pax in virtute tua.
Domine, exaudi orationem meam.

Besides the celebrated Preces of Tallis there are several settings by distinguished composers of the sixteenth and seventeenth centuries. Amongst the finest are the " First and Second Preces " of Orlando Gibbons, printed by the Rev. Sir Frederick Ouseley in his selection from the compositions of that great master (1873). The " Second Preces " were sung at the Commemoration of Orlando Gibbons at Westminster Abbey, 5th June 1907. Dr Jebb, in his " Choral Responses and Litanies of the United Church of England and Ireland " (2 vols., 1847–1857), prints Preces by Byrd, Batten, Parsons, Portman, Tomkins, William Smithe of Durham, Hooper, Holmes, Amner, Palmer and Ayleward, besides those of Tallis and Gibbons. Holmes, Byrd, Ayleward and Smithe, like Tallis, also set the Responses after the Creed. In more modern times " Preces and Responses " have been composed by Thomas Ebdon (d. 1811), Sir John Stevenson (d. 1833), the Rev. Peter Penson (d. 1849), the Rev. J. Clarke Crosthwaite (d. 1874), Rev. John Finlayson (d. 1882) and Sir Robert Stewart (d. 1894). Those (in G minor) by the last-named are very fine, and were written at the time of the obsequies of the Duke of Wellington, November 1852. A Litany in the same key is attached. They are unpublished.

It was an early custom to abstain from celebration on Good Friday. A portion of the bread consecrated on the previous day, Maundy Thursday, was reserved for the Communion
Presanctified. on the Friday, and the wine used was unconsecrated.
Mass of the, This was called the Mass of the Presanctified (*Missa Praesanctificatorum*). The idea evidently was that the Eucharist is a feast, and therefore not to be celebrated in its entirety on a fast-day. In the Church of England there is no such rite as that of the " Presanctified," and the appointment of a special Epistle and Gospel for Good Friday would seem to indicate that a Celebration on that day was intended. Bishop Andrewes, in his sermons on the Passion, speaks in such a way that there is no doubt that celebrations on Good Friday were usual in his time. Consult further : Bona, " Rer Liturg.," I, 15, 5 ; Leo Allatius, " de Eccles. Occ. et Or. Perpetua Consensione " *ad fin.* ; Neale's " Hist. of

East. Church," pt. i. c. vii. ; Blunt, "Annot. Pr. Bk.," i. 101 ; Hook, " Church Dict.," 609 (1896).

Presbytery.
Lat.
presbyterium.

The space in cathedrals and large churches between the easternmost stalls of the choir and the altar. As the word implies, it was the place assigned to the bishop and presbyters, and none else were admitted to it. It was usually elevated one step above the rest of the choir, hence the architectural term, *gradus presbyterii.*

Prime. One of the lesser canonical hours. See *sub voce* " Matins."

Prior.

The head or superior of a monastic establishment where there was no abbot. Where there was one, the prior was the next person after the abbot. The office appears to have held the same relation to the dean which a dean possessed with regard to a *Provost,* the name given to the bishop by St Cyprian and Tertullian in the early monasteries, and who ranked next to the abbot, his nomination being vested at first in the bishop and subsequently in the abbot. When the provosts gave themselves up to temporal concerns, and became too powerful in consequence, the deans were established to keep up Church discipline ; or very probably, when the chapters emancipated themselves from the bishop as head of the chapter, they exchanged the name of the provost, who had been his immediate deputy, for that of dean, allowing his merely temporal duties to devolve on an officer bearing his name, the dignity thus again becoming, as it were, a mere obedientiary. The title of provost was revived at the consecration of St Ninian's Cathedral, Perth, in 1850, the dean of a Scottish diocese being simply then an archdeacon. The office of *Prior* existed at Cologne (Innoc. III. *de Cler Excom.*) and in several Spanish cathedrals.

Processions.

According to Western usage there is a procession, *ante crucem*— that is, headed by the processional cross—every Sunday and Greater Festival before solemn Celebration. To this the old English uses add a procession after Evensong on feasts and on Saturday evenings from Easter to Advent. On Candlemas Day, or Feast of the Purification of the B. V. M. (2nd February), those in procession carry lighted tapers in allusion to the prophecy of Simeon, " A light to lighten the Gentiles " ; and on Palm Sunday branches of palm in commemoration of Our Lord's triumphal entry into Jerusalem, when the people took branches of palm and strewed them in the way. The Litany is sung in procession on the Rogation Days. The proper order of processions is this : The priest with the taper-bearers, etc., goes to the midst of the choir before the altar steps, and there puts incense into the censer ; the procession then starts from the Epistle side, and passing down the south aisle returns through the nave. The old English use was to employ the inverse order in *penitential* processions, passing down the *north* aisle, and returning by the nave. In cathedrals and large churches the procession on feast days and other solemn occasions quitted the choir by the north door of the presbytery, and passed behind the high altar, by the ")procession path," so reaching the south aisle and returning through the nave. It is usual to sing a hymn or Psalm in processions. The old office-books or " Processionals " give an anthem or antiphon for every Sunday, to which is added, except from Palm Sunday to Trinity Sunday, a " Prose with versicle, response and collect to be sung in the station "—*i.e.* standing in the nave before the choir-screen—and another antiphon on entering the choir. On festivals a hymn followed the first antiphon or " responsary " as it was called. Archbishop Cranmer wished to set forth the " Processions " in English, but was prevented from carrying out his design. In parish churches it would appear that before High Mass on all Sundays and double feasts, the priest alone, accompanied by a single boy, went and sprinkled the people and each altar with holy water, but, whether in cathedrals or parish churches, on arriving at the rood-screen, the celebrant, turning to the people, read the " Bidding Prayer "—*i.e.* a list of those who were to be prayed for at the Mass. The Sarum order of procession at High Mass was as follows :—(1) vergers or churchwardens with rods, (2) boy in surplice carrying holy water, (3) cross-bearer, (4) two candle-bearers abreast, (5) thurifer and boat-bearer, (6) sub-deacon, (7) deacon, (8) celebrant, (9) choir-boys, (10) choir-men, (11) deacons and priests intending to sit in choir, in surplices and hoods (12) the bishop wearing his mitre and with his pastoral staff in his hand, not carried before him. All those who sat in the choir were to walk, not in pairs shoulder to shoulder but wide apart, so as to form two lines with an open space between. At Evensong the order was verger, wardens, cross-bearer, candle-bearers, thurifers, priest in cope, choir-boys, choir-men, etc. No cross was carried in the Saturday evening processions at Sarum, but that " *processio ante crucem* was practically merely a ' station ' at the choir gates in front of the great Rood." The orderly processions before and after service, to which we are now so accustomed in our cathedrals, were almost unheard of sixty years ago, the choir-boys, lay clerks, and minor canons dropping in by twos and threes, as they do in the Continental cathedrals to this day, the entrance of the dean or canon-in-residence being the signal for beginning the office. From the " Life and Reminiscences of Sir George Elvey " (1894) it seems that a procession became the rule, during his organistship of St George's Chapel, Windsor, in the year 1846.   There can be no doubt that many churches set the example to the cathedrals in this respect during the early days of the Oxford movement.   But in our great diocesan churches, where perfect architecture, venerable associations, and all appliances for vocal and instrumental harmony would seem to insure to our Liturgy its fullest devotional effect, the service was sometimes turned into burlesque by the slovenly irreverence of the dignitaries.   As an example, may be mentioned a scene which occurred about the middle of the last century in one of these diocesan churches, where the prebendaries were bound to attend daily prayers for twenty-one days continuously in every year ;   the rule being that if a prebendary missed a single service he was obliged to begin his twenty-one days over again.   One day an old prebendary (high, dry, and gouty) came limping into his stall a minute after the service had begun.   The dean immediately turned to him and exclaimed : "You must begin again, sir."   "Do you hear, sir, what the dean says to you ? " shouted the prebendary to the intoning minor canon ; "he tells you to begin the service again."   The "inferior" officer humbly obeyed, and complete victory crowned the old prebendary's stratagem.   The 34th number of *The Parish Choir* (October 1848) contains an article, "A few words on Westminster Abbey by a Looker-on."   This was written not long after the reopening of the choir, with its new stall-work, etc.   The writer observes, "Let me mention one great improvement which distinguishes the new regime.   The members of the choir, instead of lounging in by ones and twos, as they used to do, now enter in procession, the juniors first, and a very pleasing and becoming sight it is.   Perhaps another day they will sing something of a hymn or anthem as they walk. This would give still more solemnity to the procession, and is, I believe, in accordance with the statutes of some Collegiate Churches."

Procession Path.   A continuation of the choir aisles behind the high altar in an apsidal and occasionally in a square-ended church.

Processional Cross.   See *sub voce* "Crucifer."

Processionale.   A name given to the book, Sarum, Gallican, or Roman, containing offices sung in procession, such as litanies, psalms, antiphons, hymns, etc.   The Processionale of Sarum was famous.

Prymer.   English versions of the *Horae* (hours of the Holy Spirit, Blessed Trinity, and of the Blessed Virgin, etc.), and occasional devotions, the Litany, Dirge, etc. (*q.v.*), may be certainly traced to the fourteenth century, under the name of the Prymer.

ECCLESIASTICAL TERMS

This word is peculiarly English ; and it is highly probable that it was derived from some small manuals, which were spread among the people, of the first lessons of religious belief and practice : and in its first state, before the middle of the sixth century, as the *Little Office* or *Officium Parvum*, it may have been known among the Anglo-Saxons as containing the Creed, the Lord's Prayer, and the Ten Commandments. There are still remaining in MS. many short expositions in the vernacular of these elements of Christian knowledge, to which are often added the seven works of mercy, the seven sacraments, the two precepts of the Gospel, and such like. Springing from such early manuals, the Prymer received its gradual additions in successive ages, until we find it commonly mentioned in the fifteenth century as a well-known book of private devotion, containing certain set prayers and offices. It was in English or in English and Latin, and sometimes in Latin, with occasional portions or collects in English. The title was "This Prymer of Salisbury Use," or " The Prymer both in English and Latin," or " The Prymer set forth by the King's Majesty." The earliest known copy, belonging most probably to the latter part of the fourteenth century, was printed by Maskell in his "Monumenta Ritualia Ecclesiæ Anglicanæ" (1846), and comparing it with the famous Prymer of King Henry VIII. (1545) it may be said that for 150 years preceding the Reformation, and probably for a much longer period, the Prymer was the book authorised by the English Church for the private devotion of the people. The contents of the Prymer (*c*. 1400) as printed by Maskell were, Matins and Hours of Our Lady, Evensong and Compline, the seven Penitential Psalms, the fifteen Psalms of Degrees (cxx.-cxxxiv.), the Litany, Placebo, Dirge, the Psalm of Commendation (Ps. cxix.), Pater Noster, Ave Maria, Creed, the Ten Commandments, the seven deadly sins. The Prymer as "set forth by the King's Majesty and his Clergy (1545) purged of much that was superstitious," comprised the Kalendar, the King's Highness' Injunction, the Prayer of Our Lord, the Salutation of the Angel (Ave Maria), the Creed, or articles of the faith, the Ten Commandments, certain graces, the Matins, the Evensong, the Compline, the seven Psalms, the Litany, the Dirge, the Commendations (Ps. cxix.), the Psalms of the Passion (xxii., lxix., lxxxviii., ii., and lix.), the Passion of Our Lord, certain godly prayers for sundry purposes, and a table of contents. Many copies of the earlier *Officium Parvum* exist in MS. and in printed editions; some, like the missals, are most beautifully illuminated, with miniatures and armorial bearings of the owners, pictures of the life and sufferings of Our Blessed Lord, of the saints and martyrs, or descriptive of

239

A DICTIONARY OF

the offices, such as of the vigils or burial. Consult Maskell, " Dissert.
on Service-Books" chap. ix., "Mon. Rit." i. p. clii. and a full
table of contents of a complete edition (Paris, 1507), p. clv. Plenty
of very early MSS. are in existence, containing expositions of the
Creed, the Lord's Prayer, Ten Commandments, etc., in the vulgar
tongue ; thus showing, for the consolation of English churchmen,
that their forefathers before the Reformation were neither so
ignorant nor so uncared for as is often represented. In fact
they had, *in English*, almost all parts of the service which we
now possess, excepting the Communion Office ; and they offered
up, day by day, the same prayers which are daily offered by
their posterity. A specimen will be found in the Collect for
Peace, now said daily at Evensong, reprinted with the Latin,
by Maskell in his English Prymer of *c.* 1400; beginning " God,
of whom ben hooli desiris, right councels and iust werkis "
(" Deus, a quo sancta desideria, recta consilia, et justa sunt
opera ").

In singing the Alleluia after the Epistle in the Mass, a custom
said by Gregory the Great to have been introduced by Damasus
(Greg. "Mag. Epist. ad Johan. Syracus," lib. x. epist.
Prose.   12), it became a common use to prolong the last syllable
Lat. *prosa.*   upon a number of notes. "Words in rhythmical prose,"
                          says Dean Hook in his " Church Dictionary," " were
afterwards arranged to these notes, and later metrical hymns, and
these were called *Prosae.*" In the eighth century, Notker, Abbot of
St Gall, in Switzerland, composed several of these *prosae*, otherwise
called *sequentiae* (sequences), which were sung after the gradual (*q.v.*).
Pope Nicholas I. first authorised their use. They soon became very
numerous, and often very ridiculous, and were retrenched by the
Council of Cologne in 1536, and of Rheims in 1564. Those retained
were the *Victimae Paschali laudes* (Easter), *Veni Sancte Spiritus*
(Whitsuntide), *Lauda Sion Salvatorem* (Corpus Christi), *Stabat
Mater Dolorosa* (Feast of the Seven Dolours of the B.V.M., Friday
after Passion Sunday), and *Dies Irae* (Mass for the Dead). A few
others will be found in graduals printed for local use in various
dioceses, and permitted to be retained. The more deeply the stores
of mediæval hymnology are studied, the more will the richness and
variety of its sequences excite admiration. Dr Daniel published
in his " Thesaurus Hymnologicus" (1843), a hundred and thirty,
besides the commencements of, or extracts from, a hundred and
fifty more. The Rev. J. M. Neale published in 1852 a hundred
and twenty-four others, and yet both collections left an enormous

ECCLESIASTICAL TERMS

field open to future students. The pages of *The Ecclesiologist*, 1853-1863, contained a collection of sequences which had not, till then, been reprinted from their original missals. This valuable series of articles was entitled " Sequentiæ Ineditæ." The materials were collected from the missals of the north-east of France and Belgium ; three printed Danish missals—Copenhagen, Sleswic and the Danish Dominican ; four Swedish missals—Upsal, Lund, Abo, and Strengnas ; the missals in the Library of the Bollandist College of St Michel at Brussels ; and sequences from Portuguese missals—not hitherto investigated. Each fasciculus was laid before the reader, appropriate to the season of the Church's year, at which the number of *The Ecclesiologist* containing it appeared.

Prothesis. The table in a church on which the elements in the Eucharist are placed, previously to their being laid as an oblation on the altar. Called also credence (*q.v.*). The word *prothesis* (προθεσις) is derived from the Temple service, in which the placing of the shewbread was called ἡ πρόθεσις τῶν ἄρτων, and the bread itself, οἱ ἄρτοι τῆς προθέσεως—*i.e.* the loaves set in order before the Lord. See further *sub voce* " Credence."

Psalter. One of the numerous service-books of the English Church before the Reformation was the *Psalterium* or Psalter, a separate book according to the use of particular churches, containing the Book of Psalms divided into certain portions so as to be sung through in the course of the week in the service of the Hours. Maskell ("Dissert.," p. xxxvi.) gives the arrangement of the Psalms from a "Psalterium cum Hymnis ad usum insignis ecclesiæ Sarum et Eboracensis." When, in 1549, our present Prayer-Book was compiled, largely from the mediæval offices, the whole Psalter was taken in order every month, instead of fixed Psalms for each service throughout the week. There was nothing unusual in making a new arrangement of the daily Psalms. Every church, and every fraternity of monks, and almost every religious house, had its own rules in this respect. In the English Church twelve Psalms had been sung in the nocturns of Matins alone. Cassian ("Instit. Coenobit." ii. 2) tells us that some churches repeated twenty or thirty Psalms, some more, and some only eighteen ; while in some monasteries in Egypt they read fifty, in others sixty Psalms. In Spain, three Psalms were sung in the nocturnal office. Cardinal Quignonez also rearranged the Psalter in his reformed Breviary, giving three Psalms to Matins, and two or three to the offices of the other Hours, so that the Psalter should be read through every week —" Psalterium dispositum in dies et horas ordine ; quo totum singulis hebdomadibus dicitur per totum annum " (Breviar. fol. 1, ed. 1537). In the Greek ritual, the Psalter was divided into twenty portions called καθίσματα, or sessions, of which the 119th Psalm formed one : each cathisma was divided into three parts by the doxology interposed between each part. These divisions were called στάσεις, or stations, and between each stasis a lesson was interposed. Jebb (" Choral Service of the Church," p. 274) gives the apportionment of the Psalter in the English unreformed offices. The repetition of the *Gloria Patri* " at the end of every Psalm throughout the year " was ordered in 1549. In the Breviary it had been appointed after some Psalms, or after a series of Psalms. " Its use," says Procter (" Book of Common Prayer "), " signifies our belief that the same God was worshipped by the Jewish Church as by us ; and we, by this addition, turn the Jewish Psalms into Christian hymns." In the unreformed offices, to every Psalm and canticle was attached an antiphon, a short verse sung before and after it, to some melody composed in the old Church modes, the Psalms being chanted in the same mode. The antiphon was of three kinds—viz. either some remarkable verse of the Psalm itself, embodying its principal sentiments, or else a short passage from Scripture, relating to the service of the day ; and lastly, on Saints' Days, it was usually a short sentence eulogistic of the saint who was commemorated. In many respects, says the Rev. J. Baden Powell (" Choralia," p. 55), the antiphon was " a perfectly beautiful adjunct to the Psalmody, bringing the special force of the Scripture of the day to bear upon the Psalms sung, and so giving them a meaning and intention ; a ' lighting up,' special to the day or season." The compilers of our Liturgy were of opinion that " anthems (antiphons), responds, invitatories, and such-like things " did " break the continual course of the reading of the Scriptures," and for this reason they were " cut off." However much we may regret the excision of these antiphons from a musical as well as from a doctrinal point of view, a little consideration will show that the reformers of the English ritual exercised a sound judgment in removing them from a Common Prayer-Book intended for the use of the poor and unlettered, for the wayfaring and hard-working man, and not merely for the scholar, the clergyman, or the member of a cathedral body ; since they would have added materially to the complexity of the book, and the task of fitting the antiphons to the Psalms would not always have been an easy one ; indeed, in these days of Anglican chants and settings of the canticles service-wise, it would be, musically, an almost impossible one. In some " advanced " churches the antiphons have been restored,

ECCLESIASTICAL TERMS

especially as regards those to the *Magnificat*, but their use has not yet extended to the daily services of cathedrals.   They may, however, be heard at St Paul's at the annual Festival of the London Gregorian Association ; and in the forms of service drawn up for use on special and solemn occasions in the same cathedral, antiphons are appointed to be sung before and after the Psalms and canticles. The apportionment of the Psalms to our two daily offices of Matins and Evensong may, on the whole, be pronounced satisfactory.   The only alteration one might wish for would be to remove the 141st Psalm from Matins to Evensong of the 29th day of the month, not only because in its very nature it is an evening Psalm—" Let my prayer be set forth in Thy sight as the incense : and let the lifting up of my hands be an evening sacrifice " (verse 2)—but because the Psalms of that evening are so unusually and unprecedently short. Our Church appoints special or " Proper" Psalms for Christmas Day, Ash Wednesday, Good Friday, Easter Day, Ascension Day, and Whitsun Day.   The occasions on which Proper Psalms might be used could be extended in the manner suggested in a series of articles, "·The Theory of the Prayer-Book," printed in *The Ecclesiologist* during the years 1856 and 1857.   At the first Evensong of the Great Festivals, the Psalms proper for the Evensong of the festivals themselves might fitly be sung.   The earliest service-books of the reformed Liturgy set forth the chants after which the ritual music of the Prayer-Book was to be ordered, and these were all of them the Gregorian tones.   In 1550 these psalm tones or chants, handed down from the earliest times by the immemorial use of Western Christendom, were set to the various portions of Edward VI.'s First Prayer-Book, under the direction of Archbishop Cranmer, by John Merbecke, organist of St George's Chapel, Windsor.   Hawkins, in his " History of Music " (1776), errs in attributing this plain-song to Merbecke as its original author.   What he did was simply to adapt the ancient music of the Latin ritual, according to its then well-known rules, *mutatis mutandis*, to the new English translation of the Breviary and Missal.   And that this course was approved at the first, and afterwards confirmed by the highest authority in the Church is plain from the 49th of Queen Elizabeth's " Injunctions," taken in connection with the well-known contemporary uses of the Chapel Royal and the cathedrals throughout the Anglican Communion, some of which continue to the present day ; while there is undoubted evidence that the Gregorian tones for the Psalms continued in use, not only immediately after the Reformation, but very far on into the seventeenth century.   Thomas Morley, in his " Intro-

A DICTIONARY OF

duction to Practical Music" (1597), says, " Churchmen have devised certain notes commonly called the eight tunes, of which the tenor be the plain-song. Here they be." And then he proceeds to give the ancient Church form of recitation in a four-part harmony. Soon after the Restoration James Clifford, in his " Divine Services and Anthems," and Edward Lowe, in his "Short Directions for the Performance of Cathedral Service," gave the eight tones, and many of their endings, the latter according to the *Tonale*, and as he himself had sung them before the Rebellion when a chorister at Salisbury. In the numerous editions of Playford's " Introduction to Music," the first of which appeared in 1674 and the last in 1730, the tones were still given as the standard chants for the Psalms, although the Anglican form of single and double chants had already been for some time in use. The interruption of the traditional use of chanting, during the overthrow of the regal and episcopal government in the middle of the seventeenth century, seems to have paralysed for a time any latent power or desire to regulate the English chant. Little, if any, knowledge of the subject seems to have remained in English choirs. Thus, unprotected by regard for the ancient rules, the chanting grew gradually worse, till no rule or guide seemed left ; choir men and boys took their own individual course, and no consent nor unity of effect remained, so far as the recitation and singing of the words were concerned. " Even in the Chapel Royal St James's," observes the Rev. Thomas Helmore (" Primer of Plain-song," p. 71), " in the beginning and middle of the last century, no common rule of division was prescribed by authority, and it was only by chance if occasionally every individual in any particular verse hit upon the same mode of verbal arrangement. It can hardly be said that cathedral choirs were in this respect much better, though they did not labour under the same disadvantage of combining the members of several choirs, no two of which divided the words exactly in the same manner." It is not easy to determine who was the inventor of the pointed psalter. One of the first to whom the idea occurred was John Marsh of Chichester, a clever amateur composer and organist. This would have been about the year 1800. At any rate, his views were carried out shortly afterwards by Dr Beckwith, organist of Norwich Cathedral, who, in 1808, published his collection of chants entitled " The First Verse of every Psalm of David, with an ancient or modern chant in score, adapted as much as possible to the sentiment of each Psalm," setting forth in the preface the following, with the force of a " strong recommendation " :—
" Suppose the organist and choir were to meet every morning and

244

ECCLESIASTICAL TERMS

afternoon for one month, and agree on the proper place in each verse of the Psalms where the reciting should end in both the first and last parts of the chant, and under that particular word or syllable place a conspicuous *red* mark : if one book were thus carefully marked, the others might be rendered similar to it. The benefit would be, all the members of the choir might recite as one person, and all come together to that word which they are previously sure is the most proper to end the recital."   In 1821, Jonathan Gray, a member of the choir of York Minster, issued a book entitled " An Enquiry into Historical Facts relative to Parochial Psalmody," wherein he sets forth the *Te Deum* "pointed to be conveniently chanted in Churches." In his " Twenty-four Chants," published in 1834, he prefixed some remarks on chanting, claiming for Dr Camidge, then organist of York Minster, " the first contrivance and publication of a method for distinguishing both the words of the chanting [reciting] note, and the places of each of the syllables which follow." These " Instructions to Chanting " were printed by Dr Camidge in the collection of his cathedral music, which appeared about the year 1831. In this book some specimens of pointing are given, from a work upon which the Doctor was then engaged.   Another gentleman resident at York, a Mr J. E. Dibb, brought out, in 1831, a " Key to Chanting the Psalter or Psalms of David . . . with a peculiar arrangement to facilitate the practice."   This seems to have furnished an interesting sequel. *The Harmonicon* of February 1832 contains a long letter freely criticising Mr Dibb's book and methods.   The communication is signed " M.H.," the writer being Miss Maria Hackett, " the choristers' friend."   Miss Hackett observes that " an edition of the Psalter, with the proper subdivision of the verses, marked throughout with bars, would furnish the most intelligible and certain direction, and might be printed at a very moderate expense."   She then proceeds to give specimen suggestions, from which she appears to have invented or foreshadowed the signs of pointing now in general use.   She evidently took a deep interest in the subject, and a second letter from her appeared in the following issue of *The Harmonicon*. The copy of the Psalter used by Miss Hackett for this work, marked in red and black ink by her own hand, is now in the possession of the writer of this notice.   It was not, however, until 1837 that the first complete pointed Psalter for use with Anglican chants was published.   This was the now well-known work of Robert Janes, organist of Ely Cathedral.   It went through several editions, and is still in use at Ely in a revised form.   This was followed in 1843 by a similar work by Dr S. S. Wesley, then organist of Leeds Parish

Church, and, in 1849, it was taken by him to Winchester Cathedral, where it was long in use. Since that time the principal pointed Psalters have been those of the Rev. R. Corbet Singleton (for the use of St Columba's College, Ireland), 1846; James Ingham of Exeter, 1848; Joseph Warren ("Chanter's Hand-Guide"), 1850; Rev. W. Mercer, 1854; Dr Stephen Elvey—one of the most sensible of all—1856; Dr E. G. Monk and the Rev. Sir F. A. Gore Ouseley, 1862; Revs. A. Beard and H. Gray ("Oxford and Cambridge Psalter"), 1863; J. Heywood ("Anglican Psalter Noted"), 1864; Benj. St J. B. Joule, 1865; James Turle (for the S.P.C.K.), 1865; E. J. Hopkins ("Temple Psalter"), 1867; Rev. J. Troutbeck ("Manchester Psalter"), 1868; Rev. L. Tuckwell, and Dr J. Stainer ("Magdalen Psalter"), about the same time; J. M. W. Young ("Lincoln Psalter"), "Cathedral Psalter," 1873, revised 1908; A. S. Cooper ("Parochial Psalter"), 1876; Arthur Henry Brown ("The Anglican Canticles and Psalter"), 1877; W. H. Monk ("Psalter and Canticles"), 1878; Dr Westcott, Bishop of Durham ("The Paragraph Psalter"), 1879; S. Stagoll Higham ("The St Mary Abbots Psalter"), 1898; Rev. H. G. Daniell-Bainbridge and Sir Frederick Bridge ("The Collegiate Psalter"), 1908. The choice of a pointed Psalter is a matter that must of necessity be left to individual taste; but whatever book is chosen, its rules must be carefully followed if uniformity in chanting is desirable. Since 1843, when the Rev. Frederick Oakeley and Richard Redhead published their Psalter, "Laudes Diurnæ," the advocates of the Gregorian style of chanting have not been inactive. Among the principal Psalters put forth for this purpose must be mentioned those of the Rev. W. B. Heathcote ("Oxford Psalter"), 1845; Rev. Thomas Helmore ("Psalter Noted"), 1849; Richard Redhead (1864); Rev. Jas. Gray (1865); W. Spenser Nottingham and Rev. J. W. Doran; Rev. Harry Sargent ("Merton Psalter"), 1867; W. T. Best (1868); Rev. E. D. Cree (1872); Dr W. H. Monk (1883); W. S. Rockstro; Rev. R. R. Chope; Arthur Henry Brown; Rev. J. B. Croft—the last-named on the Solesmes Method. In 1841, J. Alfred Novello had published his "Cantica Vespera: the Psalms chanted at Vespers and Compline, pointed and adapted to the Gregorian Tones," but this was exclusively for the use of "that other great Church." The first regular collection of chants made in this country seems to have been that entitled "Fifty Double and Single Chants, being the most Favourite as Perform'd at St Paul's, Westminster, and most of the Cathedrals in England." This, a thin octavo, now very scarce, was printed by C. & S. Thompson,

ECCLESIASTICAL TERMS

75 St Paul's Churchyard, about the year 1769. It was followed in 1770 by a much larger collection, " Divine Harmony," compiled by Thomas Vandernan, one of the Gentlemen of the Chapel Royal. It should, however, be mentioned that the first and second volumes of Dr Boyce's " Cathedral Music," published respectively in 1760 and 1768, contained a small selection from the single and double chants then in general use. Since 1770 innumerable collections of chants, both original and selected, have appeared. A list might easily be compiled, but to give it here would take up too much space.

At St Paul's (as at other Cathedrals of the Old Foundation) it was the duty of each canon or prebendary to recite daily, whether present in church or absent, a portion of the Psalter. This was ordered by Bishop Maurice, A.D. 1085. Over the stall of each prebendary in the old cathedral was the name of the estate, manor or *corpus* from whence his endowment was derived, together with the first words of one of the five Psalms which he was bound to recite " to the glory of God, and for the more fully answering the intention of the founders and benefactors" of the stalls. These inscriptions, in gilt letters on a blue ground, are preserved, in exactly the same order, in the present cathedral. Of the estates, eight only were at some distance from the cathedral, two in Bedfordshire, five in Essex, one in Middlesex. Of the other twenty-two, nine were at Willesden ; the rest were in the immediate neighbourhood of London. One of the stalls still bears the name of Consumpta per Mare ; the estate was at Walton-on-the-Naze, and the inundation which the name commemorates seems to have occurred about the time of the Conquest. Dr Simpson ("Chapters in the History of Old St Paul's," p. 32) tells us that Dean Donne, when Prebendary of Chiswick in 1619, preached a series of five sermons on " The Prebend of Chiswick's five Psalms," and in one of these sermons he says quaintly enough, " The Psalms are the manna of the Church. As the whole Book is manna, so these five Psalms are my Gomer [or Omer, as in our present English version, in allusion to Exodus xvi. 32-36] which I am to fill and empty every day of this manna." And in another place he says : " Every day God receives from us [the prebendaries], howsoever we be divided from one another in place, the Sacrifice of Praise in the Whole Booke of Psalmes. And though we may be absent from this Quire, yet wheresoever dispersed, we make up a Quire in this service of

247

A DICTIONARY OF

saying over all the Psalmes every day." Each prebendary on his installation is admonished to " turn and remember " his five Psalms. " Oh! reader, scoff not; it concerns thine own soul: try in Faith to steal from the world each day some little time for holy meditation on a Saviour's love, beside thy past and present communings. A saint of old found *years full* of lessons in one single verse (Psalm xxxix. 1). Open thy heart still oftener to Him. ' Man of Sorrows,' He will comfort thee, guide thee, delight thee, and give thee thy heart's desire. May the sweetest music of those five sweet Psalms be the balm they have yielded to thy torn heart— as constant as the undying ripple of ether may the recollection of their sweetness be " (Wm. St George Patterson, sub-chanter, priest vicar, and divinity lecturer of Lichfield Cathedral, 1857). " Going to St Paul's to morning service on Sunday the fourth of May . . . I was put into a stall, inscribed WELDLAND, with the legend, *Exaudi, Domine, justiciam*, where, kneeling down I gave myself up to the solemn worship of God " (" Impressions of England in 1851," by the Rev. A. Cleveland Coxe, afterwards Bishop of Western New York). The annexed tables will show the present arrangement of the stalls of the dignitaries, prebendaries, and others in the choir of St Paul's with the initial portion of the Psalter to be recited by each prebendary.

On the South or *Decani* side, beginning from the West:

1. Decanus.
2. Canonicus Residentiarius I.
3. Canonicus Residentiarius III.
4. Thesaurarius.
5. Canonicus Minor I.
6. Canonicus Minor III.
7.
8. Canonicus Minor V.
9. Finsbury. — *Benedictus Dominus Deus.*
10. Chamberlainwood. — *Bonum est confiteri.*
11. Holbourn. — *Salvum me fac, Deus.*
12. Harleston. — *Fundamenta ejus.*
13. Portpoole. — *Quid gloriaris in malitia.*
14. Mora. — *Confitebor Tibi in toto.*
15. Cantlers *alias* Kentish Town. — *Dominus illuminatio mea.*
16. Twyford. — *Deus misereatur nostri.*
17. Mapesbury. — *Memento Domine, David.*
18.
Stall of the Bishop of London.
19.
20. Oxgate. — *Domine, exaudi orationem*
21. Sneating. — *Deus, Deus meus.*
22. Wenlock's Barn. — *Quemadmodum desiderat.*

248

ECCLESIASTICAL TERMS

23. Brownswood.
24. Rugmere.
25. Ealdstreet.
26. Canonicus Minor VII.
27. Canonicus Minor IX.
28. Canonicus Minor XI.
29.
30.
    Throne of the Bishop of London.

Deus, judicium Tuum Regi da.
Ad Dominum cum tribularer.
Dominus regnavit, exsultet terra.

On the North or *Cantoris* side, beginning from the West:

1. Archidiaconus Londinensis.
2. Canonicus Residentiarius II.
3. Præcentor.
4. Cancellarius.
5. Canonicus Minor II.
6. Canonicus Minor IV.
7.
8. Canonicus Minor VI.
9. Totenhall.
10. Caddington Minor.
11. S. Pancratius *vel* S. Pancras.
12. Reculverland.
13. Weldland.
14. Hoxton.
15. Ealdland.
16. Islington.
17. Wilsden.
18.
    Stall of the Lord Mayor of London.
19.
20. Consumpta per mare.
21. Bromesbury *alias* Brondesbury.
22. Neasden.
23. Newington.
24. Caddington Major.
25. Chiswick.
26. Archidiaconus Middlesexiæ.
27. Canonicus Minor VIII.
28. Canonicus Minor X.
29. Canonicus Minor XII.
30.

Beatus vir, qui non abiit.
Miserere mei, Deus.
Voce mea.
Beati quorum remissae.
Exaudi, Domine, justiciam.
Deficit in salutare anima.
Deus stetit in synagoga.
In convertendo Dominus captivitatem.
Noli aemulari.

Confitemini Domino, etc., dicant qui.
Beatus vir qui timet Dominum.
Domine, ne in furore.
Confitemini Domino.
Omnes gentes plaudite.
Nonne Deo subjecta.

At Lincoln (as at St Paul's) over the stalls of each of the fifty-three Prebendaries is the name of the estate whence the stipend of the incumbent was derived, together with the initiatory portion of the Psalter enjoined to be recited daily in private. The form of installation of a Prebendary at Lincoln concludes with these words by the installer (the Dean, or in his absence the Sub-Dean or Sub-

Dean's deputy) : " Respice titulos Psalmorum quos singulis diebus, impedimento cessante, recitare debes." At Lincoln it is the duty of the " Clericus de Re et Ve " to suspend the table of preaching turns in the stall of the incoming Prebendary, whose turn it is to preach on the following Sunday. " The Office of the Clerk of Re and Ve " (says the Rev. A. R. Maddison in his Short Account of the Vicars Choral, Organists, Choristers, etc., of Lincoln Cathedral, 1878) " has been a fruitful source of perplexity. The mysterious words ' Re et Ve,' as they are written in the Chapter Acts, seem at first to have no definite meaning. However, it seems most probable that they simply signify Revestry and Vestry. In the Muniment Room of the Cathedral, a large number of the ' Rolls of Re and Ve ' are preserved, and the duties of the clerk were those of a scribe, keeping the names of the Canons who came into residence and who quitted it. The wording of the appointment of one of these clerks in a Chapter Act is : ' Ad officium scribendi Re and Ve.' " Of course, in these days the post is hardly more than nominal ; the only fragment of the old mediæval duty yet surviving being that of the suspension of the preaching turns already mentioned. Browne Willis (" Survey of Lincoln Cathedral ") is confusing when he says that there are " two clerks of the Vestry." What really is the case is this—there is the post of Vestry Clerk, and there is the clerkship of Re and Ve ; but these are perfectly distinct in their nature. At Truro, the first Bishop, Dr Benson, anxious to link the newly-formed see with the ancient memories of the early Cornish Church, attached to each stall of the Honorary Canons the name of some early Missionary Bishop or other renowned Saint from the old Celtic Kalendars, or from among those who, in early ages, gave their names to numerous villages or " Church towns " in Cornwall. The selected names are inscribed on the several stalls, together with the Latin titles of the Psalms, as at St Paul's and Lincoln. In this way the whole Psalter, of 150 Psalms, is repeated every day by the Chapter, including the Bishop and Canons, Residentiary and Honorary. The number of Psalms to be recited daily varies from one to seven according to length. The usual number is three, four, or five, but the Canons of St Piran, St Uni, St Samson and St Cybi, have one each—all long : *Attendite, populé ; Misericordias Domini ; Confitemini Domino, et invocate ; Confitemini Domino quoniam ;* while the Canon of St Winwoloc has seven short ones, beginning with *Nisi quia Dominus.* To all the rest are assigned two, three, four or five.

ECCLESIASTICAL TERMS

Pulpitum. See *sub voce* " Rood-loft " or " Rood-screen."

The vessel in which the Holy Sacrament, in the form of bread, is reserved for the need of the sick. Such a vessel was used for the purpose from early Christian times. " Super Altare

Pyx. nihil ponetur nisi . . . pyxis cum Corpore Domini
Gr. Πυξίς (a ad viaticum pro infirmis " (Leo iv. *c* A.D. 850). The
box, generally pyx is mentioned in the Council of York, 1179, and
of box-wood); enjoined by Pope Innocent III., in 1215, to be over or
Lat. *pyxis ;* near an altar. By the ancient custom it was sus-
Fr. *boite à* pended over the altar and thence sometimes spoken
hostie ; of as the " suspensio." The favourite form of a pyx
Germ. *das* was that of a dove, or occasionally a tower. Pyxes
ciborium. in the form of a dove, beautifully enamelled, may not
infrequently be seen in museums abroad ; there was
recently, and probably still is, one in use at St John's, Malta. In
the fourteenth century it was most frequently a small box, circular
in form, in accordance with the form of the Host, and with a conical
lid, usually terminating in a cross. Bishop Bleys, of Worcester,
c. 1220, ordered two pyxes, one of rich material for the Host and the
other " decent and honest " for the oblates. In 1322 the Archbishop
of Canterbury (Walter Reynolds) required the pyx to be made of
silver or ivory. There are fine examples of cup-shaped pyxes at
New and Corpus Christi Colleges, and in the Bodleian, Oxford. In
the Inventory of St Paul's, 1552, we find a " rounde pounsedd
[ornamented] pix used to reserve the sacramente, silver and all
gilte, xiij unc. di." In 1245 a silver pyx hung *ultra majus altare.*
The term *corporas* or *corporax,* seems to have been often used as a
synonym for pyx, though sometimes (as in the Prayer-Book of
Edward VI. of 1549) for a cloth placed upon the paten or in the
pyx (Rubric to Prayer-Book of 1549, Parker Society Ed., p. 85)
and at other times for the covering placed upon the pyx, which
Walcott (" Sacred Archæology," under " Corporax Cups ") states
was a thin veil of silk or muslin. That at Durham was of very fine
lawn, embroidered with gold and red silk, and finished with four
knobs and tassels. A pyx cover is mentioned in the inventory of
St Mary-at-Hill in 1485-1486 (Nichols, " Illustrations," etc., p. 114).
For such use was the bequest of John Osborne to the Church of
Purleigh, Essex in 1511 : " I bequeth my typett of sarsenett to
be hanged over the pixe with the holy Sacrament of the forsaid
high aulter " (Essex Archæolog. Soc., 2nd Series, i. p. 172). At
Chipping Barnet was " a clothe of nedyll worke, and other of silke,
for the pyxe." From the latter part of the fifteenth century an

important change took place ; the pyx was no longer suspended, but was placed in a niche in the reredos, over the altar, and necessarily furnished with a door and lock ; and to suit this changed arrangement the pyx had a foot attached, which gave it the descriptive title of a "standing pyx," and it took the form of a covered chalice. By this time the ciborium or baldacchino had been generally abandoned, and the term *ciborium* was frequently applied to a standing pyx. In the Inventory of St Paul's taken in 1552 we find "A longe pix silver and all gilte standing upon a foote and upon the over parte a greate rounde ball or pomill with a greate flower upon the same." It weighed 42 ounces. The original custom of a suspended pyx was never abandoned in this country, for in the reign of Queen Mary we find it mentioned frequently ; as in the printed "Churchwardens' Accounts of St Michael's, Cornhill " (p. 115), " Paid for a pyxe to hange over the hye awlter, iijs. iiijd " ; and in 1556 they " Paide for a corde to pull upe the sacrament iiijd." Probably in many places it hung beneath a canopy, as at Durham, where the canopy is described (" Rites of Durham," Surtees Soc., p. 7) as most sumptuous, while the pyx itself was of pure, fine gold, curiously wrought of goldsmith's work. In short nothing was deemed too beautiful or costly for the adornment of God's House in those times. The term pyx is sometimes erroneously employed to denote the box to contain the wafers or bread ready for consecration.

Quadragesima. The Latin name for Lent. It was formerly given to the First Sunday in Lent, from the fact of its being *forty* days before Easter, in round numbers.

Quadrangle. A square or court surrounded by buildings. The buildings of monasteries were generally arranged in quadrangles—*e.g.* the cloisters. Colleges and large houses are also disposed in the same way. At Oxford these squares are called " quadrangles," or more familiarly " quads." At Cambridge, the corresponding term is " court." Thus at Oxford we speak of " Peckwater Quad.," Christ Church, and at Cambridge of the " Great Court," Trinity.

Quadripartite Vaulting. Where each bay or compartment is divided by its ribs into four cells or portions.

Quatrefoil. A square panel or a piercing in the tracery of a window. etc., divided by cusps or featherings into four leaves. Bands of small quatrefoils are much used as ornaments in the Perpendicular style, and sometimes in the Decorated. When placed diagonally they appear formerly to have been called

ECCLESIASTICAL TERMS

" cross-quarters." There are fine examples of Perpendicular quatrefoils at King's College Chapel, Cambridge.

**Quinqua-
gesima.** The Sunday before the first day of Lent (Ash
Wednesday), so called because it is the fiftieth day
before Easter, reckoned in the whole numbers. The
title of this Sunday is to be found in the Lectionary
of St Jerome and in the Sacramentaries.

Amongst the adjuncts, furniture, and ornaments of the altar in
early inventories we find mention of a " Reed " (*calamus*), and
Reed. examples of the vessel itself may, though extremely
rare, be met with. At St Paul's, in 1402, a chalice of
Greek work had lost its paten, but retained its reed ; a relic of
the time when, as Dr Rock ("Church of our Fathers," i. 165-167)
says, the deacon carried the chalice down from the altar to the
people, and "each one drank of its hallowed contents through
a long narrow pipe or hollow reed, made of gold, silver, or ivory,
which was often, though not always, fastened on a pivot to the
lower inside part of the sacred vessel. The golden reed is used
to this day by the Pope whenever he solemnly pontificates, and
by the cardinals who serve him as deacon and sub-deacon,
both of whom communicate with the Supreme Pontiff under
the two kinds." Three such reeds are figured by Dr Rock. It
seems to have been in use in the Anglo-Saxon period. It was
also used, as supposed, for administration of the Blessed Sacrament to the sick, when it could not be given from the chalice
without risk of accident. Otherwise little seems to be known of
this vessel.

In the Continental churches those persons are called " regulars "
who profess to follow a certain rule (*regula*) of life, and observe the
Regular. three vows of poverty, chastity, and obedience ; in contradistinction to the " seculars " who live comparatively in the world (*saeculum*) In the Old Foundation Cathedrals of
England the canons were " secular " : those in the monastic ones,
commonly called Cathedrals of the New (or Henry VIII.'s) Foundation, were termed " regular." It is probable that the fact of certain
English cathedrals being served by "regulars"—Winchester, for
instance, which was a Benedictine monastery—gave rise to the
custom of arranging the choirs, even of those where the foundation
was " secular," after the monastic fashion, to the exclusion of the
laity from the services there performed—an encroachment on the
part of the mediæval clergy from the effect of which we still
suffer.

This was the term, as a substantive word, given in our Church
before the Reformation to persons engaged by solemn vows to the

Religious. monastic life. It is still used in this sense on the
Continent, and with us is now given to those who are
members of brotherhoods, sisterhoods, etc.

A small chest, box, or casket to contain relics. Depositories of
this kind were very common in our churches before the Reformation.

Reliquary. They were made of wood, iron, or other metal, and
occasionally of stone ; they were always more or less
ornamented, and sometimes were covered with the most costly
embellishments. Consult, J. C. Wall, " Shrines of British Saints "
(1905). See also *sub voce* " Shrine."

A generic term for all the variations of style that arose from
the resuscitation of classical architecture, simultaneously with the

Renaissance. revival of letters. In this the Pagan element re-
appeared, and superseded, sooner or later, almost
entirely over Europe, the Pointed or Christian style.

Before the Reformation, on Good Friday, a cross was set up in
front of the altar, and the clergy and people prostrated themselves

Reproaches, before it. This was called " Creeping to the Cross."
The. A proclamation dated Henry VIII. orders : " On Good
Lat. Friday it shall be declared how creepynge of the crosse
Improperia. signifyeth an humblynge of ourselfe to Christ before
the crosse." During this ceremony the *Improperia*
or " Reproaches," a selection of anthems, were sung. They are
chiefly taken, with a few verbal alterations, from the prophecy of
Micah, vi. 3, 4, beginning : " O my people, what have I done unto
thee ? " intermingled with a very ancient form of the *Kyrie Eleison*
used in the Greek Church. They set forth " the exceeding ingrati-
tude of His chosen people to our Blessed Lord, and of those who by
their sins crucify Him to themselves afresh." At the conclusion,
the hymn *Pange lingua* (" Sing, my tongue, the glorious battle "),
which commemorates the Life and Passion of Our Lord, is sung. In
the Church of Rome, the Gospel in the Mass of the Presanctified
concluded, the celebrant puts off his chasuble, and taking down
the cross, covered with a veil from the altar, he goes with the deacon
and sub-deacon to the Epistle corner of the altar, where he uncovers
the top of it, and shows it to the people, singing with the deacon
and sub-deacon the anthem, " Ecce lignum crucis, in quo salus
mundi pependit," to which the choir, prostrate on the ground,
answer, " Venite adoremus." From thence the priest proceeds
again to the Epistle corner, where he uncovers the right arm of the

cross, singing a second time, " Ecce lignum," etc., as before. Lastly he goes to the middle of the altar, and uncovers the whole cross, singing a third time, " Ecce lignum," etc. After which he carries it to a place prepared before the altar, where he himself first kisses it, and then all the clergy and laity, two and two, kneeling thrice on both knees, and kissing the foot of the cross. During this ceremony, two cantors in the midst of the choir sing the " Reproaches " as before mentioned, the choir responding antiphonally. When the ceremony is almost finished, the candles are lighted, and the cross is placed again upon the altar. Then the priest, ministers, and clergy go in procession to the place where the Blessed Sacrament was put the day before, from whence It is brought back in the same order as It was carried thither. During the procession is sung the hymn *Vexilla regis*. The Mass then proceeds. The *canto fermo* of the "Reproaches" will be found in any complete Gregorian plain-chant manual. Celebrated settings of the *Improperia* in *canto figurato* are those of Palestrina, Marco Antonio Ingegneri and Tomaso Vittoria, all sixteenth century, and published in cheap and accessible form by Breitkopf and Härtel. The same office, according to the Use of Sarum, will be found set forth in detail in " The Liturgy of the Church of Sarum," translated from the Latin by Charles Walker (1866). The singing of the Reproaches on Good Friday has, for many years, been revived in some of our parish churches, at the conclusion of the altar service in the forenoon, or at a special service in the afternoon. One of the earliest churches to adopt it (1859) was that of St Matthias, Stoke Newington. W. H. Monk, then organist and director of the choir, prepared for this purpose an excellent edition of the plain-song " Reproaches." The service then took place at 2.30, but when, some ten years later, the "Three Hours' Devotion" from 12 to 3 was established, it succeeded the Ante-Communion Service. There is also a harmonised setting of great beauty composed by the Rev. J. B. Dykes, Mus.D. It was originally written for "The People's Hymnal," in 1870, and has since been included in the complete collection of his hymn tunes, published by Novello. A metrical paraphrase of the Reproaches, by Gerard Moultrie, will be found in " The Hymnary" (No. 255), where it is set to a well-known tune by Richard Redhead. The Office of " The Reproaches," according to the ancient English use, has been printed, with notation, by the Plainsong and Mediæval Music Society.

Requiem. A musical Mass for the Dead (Lat. *Missa pro Defunctis*; Fr. *Messe des Morts*; Germ. *Seelmesse*), so called from the opening words of the introit, " Requiem æternam dona eis, Domine." It comprises, besides the introit, the *Kyrie Eleison*, the gradual, the tract, the sequence (*Dies Irae*), the offertory, the *Sanctus*, a hymn after the Elevation of the Host, or the Psalm, *De profundis*, and the Communion (*Lux aeterna luceat eis, Domine*). The *Credo* and *Gloria in Excelsis* are not sung. Among the most notable Requiem Masses are those of Anerio, Casciolini, Di Lasso, Palestrina, Vittoria, Durante, Jommelli, Sabbatini, Mozart, Winter, Cherubini, Neukomm, Gaensbacher, Verdi, Gounod, Berlioz, Rheinberger, and those of our countrymen, R. L. de Pearsall and Sir C. Villiers Stanford. In the First Prayer-Book of Edward VI. there is provided " The Celebration of the Holy Communion when there is a burial of the dead." It consists of the introit, " Like as the hart " (Ps. xlii.), Collect, substantially the same as that in our present burial service, Epistle (1 Thess. iv.) and Gospel (St John vi.). The full musical notation (plain-song) given by Merbecke in his Book of Common Prayer Noted (1550), comprises the introit, *Kyrie Eleison, Sanctus*, and *Agnus Dei*. This office was removed from the Book of 1552 and it does not occur in any of the subsequent revisions of 1559, 1604, and 1661–1662.

Reredos.

Fr. *retable*, *arrière dos ;*
Ital. *postergule ;*
Span. *retablo*.

Called by Bishop Andrewes, " the backpiece." The generic term for the wall or screen at the back of an altar, whether of carved stone, wood, metal-work, or drapery. Stone reredoses are usually enriched with a profusion of niches, buttresses, pinnacles, statues, and other decorations, which were often painted with brilliant colours. Reredoses of this kind frequently extend across the whole breadth of the church, as at St Alban's Abbey, Durham Cathedral, St Saviour's Cathedral, Southwark ; Gloucester Cathedral (Lady Chapel) ; Winchester Cathedral ; Christ Church Priory, Hants ; All Souls', New and Magdalen Colleges, Oxford, etc. In parish churches they were generally simple, and appear very frequently to have had no ornaments formed in the wall, though sometimes corbels or niches were provided to carry statues, and sometimes that part of the wall immediately over the altar was panelled. Remains of these, more or less injured, are to be found in many churches, particularly at the east ends of aisles, as St Michael's, Oxford ; Hanwell and Enstone, Oxon ; Solihull, Warwickshire, etc. At the parish church, Reigate, Surrey, in 1846, a reredos of excellent Late Decorated work was discovered, behind the woodwork underneath the east window, by Henry Woodyer, the architect engaged upon the restoration. It consists of thirteen niches, richly worked within, and surmounted by crocketed canopies of the ogee form. Remains of polychromatic decoration were found on scraping off the whitewash, and the present coloration is, as nearly as could be discovered, a restoration of the original. *The Gentleman's Magazine* of November 1846 had a woodcut representing this reredos, with a carefully written account from the pen of a contributor singing himself "W. H. A." The reredoses in the cathedrals and college chapels enumerated above were much mutilated and defaced at the time of the Reformation and the Civil War, but they have, of late years, been restored to their pristine beauty, especially those of Winchester and St Alban's, where the rood has been added. Many of our cathedrals have been equipped in modern times with reredoses of various material. Those designed by Sir Gilbert Scott in stone, marble, and alabaster for Ely (1855), Exeter (1876), Gloucester (1873), Lichfield (1863), Rochester (1875), Salisbury (1876), and Worcester (1868), are as good as anything produced at the period of their erection—namely, that of the restoration of the various cathedrals containing them. The Church of St Mary, Stoke Newington (1858), has a superb reredos by the same distinguished architect, a Cenacolo, or representation of the Last Supper, behind an arcade. A neighbouring church, All Saints', possesses a reredos of singular beauty from the chisel of Earp, illustrating the four and twenty elders falling down before the throne. The reredos in St Andrew's, Wells Street, designed by Street and executed by Redfern (1868), is remarkably beautiful, and as reverent in feeling as it is powerful in artistic conception. At St Augustine's, Haggerston, the reredos designed by Henry Woodyer, the architect of the church, and executed by Nicholls, is perhaps one of the stateliest and most beautiful works of its date (1867) in London. A wooden reredos by the same architect, of simpler design, but richly polychromed and gilded, is in the Collegiate Church of St Michael, Tenbury, and another, somewhat similar, is in the Chapel of the House of Mercy at Clewer. The present penchant is for a reredos of the triptych form of which we have so many examples from the designs of Messrs Bodley and Garner. The modern reredoses of stone in the cathedrals of Truro and Bristol, both by J. L. Pearson, are very grandiose. At Peterborough the same architect has employed the baldacchino, or ciborium. In the city churches designed by Sir Christopher Wren, the reredos or altarpiece of richly carved wood is invariably a prominent feature. Much of the carving is by Grinling Gibbons, and is worthy of the most careful study and examination. The reredos in St Paul's Cathedral, though hardly in harmony with the surroundings, is probably the most costly and elaborate one of Renaissance design erected in modern times. It dates from 1888. The parish church of St John of Jerusalem at Hackney has recently been adorned with a wooden reredos in keeping with the architecture of the church—a Classical erection of the end of the eighteenth century. Christ Church, Bristol, an Italian building of 1787, with a lofty and well-proportioned spire in the style of Wren's steeples, and a pleasing interior, has a small, but extremely beautiful, modern reredos of Renaissance design, with the Crucifixion as the central subject. The church of Hoar Cross, the munificent foundation of Mrs Meynell Ingram, in the neighbourhood of Lichfield, built by G. F. Bodley, in the style so peculiarly his own, has an exquisite reredos similar in *motif* to those at St Alban's, Winchester, etc., but of course upon a much smaller scale. On the Continent, reredoses in all styles are abundant, and many of them are very magnificent. Frequently—and especially in Belgium— a picture by some celebrated artist forms the central subject.

The capitular members of certain cathedrals, who are bound to reside a certain time at the cathedral church, to perform the ordinary duties there, and to attend more immediately to its **Residentiary** concerns. In England, all Cathedrals of the Old **Canons** Foundation have canons residentiary, and a much *(Canonici* larger number of prebendaries non-residentiary. Ori- *residentiarii).* ginally, they were bound to residence for the greater part of the year. But, various causes having rendered this inconvenient or impracticable, a regulation took place of appointing a certain number to reside every year. The number was at first variable, but in the course of time it was fixed in the different cathedrals. Among these residentiaries the revenues of the chapters were shared, as they undertook the duties of the whole body ; and this is the actual divisible revenue of the old chapters to this day. Now according to the spirit of their institution, the residentiaries, instead of dividing the year between them, and attending in rotation, ought constantly to reside simultaneously, and confine themselves to the service of the cathedral, so that any service of the Church should be attended by a numerous band of sacred ministers. In St Paul's Cathedral, the four amply endowed residentiaries were originally obliged to constant residence, and forbidden to undertake any other duty, so that all should be present every Holy Day, and each of the four present at some one service every day of the week. In the New Foundation Cathedrals there were no non-residentiary canons, and it was intended by the authors of the Cathedral Reform Act of 1840 that there should be none anywhere. But during its progress through Parliament it was altered into merely "suspending" the incomes of all non-residentiaries ; and the residentiaries were reduced to four in nearly every cathedral. At Lincoln and St Paul's a new residentiary was added to make four in the patronage of the bishop, but he must appoint an archdeacon thereto. Before that time the dean was also a residentiary at both places. The non-residentiaries, however, retain whatever ancient rights they had. But the twenty-four " honorary canons " who were invented at the same time for the New Foundation Cathedrals have no rights of voting either for proctors in Convocation, or the disposition of chapter patronage, or anything else.

In the old English offices an antiphon was so called, which was sung after reading three or four verses of a chapter ; after which
Respond, or the chapter proceeded. The responds were supposed
Responsory. to give the keynote of the lection, but frequently, as in the *Venite* with its invitatories, the sense was broken up rather than illustrated. The aspect in fact which the lectionary part of the office assumed was that of an elaborate piece of music, interrupted at intervals by a very brief recitation out of Holy Scripture as a homily. Consult Freeman, " Princ. Div. Wor." i. 340–341 ; Palmer, "Orig. Liturg." ii. 46 ; and for examples of " Responds," Procter, " Book of Common Prayer," 183.

In mediæval architecture, a half pillar or pier attached to a wall to support an arch, etc. Responds are frequently used by them-
Respond. selves, as at the entrance of chancels, etc., and are also generally employed at the terminations of ranges of pillars, such as those between the body and aisles of churches. A good example may be seen in Fotheringhay Church, Northants. In the contract for the building we find, " Ten mighty pillars, with four *responds*." At St Paul's, the eight masses of solid stonework, enriched with pilasters, festoons, and panelling, which connect the huge dome piers with those of the nave, choir, and transepts, may be termed " responds." Two similar erections at the eastern extremity of the choir have their lower portions pierced to afford egress to the aisles. Until 1860, the stalls and organ-screen occupied the two easternmost of the three bays of the choir, and a portion of the western-most one, on either side. In that year they were moved farther westward, leaving the easternmost bay open. Before 1860, egress was also afforded to the aisles by means of gates, immediately west-ward of the organ-screen, which was not placed in the position demanded by architecture—namely, flush with the great piers of the

dome. An ante-choir was thus formed, but, at the same time, a great deal of space in the choir proper was sacrificed. During the alterations of 1871–1872 the stalls were not again shifted, but the stalls of the dignitaries which before 1860 had been returned beneath the organ-screen were replaced, with the organ above them on either side, against the western responds, a proceeding which necessitated the removal of the monuments of Nelson and Cornwallis to corresponding positions in the south transept. From 1860 to 1871 the returned stalls had been set up within the pierced eastern responds, where they served as sedilia.

Retable or Gradine. A shelf or ledge behind the altar ; properly a part of the reredos. On it are placed the cross and candlesticks. The retable forming part of the reredos at St Paul's is very magnificent and deserving of close examination. The retable is often improperly called the " super-altar," a small portable slab of stone, which is placed on altars which lack a stone mensa (*q.v.*), or which have not been consecrated. The super-altar was probably in the first place used when the altar itself was in a bad condition, and was taken about, as it was called *Altare viaticum, Altare portabile,* and *Altare itinerarium.* It is the " super-table " of Archbishop Cranmer. In a Nominale of the fifteenth century, privately printed in 1857, super-altar is explained as " a hye awtyr " : evidently confusing it with the superior or high altar of the church. This shelf was covered with a super-frontal, to correspond with the frontal of the altar itself : as for example at St Mary-at-Hill—" A frontall for the schelffe standing on the altar of blue sarsenet with brydds [birds] of gold " (Accounts of St Mary-at-Hill, for the year 1486). In Italy it is called the Predella, but the same term is quite as often used to refer to the row of small scenes which usually occupied a foot or so of painted panelling at the foot of the great altar-painting, in the nature of a reredos, so customary there from the fifteenth century. Amongst the contents of the treasury of St Paul's in 1295 were " iij superaltaria benedicta." One was of jasper, *ornatum capsa argentea deaurata* (Dugdale's " St Paul's," 315) ; another, also of jasper enclosed in plates of silver-gilt, contained relics of St Andrew, St Philip, St Dionysius, and St Blaise, and a piece of the cross of St Andrew. St George's Chapel, Windsor, was rich in these superaltars, having no less than six—one of jasper, one of alabaster, and four of marble. Among the treasures of Salisbury Cathedral, 1222, was one set in gold ; and at Durham, in 1372, there was one of jet, a material occasionally employed for this purpose (Rock, " Church of our Fathers," i. 257).

ECCLESIASTICAL TERMS

Retro-choir. An aisle, or area, providing a free passage round and behind a choir and altar, as at Chichester, Durham, Ely, Exeter, Gloucester, Hereford, Lichfield, Lincoln, Peterborough, Winchester, Worcester, York, etc. At St Asaph, Bangor, Carlisle, St David's, Oxford, Ripon, Rochester, and Southwell, there is no retro-choir, the high altar being immediately under the east window. See also *sub voce* " Procession Path."

Returned Stalls. Stalls which, besides running longitudinally, are returned transversely at the western end of the choir. The English cathedrals which retain their original return stalls, with canopies, are Carlisle, Chester, St David's, Gloucester, Lincoln, Manchester, Ripon, and Winchester. These stalls are assigned to the dignitaries. At Exeter the stalls themselves are ancient, but the canopies are modern (1876). Such stalls are also to be found at St George's Chapel, Windsor ; Beverley Minster, King's College, Cambridge, and in a number of parish churches, such as Ludlow, Shropshire ; Cartmell Priory, Lancashire ; Rothwell, Northants ; Herne, Kent ; and Wantage, Berks. Some of these are without canopies. Returned stalls vary in number, according to the width of the choir. At Lincoln there are six ; at Exeter, Gloucester, and Winchester, five ; at Chester, Ripon, King's College, Cambridge, and St George's, Windsor, four ; at Beverley, St David's, and Ludlow, three, on either side of the door beneath the rood-loft. At St Patrick's Cathedral, Dublin, there were three, before the restoration of 1861–1865, and at Christ Church, before the restoration of 1872–1878, there was only one on each side of the choir door. The last-named, however, were modern, dating only from 1830. At St Paul's, until 1860, the stalls introduced by Wren, with their matchless carvings by Grinling Gibbons, were returned under the organ-screen. There were two on either side of the entrance. These were assigned to the Dean, the Precentor, the Archdeacon of London, and the Archdeacon of Essex, following the arrangement in the old cathedral. Three of these stalls were usually occupied by the canons residentiary, who had, elsewhere in the choir, stalls assigned to them as prebendaries. The cathedrals of Bristol, Chichester, Durham, Ely, Hereford, and Worcester had their returned stalls, previously to the redistribution of their choral fittings during " restorations." At Canterbury the fine returned stalls of Charles II.'s time, ascribed to Grinling Gibbons, are still happily *in situ*. Those of York date from 1831 ; those of Westminster from 1848 ; those of Eton College from 1852. Returned stalls existed at Lichfield till 1856 ; at Peterborough till 1886 ; at Salisbury until

1870 — all of inferior modern work, and replacing interesting examples of Renaissance. At Rochester the returned stalls without canopies are modern, and date from 1876 ; the whole of the misericordes had disappeared in previous restorations, nothing but the brackets which carried the divisions between the seats being in existence. At Wells, during the unfortunate restoration of the choir under the architect Salvin, in 1848, every vestige of old woodwork, except the *misereres* of the stalls, was ruthlessly cast out. Even the grand old seventeenth-century organ-case was not spared. Stone backs and laboured canopies, supported on shafts of polished Purbeck marble, were forced on to the *misereres*, which, in order to afford more room for the promiscuous crowd of a Sunday congregation, were arranged piecemeal between the pillars, so lessening their numbers that, if the whole chapter were ever to assemble, some less lucky dignitaries must sit on the laps of others. Five stalls were returned on either side of the choir door. Many of the great Continental cathedrals and churches retain their returned stalls, and where this is so the aspect of the choir is very picturesque. Consult T. F. Bumpus' " Glories of France " (1902–1905) ; " Cathedrals and Churches of North Germany " (1903–1906) ; " Cathedrals and Churches of North Italy " (1907) ; " Cathedrals and Churches of Norway, Sweden, and Denmark " (1908) ; " Cathedrals and Churches of Belgium " (1909). Also Street's " Gothic Architecture in Spain " (1865).

Rochet. A linen garment worn by bishops under the chimere (*q.v.*). It was the bishop's ordinary garment in public during the Middle Ages. The " rochette " is spoken of in the old *Ordo Romanus* under the title of *linea*, and has, no doubt, been very anciently used by bishops in the Western Church. The word " rochette," however, is not of very great antiquity, and perhaps cannot be traced further back than the thirteenth century. It is thought by Gavanti that the *linea* worn by St Cyprian was the same as the rochette, in which Baronius agrees. The chief difference between this garment and the surplice was, that it was of finer material and that its sleeves were narrower than those of the latter ; for we do not perceive in any of the ancient pictures of English bishops those very wide and full lawn sleeves which are now used, which sleeves are now improperly attached to the chimere or black satin robe. It differs also from the alb in reaching only to the knees. Hody (" History of Convocations," p. 141) says that in the reign of Henry VIII. our bishops wore a scarlet garment under the rochet ; and that in the time of Edward VI. they wore a scarlet chimere, like the doctors' dress at Oxford, over the rochet, which in the time of Queen Elizabeth was changed for the black satin chimere used at present.

Rogation Days. So-called from *rogare*, " to beseech." They are three fast days immediately before the Festival of the Ascension, and they are meant to prepare us for the Communion on that great feast to which they are as a minor Lent. Christ goes up to be our Intercessor ; hence the great subject of *prayer* as connected with sacrifice, and the mediatorial work of Christ, comes prominently into view. One of the primary purposes of rogation fasts was to supply a blessing on the fruits of the earth before harvests ; because at this time of the year the fruits of the earth are tender and easily hurt ; therefore litanies extraordinary are said to God, to avert His judgment. These rogations were not merely offered in Church, but in the open air, the people going in processions and saying them responsively with their pastors. At the Reformation the rogation processions were retained, and in some places they have been kept up to the present day. The curate, with his parishioners, used to walk round the parish, pausing at certain bounds to offer thanksgivings, and to implore a blessing on the fields and farms. He also at times repeated the Mosaic formula : " Cursed be he that removeth his neighbour's landmark." The 104th Psalm was also said or sung. Among the Homilies will be found a curious one, divided into three parts, for these days ; but they are not altogether suitable for modern use. There is no office, or even single collect, appointed for the Rogation Days in the Prayer-Book, but the Gospel for the Fifth Sunday after Easter teaches us how we may ask of God so as we may obtain. The requisitions of the Church are " abstinence " and " extraordinary acts and exercises of devotion." Suitable hymns are, however, to to be found in many modern hymnals, and for cathedral use there is no difficulty in selecting appropriate anthems. The custom of " Beating the Bounds " is observed in many parishes, especially those in the city of London, where it takes place on Ascension Day. This ancient custom is still kept up at Lichfield. Early in the morning of Ascension Day the senior choristers of the cathedral decorate several of the houses in the city and close with elm boughs, gathered the day before. At the conclusion of Matins and High Celebration in the cathedral the whole of the choristers, accompanied by their master, the priest vicars, and cathedral dignitaries, all vested in surplices, etc., and preceded by a cross-bearer, walk round the boundaries of the close, halting at eight places, where there is a record of there having been or still is a well. A portion of Scripture is read, and a hymn sung at each place, and the clergy and choristers enter the west door of the cathedral as the words : " O enter then His gates with praise," in the Old Hundredth Psalm, are sung. Prayers are said round the font, and the elm boughs are then deposited on its steps. It should be observed that there is not an atom of religiousness in the London custom of beating the boundaries of the parish. It is now merely an exhibition of ribaldry on the part of churchwardens and parish schoolboys. The early English name of Rogation Days was " Gang Days," or " gang dagas," days of perambulation. The Rogation Days are so referred to in the " Canons of Cuthbert," Archbishop of Canterbury, A.D. 747.

Rood-beam. In German churches, a beam thrown across the entrance to a choir for the support of the Crucifix and the figures of SS. Mary and John. Sometimes used in conjunction with the solid loft or jubé (*q.v.*).

A gallery running along the top of the rood-screen which, in parish churches, usually crossed the chancel arch, on which the *rood*—*i.e.* the Crucifix with SS. Mary and John—was placed.

Rood-loft.
Old Eng. *rod ;*
Saxon *roda ;*
Fr. *jubé ;*
Germ. *lettner.*
In large transeptal churches the rood-loft with its screen was usually of stone, and sometimes contained a chapel and altar within it. These more substantial rood-lofts have, in many cases, been converted into organ-lofts. Rood-screens are used to mark the separation between the nave and choir, or chancel—emblematic of the Church Militant and the Church Triumphant, which is shown by them ; also to enable the deacon to chant the Gospel to the faithful from a high place, in accordance with the practice and traditions of the Church, attested by most of the ecclesiastical writers of antiquity. This custom was continued till 1790 in most of the French cathedrals. Rood-lofts were generally used for preaching, prior to the introduction of pulpits in the thirteenth century. The Martyrology and Lections (lessons) were read from the rood-loft. Fasts and festivals were also announced from it. According to a homily of St John Chrysostom, the deacon stood on the rood-loft to say the words *Sancta Sanctis* to the people before the Communion. The emperors were crowned in the jubé or rood-loft at the great church of Constantinople ; and the French kings, down to Charles X. (on Whitsunday, 1825), were always enthroned in the rood-loft at Rheims Cathedral. Parts of the service on Christmas Day and Good Friday were chanted from the rood-loft. In large cathedrals and collegiate churches rood-lofts

were of stone, with two staircases, to enable the gospeller and epistoler to ascend different ways on their proper sides of the choir. In parochial churches rood-lofts were generally of timber, and had only one staircase, built in a pillar or in a small turret outside the walls. There are ancient rood-stairs at Lavenham and Long Melford, Suffolk ; St Martin, Stamford ; Wells, Norfolk ; Frome, Somerset ; and many other places. The ancient rood-lofts with their staircases remain at York, Lincoln, Exeter, Canterbury, Wells, Southwell, Ripon, Westminster, Norwich, St David's, etc. Consult Pugin, " Chancel Screens and Rood Lofts " (1851). The same writer in his " Present State of Architecture in England," 1840 (p. 29), observes : " It is worthy of remark that the first rood erected in England since their destruction by Act of Parliament, was set up in the private chapel of Ambrose Lisle Phillipps, Esq., of Grace Dieu Manor, a zealous restorer of Anglo-Catholic antiquity. In this chapel most solemn service is performed on Sundays and Festivals, the Gradual chanted from the Lettern, and the whole Office sung by men and choristers in the devotional and sublime plain chant." Until the middle of the eighteenth century or so, every great church in France had its *jubé* or rood-loft, often a magnificent specimen of handicraft. But the age of Louis XV. was inimical to mediæval tradition, and rood-loft after rood-loft was pulled down to be replaced by an erection in one of the Classical Orders, such as the Doric loft which existed until some twenty years ago at Rouen. When the tide of church restoration set in under the Second Empire (1852–1870) these pseudo-Classical screens succumbed in their turn, and were, in most cases, replaced by little else than a mere grille of iron. Modern French ecclesiologists seem to have no idea of the light open screen of stone, wood or brass with which our cathedrals of Bristol, Chichester, Ely, Hereford, Lichfield, Salisbury and Worcester have been equipped since the Gothic revival, nor of the suspended or elevated rood and attendant figures, modern examples of which have, with the approval of the clergy and to the delight of many a devout congregation, been placed of late years in not a few of our ancient and modern parish churches. The absence of the screen is a great drawback to the complete enjoyment of a French cathedral interior. There is an absence of that mystery which is so charming in the cathedrals of England and Northern Germany.

Rubric. From the Latin *rubere*, to be red. A direction printed in service-books pointing out how, when, and where all things with regard to divine service are to be performed. This direction was formerly written or printed in *red* ink, after the

A DICTIONARY OF

example of the old Roman law-books, in which the titles and remarks were so written, hence the name. In our Prayer-Book the rubrics are now generally printed in italics, and sometimes in red.

Rulers of the Choir, or Rectors of the Choir. Two persons in cathedrals, etc., who presided over the singing, and especially over that of the Psalms, that all might be done reverently and in order. On all the major feasts, and on minors of the two highest classes, the precentor in person " ruled " the choir. The rulers walked to and fro and on either side of the choir, with staves in their hands, to mark the time of the chant. At Exeter they noted the absence or irregularity of the vicars and delated them to the president of chapter. At York they wore copes, and delated vicars who did not sing. At Lincoln they sang with the precentor at the bench in the choir (Wilkins' " Concilia," i. 537). At Exeter (MS. Harl. 1027) they had faldstools covered with leather, and carried staves of ivory and boxwood, as apparently they did at St Paul's. From the " Chronicle of the Grey Friars of London " (edited for the Camden Society in 1852, from a MS. in the British Museum, Cotton Library) we learn that " at Crystmas [1550] was put downe in Powlles the *Rectores Chori* wyth all their coppys (copes) at processione, and no more to be usyd." At Lichfield the choir rulers invariably wore " silk copes in choir, precious copes on Christmas Day, white at Easter, red on certain feasts, and embroidered or changeable on some other days, at the Sacrist's direction." (Walcott, " Cathedralia," 183). At Hereford they began the offices and the *Kyrie* in the Mass. At Wells (1298) they forfeited their day's wages if they did not know the hymns and intonation of the Psalms. At Salisbury the choir was ruled every Sunday and double feast, and feast of lections ; from the first vespers of Christmas to the octave of Epiphany ; on its octave and vigil when not falling on a Sunday ; through the weeks of Easter and Pentecost, and on certain feasts falling in Easter time—viz. St Mark, SS. Philip and James, St Barnabas, etc. ; in the octave of the Ascension, the octave of SS. Peter and Paul, the octave of the dedication of the church, etc. (MS. Harl. 1001, p. 121 *b*). The choir, by weeks alternately, was called the dean's or cantor's (precentor's) choir ; but on all double feasts was always the dean's throughout the year, if he were present to do his office, except at Christmas, Easter and Whitsun weeks, when the choir was united. In collegiate churches, as Chester-le-Street and Astley, the dean acted as Rector Chori, there being no precentor. The title " Rector Chori " is borne by the organist of Southwell Minster to this day. The Rectores Chori are

266

ECCLESIASTICAL TERMS

the Spanish Præcentores Sceptrigeri. Martene ("De Ant. Eccles.," i. 240) thus alludes to the rulers of the choir: "Rectores chori cum duo tantum habentur sequantur regulam clericorum de secunda forma. Cantor stat in medio chori cum ceteris rectoribus chori scil. in festis majoribus duplicibus tantum; deinde principales rectores chori ex utraque parte sui; exinde duo rectores secundarii, postea chorus more solito." Charles Wild, in his fine coloured plate representing the interior of the choir of Amiens Cathedral during High Mass, depicts the two choir rulers vested in green copes, wearing conical caps and holding their staves. This picture is one of a series of twelve of the cathedrals of France and Germany published about 1833. The architectural drawings of Wild are as remarkable for their fidelity as for their freedom and effect. The subjects are well chosen, the architecture is grand and rich almost to redundancy, and the various ceremonies are represented with great spirit and correctness. With all respect for Prout, and some others, it must be admitted that there never was an artist who touched on Gothic architecture with the same severe truth and fidelity as Charles Wild. J. D. Chambers ("Divine Worship in the Church of England in the XIII. and XIV. Centuries," 1877) cites several examples of staves carried by precentors and choir-rulers. Such staves were about the height of a man, usually of wood, metal or ivory, having richly carved and ornamented heads. "In the woodcuts of the Sarum *Processionale*, the Rulers are represented by T-headed staves. These are, of course, only symbols, and do not show the size, but they doubtless prove that the staves at Salisbury had heads of this shape" (Dearmer, "Parson's Handbook," 143 fn.). In 1050 Bishop Leofric gave three "Cantorstaffae" to the Cathedral of Exeter (*Codex Diplom*. Anglo-Sax. iv. 275). In the Inventory, they are described as "Baculi co-operti cum argento." There were also three of ivory. Pugin ("Glossary of Ornament," 190) enumerates as in St George's Chapel, Windsor, in the fifteenth century: " A staff for the Precentor in the choir having five bands in the height, and a crosspiece of ivory set in silver with a crystal knob at the top. Also two staves of one suit for the cantors at Principal Feasts; and two staves of one suit for ordinary days." Pugin mentions others at York, etc., which, however, seem to be processional. At Canterbury in 1287 (Appendix to Dart's "History and Antiquities of the Cathedral Church of Canterbury," 1726, p. 15), the "Baculi Cantorum" were, one of St Thomas, silver-gilt, adorned with gems; one of St Dunstan, silver, with the head of ivory; a larger one partly of silver, jewelled; four of horn, with he heads of ivory ; and two of wood for the daily service. Bonneau (" Inventaire du Trésor de la Cathédrale d' Auxerre," 1892, p. 72) describes a cantoral staff as " garni de son baton d'argent couvert de fleurs de lys depuis le haut jusqu'en bas, au dessus un aigle tenant en son bec une châinette avec une petite boulette de verre blanc, donné par feu M. Thévenon chanoine et chantre, pesaut sept marcs deux onces, y compris le bois." Also " Un autre bâton de chantre, de vermeil doré, au-dessus de la pomme d'iceluy un aigle aussi de vermeil doré tenant en son bec une châinette avec ruby. Donné a l'église par feu M. Lauverjat, chanoine et chantre, avec son étuy de cuir noir garni de crochets ; l'oiseau et la pomme du dit bâton pesants sept marcs. Le bâton pèse neuf marcs deux onces, compris le bois." In his " Divine Worship " (p. 42) J. D. Chambers figures the head of a cantor's staff from the Collection Bonvier, Amiens, and another from Cologne Cathedral. At the summit of the latter is a representation of the three Wise Men (who are especially venerated at Cologne) presenting their gifts to the Infant Saviour. Dr Bock (" Liturgische Gewänder ") and Pugin (" Glossary of Ecclesiastical Art ") have each figured examples of cantoral staves, but neither states where the originals are. In the Musée de Cluny at Paris there is a piece of wood carving, probably the panel of a stall end, representing a Precentor (Grand Chantre) vested in cope and alb, and holding a plain staff. It is of sixteenth-century German workmanship. At St Paul's, in 1295, an iron chair with gilded heads and balls was set apart for the Precentor's use.

Sacrist. An officer described in the canon law as keeper of the church ornaments ("Decret. Greg.," ix. l. i. tit. xxvi., xxvii.). Where there was no permanent sacrist, a canon named Præfect of the Sacristy was appointed, with a clerk as sub-sacrist. There were two sacristies in large churches, one for the canons, the other for the chaplains. He was the treasurer's vice-custos, being the treasurer's vicar or deputy. At St Paul's he opened at Matins and Vespers the doors of the sacristy, which contained three rooms for the choirmasters, and kept the approaches to it clear of idlers. Under him were three vergers. He kept the choir clean and the vessels clean, repaired breakages, and saw the books were bound. One of the minor canons still bears the title of sacrist. In the Old Foundation Cathedrals generally he represented the treasurer (*q.v.*), in taking charge of the fabric, altars, vestments, books and *instrumenta* of Divine worship. At Lichfield he is now a priest vicar. In France he was the cheficier, the keeper of the chevet (*capitium*) or sanctuary, in charge of the furniture

ECCLESIASTICAL TERMS

and ornaments necessary for service. The office still exists at Canterbury, Carlisle, Durham, Ely, Gloucester, Norwich, Peterborough, Rochester and Worcester—all New Foundation Cathedrals. In our own day, in churches where full ritual is carried out, the duties of the sacristan are multifarious and important. Our present word " sexton " is a corruption of " sacristan " or " sacrist."

Saddleback, or Pack- saddle Roofed Tower. One not having its sides of equal height, but two of them raised in gables, over which is constructed a common roof, which in some instances gables transversely to the axis of the church. Although uncommon in English architecture, the saddleback tower is of frequent occurrence in certain districts of Germany and France. In the latter country it abounds in the villages near Caen and in other parts of Normandy. Since the revival of Pointed architecture in England this type of tower has been employed with considerable frequency both in town and village churches, and, as a rule, with pleasing results. Good examples are at St Matthias', Stoke Newington, and St Alban's, Holborn (both by Butterfield); at St Luke's, Kentish Town (Basil Champneys), and at St Bartholomew's, Armley near Leeds (Walker and Athron).

Sancte-Bell, Sanctus-Bell, Sacring-Bell. A small bell used in the Roman Church to call attention to the more solemn parts of the Mass, as at the conclusion of the ordinary, when the words *Sanctus, Sanctus, Dominus Deus Sabaoth* are sung, and on the elevation of the Host at the Consecration. It is now usually, if not always, a small hand-bell carried by a server, and was generally of this kind in England previous to the Reformation, made sometimes of silver; but in some instances a larger bell was used, and was suspended on the outside of the church in a small turret, made to receive it, over the archway leading from the nave into the chancel, and rung by a rope from within. Many examples remain in England, but the practice does not seem to have been usual, although it was ordered by the canons of Archbishop Peckham, in 1281, that bells should be tolled at the elevation of the Body of Christ, in order that people who had not leisure daily to be present at Mass might, wherever they were, in houses or fields, bow their knees, in order to the obtaining the indulgences granted by many bishops. The hand-bell was one of the items of church goods which in the time of Edward VI. were sold, if of any value, or else otherwise disposed of; as at Waddington St Peter, Lincolnshire, where the churchwardens reported to the Commissioners that there had been " one sacringe bell which honge at a may pole topp, and what

269

is become of it we know not." It was forbidden, by the Royal Injunctions in 1549, and by Ridley's Visitation Articles in 1550, but was revived in the following (Queen Mary's) reign ; as at St Michael's, Cornhill, the churchwardens in 1556 " paide to a carpenter for mendinge the saintes bell, for boltes and iron of the same, ij^s." In some parts of Tyrol these bells are arranged on a triangular frame, and necessarily rung together ; they are often left carelessly on the altar-step. At Gerona in Spain is a number of such little bells arranged on a wheel, with delicate carvings in wood of the fifteenth century, and set ringing as the wheel revolves. An engraving in Lübke's " Ecclesiastical Art during the Middle Ages " (p. 154) illustrates this arrangement at Gerona. The largest arrangement of bells of this kind is in the Abbey Church of Fulda. It is of bronze, in the form of a large star, and richly mounted with bells. At the Church of St Matthias, Stoke Newington, the ordinary " five minutes " or " service " bell, has for many years been used at the Consecration in the Communion Service. Sacring-bell cotes remain at many churches, as at Isham, Rothwell and Desborough, Northants; Boston, Lincolnshire; Bloxham, Brize-Norton, Coombe and Swalcliffe, Oxon ; and in Wiltshire they are very common. At Long Compton, Warwickshire, there is a beautiful Decorated example. At Deddington, Oxon, the bell itself was found in the wall.

Sanctuary. The presbytery or eastern part of the choir of a church, in which the altar is placed. See also *sub voce* " Choir" and " Presbytery."

Santoral. The Spanish name for a church choir-book.

The office-books called " of Sarum " were drawn up by St Osmund, Bishop, and founder, of the Cathedral Church of Salisbury (A.D. 1078–1099), in order to consolidate the Anglo-**Sarum Office-** Saxon ritual which had been disturbed by the Norman **books.** invasion, and immediately became the secular use in all churches in the southern dioceses. The province of York and the diocese of Lincoln had " uses " of their own. In South Wales the Hereford Breviary and Missal were used; in North Wales that of Bangor. These varied slightly from the Salisbury office-books. But the Sarum *Ordinale* (*i.e.* the " pica " or " pye ") was in use not only throughout all England and Wales, but all Ireland also ; the nucleus, probably, of the " United Church of England and Ireland." The principal office-books of Sarum use were these : (1) The " *Missale*," of which editions of 1492, 1494, 1498, 1510, 1527, 1534, 1554, etc., are preserved. This contained the Ordinary and Canon of the Mass (translated, with a preface

ECCLESIASTICAL TERMS

and explanatory notes, by Charles Walker, 1866), together with the introits, collects, epistles, graduals, alleluia, tracts, sequences gospels, offertories, Communions, and Post-Communions, throughout the year. It was divided into the " Temporale," containing the services for the Sundays and ferias from Advent to Advent ; and the " Sanctorale," containing the services proper for the feasts of saints. (2) The " *Grayle*," or *Graduale*, which contained the musical notation to the introits, graduals (whence the name), tracts, sequences, etc., together with the musical notation to the *Credo, Gloria in Excelsis*, preface, and such other parts of the ordinary and canon as were sung. (3) The " *Processionale*," containing such parts of the services as were sung in processions. (4) The " *Ordinale*," a handbook of directions to the priest, so far as regards the Mass. For the choir service were : (5) The " *Portiforium*" or " Breviary," containing the service for Matins, Lauds, Prime, Tierce, Sext, None, Vespers, and Compline, throughout the year, together with the Litany and the Vigils for the Dead. It was divided into two parts—" pars hyemalis," containing the services from the First Sunday in Advent to the end of Whitsun Week ; and " pars æstivalis," beginning with Trinity Sunday, and giving the services thence to Advent. (6) The "*Legenda*," containing the lessons read at Matins. (7) The " Pica " or Pye, a kind of directory as to the order in which the services were to be said. (8) The " *Tonale*," containing the Gregorian Tones for the Psalms, canticles, etc., with directions. (9) The *Antiphonarium*, or "Antiphoner," containing the musical notation to the antiphons. Lastly, for the occasional offices, was (10) The " *Manuale* " or " *Sacerdotale*," containing the offices of baptism, matrimony, visitation, and anointing of the sick, burial of the dead, etc., and (11) The *Pontificale*, containing those peculiar to a bishop—as confirmation, ordination of priests and deacons, consecration of bishops, ordering of sub-deacons, readers, exorcists, acolytes, doorkeepers, etc. Consult further— " Missale ad usum insignis et præclaræ Ecclesiæ Sarum. Pars Prima : Temporale. Londini : Veneunt apud C. J. Stewart," 1861 ; " The Psalter, or Seven Ordinary Hours of Prayer, according to the use of the illustrious and excellent Church of Sarum ; with explanatory notes and comments," by J. D. Chambers, London : J. Masters, 1852.

A piece of (black) silk or other stuff which hangs from the neck, and is worn over the rochet or surplice. It is not mentioned in the **Scarf.** rubric of the English ritual, but is worn by our bishops and dignitaries of the Church, and by D.D.'s in the universities (see 74th Canon). It is used from long custom, and

271

may be referred to the ancient practice of the Church, according to which presbyters and bishops wore a scarf or stole in the administration of the Sacraments, and on some other occasions. For some years scarfs were supposed to belong to bishops' and peers' chaplains, but for no good reason. They were wider than the now common stole, and may probably be identified with the "black tippet" of the canon (Hook's "Church Dictionary"). Priests in Ordinary of the Chapel Royal were entitled to wear the scarf, as were also minor canons of St Paul's and Westminster who held the same office (see the anecdote in Life of Rev. R. H. Barham, Minor Canon of St Paul's and Priest of the Chapel Royal ; author of the "Ingoldsby Legends," 2nd edit., 1880). In his Charge of 1842 Bishop Blomfield ordered all the London clergy to wear the scarf. See also *sub voce* "Stole" and "Tippet."

Screen. A word evidently derived from the root of Latin *cerno*, Greek κρίνω, to separate. Any separation of one part of a church from another. Screens are sometimes large and deep structures of stone, with only a wide door in the middle, in pre-Reformation times supporting the rood, but since, generally, the organ. At St Alban's Abbey the screen has two doors with the old altar space between it, and there are instances of such an arrangement in Germany, Spain, and other parts of the Continent. Frequently screens are of light construction, tabernacle work, open arcading, wood tracery, or metal. Consult A. W. Pugin, "Chancel Screens and Rood Lofts" (1851) ; Bligh-Bond, "Chancel Screens" (1909). It is impossible not to regret the destruction of the organ-screen and of much of the woodwork erected by Bishop Cosin in and about the choir of Durham Cathedral. The whole of this screen-work was of oak, elaborately and richly carved, and most characteristic of the period of its execution (1663). There was no attempt, in the organ-screen, and in the screens giving access to the choir aisles, to imitate the architectural features of an earlier time, "though," says the Rev. W. Greenwell in his little book on Durham Cathedral (5th edition, 1897), "it was evident that the artist who designed them was actuated by the reasonable desire to make them, by a bold and vigorous treatment, harmonise in their general effect with the building in which they were placed." The greater part of the organ-screen, broken up and destroyed as a whole, is dispersed in various places in the castle. Upon the screen was placed the organ originally built by Bernard Schmidt, commonly called Father Smith, under an agreement with the Dean and Chapter, dated 18th August 1683. It was contained in a very handsome oak case, with richly gilded and diapered pipes, erected during the episcopate of Lord Crewe (1674–1721), whose arms it bore. At the time of the destruction of the screen, 1846–1847, it was placed on the floor in the north choir aisle. It was removed from the cathedral in 1876, the " choir organ," containing two of Father Smith's stops, being placed in the Castle Chapel, and the other parts of the case dispersed. The remainder of the stops, among them some of Father Smith's make, were carelessly stowed away in the south triforium of the nave, where they have been destroyed for any useful purpose by the children of cathedral dignitaries while amusing themselves there. They still remain a melancholy instance of the neglect and indifference with which articles of interest and value have too often been treated in this cathedral. A privately issued book, " A Record of Works done in and upon the Cathedral and Collegiate Buildings of Durham," printed for the Dean and Chapter in 1858 and again in 1864, is an admirable record of destructive work. Much of the interesting post-Reformation woodwork in Durham Cathedral (not omitting the oak screen which, until 1847, surmounted the rectangular platform in the Nine Altars, upon which the shrine of St Cuthbert was placed) is represented in Surtees' "History of Durham," and in Billings' "Durham Cathedral," Plates XLI., XLII., L., LVI., LXVI., LXVII. and LXVIII.

Scriptor Tabulæ. The officer who drew up the weekly rota or table of duties in old St Paul's.

Secondaries. A generic term for the inferior members of cathedrals as vicars choral, minor canons, etc. ; the *clerici secundae formae*—that is, of the second or lower range of stalls—called the *bas choeur* in France. Sometimes the priest vicars and minor canons were included in the superior form. At Chichester a secondary sang the daily Requiem Mass in the Lady Chapel. Some of the lay singers at Exeter are still so called. Sometimes the term was applied to the assistant priest in course, even though not of the second form. At Hereford the second vicar choral who assists in chanting the Litany is called the " Secondary."

Secret of the Mass. The secret prayers said by the celebrant at the conclusion of the offertory, so called because they are said at the setting apart (Lat. *secernere, secrevi, secretum*, to set aside) of the bread and wine for consecration. The custom of praying silently and raising the voice at the conclusion, " Per omnia sæcula sæculorum," termed *ecphony*, is ancient. The Canon of the Mass, or Anaphora, immediately follows, beginning with the *Dominus vobiscum* and *Sursum corda*. (In modern terminology the canon begins a little later, with the prayer, *Te igitur*.) This has not been appreciably altered since the fourth century.

Theologians distinguish three states of life—the lay, the religious, and the ecclesiastical. Many who serve God in the religious state are also in Holy Orders. Hence the clergy are known **Secular Clergy.** as "regular" and "secular" clergy; the former living under monastic rule (*regula*), the latter as ordinary ecclesiastics in the world. The term "secular" is not by any means of necessity a word of reproach, though frequently used in such a sense. A parallel case is the use of the word "profane," which, as applied to individuals, is a heavy stigma, and is yet used quite harmlessly as a technical phrase to distinguish ordinary from "sacred" history. See also *sub voce* "Regular."

The seats near an altar, almost universally on the south side, for the ministers officiating at the Holy Eucharist to retire to during **Sedilia.** the singing of certain portions of the service. They are generally three in number—for the celebrant, epistoler, and gospeller. In our churches they are occupied during the sermon. They were sometimes movable, but more usually in this country were formed of masonry and recessed in the wall like niches. Numerous examples remain in our ancient churches, a few of which are of as early date as the latter part of the twelfth century, but the majority are later, extending to the end of the Perpendicular style. Occasionally there are four seats, as at Rothwell, Northamptonshire; or five, as at Southwell Minster. At Lichfield there are six, but these were not originally sedilia. Sometimes a single seat, under one arch, or formed on the back of a window, is found, long enough for two or three persons. They are very commonly placed at different levels, the eastern seat being a step the highest, and the western one the lowest, as at Exeter Cathedral, Cherry Hinton Church, Cambridgeshire, and Preston—an interesting little Early English church near Brighton.[1] Sometimes, however, when three seats are used, the two western ones are on the same level, and sometimes the two eastern are level, and the western a step below them. The decorations used about them are various, and in enriched buildings they are often highly ornamented, and sometimes surmounted with tabernacle-work, pinnacles, etc. There is a curious example of early date of a single sedile at Lenham, Kent. It projects considerably from the wall (though the back is slightly recessed) with stone elbows resembling an arm-chair. At Beckley, Oxon, and St John's, Winchester, are examples of single

[1] The Preston sedilia were unfortunately destroyed by fire some years ago.

sedile. Good examples of modern triple sedilia may be seen at Llandaff Cathedral, St Andrew's, Wells Street (1847), St Barnabas', Pimlico (1850), St Stephen's, Shepherd's Bush (1850), St Stephen's, Westminster (1850), St Matthias', Stoke Newington (1853) and St Michael's College, Tenbury (1856). At St Paul's are modern sedilia of oak, of excellent design, and in harmony with the architecture of the cathedral. On the Continent examples are not very common. In the Pfarrkirche at Kempen, north-west Germany, are magnificent triple sedilia (*celebrantenstuhl*) in oak, of the year 1486. Those in the Church of St Elizabeth at Marburg, Westphalia, are illustrated in King's " Study-Book of Mediæval Architecture," vol. ii., 1857. Perhaps one of the most beautiful examples of sedilia in England is to be seen in the Church of St Thomas (the Archbishop and not the Apostle), Winchelsea, Sussex. These sedilia, of equal height, are rich Decorated, and diapered at the backs. Attached is a piscina of the same date. They are figured by W. D. Cooper in his " History of Winchelsea," 1850.

See.
Lat. *sedes*.
The seat of episcopal dignity and jurisdiction, where the Bishop has his throne or *cathedra*. Hence the word " Cathedral."

The Sunday which in round numbers is seventy days before Easter, hence the name. There being exactly fifty days between the Sunday next before Lent and Easter Day, inclusive, that **Septuagesima.** Sunday is termed Quinquagesima — *i.e.* the fiftieth. The two Sundays immediately preceding are called, from the next round numbers, Sexagesima and Septuagesima, sixtieth and seventieth. Septuagesima is really the sixty-third day before Easter. The title of this Sunday is to be found in the Lectionary of St Jerome and in the Sacramentaries. The period between Septuagesima and Easter is sometimes called the " Greater Lent," and is supposed to refer to the seventy years' captivity of the children of Israel, when they hung their harps by the waters of Babylon, saying, " How shall we sing the Lord's song in a strange land ? " Hence the word " Alleluia," which signifies " Praise the Lord," and is a joyful song, is omitted during these seventy days. It was formerly the custom to sing the " Alleluia " many times over in the service, just before Septuagesima. This was called the "farewell to Alleluia." The " Alleluiatic Sequence "—*i.e.* the hymn beginning " The strain upraise of joy and praise "—was so employed in Germany, and the hymn, " Alleluia, song of sweetness," by the Anglo-Saxon Church, and later in the diocese of Worcester. Septuagesima, Sexagesima, and Quinquagesima form a season of preparation for the Lenten fast, whence the Church begins to read in her Lessons the Book of Genesis, which tells of man's fall, to dispose us to repent of and put away that sin by which death and sorrow came into the world. It seems appropriate to sing the canticle *Benedicite Omnia Opera* at Matins on Septuagesima Sunday, after the first chapter of Genesis has been read as the First Lesson. In some churches it is sung daily, in place of *Te Deum*, from Septuagesima to Easter. At many places, notably in the Cathedral of Soissons, France, an absurd custom formerly prevailed. At the conclusion of the evening offices on the day preceding Septuagesima Sunday, a top, marked with "Alleluia" in gold letters, was whipped by a chorister down the choir and out into the cloisters. This was called "whipping Alleluia out of Church until Easter." In other places a ceremony took place on the same day called "The Burial of Alleluia." Hone ("Every-Day Book," i. 104) gives some particulars, such as they are, of this custom.

Septum. The enclosure of the Holy Table made by the altar-rails.

Sepulchre (Easter). A representation of the entombment of Our Saviour, set up in the Latin Church at Easter, on the north side of the chancel near the altar. In this country, before the Reformation, it was usually a wooden erection, and placed within a recess in the wall or upon a tomb. Several churches, however, still contain permanent stone structures that were built for the purpose, some of which are very elaborate. There are fine specimens of the Decorated style at Heckington and Navenby, Lincs.; Hawton, Notts, and one somewhat earlier at St John's, Winchester. At Eastbourne, Sussex, there is one of Perpendicular date. On Good Friday, the altar cross, having received the veneration of the clergy and people after the singing of the *Improperia* or "Reproaches" at the Mass of the Presanctified, was taken back—Vespers having been sung *sine cantu*—to the sepulchre and, together with the Host, was incensed. It was brought back with the Host to the high altar on Easter Day, at a short service introductory to Matins, when the anthem *Christus resurgens* was sung and a short office said. This office is given at full length by Procter in his "History of the Book of Common Prayer," pp. 284, 285.

Sequence. See *sub voce* "Prose."

Service. What the Mass has been to composers who have written for the Roman Communion—a theme to test their highest powers, and to inspire the noblest emanations of their genius—has been the English substitution for the Mass, and the songs of praise special to Matins and Evensong to musicians who have wrought for the Church of this country. These compositions for our Liturgy are technically and collectively called " Services." A " service " or a " set " of pieces for the whole of the canticles and Communion Service would comprise in all its fulness the *Te Deum, Benedicite, Benedictus, Jubilate,* at Matins ; the *Magnificat, Nunc dimittis, Cantate Domino, Deus misereatur,* at Evensong ; and the *Kyrie, Credo, Sanctus, Gloria in Excelsis*—to which some modern composers have added the introit, gospel thanksgivings, offertory sentences, *Sursum corda, Benedictus qui venit* and *Agnus Dei*—in the Office of the Holy Communion. The first collection of polyphonic Church music to contain services, published in this country, appeared in 1560, just ten years after the publication of Merbecke's arrangement of the canticles and Communion Service, to the ancient plainsong. Ample material for the study of services by composers from the time of the Reformation to the end of the eighteenth century, is afforded by Day's " Service-Book " (the collection of 1560 above alluded to) ; Barnard's " First Book of Selected Church Music " (1641) ; Boyce's " Cathedral Music " (3 vols., 1760–1778); Arnold's " Cathedral Music " (3 vols., 1790); Rimbault's " Cathedral Music," (1847); and Ouseley's " Cathedral Services by English Masters " (1853). Since that time it has been the custom to publish services separately rather than in collections and expensive volumes. Many of the older services have been published under the superintendence of competent editors in cheap octavo form. A glance at the catalogue issued by Messrs Novello will show how wide, comprehensive, and varied in style is our repertory of cathedral services, both ancient and modern ; ranging from Tallis and Tye to the present day.

The following is a list of some of the most important Service-Books, Consuetudinaries, etc., English and Roman, **Service-Books.** which have been edited in this country in modern times :—

Breviaries :

" Breviarum ad usum insignis Ecclesiae Sarum, 1531 " ; edited by F. Procter and C. Wordsworth (1879–1886).

" The Aberdeen Breviary," 2 vols. (1) Pars Estiva, (2) Pars Hyemalis, 1854.

" The Hereford Breviary," edited by W. H. Frere and L. E. G. Brown (1904).

" The Roman Breviary, reformed by the Œcumenical Council of Trent," translated by the Marquis of Bute, 2 vols. (1879).

"Quignon's Reformed Breviary of 1535," edited by Dr J. Wickham Legg (1882).

"The Second Recension of the Same," edited by Dr J. Wickham Legg (1908).

Missals :

"Missal in English." The Sarum Missal done into English by A. H. Pearson, 1884.

"Missale ad usum insignis et praeclarae Ecclesiae Sarum," edited by F. H. Dickinson. Burntisland (1861–1883).

"The Sarum Missal" (Church Press Co., 1869).

"Altar-Book, containing the Order of Holy Communion according to the Use of the Church of England, with additions from the Sarum Missal," edited by a Committee of Priests (1902).

"The Liturgy of the Church of Sarum," translated from the Latin, with a preface and explanatory notes, by Chas. Walker, with an Introduction by the Rev. T. T. Carter (1866).

"Missale ad usum insignis Ecclesiae Eboracencis," edited by W. G. Henderson (1874).

"Missale ad usum insignis et praeclarae Ecclesiae Herefordensis," edited by W. G. Henderson (1874).

"Missale ad usum Ecclesiae Westmonstariensis," edited by J. Wickham Legg, (Henry Bradshaw Society, 1891).

"The Missale de Arbuthnott, according to the Use of St Andrew's, Scotland," edited by A. P. Forbes (Bishop of Brechin), 1864.

"The Leofric Missal, as used in the Cathedral of Exeter, during the Episcopate of its first Bishop, 1050–1072," edited by the Rev. F. E. Warren, B.D. (1883).

"Missale Romanum Mediolani 1474," edited by Rt. Lippe, D.D. (1907).

Miscellaneous :

"Processionale ad usum insignis ac praeclarae Ecclesiae Sarum," edited by W. G. Henderson (1882).

"Ordinale Exon," edited by Rev. J. N. Dalton, 2 vols. (1909).

"The Psalter, or Seven Ordinary Hours of Prayer, after the Sarum Use, with the Hymns, Antiphons and Collects," edited by J. D. Chambers (1852).

"Manuale et Processionale ad usum insignis Ecclesiae Eboracensis," edited by W. G. Henderson (Surtees Society, 1875).

"The Antiphonary of Bangor," edited by the Rev. F. E. Warren, B.D., 2 vols. (1893).

"Ordinale secundum usum Exon," edited by Rev. H. E. Reynolds, M.A.

ECCLESIASTICAL TERMS

"Legenda Sanctorum : the Proper Lessons for Saints' Days, etc., according to the Use of Exeter, compiled by John de Grandisson, Bishop, 1327," edited by Rev. H. E. Reynolds, M.A. (1880).

"The Winchester Troper, from MSS. of the X. and XI. Centuries," edited by W. H. Frere (1894).

"The Irish Liber Hymnorum," edited by J. H. Bernard, Dean of St Patrick's, and R. Atkinson, LL.D., 2 vols. (1898).

"Facsimiles of the Creeds from Early MSS," edited by A. E. Burn, D.D. (Henry Bradshaw Text Society).

"The Use of Sarum: the Sarum Customs as set forth in the Consuetudinary and Customary," edited by W. H. Frere (1898).

"Consuetudinarium Ecclesiae Lincolniensis, tempori Richardi Gravesend Episcopi (A.D: 1258–1279) redactum," with Introductory Notes by Christopher Wordsworth, M.A. (1880).

"Registrum Statutorum et Consuetudinum Ecclesiae Cathedralis Sancti Pauli Londinensis," edited by the Rev. W. Sparrow Simpson, D.D., 1873. Appendix 1897.

See also the publications of the Plainsong and Mediæval Music Society and an important list of printed service-books of English Uses, published in *The Ecclesiologist*, No. LXXVI. (February 1850).

Severy. Old Eng civery. In architecture, a bay or compartment of a vaulted ceiling. In the contract for vaulting the choir of St George's Chapel, Windsor, 21 Henry VII. "Reliq. Antiq." vol. ii. p. 115, we find: "John Hylmer and William Vertue . . . shall vawlte or doo to bee vawlted with free stone the roof of the quere of the College Roiall of our Lady and Saint George within the Castell of Wyndsore, according to the roof of the body of the said College ther, which roof conteyneth vij seuereys."

Sexagesima. The Sunday but one before Lent, so-called as being about sixty days before Easter. It is really the fifty-sixth day before the great festival. See also *sub voce* "Septuagesima."

Sext. One of the "lesser" canonical hours. The service for noon, the hour at which Our Lord was nailed to the Cross. In the Roman Breviary it consists of *Paternoster, Ave Maria, Deus in adjutorium*, the hymn, *Rector potens*, Psalm cxix., from *Deficit in salutare* to *Iniquos odio habui* — with antiphons according to the season, a short chapter of Holy Scripture, Scriptural versicles, and the Collect of the Day. Where the capitular offices are recited daily, Sext follows High Mass.

Shaft. The body of a column or pillar ; the part between the capital and the base. In mediæval architecture the term is particularly applied to the small columns which are clustered round pillars or used in the jambs of doors and windows, in arcades and various other situations. There are beautiful examples of Early English shafts in the triforium of St John's Church, Chester. During the Early English period it became the fashion to form detached shafts of marble. The extent to which this charming custom was carried may be seen at Westminster Abbey, at Salisbury, and the Temple Church. It had its inconveniences, however, in construction, as these collections of columns depended on their caps, bands, and bases for holding them together, and therefore for their strength ; and it was found, before the end of the thirteenth century, that safer buildings could be constructed with stones built in courses, and so gradually marble shafts went out of fashion. But they are one of the special and most beautiful features of the thirteenth century.

Shawm, or Schalmey. An obsolete instrument, precursor of the oboe and clarinet ; a religious instrument of the Jews. By the French, the lower register of the clarinet and basset-horn is called the *chalumeau* (stem, or straw-pipe) tone, a derivation of *shawm*, or from the Latin *calamus*, a reed. The word " shawm " occurs in the *Cantate Domino* (Ps. xcviii.)—"With trumpets also, and shawms, O shew yourselves joyful before the Lord the King " (v. 7). The word always puzzled the Duke of Cambridge, father of the late duke. It is related that on one occasion while hearing the *Cantate Domino* of Attwood, at the Festival of the Sons of the Clergy at St Paul's, he exclaimed aloud, " Shawms, shawms—what *are* they ? "

Shrine. A repository for relics, whether fixed, such as a tomb, or movable. The term is also sometimes applied to the tomb of a person not canonised. The most splendid and costly materials were used in the construction of shrines, and enriched with jewellery in profusion, such as those of St Taurin, at Evreux, in Normandy, and the Three Kings (the Magi who came from the East) in Cologne Cathedral. There are also very magnificent shrines at Aix-la-Chapelle, and in many other foreign cathedrals. Those shrines which were movable were on certain occasions carried in religious processions. Others were substantial erections, generally the tombs of saints, as that of St Ethelreda, formerly at Ely ; that of Edward the Confessor in Westminster Abbey ; that of St Erkenwald, Bishop of London, in old St Paul's ; and that of St Cuthbert,

ECCLESIASTICAL TERMS

formerly in Durham Cathedral. These were often rebuilt with additional splendour subsequently to their first erection. That of St Thomas à Becket at Canterbury was world-famed. Consult J. C. Wall, " Shrines of British Saints " (1905).

Slype. The term for the slip of ground or passage which led to the cemetery, lying usually between the transept and the chapter-house in the monastic cathedrals, as at Chester, Durham, Gloucester, Norwich and Winchester. At Chester it was called the Maiden's Aisle. At Durham the bench for the almsmen at the Maundy was set between the prior's door of the church and the slype. At New College, Oxford, the " slype " was a slip of ground on the north side of the hall and chapel, where were the stables and other offices. Here, in 1878, a huge new pile of college buildings was erected by Sir Gilbert Scott. The slype at Winchester has a Latin motto to the effect, that one way led to the choir and the other to the market. It was opened in 1632, in order to prevent the indecency of leaving the cathedral open as a common thoroughfare to the close and college (Milner, " History and Survey of Winchester," ii. 132). Archbishop Parker forbade the church and cloister of Canterbury to be a highway or passage for market-folk (Strypes' Parker, ii. 21, 23). The scandal of a public thoroughfare long continued at Durham ; and at Worcester in 1750, the opening of the slype at the west end " removed the indecent annoyance of passengers conveying every kind of burden through the principal north entrance across the nave to the cloisters, even during the time of Divine service" (Chambers' "Worcester," 132). At Salisbury, Laud, in his Visitation Articles, inquired whether the church and close were made a common thoroughfare (Works, v. 461), and at Norwich, early in 1740, Bishop Gooch suppressed the indecent thoroughfare through the nave and north transept.

Soffit. The under side of an arch, plain in Early and richly moulded in the Middle and Complete Gothic epochs. See also under " Intrados."

Solo Anthem. An anthem written for a single voice (treble, counter-tenor, tenor or bass) with organ accompaniment, and concluded by a short chorus. Several of the compositions of Purcell, Blow, Clark, Croft, Weldon, Greene, Travers, Boyce, Kent, Nares, Hayes, Battishill, and Sir John Stevenson are favourable specimens of this class of sacred composition. In certain cases, solo anthems were written to display the voice of some famous cathedral singer of the day. Thus, for example, Purcell wrote many of his deep bass solos for the Rev. John Gostling, Sub-dean of St Paul's,

Precentor of Canterbury and one of the gentlemen of the Chapel Royal (d. 1733) ; Croft and Weldon composed for Richard Elford, the counter-tenor, a member of the choirs of St Paul's, Westminster, and the Chapel Royal (d. 1714) ; Boyce admired the high bass of Richard Bellamy, a member of the same three choirs half-a-century later ; Kent wrote many of his treble solos for Charles Dibdin when a chorister of Winchester College ; while the tenor solos in Sir John Stevenson's anthems were intended for John Spray, one of the vicars choral of the cathedrals of Christ Church and St Patrick, Dublin (d. 1827), in his day " the first tenor singer in this Empire," as recorded on his monument in the Lady Chapel of St Patrick's. Several more modern instances might be adduced.

Sonata di Chiesa. The Italian term for an organ sonata, suitable for performance in church, with or without orchestral accompaniment. Such a sonata intended for secular occasions was termed a *Sonata di camera*. There is a fine example of a *Sonata di chiesa* by Mozart, for strings and organ in the key of C major. It was written for Saltzburg Cathedral in 1780, at which time it was the custom to perform, between the reading of the Epistle and Gospel at High Mass, a short movement for orchestral instruments and organ. This beautiful little piece was performed at the Commemoration of Mozart in Trinity College Chapel, Cambridge, on 5th December 1891, the centenary of the composer's death. The organ, however, in this composition merely supplies an accompaniment of the simplest kind, and nowhere plays an independent part, the violins being treated throughout as the principal instruments.

Song-men. A name for the lay singers in York and some other cathedrals.

Song-school. A room set apart in cathedrals for the practice and musical instruction of the chorister-boys. At Durham the song-school was in the cemetery adjoining the south side of the nine altars. It was wainscoted with wood all round and furnished with forms and a long desk. The master here taught the choristers, who sang at High Mass and Vespers, the services at which he played on the organs. There was a second school in the south transept, furnished also as a chapel for the 6 A.M. service. At Wells the song-school remains over the west walk of the cloister. At Lincoln it is an upper room adjoining the south-east transept. At Lichfield the boys are taught in a separate building in the close. The Westminster choristers have their song-school in the Little Cloisters, while those of St Paul's are instructed in their very complete school-house adjacent to the deanery. In some places, where there is no regular song-school, the boys attend the organist at his own residence. The song-school at Ripon is very complete and commodious, and serves partly as a library for the cathedral music. At Hereford the song-school is adorned with some interesting portraits of former organists of the cathedral. At St Michael's, Tenbury, the choristers practise daily in the College Hall under the direction of the Warden, who is also Precentor. A rehearsal with the full choir is held every Wednesday evening in the same place. Under no circumstances are practices ever held in the church.

In architecture, the triangular spaces included between an arch
Spandrel. and a rectangle formed by the string course over it.
The string course is a projecting horizontal (or occasionally sloping) band or line of mouldings.

In olden times, choristers were privileged to demand a fee from every newly installed officer of the church and to levy " spur money "
from all who attended the service in riding gear.
Spur Money In the former case the fee varied according to the
in Cathedrals. position of the installed officer, and was paid without
conditions being imposed in return ; in the latter, the wearer of spurs could require the youthful tax-gatherer to repeat his " gamut " perfectly ; if he hesitated he lost his spur money. Royalty was not even exempt from this fine, for one of the items in the Privy Purse Expenses of Henry VII. is as follows :—" 1485, Oct. 1. To the children of the Chapell, for the King's spoures, 4ˢ." Thrice in the reign of Henry VIII., in the year 1530, a similar entry occurs. At Hereford, once, a person applied to the magistrates for redress, the choristers having decamped with his hat, on his refusal to pay the customary fine. The magistrates decided in favour of the boys. A correspondent in *Notes and Queries* (2nd series, xii. 229) says : " Fifty years ago " [*i.e.* early in the last century], " when in uniform, and having spurs screwed into my boots, I entered the Cathedral of Bristol, some choir lads accosted me, telling me I must pay forfeit for wearing spurs. To satisfy myself that they were not wanting to ' levy mail upon me,' I asked the verger, who accompanied myself and a friend about the church, who smiled and said it was customary ; and so, lugging out half-a-crown, the young *fry* soon vanished." Charles Knight, in the chapter " Items of the Obsolete," in his delightful book, " Once upon a Time," thus illustrates the same subject : " It was a dangerous thing for a stranger civilian to wear that spur at Windsor. He stalked into St George's Chapel. No matter what the choristers were chanting,

in an instant the spur was detected, and the distracted man, as he left the nave, after a little gazing at the painted windows, was surrounded by a bevy of white surplices demanding ' spur money.' " The custom is alluded to by Thomas Decker in his " Gul's Horn-booke," published in 1609 : " Never be seen to mount the steps into the choir [of St Paul's] but upon a high festival day, to prefer the fashion of your doublet : and especially if the singing-boys seem to take note of you, for they are able to buzz your praises above their anthems, if their voices have not lost their maidenheads. But be sure your silver spurs dog your heels, and then the boys will swarm about you like so many white butterflies ; when you in the open choir shall draw forth a perfumed embroidered purse, the glorious sight of which will entice many countrymen from their devotion to wondering. and quoit silver into the boys' hands that it may be heard above the first lesson, although it be read in a voice as big as one of the great organs." This singular custom lingered long in our cathedrals ; at Peterborough so comparatively recently as 1850. In that year some officers of the Sappers and Miners walked into the church with spurs on, and were instantly mulcted. When spur money was no longer to be obtained, the boys contrived to squeeze an equivalent by " turning " an anthem-book, taking the volume to any likely-looking stranger in the stalls and " waiting " on him until paid to go away. In North's " Lives of the Norths " (i. 279) we are told that Lord Keeper Guildford " being well known in all the choirs wherever he came, the boys failed not to bring him a fair book of the anthem and service, and sometimes the score if they had it, expecting, as they always had, a compensation for their pains." Asking for spur money was an old custom at Canterbury when Sir George Elvey and Dr Longhurst were choristers there. The former used to relate with amusement how startled an old farmer would often be when, having wandered into the cathedral on market-day, the choristers, ever on the watch, pounced on him for this fine. Elvey, when he became organist of St George's Chapel, Windsor, in 1835, reintroduced the custom there, greatly to the surprise of some unwary gentlemen who rode into Windsor to attend the service, and clinked all unheeding into the chapel with their spurs. They were caught as soon as service was over, and not permitted to quit the building until some of their superfluous cash was transferred to the pockets of the eager boys. In a quaint pamphlet published in 1598, " The Children of the Chapel [Royal] stript and whipt," occurs the following passage :—" We think yt very necessarye that euerie querister should bring wyth him to church a Testament in English,

284

and turne to euerie chapter as it is daily read, or some other good and Godly prayer-book, rather than spend theyr time in talk and hunting after 'spur money,' whereon they set theyr whole mindes, and do often abuse dyvers, if they doe not bestowe somewhat on them." In 1622 the Dean of the Chapel Royal issued an order by which it was decreed "That if any Knight or other person intituled to wear spurs, enter yᵉ Chappell in that guise, he shall pay to yᵉ quiristers yᵉ accustomed fine ; but if he command yᵉ youngest quirister to repeat hys 'gamut,' and he faile in yᵉ so doing, yᵉ same Knight or other, shall not pay yᵉ fine." On one occasion the Duke of Wellington walked into the Chapel Royal, St James', booted and spurred, and was instantly pounced upon. "Repeat your gamut," said his Grace to the youngest chorister, but the little urchin failed to do so, and the impost was not demanded. The Duke (an excellent musician) was equal to the occasion. The "gamut"—*i.e. gamma ut*—was the note G, the *Ut* or *Do* of the lowest hexachord of the ancient system of Guido d'Arezzo. As these hexachords in ascending overlapped one another, and as the notes were named by *combining* the overlapping names, the task was a fair test of the boy's musical knowledge, and amounted to the same thing as asking a sailor to "box the compass." With many of our old cathedral writers "gamut" means the key of G. Blow's Service in G (printed in Boyce's "Cathedral Music," vol. i.) was commonly called his "Gamut Service"—"Blow in Gamut." Spur money can be traced back to 1228, when it was decided that the priors of Binham and Wymondham might attend the synod at Norwich in copes and with spurs, without changing their travelling garb ("Gesta Ab. St Albani," i. 278). At St Paul's the choristers threatened imprisonment in the choir for a whole night to all who refused them money ! Robert Finch, one of the prebendaries of Westminster (1781-1803), once paid eighteen-pence as an offender, but the Duke of Cumberland pleaded successfully that it was hard if he could not wear his spurs where they had been first buckled on. At the installation of the Knights of the Bath in Henry VII.'s Chapel the Cook of Westminster stood with a cleaver at the door, threatening to strike off the spurs of any unworthy of their honour. He received a fee for his speech. The practice was not confined to England, it seems, if we may credit a story quoted by Ménage from "L'Histoire et Plaisante Chronique du Petit Jean du Saintré." (1523).

Squinch. The architectural term for a small arch or projecting course of stone formed across the angles of towers, etc., in Gothic architecture, to support the alternate sides of octagonal spires above.

Squint. See *sub voce* " Hagioscope."

The sequence for the Feast of the Seven Dolours of the B. V. M. observed in the Church of Rome on the Friday in Passion Week.

Stabat Mater Dolorosa. This noble poem, used both as a sequence and a hymn, has been, not unjustly, styled the most pathetic of mediæval hymns. The vividness with which it pictures the weeping mother at the Cross, its tenderness, its rhythmical beauty, its melodious double rhymes almost defying reproduction in another language, and its impressiveness when sung either to the fine plain-song melody, or to the noble strains to which many of the great masters of music, from Palestrina in the sixteenth to Dvořák in the nineteenth century, have set it, go far to justify the place it holds, and has long held, in the Catholic Church. Concerning the authorship of this poem, there has been, and still is, a great amount of uncertainty. The verse form is not earlier than about 1150. The only ascriptions which bear any impress of probability are those to Pope Innocent III. (d. 1216), and to Jacobus de Benedictis (d. 1306). There is quite a literature on the subject of this sequence, the best and most complete summary of it being that by Dr J. Kayser in his " Beitrage zur Geschichte und Erklärung der ältesten Kirchen Kymnen " (vol. ii. 110–192, Paderborn, 1886), where the different forms of the text are printed in full, with an elaborate commentary and a full apparatus of various readings. The best English translation is that partly by the Rev. Edward Caswall, Bishop Mant, and the compilers of " Hymns, Ancient and Modern." In cantata form the most popular setting has long been the luscious one of Rossini. It may be mentioned as an interesting fact that the first person to bring this work out in London was James Bennett, one of the gentlemen of the Chapel Royal, a noted tenor singer, and extensively known as a teacher. He had seen, by mere accident, the MS. score of the work at D'Almaine's, the music publisher in Soho Square. He borrowed it, and, at considerable cost, obtained permission to produce it and perform it, and it was sung privately before a large assembly of musical connoisseurs, at his house in Charlotte Street, Portland Place, in 1842. It was a success, and, it may be, gave an impetus to the future fame of this (for Rossini) unique work in this country. Among the numerous composers who have set the hymn in addition to those above mentioned are Josquin des Près (d.1521) ; Steffani (d. 1730) ; Astorga (d. 1736) ; Pergolesi (d. 1736) ; Clari (d. 1745) ; Durante (d. 1755) ; Scarlatti (d. 1757) ; Abos (d. 1787) ; Caffaro (d. 1787) ; Boccherini (d. 1805) ; Haydn (d. 1809) ; Winter (d. 1825) ; Schubert

ECCLESIASTICAL TERMS

(d. 1828) ; Ledesma (d. 1847) ; Neukomm (d. 1858), and in more modern times, Gounod, Henschell, Rheinberger, Turpin, and Hunt. Gounod's " Stabat Mater " is to a French paraphrase by the Abbé Castaing. It begins, "Debout, près de la Croix qui d'angoisse. l'inonde." This grand and effective composition is familiar in this country as an anthem for Lent and Holy Week under the title of " O come near to the Cross," the English adaptation having been primarily made by the Rev. Benjamin Webb for the use of St Andrew's, Wells Street, in 1868.

Stall. A fixed seat of wood enclosed, either wholly or partially, at the back and sides. All large churches, and most small ones previous to the Reformation, had a range of wooden stalls on each side and at the west end of the choir, which were separated from each other by large projecting elbows, with desks fixed before them. In cathedrals and other large buildings they were enclosed at the back with panelling, and were surmounted by over-hanging canopies of open tabernacle-work, which were often carried up to a great height, and highly enriched with pinnacles, crockets, pierced tracery, and other ornaments. Examples of stalls of this kind remain in many of our cathedrals and other churches. In some cases there were two rows of stalls on either side, the back rows of course being only surmounted by canopies. In parish churches the stalls were without canopies, and frequently had no panelling at the back above the level of the elbows, but in many instances the walls above them were lined with wooden panels, with a cornice above, corresponding with the screen under the rood-loft. The earliest English stalls—*i.e.* as regards the actual seats—are those of Exeter. The earliest canopies are those of Winchester, being Geometrical or Early Decorated. After those of Winchester the finest canopied stalls, ranging from the Decorated period to that of the Renaissance, are to be seen at Canterbury, Carlisle, Chester, Chichester, St David's, Durham, Ely, Gloucester, Hereford, Lincoln, Manchester, Norwich, St Paul's, Ripon, St George's Chapel, Windsor ; King's College Chapel, Cambridge ; Henry VII.'s Chapel, Westminster ; Beverley Minster ; Ludlow Church, Shropshire ; Nantwich Church, Cheshire ; All Saints', Hereford ; Newark-on-Trent ; Boston Church, Lincolnshire, the last partly modern. At Westminster Abbey, the original stalls, dating probably from about 1253, were destroyed in 1775 by Keene, the Abbey Surveyor, who put up new ones in what then passed for Gothic. A plan of the Abbey choir made in 1715 shows sixty-four stalls in all, and agrees with a description printed three years later, which says there were twenty-eight stalls on each side, and eight at the west end (returned) —*i.e.* four on either side of the choir door. The stalls are shown in Sandford's " Coronation of James II. " ; their arched canopies were supported by slender shafts, with moulded annulets and capitals. Two of the misericordes still exist, and also what is probably a portion of one of the carved divisions. Dart, in his " Westmonasterium " (1725), says the stalls were crowned with acute Gothic arches, supported by pillars, and that the abbot's and prior's stalls (now the dean's and sub-dean's) were to the right and left on entering the choir. Keene's stalls were removed in 1847–1848 during the refitting of the choir under Edward Blore with whom, as surveyor, the worthy dean and chapter of that date were unfortunately saddled. Blore's stalls, of oak in Middle Pointed, are certainly elaborate and varied in their design, and show that he took considerable pains with them, but he made the strange mistake of copying stonework in wood, the details of the tomb of Aymer de Valence being expressly named by him as models, overlooking the difference of the treatment proper to such different materials. Hence, the general effect is heavy and machine-like, and totally lacking in the poetry of the mediæval work. The subsellæ, also, are cumbersome and take up far too much space. Blore resigned his post as Abbey Architect soon after the completion of this new stallwork and Mr (afterwards Sir) Gilbert Scott was appointed as his successor. Had this work been delayed a year or two longer we might have had choir fittings in the Abbey in no way inferior to those of Ely, upon the restoration of which cathedral Scott was about the same time engaged. Modern examples of canopied stalls are too numerous to be mentioned, but those at Peterborough Cathedral and St Nicholas, Great Yarmouth, are perhaps as good as any. Those put up in Eton College Chapel, during its restoration under Deeson in 1852, are commendable. In Continental ecclesiology examples of fine canopied stallwork may be mentioned at the following places:—the cathedrals of Albi and Auch, and the church at Brou (French Gothic) ; the cathedrals of Bayeux and Nôtre Dame, Paris; the Church of St Riquier (French Renaissance) ; the cathedrals of Ratzeburg, Magdeburg, Meissen, Naumberg—where there are two sets, one of wood in the eastern choir, the other of stone in the western—the Dom, Erfurt, and the Minster, Ulm (German Gothic); the Kloster-Kirche, Gaesdonk, in the Rhine Provinces (German Renaissance) ; St Gertrude, Louvain ; Bruges Cathedral ; the parish church at Aerschot (Belgian Gothic) ; the cathedral, Roeskilde, and the Church of St Knude, Odense (Danish Gothic) ; the Cistercian Church, Soro (Danish Renaissance).

ECCLESIASTICAL TERMS

In Italy and Spain finely carved stalls of various periods abound, of which instances might be multiplied *ad infinitum*. In the English mother-church of Sarum (*i.e.* Salisbury Cathedral), which served as a model for all churches of the same rite, the stalls at the four extremities of the choir were assigned to the four principal dignitaries. Entering the choir through the rood-screen, on the right was the stall of the Dean, on the left that of the Precentor. Nearest the sanctuary on the right was the stall of the Chancellor, opposite that of the Treasurer. Next to the Dean stood the Archdeacon of Dorset, then the Sub-dean. Next to the Chancellor stood the Archdeacon of Wilts; next to the Precentor stood the Archdeacon of Berks, then the Succentor; and next to the Treasurer the other Archdeacon of Wilts; in the midst, on either side, the Canons who were prior in dignity. This constituted the superior grade. Below these sat the Minor Canons, the deacons and other clerks in similar order. This was called the " second form," and below these again the boys on stools. The rulers of the choir sat in the midst at the western extremity of the choir, facing the altar, on seats prepared for them, and executed their office at a lectern *in medio chori*.

Stanchion.
Fr. *etancon*.
The upright iron bar between the mullions of a window, screen, etc. Stanchions were usually square bars, and were frequently ornamented at the top with *fleurs-de-lis*, leaves, etc. There is a good example, with *fleurs-de-lis* head, at Warborough Church, Oxon.

Stipendiaries.
Members of cathedral and collegiate choirs, who do not possess an independent estate, but are paid stipends. At Christ Church and St Patrick's Cathedrals, Dublin, those singers supernumerary to the vicars choral are termed " Stipendiaries." At St Paul's, since 1873, such singers have been called " Assistant Vicars Choral." Milman, soon after his appointment to the deanery of St Paul's in 1849, engaged a certain number of extra singers for the Sunday services, in addition to the six vicars choral on the foundation. At Exeter, such singers are termed " Secondaries."

Stole, or
Orarium.
Gr.
στόλη, ὡράριον.
A tippet (*q.v.*) or narrow scarf. The Council of Laodicea has two canons (22, 23) concerning the use of the orarium, which might be used by presbyters and deacons, but not by the inferior orders. Other councils give directions as to its use, and many writers refer to it. The word " stole " did not come into use till later. The στόλη (literally, an equipment) meant any dress, but in Latin (*stola*) implied in the first instance the dress of a Roman matron. How it came to mean the vestment the word afterwards

289

was used for is a matter of conjecture. The stole is a narrow strip of silk passed over the neck, and hanging in front to about the knees of the wearer. It is usually ornamented with a cross at the neck and at either extremity. The ends are slightly expanded and fringed. It varies in colour with the season. It is a eucharistic vestment, but is also worn in choir offices. The deacon wears it across the left shoulder only. At the Holy Eucharist it is crossed over the breast and fastened under the girdle, the ends appearing below the chasuble. It signifies the yoke of obedience of the priesthood to Christ ; and also the rope put around the neck of our Blessed Lord, to drag Him to Calvary. See also " Scarf " and " Tippet." Mr J. D. Chambers, in his book, " Divine Worship in the Church of England in the XIII., XIV. and XIX. Centuries," 1877, devotes considerable space to a description of the stole from the earliest times, together with much interesting historical matter. He figures examples of ancient stoles richly worked and embroidered. Among his delineations are two of the thirteenth and fourteenth centuries ; part of the stole of St Thomas of Canterbury, preserved at Sens, and that found on the body of St Cuthbert when his tomb was opened at Durham in 1829. In the Inventories of St Paul's (*Dugdale*), Canterbury (*Dart*), and Exeter (*Oliver*), many stoles are enumerated of great magnificence, of silk, velvet and gold thread, with jewels of various colours. These, however, were all of the same suit with the chasuble, etc., and are not catalogued separately but all included under the term " Vestimentum." For instance, at St Paul's, in 1295 (*Dugdale*, 311), the vestment of Henry de Wengham, Bishop of London, 1259–1262, was embroidered with gold and silver with his arms, with amice, stole and maniple of the same kind. A vestment of John de Northampton, Prebendary of Willesden, had apparels of purple samite embroidered with lions, eagles and trees, with stole and maniple of the same cloth embroidered with images, the amice being of fine thread adorned with flowers. Stoles were frequently decorated with fringes or lappets, or jewelled pendants at the extremities. At Canterbury, in 1321, were eight pairs of stoles and maniples, all with pendants of pearls and gems (Append. to Dart's " Canterbury," viii.). Sometimes, as also like the copes, at these extremities were pendants of lumps of gold and often a number of small bells. At St Paul's, in 1295, were stoles and maniples with images, and at their ends angels with little silver bells. Godfred of Croyland, in 1299, had a stole of red velvet with little bells, and acorns of gold and silver and jewels sewn on. Stoles, as a rule, should not be expanded at the extremities, certainly not in the case

ECCLESIASTICAL TERMS

The deputy of the precentor in Cathedrals of the Old Foundation.
The title probably answers to the ὑποβολεῖς mentioned by Socrates,
the ecclesiastical historian of the fifth century. It

Succentor, or would seem that originally the succentor led the anti-
Sub-chanter. phonal chant on the side opposite the precentor, as
Fr. sous- St Augustine includes under cantors the precentor,
chantre or " qui vocem præmittit in cantu " ; and succentor,
chantre; " qui subsequenter canendo respondet." At Salis-
Span. bury he ranks before the prebendaries and after the
sochantre. sub-dean, being regarded as a dignitary, and by the
Statutes of Osmund has one preaching turn. Bishop
Burnet relieved the succentor from residence in 1695. At the other
cathedrals the succentor is one of the minor canons or priest vicars.
One of his principal duties now is to draw up the table of services
and anthems for the week. At St Paul's he attends the periodical
full rehearsals of the choir, and checks the attendance of the vicars
and assistant vicars choral. At York there is a *Succentor Canonicorum* and a *Succentor Vicariorum*, the former being a dignitary,
the latter a priest vicar choral. At Hereford his duty was to bear
the " burden " of the chant and psalmody ; to table the choir for
singing and direct the rulers of the choir ; to distribute copes on
the greater feasts ; to order processions. He took care that the
singing was reverently conducted, and appointed five boys as clerks
of the first form, removable at his will, to sing the antiphons, and
to carry tapers and censers, who were to wear " an honest robe,
shoes and stockings." At Lichfield he supplied the precentor's
place when absent, and ruled the song-school by his official. He
also arranged the method and order of processions ; enjoined lections
on Greater Doubles and in Masses ; watched and observed the time
for beginning the Mass and the Hours, and on Saturday, after the
recitation of *Benedicite* in chapter, arranged the services publicly
for the ensuing week. At Chichester (1232) he gave seven or fourteen
stripes to boys misbehaving in choir, and received 40s. a year from
the precentor out of the Archdeacon of Chichester's synodals. At
York, to the vicars' succentor it belonged to delate offending vicars
on Saturdays, mark out the table, and warn those whose names were
on it, or in their absence appoint others to supply their turn ; to
hear them sing their part for the first time, and punish them if necessary. In the name of the precentor he ruled the choir, ordered its
services, and gave the note of the antiphon to the dean. The canons'
succentor directed the major canons. At Exeter the organist was,
in the eighteenth century and early in the last, succentor and

293

Informator Puerorum, or Teacher of the Boys. William Jackson held these offices from 1777 to 1803, and later on, from 1835 to 1842, Dr S. S. Wesley. Early in the eighteenth century, and certainly down to 1762, the succentorship was held (as now) by one of the priest vicars. An inscription on a tomb in the cathedral runs : " Here lie y* reliques of y* Rev. Mr Tobias Langdon, Master of Musick, Priest Vicar and Sub-chaunter of this Church, and Prebendary of Bodmyn in Cornwall. He was generally beloved by those y* knew him and his loss was as generally lamented which happened on the 14th of September 1712." This was the grandfather of Richard Langdon, afterwards (1753–1777) organist of the same cathedral, and the composer of some well-known chants. At Hereford, within the last two or three years, the office of succentor has been united with that of organist, an arrangement which has been found to work extremely well. Several names of considerable interest will be found among those who have held the office of succentor in our cathedrals at various times. At Amiens, as chanter, the succentor ranked next the precentor, or préchantre. He installed canons in the lower stalls, governed the choristers, and, with the precentor, admitted and dismissed them. His stipend was 260 livres. In 1530 the sub-chanter at Rouen had a prebend attached to his office, but had no precedence, except that on certain days he occupied a particular stall. He ruled the choral Mass, beginning all the offices on Double Feasts, and on Sundays informed the chaplains what was to be sung. He also gave the note for the response and anthems in processions, except the anthem at the entry of the choir, which belonged to the precentor. He also had charge of all processions. At Seville he tabled the ministers for Church service, and was the precentor's deputy in ruling the choir. At Placentia, the succentor, in the precentor's absence, made out the " matricula," tabled the chanters and readers ; while the precentor's duties were " disponere chorum et idoneos in chorum introducere." At Nôtre Dame, Paris, he was a dignitary appointed by the chapter. See also *sub voce* " Precentor." For a list of the succentors of St Paul's since 1672 see J. S. Bumpus, " History of English Cathedral Music," 190. Much of interest concerning the succentors and the College of Vicars Choral at Hereford will be found in the Rev. F. T. Havergal's " Fasti Herefordienses " (1869), the information being mainly derived from the MSS. of the Rev. Wm. Cooke (succentor, 1808–1836), who made large collections for a history of the college. A list of the sub-chanters of Lichfield from the year 1228 is given in a volume of the records, etc., of that cathedral compiled by Dr J. Charles Cox.

ECCLESIASTICAL TERMS

A vote, token of assent and approbation, or, as in public worship, the united voice and consent of the people in the petitions offered.

Suffrage. The term is also used in the Prayer-Book to designate a short form of petition, as in the Litany. Thus, in the Order for the Consecration of Bishops, we read that in the Litany as then used, after the words, " That it may please Thee to illuminate all bishops," etc., the proper *suffrage* shall be, " That it may please Thee to bless this our brother elected," etc. The versicles immediately after the Creed at Matins and Evensong are also denominated " suffrages," in the forms of " Prayer with Thanksgiving " formerly appointed for 5th November, 29th May and 20th June: " the Suffrages next after the Creed shall stand thus," etc. The Litany in the Ordering of Deacons is headed " The Litany and Suffrages." By " suffrages " here seems to be meant the latter part of the Litany—*i.e.* after the Lord's Prayer—called by Wheatley (" Book of Common Prayer ") the " supplications." See also *sub voce* " Litany."

Super-altar. See *sub voce* " Retable."

Originally a term applied to the decoration attached to the wall behind and above the altar. It is now taken to mean the decorative **Super-frontal.** hanging which overlaps the frontal (*q.v.*), hanging over it for about six or eight inches. The colour of the super-frontal should be violet in penitential seasons, and red, green, or cloth of gold, at all other times.

A long linen robe with large sleeves, used by all clergy under the episcopal order, by choirs and other persons specially engaged in **Surplice.** the celebration of divine service, and also, on certain days, by members of colleges, whether clerical or lay. It may be called the uniform of the Church in divine service. The word is derived from *super*, over, and *pelliceum*, a robe of fur, which was worn in England and other northern countries as a protection from cold. In the early English Church it was a majestic, graceful garment, very full, and reaching nearly to the ankles ; and having ample sleeves, widening down to the hands, and hanging in graceful folds. This is evident from old brasses, and from various episcopal injunctions for a long and full surplice with long sleeves. The long English surplice, reaching nearly to the ground, with flowing sleeves, is acknowledged even by the Roman ritualists (*vide* Goar and Dr Rock) to be more primitive than the short, poor little foreign garment which disfigures so many of our churches at the present day. The surplice was in fact originally an alb enlarged both in the body and the sleeves, to enable it to be worn over the *pelliceum*. The short surplice adopted in the Roman Church is a corruption, as Cardinal

Bona confesses ("Rer. Liturg."). He says that Stephen of Tournai, who lived A.D. 1180, shows that the surplice formerly reached to the feet, and that in the course of time it was shortened, as it appears from the Council of Basle, Sess. 21, which commanded the clergy to have surplices reaching to the middle of the leg. He adds that they are now so much shortened as scarcely to reach the knees. A fashion of wearing such short surplices, and, even if not short, as scanty and free from folds as possible has for some years been in vogue among many of the clergy and choirs in the Church of England, but of late a return to ancient and primitive usage has been made in a few quarters. Almost the only choral foundation in this country in which the use of the ample surplice is maintained is that of St Michael's, Tenbury. The woodcut, representing two choir-boys, prefixed to the Rev. J. E. Millard's little book, "Historical Notices of the Office of Choristers" (1848), exhibits the English surplice in its true form. See also under "Cassock." The open buttoned surplice, still to be seen in many cathedrals and at Oxford and Cambridge, St Michael's College, Tenbury, etc., came in about the end of the seventeenth century, owing, it is said, to the growing habit among the clergy at that time of wearing a wig. Before that time surplices were very much like the long ones worn at present, except that they were closed in front, but with a circular hole in the middle for the head to pass through; which aperture was curiously coloured or ornamented with elegantly wrought needlework, done sometimes in scarlet, but more frequently in dark blue thread.

According to the 17th Canon, " all masters and fellows of colleges or halls, and all the scholars or students in either of the universities, **Surplice Days.** shall in their churches and chapels, upon all Sundays, Holy Days, and their eves, at the time of divine service, wear surplices according to the order of the Church of England; and such as are graduates shall agreeably wear with their surplices such hoods as do severally appertain unto their degrees." Saturday evening, it is to be observed, as the eve of Sunday, has always been considered as coming within this rule. The colleges in the universities of Cambridge and Dublin construe this rule as applying to *all* their members; those of Oxford—Christ Church excepted—to the *foundation* members only; and at Cambridge, too, noblemen do not wear surplices. By the 25th Canon the use of the surplice is prescribed daily to the deans, masters, heads of collegiate churches, canons and prebendaries. In the universities, the choirs and chaplains wear surplices whether it be a " surplice

ECCLESIASTICAL TERMS

day " or no. Formerly, at King's College, Cambridge, the boys of the choir wore black gowns on non-surplice days.

Tabernacle. The receptacle for the monstrance or pyx (*q.v.*) It was not in use in England till five or six years before the Reformation, or until Queen Mary's reign, notwithstanding the Constitutions of Archbishop Peckham in 1279 headed " Eucharistia in tabernaculo clauso, idque in pixide decenti, ne alteratur, custodiatur, et singulis Dominicis innovetur." The distinction between the tabernacle and the pyx is specified by Lyndwood, the great English canonist (d. 1446), who thinks it necessary to observe in his Glossary, " Sic ergo tabernaculum et pyxis non supponunt pro eodem quia pyxis poni debet in tabernaculo, sicut hic patet "; and " Tabernaculum—Sic dictum, quia de tabulis sit factum, vel quia tabulis vel lignis sit impensum." On the Continent, especially in Germany (where it is called the " Sacrament-Hauslein "), many earlier tabernacles may be seen, dating back some fifty years previously. It will suffice to refer to the magnificent specimen of Adam Kraft's work at Nuremburg, which is a canopy of open pinnacles and tracery 64 feet high ; and to those at Limburg, Meissen, Paderborn, Ratisbon and Ulm. The grandest of all is at Seville Cathedral, called *El Monumento* ; it was designed by Antonio Florentin in 1544, and added to in 1624 and 1688. It is composed of twenty-four columns in each stage, and rises to a height disproportionate even to the cathedral itself, which is 145 feet to the vaulting. It is, however, not a permanent structure, but takes to pieces, and is only put up for the festival of Corpus Christi and the ceremony of the Easter Sepulchre. It is erected over the tomb of Fernando, son of Christopher Columbus, at the west end of the nave of the cathedral, and when lighted upon the night of Good Friday, when the Host is enclosed in the silver *custodia*, the effect is truly marvellous. Camille Enlart (" Manuel d'Archéologie Française," 1902) gives illustrations of two curious and interesting French tabernacles, one of wood, at Senanque (Vaucluse), beginning of the thirteenth century : the other of stone at Semur (Côte d'Or), fifteenth century.

Te Deum Laudamus (" We praise Thee, O God "). It is probable that, from very ancient times, Psalms or canticles have been intermingled with the reading of the Scriptures in the public service : and those which we now use occupy, as nearly as possible, the places where they have been sung for centuries. The tradition that ascribes the authorship of the noble hymn, *Te Deum*, jointly to SS. Ambrose and Augustine cannot be deemed deserving of credit ; this has

A DICTIONARY OF

been demonstrated by Tentzel ; but its absolute and definite authorship has not yet been fixed. It has been attributed, in addition to the two celebrated writers above named, to Athanasius, *c.* A.D. 340 ; to Hilary of Poictiers, *c.* A.D. 368 ; to Hilary of Arles, *c.* A.D. 440, and to Abondius. Koch asserts it to be an *evening* hymn of primitive antiquity written in Greek and translated into Latin by St Ambrose, for the use of his church at Milan ; and to have been subsequently introduced into the North African churches by St Augustine. He adds that, owing to the respect in which St Ambrose was held, it spread throughout the whole West, under the name of the Ambrosian Hymn of Praise, and was universally adopted by the first half of the sixth century. He further asserts (but gives no authority) that it is found in Greek in one of the earlier MSS. of the sixth century *together with a morning hymn,* immediately after the Psalter ; and, that it begins in the Alexandrine Codex with the words, Καθ'ἑκαστην ἡμέραν εὐλογήσω σε. Blunt, however (" Annotated Prayer-Book "), is more accurate when he says that to the Psalter in the Alexandrine Codex there is a *morning* hymn appended, corresponding in several of its verses with the *Te Deum.* It is the last of fourteen ; and begins with the *Gloria in Excelsis,* which is followed by three verses of the *Te Deum* beginning, " Day by day we magnify Thee." To these succeed a verse from the *Benedicite,* and some half-dozen verses selected from different Psalms. Bingham (the best authority for clearness and brevity) says it was composed by a French writer, about 100 years after St Ambrose's death, for the use of the Gallican Church. This writer was most probably Nicetius, Bishop of Trêves *c.* A. D. 535. The most ancient mentions of it are found in the Rule of Cæsarius, Bishop of Arles (fifth century). Aurelian, successor of Cæsarius, appointed it to be sung in the *morning.* St Benedict, in his rule, directed it to be sung in the *nocturnal* office on Sundays. There is no doubt that this ancient and glorious hymn has been in *daily use* in the English Church ever since the Conquest. It was inserted by St Osmund, *c.* 1085, in the Salisbury Portiforium or Breviary, where it is called the " Psalm Te Deum," or the " Canticle of Ambrose and Augustine," from the old legend that, at the baptism of Augustine by Ambrose, it was sung alternately by the two saints, as it was composed by inspiration. The rubric of the Sarum Breviary appointed it at Matins on Sundays and festivals. It is also to be found in early copies of the Breviary of York. In the Roman Breviary it is only appointed on Sundays and certain feasts ; but even on these it is omitted at certain seasons of the year. Our Prayer-Book orders it for daily use, but the *Benedicite* is generally

298

substituted for it in Advent and Lent. The *Te Deum* has three divisions : (1) An act of adoration to God the Father, and to the Trinity ; vv. 1-13. (2) An intercessory rehearsal to Christ the Lord, of His redemptive work for man ; vv. 14-21. (3) General suffrages for peace and deliverance ; vv. 22-29. In Merbecke's "Boke of Common Praier Noted" (1550), the *Te Deum* is given to a mutilated form of the ancient Ambrosian melody. There is a better version in Helmore's "Canticles Noted," but perhaps the most authentic arrangement is that sung at the Church Pageant in June 1909, and printed in the illustrated quarto "Handbook." The melody as given by Merbecke forms the tenor part of a *Te Deum* by Heath, printed in Day's "Service-Book," 1560, and again in 1565. In the twelfth number of *The Parish Choir* (Jan. 1847) will be found an arrangement of the *Te Deum*, Heath's tenor forming the melody, the other parts being thrown into the form of an accompaniment, without, however, in any way altering Heath's modulations or harmonies. There is a form of the Ambrosian Chant adapted from the *Modus Simplex* in the Appendix to the Ratisbon "Ordinarium." This was published in 1881, in the Service-Book of the London Gregorian Association, set to the English words by J. W. Doran and W. Spenser Nottingham, with organ harmonies by the Rev. G. H. Palmer. Apart from practical considerations, this is interesting as an example of what Merbecke might have done, had he not fettered himself by a too rigid adherence to Cranmer's recommendation to put "a syllable to a note as near as may be." Since Merbecke's time the *Te Deum* has formed part of every cathedral "Service," and innumerable settings have also been written, and published separately by modern composers, especially adapted for the use of parochial choirs who desire something more than the ordinary chant. Of settings in this latter style an infinite variety will be found in Novello's series, "The Parish Choir-Book," begun in 1866 under the auspices of the Ely Diocesan Choral Association, and still flourishing. Apart from its regular place in the Office of Matins, the *Te Deum* (as in the Roman Church) has invariably been used upon occasions of national thanksgiving. Thus, we have Handel's famous *Te Deum* for the Victory of Dettingen, 1743 ; that of Sir John Goss for the Restoration to Health of his late Majesty when Prince of Wales, 1872 ; a "Festival Te Deum" by Sir Arthur Sullivan for the same event ; that, also by Sir Arthur Sullivan, for the Thanksgiving for the Restoration of Peace, 1902 ; and that by Sir George Martin for the Diamond Jubilee of Queen Victoria, 1897. With the exception of those by Sir John Goss and Sir George

Martin all the settings above mentioned are lengthy compositions, and suitable only for use with a short form of prayer on special occasions. The well-known short and full *Te Deum* in A by Dr Boyce was composed for the Coronation of George III., 1761. The *Te Deum* of Gounod, primarily intended for use at St Paul's at the 1872 Thanksgiving, should be mentioned. It is short, and adapted for liturgical use. The fine *Te Deum* in D major of Henry Purcell was written for the Celebration of St Cecilia's Day in 1694, and there are similar compositions by other English composers of the later seventeenth century. The *Te Deum* is said to have been first sung in English in the Church of St Martin, Herne, Kent. Nicholas Ridley, Bishop of Rochester and afterwards of London, was Vicar of Herne in 1541, and " articles were exhibited against him for preaching against Auricular Confession, and directing the *Te Deum* to be sung in English in Herne Church." This was eight years before the publication of the first English Prayer-Book. In his " farewell " to Herne, Ridley addresses it as " thou worshipful and wealthy parish, the first cure whereunto I was called to minister God's word. Thou hast heard of my mouth oft time the Word of God preached, not after the popish trade, but after God's gospel. Oh that the fruit had answered to the seed ! " The *Te Deum* has been elaborately set by almost every composer for the Roman Church. Those of Anerio, Bononcini, Graun, Hasse, Jommelli, Mozart, Haydn, Schicht, Portogallo, Cherubini, Romberg and Berlioz are celebrated. For the history and theology of the *Te Deum* consult the " Sketch " by Dr Mackenzie, Bishop Suffragan of Nottingham and Sub-dean of Lincoln, prefixed to the Morning Service in C major by John M. W. Young, organist (1850-1895) of Lincoln Cathedral.

Tenebræ. An office used in the Church of Rome on the Wednesday, Thursday and Friday of Holy Week, and so-called from the extinguishing of the lights (*tenebrae*, or darkness), symbolising the darkness which covered the whole earth at the time of Our Lord's Crucifixion, and the desolation and abandonment which Our Saviour endured in His Passion. The Responsorium, " Tenebræ factæ sunt, dum crucifixissent Jesum Judæi," occurs in the second nocturn of Matins on Good Friday. The Tenebræ offices for Maundy Thursday, Good Friday and Holy Saturday, which in the primitive ages were said at a very early hour in the mornings of those days, are now said or sung, by " anticipation," on Wednesday, Thursday and Friday evenings. At the close of each Psalm, both at Matins and Lauds, *Gloria Patri* is omitted, and one of the fifteen candles of unbleached wax arranged in a triangular

ECCLESIASTICAL TERMS

candlestick is extinguished, except that at the top. While the *Benedictus* is being sung, the six candles on the altar are also extinguished, one by one, at every second verse, so that the whole may be put out by the last verse. In like manner, all the lamps and lights about the church are put out. On the repetition of the antiphon to the *Benedictus*, "Traditor autem dedit eis signum," the candle is taken from the top of the triangular candlestick, and hidden, still lighted, under the Epistle side of the altar, whilst all kneel and say or sing the versicle, "Christus factus est pro nobis obediens, usque ad mortem," to which, on the second night, is added "Mortem autem crucis," and on the third, "Propter quod et Deus exaltavit illum, et dedit, illi nomen, quod est super omne nomen." The Paternoster is then said, *silentio*, and the *Miserere* (Ps. li.) follows (see *sub voce* "Miserere"). This is succeeded by the prayer, "Respice, quæsumus Domine, super hanc familiam Tuam," etc. (the same as our first collect for Good Friday), after which a noise is made to represent the confusion of nature at the death of its Author; and when the lighted candle, to denote His resurrection from the dead, is produced from beneath the altar, all rise up and depart in silence. In this office at Siena the lighted candles are extinguished with a sponge, one of the many ritual customs peculiar to that cathedral. Palestrina has set the office of Tenebræ very finely, including the Lamentations of Jeremiah. The music of the Responsorium, "Tenebræ factæ sunt," by the later composers, Salvatore, Perez and Michael Haydn, is also extremely beautiful; while the *Misereres* of Allegri and Bai are great features in the office as performed in the Sistine Chapel at Rome. Where *canto figurato* is not used for the various antiphons, responsoria, etc., the whole is sung in *canto fermo*. In some of our churches Tenebræ is sung, according to the use of the diocese of Rouen. The whole of the offices of Holy Week will be found completely noted in any large Roman plain-chant manual. One of the best of such manuals is that compiled by Wm. Kelly, M. Ap. L.D., published by Richardson of London and Dublin, 1849. The service of Tenebræ, or Matins and Lauds of the last three days of Holy Week, has been done into English, and adapted to the original note, from the Sarum Breviary, by the Rev. G. H. Palmer, B.A., and printed at the Convent of St Mary, Wantage.

Terce, or Tierce. One of the lesser canonical hours, sung at 9 A.M.—*i.e.* the third hour (*tertia hora*). It consists of the Paternoster, Ave Maria, *Deus in adjutorium*, the hymn, *Nunc sancte nobis Spiritus*, three portions of Psalm cxix., beginning with *Legem pone* and ending with *Bonitatem fecisti*, versicles, responses and antiphons varying with the season, a short chapter of Holy Scripture, and the Collect for the day. When the whole of the offices are recited daily, Terce is followed by High Mass. The Rev. Benjamin Webb ("Sketches of Continental Ecclesiology," p. 321) thus describes Terce at the Duomo, Florence, on Sunday, 22nd September 1844: "At 9 A.M. a low mass was said at the high altar; when it was over, the green frontal was moved away and showed a white one. The choir had now assembled; the canons in the upper stalls wore brown capes and gowns over their arms; the minor canons in the middle row had crimson capes; and the third row was occupied by acolyths and singers. Terce was nobly sung. Two acolyths stood by the central lettern, which, under a strong lamp, bore a vast illuminated antiphonary; at the antiphons the precentor, attended by two succentors [choir-rulers are probably meant] in copes, and holding cantoral staves, stood at some distance from it facing east, and twelve singers grouped themselves between them and the lettern; and so the antiphons were sung. The celebrant, deacon, sub-deacon, and an assistant in a cope, came in in procession, and Mass was sung to true Church music with occasional organ accompaniment."

Throne. The bishop's *cathedra*, or seat, in the principal church of the diocese. Hence the word "cathedral." In our cathedrals the bishop's throne is invariably on the south side; it forms a part of the stalls at their eastern extremity, and is readily distinguished by the height of its canopy and by the redundancy of its carving and ornaments. At St Paul's the bishop has two thrones; that at the east end of the south stalls; that more to the west, his ordinary seat or stall. In Hollar's view of the interior of the choir of old St Paul's, as given in the well-known work of Dugdale, no throne is observable. In old times the Bishop of London often occupied the stall assigned to the dean. Unquestionably the most magnificent bishop's throne in England is that at Exeter Cathedral. It rises in airy state to the height of 57 feet (nearly to the roof) at the east end of the southern range of stalls. It dates from the time of Bishop Stapledon (1308–1326), the oak used in its construction having been cut down at Newton and Chudleigh, at a cost of £6, 12s. 8½d. Four years later, Robert de Galmeston, an Exeter man, was paid £4 for making this throne, exclusive of the painted decoration and statuary, now all but completely lost. During the Commonwealth it was taken down and concealed, but replaced at the Restoration, when Bishop Seth Ward, like Cosin at Durham, Sanderson at Lincoln, and Hacket at Lichfield, was most assiduous in his endeavours to bring back the cathedral to as much of its former splendour as his day permitted. At Chester Cathedral, when the shrine of St Werburgha was removed at the time of the Reformation, the lower part was converted into a throne, for Bird, the newly constituted bishop, and it so remained until Scott's restoration of the choir in 1874, when an entirely new throne was erected, and the shrine removed to the Lady Chapel. At Durham the monument of Bishop Hatfield (d. 1381), on the south side of the choir, was built during his lifetime to serve at once as his tomb and as an episcopal throne for his successor. When Sir Gilbert Scott was engaged upon the restoration of the choir of Ely Cathedral (1848–1852) the precedent existing in Henry VII.'s Chapel at Westminster of retaining only one return stall on either side the entrance of the choir was followed. These stalls are those of the bishop and dean. At Ely, at the time of the Reformation, the bishop took the place of the former abbot, the abbot's stall having been on the south side of the entrance, and that of the prior the corresponding one on the north. When, at the Dissolution, the dean superseded the prior he took his stall on the north side, and every succeeding dean has occupied the same seat, so that at Ely Cathedral alone there is no bishop's throne in the usual position —viz. the east end of the southern range of stalls—while the dean occupies, traditionally, the side opposite to his customary position. Bishop Turton, the occupant of the see of Ely while the works of restoration were in progress, much wished to have a throne in the usual place, but Sir Gilbert Scott would not consent to this obliteration of an early tradition. In the French cathedrals the bishop's throne is always on the north side, but it does not form part of the stalls, being placed in the sanctuary, having a canopy, and hangings of needlework. In many of the German cathedrals (now Lutheranised) where there is a solid choir-screen with two doors, the bishop's throne was placed between these doors. In the ancient basilicas and churches the throne was at the apex of the apse, behind the altar. The marble chair of the Archbishop at Canterbury, in which he is enthroned, was formerly in this situation. For a full description of the bishops' thrones in the various English cathedrals consult T. F. Bumpus, " Cathedrals of England and Wales, " 3 vols. (1905–1907).

In the 74th Canon, in which decency in apparel is enjoined to ministers, it is appointed that " All deans, masters of colleges, archdeacons, and prebendaries, in cathedral and collegiate churches (being priests or deacons), doctors in divinity, law and physic, bachelors of divinity, masters of arts, and bachelors

Tippet.

of law, having any ecclesiastical living, shall usually wear gowns with standing collars and sleeves straight at the hands, or wide sleeves, as is used at the Universities, with hoods or *tippets* of silk or sarsenet, and square caps. And that all other ministers admitted, or to be admitted, into that function shall also usually wear the like apparel as is aforesaid, except tippets only." And in the 58th Canon : " It shall be lawful for such ministers as are not graduates to wear upon their surplices, instead of hoods, some decent tippet of black, so it be not silk." It is supposed that the present black scarf worn by the English clergy represents three things : (1) the stole ; (2) the chaplain's scarf ; (3) the choir tippet. The chaplain's scarf is a remnant of the ancient badges, or liveries, worn by the members of noblemen's households, their chaplains included. The choir tippet grew out of the ancient *almutium* or amess—that is, a vestment which covered the shoulders, and included the hood ; the *liripipium,* or pendant part of the hood, sometimes hanging singly behind (as in our modern hoods), sometimes in duplicate before, like the scarf. In process of time the hood became separated from this pendant part in front, and hence the choir tippet. It is certain that the tippet so called, often made of sables or furs, was worn, in the form of the scarf, by dignitaries of the Church and State for many ages in England. The scarf has been called a tippet immemoriably in Ireland, and within memory in many parts of England. The law of the Church therefore seems to be this, that all ecclesiastics (whether priests *or deacons*) being prebendaries or of higher rank in cathedral and collegiate churches, and all priests *or deacons* being Masters of Arts or of higher degree, may wear either hoods or *tippets of silk* ; and *all* non-graduate ministers (whether priests *or deacons*) may not wear hoods, but only *tippets* not of silk. Whence the tippet is to be worn by all clergymen. The 58th Canon is, however, explicit as to the use of hoods by graduates. By the constant usage of cathedrals, and now almost everywhere, both hood and scarf are now worn by all graduates. [Article " Tippet " in Hook's " Church Dictionary," compiled from G. J. French, " Tippets of the Canons Ecclesiastic," 1850 ; Jebb (Bp.), " Charge to the Clergy of Limerick " ; Jebb (Dr J.), " Choral Service of the Church " (1843), p. 215.]

Tooth Ornament.
Fr. *dent de scie.*

A name given to an ornament very extensively used in the Early English style of architecture. It consists of a square four-leaved flower, the centre of which projects in a point. Although characteristic of Early English, it is occasionally met with in late Norman work, as at the west window of the south aisle of the nave of Rochester Cathedral.

ECCLESIASTICAL TERMS

Tracery. The term for the ramifications of the mullions in Gothic windows, forming geometrical and other figures. The various styles, are, perhaps, more readily distinguished by their tracery than by any other means.

Transition. A term employed in reference to mediæval architecture, while it is in progress of changing from one style to another. There are three periods of transition—viz. from the Romanesque, or Norman, style to the Early English; from the Early English to the Decorated; and from the Decorated to the Perpendicular. Buildings erected at these particular times frequently have the features of two styles so blended together that they cannot be properly considered to belong to either. Sometimes the details of the later style are associated with the general forms and arrangements of the earlier, and *vice versa*. The transition, *par excellence*, is, however, that from the Anglo-Norman to the pure, Early Pointed, free from any trace of Romanesque influence, but the change was so gradual that it is quite impossible to say when one style left off and another began, the round arch dying much harder in some districts than in others. In England this particular period of transition occupied the latter part of the reign of Henry II. Examples are the Church of St Cross, Winchester, the choir of Canterbury Cathedral, the transepts of Ripon, the western tower and transept of Ely, the western transept of Peterborough, the nave of Malmesbury, portions of Fountains, Kirkstall, Glastonbury, and Buildwas Abbeys, New Shoreham Church, Sussex, the retro-choir of Chichester Cathedral, the two western bays of the nave at Worcester, and the " Round " of the Temple Church, London. Consult paper, " Transitional," read before the St Paul's Ecclesiological Society by John P. Seddon, 7th May 1879, printed in the Society's Transactions.

Transom.
Fr. *traverse ;*
Germ.
querbalken
(cross-beam).
A horizontal mullion in windows, much used in the Third Pointed or Perpendicular style. The most ancient examples of transoms are found in the Early English style (as at Witney and Bampton, Oxon.), at which period they were mere straight bars of stone, and, except in unglazed windows of very great length, were introduced but once in the height of the opening. In the Decorated style the use of transoms increased, and examples of them in the unglazed openings of towers and spires are by no means uncommon, as in the churches of Exton, Rutland; St Mary, Stamford; King's Sutton, Northants; and St Mary, Oxford. In glazed church windows they were still very rarely employed, though they

may be seen in the cathedral at Bristol. In the Perpendicular style the use of transoms was very general in windows of all kinds ; they were often repeated several times in the height, and were also sometimes introduced in the tracery.

Transverse-triapsal. The term applied by Professor Whewell (Master of Trinity, Cambridge, 1841–1866) to churches with three apses, two of which end the transepts, and are consequently transverse. It is used by the Rev. Benjamin Webb in his " Sketches of Continental Ecclesiology, or Church Notes in Belgium, Germany, and Italy " (1848).

Treasurer. Lat. *Thesaurarius.* A dignitary to whose stall duties are attached in certain Cathedrals of the Old Foundation. At St Paul's his stall is the fourth on the south side on entering the choir from the west, but since 1882 his duties have been discharged by one of the residentiaries. Before the Reformation his office was one of considerable importance at St Paul's ; as elsewhere, he had the custody of all the goods of the church, such as the relics, books, sacred vessels, vestments, altarfrontals, and the multifarious *instrumenta* of divine worship. He appointed the sacrist (*q.v.*) as his deputy. Walcott (" Cathedralia," 57–61) gives minute details of the duties of both these officers in the English and Continental cathedrals. The present statutes of Hereford thus define the Treasurer's duties. He " shall be the Treasurer and Receiver of the Cathedral, and shall, as such, keep a full and true account of the property used in the Cathedral in such form as the Dean and Chapter shall from time to time appoint," etc. The statutes of Wells say, " He shall have supervision of receipts and expenditure, and advise the Chapter concerning the same. He shall have special charge of the bells, ornaments, utensils, and books, and all other things in the church, and shall be responsible for the good order of the church and its precincts." At Exeter he is to have " special charge of the bells, ornaments, utensils, furniture, and books, except such as are under the care of the Precentor or Chancellor, and the ordering of the seats in the church, and shall be responsible for the good order of the precinct of the Close." At Salisbury " he shall hold the ancient office of Communar, and, as such, he shall act as Bursar of the body. He shall also have charge of the muniments." At Lichfield he was called Perpetual Sacristan. The office does not exist now at York, where it became obsolete after the Reformation ; or at Lincoln, being dissolved at the same period ; or at Lichfield. In Cathedrals of the New Foundation the Treasurer is a canon, and elected annually, but not a

ECCLESIASTICAL TERMS

dignitary ; acting as the paymaster, the sacristan, and master of the fabric.

Trefoil. An ornamental foliation or feathering used in Gothic architecture in the heads of window lights, tracery, panellings, etc., in which the spaces between the cusps represent the form of a three-lobed leaf.

Triforium. A generic term applied to the storey in a large church, intermediate between the arcade separating the nave from its aisles and the clerestory. Only when this forms a passage-way is this term strictly appropriate, as in many cases in Germany this space presents merely a shallow arcading or perfectly plain surface intended for pictorial enrichment. In France this storey, which appears in its most developed form in the Early Gothic churches of the north-east, is styled the Tribune, and in Germany, where its use seems confined almost exclusively to the Rhine Provinces, the " Männerchor " (q.v.). The definition " thoroughfare " is expressive, but must be accepted with caution. At Rochester, Rouen, Eu (the two last in Normandy), and at the cathedrals of Genoa and Modena in Italy, the triforium has no flooring, but is open to the side aisles.

Troperium. One of the English pre-Reformation service-books. It contained the sequences (q.v.), and was required only when they were not to be found in the Graduale or Antiphonarium.

Tufa.
Fr. tuf ;
Ita. tufo. A porous stone deposited by calcareous waters : when compact it is called travertine. Some of the streams in Gloucestershire deposit tufa, and it is there known by the name of puff-stone. It is used principally for vaulting on account of its lightness.

Tunicle. The vestment worn by the sub-deacon at the Holy Eucharist. It is similar to the dalmatic, (q.v.) only shorter and smaller.

Turba. The chorus part, or voice of the multitude, in a setting of the " Passion Music." The responses of the turba, or crowd, in Christopher Tye's setting of the " Passion according to St John " is a remarkable composition for its period (sixteenth century). The great double choruses of the same kind in Bach's " St Matthew Passion " are marvellous in their construction and effect. In Greene's anthem, "My God, my God, look upon me," published in 1743, the chorus for four voices, " He trusted in God," is most dramatic, and suggests the *Turba*.

A DICTIONARY OF

Turning the Books. The technical term in cathedrals for marking the places in the music-books of the precentor, minor canons, vicars choral, organist, choristers, etc. This is generally performed by one or more of the chorister-boys, who are called "book-turners." When, during the earlier years of her reign, Queen Victoria attended the Sunday morning service at St George's Chapel, Windsor, the head boy went up to the royal closet, on the north side near the altar, and handed an anthem-book to her Majesty. This, and " turning " her books before the service, constituted a much-esteemed privilege. At Lichfield the boys " turn " the books vested in surplice and cassock. At St Paul's this duty is performed by the junior verger. At Salisbury, in 1884, £85 per annum were paid to a superannuated lay vicar, on condition of his " turning " the cathedral music, attending the cathedral service once every week-day and twice on Sundays. He was also clerk of the cathedral and " church pricker," or registrar of attendance of those in choir (Report of Her Majesty's Commissioners upon the Cathedral Church of Salisbury, 1884).

Tuscan Order. The simplest of the five orders of Classical architecture. It was unknown to the Greeks, and by many is considered only as a Roman variety of the Doric Order (q.v.). The capital has a square abacus, with a small projecting fillet on the upper edge ; the shaft is never fluted ; and the base consists of a square plinth and a large torus or moulding. Some authorities consider that the Tuscan is not entitled to rank as a distinct order, being, in fact, nothing more than a simplified, if not a spurious and debased, variety of the Doric. The finest of the few examples of Tuscan employed for the ecclesiastical architecture of this country is Inigo Jones's portico of St Paul's, Covent Garden. Consult Smith, " Synopsis of the Origin and Progress of Architecture " (1831) ; Leeds, " The Orders and their Æsthetic Principles " (1848).

Tympanum. See *sub voce* " Lintel."

Veni, Creator Spiritus. The Latin title of the two hymns given in the services for the Ordering of Priests and the Consecration of Bishops. The English translation of one begins " Come, Holy Ghost, our souls inspire," and that of the other, " Come, Holy Ghost, Eternal God." Of these the second is alone given in the book of 1549 ; the first was not inserted until 1661. The second hymn, now only used as an alternative, appears to have been introduced into the Ordinal of the Western Church late in the eleventh century. Its composition has been attributed to St Ambrose, but it is not claimed by his Benedictine

308

editors. It may be assigned to Rhabanus Maurus, abbot and bishop of the ninth century. Of the first hymn, the authorship has been attributed by the hymnologists Mone and Wackernagel to Gregory the Great (540-604). It is more concise than the second, which is diffuse and paraphrastic. The first music we have to the longer hymn is by Tallis, being one of the nine tunes contributed by him to Archbishop Parker's Psalter in 1560. It is now commonly known as "Tallis's Ordinal," and it is one of the very few specimens from the old harmonists which can be used at the present day without inversion—the melody being given to the treble, and not, as formerly the custom, to the tenor. Notwithstanding the great reputation of its composer, the tune appears to have been consigned to oblivion during a long period. It is neither in the collections of Ravenscroft (1621), Playford (1686), nor the "Harmonia Perfecta" (1730), nor can it be traced in any of the numerous collections of the eighteenth century. The Rev. W. H. Havergal seems to have been the first in modern times to call attention to it, and in his "Old Church Psalmody" (1847) passes the high encomium—"A child may sing the tune, while manly genius will admire it." This "Ordinal" will be found in "Hymns, Ancient and Modern" (edition of 1889), set to hymns 72, 78, and 208. Those responsible for the selection of music sung at the Church Pageant in June 1909 apparently overlooked the fact that the first music for the English translation of this hymn was composed by Tallis, for, in the scene representing the consecration of Archbishop Parker at Lambeth Palace, in 1559, the four concluding verses of the *Veni Creator* were sung to an adaptation from Psalm 132 in Day's Psalter, 1563, a tune which occurs several times in "Hymns, Ancient and Modern" with the title of St Flavian. Thus a most interesting association of music with words was lost sight of. There are good modern settings of the hymn by John Hopkins, late organist of Rochester Cathedral, and Mr Arthur Henry Brown, the latter in anthem form. Gilbert Heathcote, Archdeacon of Winchester, set the hymn to music about 1800. In the Prayer-Book of 1549 and 1552 this hymn is directed to be used after the Gospel. It was removed to its present place—before the prayer which precedes the imposition of hands—in the book of 1661. At the same time the shorter hymn, "Come, Holy Ghost, our souls inspire" was inserted, the longer paraphrase, now seldom used, being regarded (as already mentioned) as an alternative. Our present translation is that of John Cosin, Prebendary of Durham (1626), afterwards (1660) Bishop. It will be found in "The Manner of the Coronation of King Charles I. of England at Westminster,

2nd February 1626," edited for the Henry Bradshaw Liturgical
Text Society, 1892. Here it was written on one leaf (p. 69) in the
King's book, as a supplement or appendix, the preceding page (68)
being left blank. A very poor translation, probably the work of one
of the Reformers, was used at the Coronation of Queen Victoria
in 1838, and at some of the previous Hanoverian sovereigns. In 1838
it was sung to the " Grand Chant," usually considered as the composition of Pelham Humphreys, *temp.* Charles II. The *Veni Creator*
was the hymn appointed for use at the first Vespers of Whitsun Day,
at those of the feast itself, and until the Friday following. It was
also the hymn at Terce throughout the week. The traditional
plain-song melody varies in many choral-books. That now most
generally accepted is given in "Hymns, Ancient and Modern,"
and to this version it was sung with Cosin's translation, at the corona-
of our late King. Many English Church composers have reset
the hymn primarily for use at ordinations, and consecrations of
bishops. Among the most noteworthy of such compositions are
those of the Rev. Tobias Langdon, *c.* 1680; Dr Richard Woodward,
1767 ; Dr William Boyce, 1769 ; Dr Philip Hayes, 1783 ; Thomas
Garland, *c.* 1790 ; James Targett, 1800 ; Richard Bellamy, *c.* 1790 ;
Thomas Attwood, 1831 ; Dr Joseph Pring, 1805 ; Dr John Smith
of Dublin, 1828 ; A. T. Corfe (arranged from Handel), *c.* 1830 ;
George Bates, 1840; J. L. Hatton, 1864; Rev. Sir Frederick A.
Gore Ouseley, 1868 ; Sir George Elvey, 1871 ; Sir Robert Stewart,
1872, and Dr E. G. Monk, the last-named being for men's voices and
four-part chorus. Ouseley's setting is alternately for bishop and
choir. Settings by living writers are those of Frederick Cambridge,
Thomas Adams, and C. Lee Williams. A setting printed anonymously in Ed. Lowe's (organist of Christ Church Cathedral, Oxford)
" Review of Brief Directions for the Performance of Choral Service "
(1664) was reprinted by Dr Crotch in his " Collection of Old Psalm
Tunes " in 1803, and again in 1807. Crotch attributed it to Tallis,
but on what authority does not appear. It is not to be found among
any of his compositions, set either to English or Latin words. It
may be Lowe's own composition, although its style very much
resembles that of his contemporary at Oxford, Benjamin Rogers,
organist of Magdalen College. Its first publication in vocal score after
Lowe's arrangement (Crotch's being merely for a treble and bass,
figured) seems to have been in *The Parish Choir*, July 1847. It was
sung in this form at the memorable consecration of the bishops of
Adelaide, Melbourne, Newcastle and Capetown, at Westminster
Abbey, on the previous St Peter's Day (29th June). There is an

ECCLESIASTICAL TERMS

arrangement for the *Veni Creator* from the *Magnificat Tertii Toni,* contained in the work " Magnificat Octo Tonorum," published by Palestrina in 1591. This was made by Thomas Ingram, organist of All Souls', Langham Place, and an active member of the Motett Society. It was first printed in " Select Anthems for Church Choirs," edited by Ingram, and published by George Bell, 186 Fleet Street, 1850. About the same time it appeared in a collection of metrical psalmody, given as one of the musical supplements to *The Parish Choir.* This adaptation was first sung at the Consecration of Dr Fulford, as Bishop of Montreal, in Westminster Abbey, St James's Day, 25th July 1850. There is a garbled version set to the Easter Hymn, " The strife is o'er " in " Hymns, Ancient and Modern." Palestrina's own setting of the hymn for four voices will be found in the eighth volume of Breitkopf and Härtel's edition of his complete works. Dryden's paraphrase of the *Veni Creator,* beginning, " Creator Spirit, by whose aid," was set by Ralph Banks, organist of Rochester Cathedral, and included in a volume of his Cathedral Music, published after his death in 1841. Another paraphrase, beginning " Come, Holy Ghost, Creator come," will be found amongst the metrical psalmody appended to many old editions of the present Book of Common Prayer. Vincent Novello (1781-1861) set this version in its entirety as " A Hymn for Whitsuntide." The fifth stanza, " Drive far from us the mortal foe," etc., a smooth and melodious piece of four-part writing, eminently characteristic of its composer, was published in *The Musical Times* of February 1862. There is a questionable adaptation of the same version to John Dowland's madrigal " Awake, sweet love "(!) It was printed in *The Musical Times* of June 1864.

    This, known to mediæval writers as the " Golden Sequence," was the composition of King Robert II. of France. It is the sequence **Veni, Sancte** for the Feast of Pentecost. The plain-song melody **Spiritus.** from the Mechlin Gradual, with harmonies by the Rev. S. S. Greatheed, will be found in the " Hymnal Noted " (1858). There are translations by various hands. That in " Hymns, Ancient and Modern " is mainly by the Rev. Edward Caswall. The tune to which it is there set is by Samuel Webbe, originally published, and fitted to the original Latin, in his " Collection of Motetts and Antiphons, for one, two, three and four Voices, or Chorus" (1792). Sir George Martin's masterly setting, originally composed for the Latin service at the Opening of Convocation of the Province of Canterbury in St Paul's Cathedral, 30th April 1880, has been republished with a very spirited translation by the

Rev. W. Russell, sometime Minor Canon and Succentor of St Paul's and, since 1898, Vicar of Sunbury-on-Thames.

Venite, exultemus Domino. The 95th Psalm (" O come, let us sing unto the Lord "). This has been sung in the Western Church from a very remote period, before the Psalms of the first nocturn at Matins. It has generally been termed the Invitatory Psalm. The Invitatory (*Venite, adoremus*) was an antiphon sung before it, and repeated in part or entirely after each verse. The rubric of 1549 directed it to be " sung without any Invitatory " (see *s.v.* " Invitatory "). St Athanasius says that before the beginning of their prayers the Christians (of Constantinople) invited and exhorted one another in the words of this Psalm. In Henry VIII.'s Prymer it is entitled " A Song stirring to the praise of God." Merbecke noted the first verse only of the *Venite* to the 8th Tone, 1st Ending, with this brief direction : " And so forth wyth the rest of the Psalmes as they be appoynted." Thus, the most important section of the Prayer-Book left untouched by Merbecke was the Psalter. Just 300 years later this unaccountable omission was rectified by the Rev. Thos. Helmore in his " Directory of Plainsong," which included the " Psalter Noted." Ed. Lowe in his " Directions " (1661) provides a chant for the *Venite* for each day of the week, and these chants (all Gregorian Tones) are to be sung to the whole of the Psalms, " for sides "—*i.e.* by *Decani* and *Cantoris,* or antiphonally. Playford, in the " Order of Performing the Divine Service in Cathedrals and Collegiate Chapels," prefixed to his " Introduction to the Skill of Practical Music " (1674-1730), gives a similar weekly selection for the *Venite,* but his tones vary from those of Lowe, and he adds the " Canterbury " and " Imperial " tunes in four parts as " proper for choirs to sing the Psalms, Te Deum, Benedictus or Jubilate, to the Organ, or sometimes without it." Many of our earlier Church writers set the *Venite* in an ornate way—that is, anthemwise, like the *Te Deum* and the rest of the canticles, and the Psalms used as such. Specimens exist from the time of Tallis down to that of Dr Child in the reign of Charles I., but few have been printed in the collections of cathedral music made by various hands. Ouseley (" Cathedral Services by English Masters," 1853) printed that in C by Thos. Tomkins from a complete Service in his " Musica Deo Sacra," 1656, and Rimbault that in the Dorian Mode by Adrian Batten, in *The Choir,* 21st November 1863. At the Restoration, when the choral service was resumed, this practice of setting the *Venite* appears to have been dropped, and there are no more examples until almost our own day,

ECCLESIASTICAL TERMS

when it is met with in the services of C. E. Stephens in F (1847), J. L. Hatton in E (1855), and Sir Frederick Ouseley in C (1856). Amongst the unpublished compositions of Sir Robert Stewart (Professor of Music in the University of Dublin, 1862-1894) there is a *Venite* constructed in the sixteenth-century manner, the style being a very clever imitation of that of Tallis. A writer in *The Parish Choir*, February 1848, observes : " We once, and once only, heard the *Venite* sung (and very well sung) to a varied composition like a ' Service,' with solos, duets, etc. This was in the Church of St Saviour, Southwark, where considerable pains are taken with the music, although not in quite so church-like a manner as we should like." On the whole, it is well that the setting of the *Venite* " service-wise " has not found much favour. The invitatory character of the Psalm implies that it should be sung to a chant, in which all can join, rather than to variable strains. Where Anglican chants are the rule, a single chant should be used for preference.

The official who carries the silver mace before the dean and canons in a cathedral or collegiate church. As the word is derived from *virga*, a rod, it clearly ought to be spelt " virger."

Verger, or Virger. In most cathedrals the dean has his own virger and the canons have theirs. The number on the foundation varies in the different cathedrals. At St Paul's there are four, including the dean's virger. At Salisbury there are three. Other cathedrals have two, and some only one. The dean's virger of St Paul's is Ostiarius, or doorkeeper, of the Lower House of Convocation. Many persons seems to imagine that the office of virger is one of " Protestant " institution. It is nothing whatever of the kind. At Wells in 1338 the order of procession was : *virgers*, choristers, sub-deacon, deacon, priest vicars, canons, dean, bishop, archdeacons, and chaplains. As early as 1465 virgers' staves were of silver. William Gregory in his quaint " Chronicle of London," printed by the Camden Society, tells us (p. 231) that " Befor thys time . . . Docter Ive kept the scholys at Poulys [*i.e.* the ancient School of St Paul's, for Dean Colet's school was not founded till 1512] that ys undye yᵉ Chapter House, and there he redde many full notyble lessonys to prove that Cryste was lord of alle and noo beggar, and he dyd hyt after yᵉ forme of scholys, for he hadde hys abyte and hys pelyon [his habit and his furred gown] and a vyrger with a sylvyr rodde waytynge uppon hym." Mr Edwin Freshfield in his interesting book, " Notes on Church Plate," gives us some particulars of the silver staves carried by the virgers of St Paul's. Three of these are plain rods, thirty-four inches long, tapering from

313

a circular knob at the base to an acorn at the top. The staff of the preacher's virger has the date mark for 1781, and a maker's mark, " H.B.," possibly Hester Bateman. The canon's and junior virger's staves are like it and probably of the same date, but the marks are effaced. The mace of the dean's virger has the date mark for 1782, and a maker's mark, " B.D." It is about forty-six inches long, more substantial than the others, and the knob at the base is rather more elaborate. In place of the acorn at the top, there is a disc with the exterior of St Paul's in relief on one side, and inscribed round it is " Virga Decani Ecclesiæ Cathedralis Sancti Pauli Lond. John Lingard, 1 June 1798." On the other side are the arms of the dean and chapter, the two swords in saltire, with the letter D, and the same inscription with the name of E. M. Cummings, 1845. Round the base of the wand is inscribed, " R. R. Green, Vergifer Decani, 5 July 1871." Mr James Brown, appointed November 1899, *vice* R. R. Green resigned, is the present holder. By a Minute of Chapter, 22nd June 1871, it was agreed that " on the promotion of Robert Russell Green to be Dean's Virger, and the appointment of a successor to Green, the virges belonging to Cummings' executors, and to Green, be purchased by the Dean and Chapter, and that for the future the Dean and Chapter provide virges and gowns for each virger on his appointment ; such virge and gown to remain the property of the Dean and Chapter." At the Chapel Royal, St James's, the title of the virger is Sergeant of the Vestry. In many of the foreign cathedrals virgers are to be seen, wearing their black gowns, and carrying their silver maces, as in ours. Usually they wear, in addition, a black skull cap. In Wild's fine coloured drawing of the interior of the nave of Amiens Cathedral, in which the clergy and others are depicted as leaving the choir after High Mass, the virger is shown, preceded by the two " Suisses," or beadles, and followed by the crucifer and taper-bearers. He also appears in a drawing of the interior of the Church of St Ouen, by the same artist. The Archbishop of Canterbury has his virger or " apparitor," who attends him on certain occasions at St Paul's and elsewhere. The silver mace of this official is surmounted by a mitre. In some of our cathedrals—Chichester, Lichfield, Wells, and Worcester, among the number—it is the custom for the virgers of the dean and canon-in-residence to proceed a few minutes before the beginning of each service to the houses of those dignitaries, in order to escort them in their robes across the close, or through the cloisters to the Cathedral. At Lincoln the dean's virger waits for the dean at the door of the north-west transept and precedes him to the south aisle of the choir for the preliminary prayer. The other dignitaries are similarly met by their virger at the western end of the nave. At Ely, whenever the Lord Bishop attends the service, he is met by the virger at the Galilee Porch and escorted through the vast length of the nave to the choir. At the conclusion of the service the same proceeding is observed. At King's College, Cambridge, after service, the chapel virger precedes the Provost or Fellow-in-Residence through the ante-chapel to the south-west door. Formerly, at Eton, when the Provost of King's and two " Posers " arrived by road from Cambridge in full academicals, to examine at " Election " time, they were met at the gate by the chapel virger with his silver mace who led the potentate and his suite across the school yard to the entrance of the cloisters, where they were received by the Provost of Eton. It was once the custom for the two provosts to kiss when they met, but this fell into desuetude after the death of Dr Hodgson in 1840, his successor, Dr Hawtrey simply greeting Dr Okes, the Provost of King's in 1858, with a bland smile and shake of the hand. The custody of the material fabric of a cathedral devolves in a great measure upon virgers, a most useful body of men. Their duties, besides those already mentioned, consist in assisting at all services, ordinary and extraordinary, in cathedrals ; in preserving order during the services, and at all other times ; in acting as guides to visitors ; and in superintending all persons engaged in cleaning or arranging the cathedral. At St Paul's, the duties of the virgers— *servientes, virgiferarii*, as they were called—are set forth at some length in the Statutes of St Paul's, compiled by Deans Baldock and Lisieux ; the former of whom held the deanery from 1294 to 1305, the latter from 1441 to 1456. The method of their selection was that upon a vacancy amongst the virgers, the Treasurer nominated a fit and proper person to the Dean, by whom the appointment made by the Treasurer was confirmed. Dr Simpson (" Gleanings from Old St Paul's," ch. v.) gives an account of their multifarious labours in the form of a translation from Baldock's Statutes, as well as a *resumé* of a very interesting Note Book, kept by Michael Shaller, one of the virgers of St Paul's, and " Vnderchamberlein " to the " Deane and chapiter," 1566. This Note Book is preserved in the Cathedral Library. Baldock's Statute entitled *De Servientibus*, printed by Dr Simpson in his *Registrum Statutorum et Consuetudinum Ecclesiae Cathedralis Sancti Pauli Londinensis* (1873) was repealed in 1878, and a new Statute concerning the virgers was made. One rule was that the whole time of the virgers should be devoted to their duties in the cathedral. In the Appendix to his *Registrum*

(1897) Dr Simpson prints a list of the virgers of St Paul's from the year 1661. At the present day our noble Cathedral of St Paul is fortunate in possessing in its four virgers, Messrs Brown, Skinner, Powell and Mauler, men so painstaking, well-informed, obliging and attentive, and, at the same time, knowing thoroughly well how to combine the *suaviter in modo* with the *fortiter in re*. The same remarks, it may be safely affirmed, will apply equally to the cathedral virgers all over England at the present day. When, after the Restoration (1660), the dean and prebendaries of Worcester began " to resettle the church in its service, and also to repair the same by degrees, which hardly £10,000 will put the whole fabric in that order it was before the barbarous civil wars," two silver virges were " bought of Nat. Potter at yᵉ Bunch of Grapes in Cheapside, £5 " (Noake, " Monastery and Cathedral of Worcester," 1866). In the Inventory of St Peter Mancroft, Norwich, printed by J. C. Micklethwaite (" Ornaments of the Rubric." Alcuin Club, Longmans, 1897), is mentioned " a virge of silver with the cross keys and the mitre on top." The Rev. Percy Dearmer, in his " Parson's Handbook," tells us (p. 142) that the virger's gown is a very ancient garment, and that the present tendency to put the virger into a cassock is much to be regretted.

Verse. From the Latin *versiculus*, a short sentence. This word, as opposed to " full," signifies such portions of a service or anthem as are sung by a single voice to each part. In the Latin rite the term is used to distinguish the short sentences said by the hebdomadarius from those sung by the choir ; hence it came to signify the portions of a service or anthem which are allotted to the principal voices. In the Services of certain of our composers the verses are directed to be sung antiphonally— that is, by the select voices on the *Decani* and *Cantoris* sides of the choir. In such verses the direction " both sides " may sometimes be met with. This means that both choirs of *select* voices are to sing the portions so marked, but by many who have the direction of our choirs it is frequently taken to mean that the *whole* choir is to join in. Examples of verses so constructed may be seen in the passages, " And thou, child, shalt be called the Prophet of the Highest," in Hopkins' *Benedictus* in F, and " We believe that Thou shalt come to be our Judge," in Croft's *Te Deum* in B minor. When the composer's intentions are properly carried out the effect is very beautiful : otherwise it is entirely lost.

ECCLESIASTICAL TERMS

One that *begins* with portions intended by the composer to be sung by a single voice to a part, the word " verse " probably meaning **Verse Anthem.** a turn of thought to be forcibly or clearly expressed, a change of treatment or sentiment properly echoed in the style of the music. The words of the " verse " are often chosen from portions of Scripture other than the main body of the anthem by way of gloss. The chief voices on one side, *Decani* or *Cantoris*, usually sing the " verse," and the whole choir the chorus or " full " part. The verse anthem in its best period, from the time of the Restoration to the beginning of the nineteenth century, is exemplified in the compositions of Humphreys, Blow, Wise, Purcell, Clark, Croft, Weldon, Greene, Boyce, Hayes, Dupuis, Arnold, Battishill, Pring, Crotch, Sir John Stevenson, and Attwood. In a lighter style are the compositions, in like form, of Kent, Nares, Ebdon, and Clarke Whitfeld.

Short or diminutive verses, said alternately by the officiant and choir or people, such as those following the Lord's Prayer at its **Versicles.** second repetition at Matins and Evensong. The versicles, properly so called, with their responses, are in most instances passages from the Psalms, and are thus distinguished from other suffrages, which are neither verses from the Psalms, nor form in each petition and response a continuous sentence. In the Litany, the two versicles with their responses, " O Lord, deal not with us after our sins," and " O Lord, let Thy mercy be shewed upon us," are distinguished from the other suffrages (in the Litany) by having the words *Priest* and *Answer* prefixed ; and by each being a verse from the Psalms. Till the last review (1662) these had been always prefaced in the English Litany, since the Reformation, by the words "The Versicles" (see also *sub voce* " Preces "). One of the most interesting of the lectures given by the late Sir John Stainer, while Professor of Music at Oxford, was that delivered in the Sheldonian Theatre, 5th December 1894. On that occasion the Professor took as his subject " The Musical Treatment of the Versicles and Responses, etc., of the Prayer-Book." The lecture itself does not appear to have been printed, but the examples by which it was musically illustrated were lithographed by the firm of Dinham & Blyth, 28 Fenchurch Street, and are probably still to be had. Among these examples was a very noble twofold " Amen after the Third Collect," by William Byrd. When Byrd wrote, both Matins and Evensong ended with the Third Collect. The prayers for the sovereign, royal family, clergy, and people, the Prayer of St Chrysostom, and the Apostolic Benediction, were not added until

1662. In the Prayer-Book for Scotland (1637) a rubric was added after the Third Collect of Matins and Evensong, directing our present usage : " After this Collect ended, followeth the Litany : and if the Litany be not appointed to be said or sung that morning, then shall next be said the Prayers for the King's Majesty, with the rest of the prayers following at the end of the Litany, and the Benediction." Thus, although this conclusion of our service is of so late introduction, it belongs to a time when ancient customs were quite well understood. According to the old offices, such prayers would be termed Memoriæ, or Commendations, *de Pace, de Gratia, pro Rege*, etc. For the sources and musical treatment of our versicles and responses, consult Stainer's examples *ut supra* ; also Jebb's " Choral Service of the Church " (1843) and the same writer's " Choral Responses and Litanies " (1847–1857).

A name applied by Albert Durer to a pointed oval figure in the shape of a bladder (*vesica*), and formed by two equal circles cutting each other in their centres. It is a very common form

Vesica, or given to the *aureole* or *glory*, by which the representa-
Vesica Piscis. tions of the Three Persons of the Holy Trinity and the Blessed Virgin are surrounded in the mosaics, sculptures, or paintings of the Middle Ages. " It has been conjectured," says Parker (" Glossary of Architecture "), " that it was adopted from the idea that this figure is symbolical and significant of the Greek word ἰχθύς (a fish), which contains the initial letters and titles of the Saviour ; this form, however, is by no means always given to the aureole, and the idea of any peculiar symbolical meaning being attached to it appears to have been adapted almost exclusively by English antiquaries." The seals and crests of cathedral, monastic, and collegiate establishments, as well as those of bishops, are frequently in the form of a vesica. The seal of the ancient College of Minor Canons of St Paul's is circular. See also *sub voce* " Fish."

One of the greater canonical hours : the evening service corresponding to the *Lucernarium* of the early Christians. The usual hour

Vespers. for Vespers in religious houses is 6 P.M., but in the cathedrals they are now sung or recited at 2, 2.30, or
Lat. *vesperae ;* more generally 3, following None. Sometimes they
Fr. *vêpres ;* take the form of a special or late evening service at
Germ. *vesper.* 7 or 8 o'clock. In the offices of the last three days of Holy Week Vespers follow immediately after High Mass. The office consists of five Psalms, with antiphons, a short chapter of Holy Scripture, the office hymn, the *Magnificat*, and

ECCLESIASTICAL TERMS

collects. On Sundays the Psalms (109 to 114) are always the same. On week-days, or when a Holy Day falls on a Sunday, they are varied. The arrangements may, however, easily be followed by means of a breviary and calendar. Vespers, like all the other "Hours," are prefaced by the versicles and responses: "Deus in adjutorium meum intende" ("O God, make speed to save me"), and "Domine ad adjuvandum me festina" ("O Lord, make haste to help me"), followed by the "Gloria Patri" and "Alleluia" or "Laus tibi, Domine, Rex eternæ gloriæ," much as in our own office. Matins have, in addition, the versicle, "Domine, labia mea aperies" ("O Lord, open Thou my lips"), with its response, "Et os meum annuntiabit laudem Tuam," ("And my mouth shall show forth Thy praise"). Our Church still calls her Vesper office, as she did of old, by the good old Saxon name of "Evensong." The Vesper Psalms for Sundays and Ferias, pointed to the eight Gregorian Tones, have been edited by the Rev. G. H. Palmer (Wantage, 1890).

The assistants or deputies of the canons or prebendaries in Cathedrals of the Old Foundation, in the discharge of those duties, **Vicars Choral.** especially, though not exclusively, those performed in the choir, as distinguished from those belonging to the altar and the pulpit. The vicars choral, as their name implies, were originally appointed to provide for the absence or incapacity of the great body of capitular members ; the clerical vicars to chant in rotation the prayers at Matins and Evensong, etc., and the whole body to form a sufficient and permanent choir for the performance of the daily service ; a duty which the canons were originally required to perform in person. The presbyteral members were usually four, being the vicars of the four dignitaries, *personae principales*—dean, precentor, chancellor, and treasurer. Sometimes (as at Lichfield) they were five, but they are now reduced there to four. The fifth was called the Prebendary of Offley's Vicar. The rest were deacons and in minor orders, in later times they were laymen. In all Cathedrals of the Old Foundation, including St Patrick's Cathedral, Dublin, and all the Irish Cathedrals, where there were choirs, the vicars choral formed a minor corporation ; in some way under the control of the dean and chapter, but with separate estates, with collegiate buildings, halls, and chapels, some of which still exist. Their presidents are styled custos or warden, sub-dean, and sub-chanter. At St Paul's there were originally thirty vicars, one for each prebendary. Their dress was a surplice and a cope. In Dean Colet's time (1510) their number had, somehow or other, dwindled down to six laymen. These, with the twelve minor canons, constituted the adult choir until far on into the last century. In 1873, by which time the minor canons had ceased to have any direct musical connection with the choir, additional lay singers were engaged until the number was gradually raised to twelve. They received the title of assistant vicars choral. At Chichester the vicars choral were incorporated, 1334, and confirmed in 1464. At Lincoln they were first established by Bishop Hugh, and were incorporated, 1441. At Lichfield they were incorporated in 1240 ; at Salisbury in 1410 ; at Wells in 1223. At Hereford the charter of incorporation was granted to the vicars choral by Richard II., 6th September 1396. In 1534 there were a custos, or warden, and twenty-six vicars. In 1583 this number was reduced to twelve, but before the Civil War there were sixteen, all graduates, and in Holy Orders. From 1660 to 1840 twelve vicars choral, all in Holy Orders, were constantly engaged in the daily service. The organists, Hugh Davis (1630), John Badham (1661), Henry Hall, sen. (1688), and Richard Clack (1754–1779), were members of the college and consequently in Orders. The Service in E flat, by Dr John Clarke Whitfeld, organist from 1820 to 1832, composed in May 1826 but not published till 1863, bears on the original MS. score a dedication to " his kind friends, the Custos and Vicars of the College, Hereford." By the Act 3 & 4 Vict. c. 113, the number of twelve vicars was reduced to six, but arrangements were made between 1865 and 1868 for the gradual restoration of the full number. In 1869 there were a custos, three vicars choral, and six assistant priest vicars. Previous to 1840, as aforesaid, the adult portion of the choir of Hereford Cathedral was composed *solely* of the priest vicars choral, who corresponded in number with the twelve minor canons of St Paul's. In consequence of the great reduction in the members of the college after 1840, it became necessary to secure further vocal assistance, when a staff of lay singers was engaged by the dean and chapter, the custos and vicars choral paying a fixed sum towards their support. In Cathedrals of the New Foundation the title of vicar choral was generally superseded by that of minor canon for the clergy, and lay clerk for the laity. The college for the vicars choral remains at Wells on the north side of the church, with its hall, chapel, and library, and forty chambers of two rooms each, arranged in an elongated court. At Hereford it forms a fine Perpendicular quadrangle, with rooms over a cloister, a chapel, hall, and library, south of the choir, and approached by a covered way and small gatehouse. The bedern at York on the east, and portions of the colleges at Chichester and Lincoln remain on the south. The halls remain at Chichester, with the pulpit, chamber for the table furniture, and lavatory of the fourteenth century, and at Exeter, 1388. At Old St Paul's the College of Minor Canons lay to the north of the cathedral, adjoining Pardon Church Haugh (or Yard). The house was called "Pettie Canons." The thirty vicars also had their common hall. After the Great Fire, houses were built for the minor canons in a court at the extreme south-west corner of St Paul's Churchyard. This was called St Paul's College. The first minor canon who went to reside there in 1682 was the Rev. James Clifford. Those of the minor canons, who chose, lived there until early in the last century, when the locality disappeared to make way for some "improvements." A collection of madrigals, made by the Rev. Richard Webb, minor canon, is dated "St Paul's College, 12th May 1808." At Lichfield and Salisbury (both Cathedrals of the Old Foundation) one of the lay vicars choral is organist and master of the choristers. At St Paul's one of the vicars choral was organist until the retirement of Sir John Stainer in 1888. At Lichfield, in 1863, the general chapter, with the assent of Bishop Lonsdale, revised the cathedral statutes, so far as they affected the vicars choral, and did the utmost which, after taking legal advice, seemed possible in order to correct abuses which had crept in among the occupants of these freehold offices. In 1876, the vicars choral handed over their estates, except some houses in the close, to the Ecclesiastical Commissioners, receiving in lieu a fixed money payment. "Under this changed condition of affairs," wrote Dean Bickersteth to the Commissioners in 1879, "it is worthy of consideration whether provision should not be made for further alterations, which might enable the dean and chapter to exercise a sufficient control over the discipline and general efficiency of the cathedral body. The example of St Paul's Cathedral is sufficient to show the advantages which would ensue from the arrangements here suggested" (Report on Lichfield Cathedral, 1884).

The sequence for Easter Day ; one of the five sequences retained in the Church of Rome. The first line runs thus : " Victimæ Paschali laudes immolent Christiani " (" To the Paschal **Victimæ** Victim, Christians, bring the sacrifice of praise "). **Paschali.** Like the Christmas motett, *Quem vidistis pastores*, it partakes of the dramatic, introducing, as interlocutors, Mary, who returns from the Sepulchre, and the Disciples, who question her what she has seen. The traditional plain-song melody, with harmonies by Charles Child Spencer and the Rev. S. S. Greatheed, is given in the " Hymnal Noted " (1852), the translation being that of the Rev. J. M. Neale. Among polyphonic settings the most celebrated are those of Palestrina (sixteenth century), Simonelli (seventeenth century), Jommelli (eighteenth century), and H. G. Nixon (early nineteenth century). A modern setting with English words, for use as an Easter anthem, is from the facile yet masterly pen of Mr John E. West. The " Hymnary " (1872) contains a setting in hymn-tune form by Dr Gauntlett.

The evenings before certain feast days are observed as fasts. In former days it was customary to have religious services on these
Vigils. eves, and sometimes to spend a great part of the night in prayer and other devotions, to qualify the soul for the better observance of the festival itself on the morrow. These nights thus spent were called *vigils* or *watchings*, from the Latin *vigilare*, to watch. They are still observed in the Church of England to prepare us for the proper observance of these feasts in a spirit of sober joy ; and as teaching us that we must *suffer* here in order to *rejoice* hereafter. They are symbolical of the sorrows of Our Lord's earthly life, and of the probation which the saints underwent before they were fitted to reign with Christ. Every festival has not a vigil preceding it. Those appointed by the Church are as follows :— before the Nativity of our Lord ; the Purification and Annunciation of the B. V. M.; Easter Day; Ascension Day; Whitsun Day; St Matthias ; St John Baptist ; St Peter ; St James ; St Bartholomew ; St Matthew ; SS. Simon and Jude ; All Saints ; St Andrew ; St Thomas. It has been given as a reason why the other Holy Days have no vigils before them, that they generally happen between Christmas and the Purification, or between Easter and Whitsuntide ; seasons of joy which the Church did not think fit to break into by fasting and humiliation. In the " Tables and Rules " prefixed to our Book of Common Prayer there is a note to the effect that if any of the feast days *with vigils* above enumerated " fall upon a Monday, then the vigil or fast day shall be kept upon the Saturday, and not upon the Sunday next before it," Sunday being invariably regarded as a feast—the weekly commemoration, in fact, of Our Lord's Resurrection.

A piece of music formerly played on the organ, usually after the Psalms, sometimes after the Second Lesson, and so called because
Voluntary. the choice of the music was left to the will (*voluntas*) of the organist. It is mentioned by Archbishop Secker (1693–1768) as having long been customary in his day. Lord Bacon approved of voluntaries as affording time for meditation. The custom of having a " middle voluntary " is kept up in some

churches, and the effect so produced is solemn. From the account of the manner of performing the Sunday services at St Paul's, prefixed to Minor Canon Clifford's duodecimo black-letter anthembook (1664) we learn that at " the first service in the morning"—*i.e.* Matins—there was a voluntary after the Psalms "upon the organ alone" and another before the "second" or Communion Service. There was also a voluntary after the Psalms at the evening serivce. At Durham, on Sundays when there is a choral celebration, it has, for the last 300 years, been the custom to have a soft voluntary during the Communion of the laity. This seems to have been substituted for the *Agnus Dei*, which was previously sung in this place. The term "voluntary" is now generally applied to the pieces of music played by the organist at the beginning and end of the service. In the French cathedrals a voluntary is usually played during the offertory. This is called the Offertorium. A similar custom obtains in the cathedrals of Christ Church and St Patrick, Dublin. The voluntary before the service, to which we are now so accustomed in cathedrals, was by no means the rule half-a-century ago; nor is there in Continental cathedrals, where the daily offices are performed chorally, anything of the kind at the present day. At St Michael's College, Tenbury, on weekdays which are ferias, there is never any opening voluntary. This is reserved for surplice days—that is, Saturday evenings, Sundays, Saints' Days, and eves of Saints' Days. This is also the custom at St Andrew's, Wells Street, where there has been daily choral service without intermission since the consecration of the church in 1847. A concluding voluntary, however, seems to have always been pretty general in England, but abroad there is little or nothing corresponding with it ; voluntaries, as a rule, being reserved for the Offertorium at High Mass. The *sortie*, or concluding voluntary, is a comparatively modern French practice.

    The title of the head of certain colleges, and other corporate bodies. At Oxford, there is the Warden of Merton, of New, of All

Warden.
Lat. *custos.*

Souls, and of Wadham Colleges. Other heads are styled Master, Principal, Provost, President, and Rector. At Christ Church, the Dean is the head. The title of Warden is unknown at Cambridge. There is one Provost, that of King's, and one President, that of Queens'. Heads of all other colleges are styled Master. The heads of Winchester College, St Peter's College, Radley, St Columba's College, near Dublin, and St Michael's College, Tenbury, are termed Warden. This was also the case at the Collegiate Church, Manchester, until 1840, when the Warden became "Dean" and the Fellows "Canons"

—apparently an adumbration of the bishopric, founded seven years later.

Watching-loft. Positions from which the great shrines were watched. At Oxford and St Alban's the loft is a beautiful structure of wood. At Lichfield it is a gallery over the door of the sacristy. At Worcester it is a stone oriel of Perpendicular date in the north choir aisle. The parvise chambers over certain church porches were, in all probability, used as watching-lofts.

Zigzag. A decoration peculiar to the Romanesque or Norman style of architecture, consisting of mouldings running in zigzag lines. Considerable variety is given to this class of ornaments by changing the arrangement of the different suits of mouldings, and by turning the points of the zigzags in different directions. This kind of decoration is not found in buildings of the earliest Norman work, but in the more advanced specimens it is most abundantly employed about the doorways, windows, arches, etc. Examples are to be found in most churches of the Norman style.